PLANETARY LONGINGS |

DISSIDENT ACTS   A series edited by
Macarena Gómez-Barris and Diana Taylor

PLANETARY LONGINGS |

MARY LOUISE PRATT

DUKE UNIVERSITY PRESS   DURHAM AND LONDON   2022

© 2022 DUKE UNIVERSITY PRESS | All rights reserved
Designed by Aimee C. Harrison
Typeset in Minion Pro by Westchester Publishing Services

Library of Congress Cataloging-in-Publication Data
Names: Pratt, Mary Louise, [date] author.
Title: Planetary longings / Mary Louise Pratt.
Other titles: Dissident acts.
Description: Durham : Duke University Press, 2022. | Series:
Dissident acts | Includes bibliographical references and index.
Identifiers: LCCN 2021040564 (print)
LCCN 2021040565 (ebook)
ISBN 9781478015666 (hardcover)
ISBN 9781478018292 (paperback)
ISBN 9781478022909 (ebook)
Subjects: LCSH: Decolonization—LatinAmer ica.| Postcolonialism—
LatinAmer ica.|LatinAmer ica—Civilization.| LatinAmer ica—
Colonization.|B ISAC: HISTORY / Latin America / General | SOCIAL
SCIENCE / Sociology / Social Theory Classification: LCC
F1408.3.P735 2022 (print) | LCC F1408.3 (ebook) | DDC 325/.30098—
dc23/eng/20211103
LC recordavailableathttps:// lccn.loc.gov/2021040564
LC ebookrec ordavailableathttps:// lccn.loc.gov/2021040565

Cover art: Edward Burtynsky, *Nickel Tailings #35*, Sudbury, Ontario,
1996 (detail). © Edward Burtynsky, courtesy Howard Greenberg
Gallery and Bryce Wolkowitz Gallery, New York / Nicholas Metivier
Gallery, Toronto.

CONTENTS |

ACKNOWLEDGMENTS |

Spouses always come last in acknowledgments, and I've never liked that. So let me start by saying that I will toast the book's appearance with Renato Rosaldo, my lifelong partner in thought, creation, love, and the arts of living. We take none of it for granted. The thinking for this book began at the turn of the millennium, during a transformative year spent at the Centro de Investigación y Estudios Superiores de Antropología Social (CIESAS) in Guadalajara, Mexico (1998–99). Three of the chapters (chapters 1, 4, and 11) were originally drafted there, and two others (chapters 2 and 3) were researched there. I am grateful to the generous colleagues with whom I shared conversations and experiences, who took the time to teach me and show me what I needed to know. Deep thanks to Rossana Reguillo, Magda Villarreal, Gabriel Torres, Renée de la Torre, Meche González de la Rocha, Santiago Bastos, Susan Street, María de la O, Doc Alonso, Gerardo Bernache, Jorge Alonso, Pati Safa, Guillermo de la Peña, Patricia Arias, and Jorge Durán, and to México. The book took shape after another transformative dislocation, from Stanford to New York University, where I began an association with the Hemispheric Institute for Performance and Politics. I am grateful to its founder, my colleague and friend Diana Taylor, for life-changing experiences in the United States and Latin America, and for her faith in my work and this book. It would not be here if it were not for her. Heartfelt thanks to Marianne Hirsch for help with the introduction and for her warm and generous friendship, and to Claire Fox for thoughtful suggestions too numerous to count. I thank Ed Cohen for introducing me to the work of Elizabeth Grosz, and Anna Tsing for her brilliance and her intellectual generosity. Krystal Roberts provided expert editorial support all along the way, and I am grateful to Chiapas photographer Moysés Zuñiga Santiago for permission to use his image. Thanks to my colleagues in the Department of Social and Cultural Analysis, the Department of Spanish and Portuguese, and the Center for Latin American and Caribbean Studies at New York University for their inspiration and commitment. Without gratitude, I acknowledge the COVID-19 virus for the confinement that made creativity so necessary. It has taught us many things.

Lastly, I am thrilled that one of Edward Burtynsky's photographic masterpieces graces the cover. His work is sometimes seen as so desolate and distanced as to allow only for despair. For me, his work's combination of beauty and devastation incarnate what I call planetary longing. The images allow for only one human presence, the viewer, who is not given the luxury of looking at someone else's actions and desires but, rather, is present to their own.

SITTING IN THE LIGHT
OF THE GREAT SOLAR TV

In the summer of 2002, I found myself in a hole-in-the-wall restaurant in the city of Cuzco, Peru, in the company of my twenty-something vegetarian son. It was a simple, out-of-the-way place where a tasty, meatless meal was served for pennies to a local, mainly working-class male clientele. The walls, I noticed, were decorated with painted space-age images of stars, suns, and flying saucers. Shortly after sitting down, we realized that the customers were intently watching a TV screen mounted from the ceiling. It was broadcasting not the national networks but a string of videotapes from abroad documenting the visits of extraterrestrial beings over the history of the earth.

The little restaurant, it turned out, was run by a religious sect of "divine revelation" based in Peru, called Alfa y Omega. Its two central symbols are the Lamb of God and a flying saucer.

According to the pamphlets on sale, Alfa y Omega's doctrines are recorded in thousands of scrolls dictated telepathically by a "divine solar (extraterrestrial) father from the distant suns of Alpha and Omega in the Trino galaxy of the microcosm or kingdom of the heavens" (Alfa y Omega 2001).[1]

1.1 — Alfa y Omega flyer, Cuzco, July 2002. FROM THE AUTHOR'S COLLECTION.

I.2 — Alfa y Omega flyer, Cuzco, July 2002. FROM THE AUTHOR'S COLLECTION.

These "doctrines for the third millennium" explain "the origin, cause, and destiny of all things known and unknown." "Have you joined?" the waiter asked me when I bought the pamphlet. "Not yet," I said.

Unlike some other post- and neo-Christian spiritual movements at the turn of the millennium, Alfa y Omega emphasizes not belief or faith but knowledge and understanding. Its adherents are driven by a permanent search for knowledge, which includes gatherings to discuss and interpret the telepathically delivered scrolls. Like other such movements, it is strongly antimaterialist and anticapitalist, aimed at working-class people. In its writings, Alfa y Omega refers to capitalism as "the strange law of gold" (la extraña ley del oro; Alfa y Omega 2001, 22) and announces "a new kingdom of truth, justice, and equality with a new heaven, a new earth, and new knowledge" (2). Its signifying machines are elaborate and operate in the micro and the macro. For example, the pamphlets from the restaurant describe a moral calculus that assesses a person's state of virtue by assigning points of darkness and light according to the number of molecules in the bodies of the people one has hindered or helped. Adopting orphans is an act that gains many points of light (16). Then there is the Gran Televisor Solar, the Great Solar TV, a huge screen in the sky that sometime in the future will display everyone's sins "in the presence of all humanity" (39). The TV set in the restaurant was part of the message. These tropes operate as figures, that is, semantic formations whose meaning is not reducible to analysis (see Spivak 2003). The aspects of all this I want to underscore are these: first, the emphasis on knowledge; second, the planetary optic; and third, the millennial framing, including the call for the new. The extraterrestrial visitors, it seems, establish an imagined standpoint from which to define the terrestrial and the human in planetary terms.

Alfa y Omega was founded in the 1980s by a self-taught man from the Andean province of Ancash in central Peru. It is one of many popular philosophical-religious-cosmological formations that formed in the context of the approaching millennium and the devastating impact of neoliberal capitalism on working people in many parts of the world. Peruvians had suffered especially hard from crashing standards of living, state failure, and years of violence and terror from the Shining Path guerrilla movement.[2] Alfa y Omega offered practices of knowledge making and signification that rejected materialism, consumerism, and failed narratives of development. It constructed a global and planetary imaginary with a knowledge-driven, spiritualized moral vision. It interpellated all humanity in dense webs of meaning and meaningfulness, like a centripetal force.

Alfa y Omega's call for new knowledge for the new millennium reminded me of a curious textual trope that turned up in Latin American fiction also during the 1990s. In a number of novels of that decade, elaborate signifying structures appear that the protagonist of the novel recognizes as meaningful but is unable to decipher. For example, in a novel by Chilean writer Diamela Eltit, called *Los vigilantes* (*Custody of the Eyes*; 1994), the obsessive and maladapted child of the female narrator spends his days alone in a room creating elaborate structures with a set of containers. The narrator recognizes these as laden with meaning, yet they are indecipherable to her. She writes the boy's father: "The games your son plays are more and more impenetrable to me, and I no longer understand what role the objects play and what relation they have with his body. The containers are rigorously laid out in the center of his room forming a figure whose beginning and end I cannot comprehend" (76).

Here again, a figure. The child appears to be founding a new regime of subject-object relations, an order in which his mother may have no place. If there is a future, the figure suggests, it is not in her hands. In *Salón de belleza* (*Beauty Salon*; 1994) by Peruvian novelist Mario Bellatin, a novel about the AIDS epidemic, the novel's gay protagonist adorns his hair salon with large aquariums inside which multiple varieties of fish create parallel social and reproductive orders that are clearly rule governed but incomprehensible to the narrator. The predatory violence among males, females, and babies is particularly indecipherable.[3] (Both these novels are discussed further in chapter 4.) Tropes of this sort abound in the work of the prolific and popular Argentine novelist César Aira. A text called *La villa* (*Shantytown*; 2000), for instance, takes place in a huge poor neighborhood on the outskirts of Buenos Aires, suspected of being a center for the drug trade. The detective assigned to investigate is completely unable to make sense of how the place works, even though his profession is to *figure* such things out. At the end, the shantytown is revealed to be an elaborate, self-regulating spatial, social, semiotic, and economic order completely opaque to him. Whatever future is being constructed here, he is not part of it.

Like Alfa y Omega's extraterrestrial scrolls, these unusual figures with their elaborate hidden meanings allegorize the crisis of knowledge and futurity experienced by many sectors of humankind in the 1990s. It was not only the approaching millennium, though that was surely part of it (remember the Y2K crisis?). Neoliberal capitalism was transforming the world, bringing ecological catastrophe with it. No one has summed up more clearly than Anna Lowenhaupt Tsing the vast economic restructurings that inform this book: "In the last two decades of the twentieth century, capitalism was transformed by the establishment of new international rules of trade that offered tremendous advantages for the world's most powerful corporations. Capital whizzed around the globe. Free-trade zones and new technologies of communication encouraged companies to spread their operations to ever-cheaper locations. Transnational specializations—such as currency traders, energy traders—flourished. Privatization initiatives and free-trade regulations dismantled national economies, making once-public resources available for private appropriation. Social scientists were awed by the scope of the project" (2005, 11–12). As the millennium approached, multinational enterprises invaded vast new territories with extractive industry and ecological devastation. Traditional knowledges became less and less able to explain the worlds they inhabited, and traditional lifeways less able to offer viable futures for the young. As standards of living for many fell in the face of demands for cheap labor, narratives of progress collapsed, along with hopes for more prosperous futures. Modernity also lost its power to map credible aspirations (chapter 1), while binary orders of gender, sexuality, and family shook at their foundations, not least because women were pressed into the underpaid workforce. The myth of development was increasingly challenged by the emerging narrative of unsustainability. No wonder the head of Alfa y Omega declared himself a *futurólogo*, a futurologist. Not just humanity but the whole biosphere was headed toward increasingly unrecognizable, possibly apocalyptic, futures. As the novelists prefigured, those futures called for new kinds of knowledge and new interpreters to decipher—and to make—the postmillennial world. The Zapatistas saw it, too, in the stream of communiqués they launched into the world after their uprising in 1994 (Ejército 1997; see chapter 3). As is often the case, popular culture anticipates what is coming: the new knowledges will be planetary, and they will address all of humanity, linked now by a shared fate.

This book reflects on these and other planetary figurations from a vast but specific location: the Americas. It is written from a conviction that the turn of the millennium—the last decade of the twentieth century and the first decade of the twenty-first—has marked a critical turning point in the human and planetary condition. This is not a book "about" the Americas. It is about a range of planetarized processes, forces, and aspirations, observed and thought about mainly from the Americas. Like Alfa y Omega, I think *from* the Americas *about* the planet. I am a student of Latin America raised in Canada and living in the United States—as Barack Obama quipped after nailing a nonchalant three-pointer in 2020—that's what I do.[4] To think from the Americas is to think from unique civilizational and ecosystemic and geophysical histories that unfolded separately from those of the Afro-Eurasian landmass. The civilizations of the Americas had no "cradle" in the Middle East. Agriculture did not spread to the Americas from somewhere else. They had their own Neolithic(s). The sciences, empires, cities, writing systems, mathematics, music, astronomy, agriculture, manufacturing, and art forms that developed in the Americas after 14,000 BCE did not share a "common origin" with other sectors of humankind. Nor did their animals and plants for more than 200 million years.[5] Looking out from here, both the constants and the differences with other regions astound.

To think from the Americas is also to think from the history of European expansionism, colonialism and indigeneity, invasion and dispossession, extractive capitalism and slavery, experienced from the arrival site or receiving end of these forces. From the moment they acquired their name in 1507, the Americas have lived a history of transaction, contestation, exploitation, and invention. Such dynamics are the focus of this book. The first half centers on the turn of the millennium, from the 1990s through to 2020. The second half widens the chronology to the past two hundred years or so, and their echoes in the present. Two preoccupations recur throughout: futurity and force. Futurity is central because of the unprecedented crisis of futurity that human agency has brought about but is less and less able to imagine or control. This dire predicament offers a fruitful standpoint from which to think back to other crises of futurity, to become aware that agency and being require a projection into a future that is by definition imaginary, even if apparently certain. Thinking through futurity seems a gift of our apocalyptic moment. My other keyword, *force*, likewise derives from the unspecifiable, unpredictable dynamism of our Anthropocenic "nonanalogue" state, in which agency, intent, and governability determine less and less. As humans and other life-forms are increasingly subject to processes they do not control, knowledge makers are oddly freed from the demand to predict, model, specify, explain. A new openness to unpredictability enables a shift out of the systemic. Things that used to look like categories, structures, or systems start appearing as forces that can operate at any range and scale and have the ability to make things happen in any context in which they come into play—in the way we know warming temperatures will make things happen but no longer expect to fully know what things. With that kind of unpredictability comes improvisation. At different points in the book, I suggest the fruitfulness of conceiving indigeneity, coloniality, modernity, or decolonization in this way, as forces rather than systems or structures. This perspective enables thinking across massively varying scales and ranges, another postmillennial imperative.

World-Making at the Millennium

That 2002 Alfa y Omega moment in Cuzco makes a pretty good pivot from which to look first back at the end of the second millennium and then ahead to the beginning of the third, as I do in the first half of this book. On one side of the pivot, chapters 1–4 look at how the turbulent 1990s were lived and imagined. On the other side of the pivot, chapters 5–9 engage postmillennial anxieties, desires, and repositionings. On both sides of that pivot, one of my main interests is world-making, meaning the actions, practices, and creations by which people craft meaningful realities and stories for themselves out of their engagements with what is around them, even as they contend with hostile circumstances. As I argue in chapter 2, in response to imposed loss and hardship, like forced migration or the destruction of small-scale agriculture, communities imagine those forces in their own terms. The early chapters of the book are populated by such inventions—vampires, recycled travel tales, apocalyptic denouements, Indigenous experiments in citizenship and mobility, and an Andean ghost-mother who won't go away. Worlds are made by other means.

The emphasis on world-making is shared by scholars across disciplines who seem to engage with the disruptive impacts of capitalist globalization. After working for thirty years with an Australian aboriginal group, anthropologist Elizabeth Povinelli sidestepped the lexicon of dispossession and loss to describe their situation. In the face of what she called economies of abandonment, Povinelli (2016) concluded that in this small group, the older generation had taken on the project of creating a "science of dwelling" (such an evocative phrase) that would give the young a viable way of being and living in the hostile environments they would face. The aim was not to preserve traditions but to create futures for the young. Anna Lowenhaupt Tsing in her remarkable treatise *Friction* (2004) reports on fieldwork in Kalimantan, Indonesia, where she went to find out how the Meratus, the forest people she had studied before, were interacting with the forces of globalization, especially the multinational lumber interests that had invaded their territory. She was consciously seeking an understanding that went beyond the predictable rage and despair at seeing their lifeways disrupted. She found it through the concept of friction, which enabled her to see the world-making dimensions of inhabitants' interactions with global forces. Everything that enters from outside can do so only through traction with something that is already there, and that friction between the given and the new produces unplanned effects and possibilities. The challenge for the ethnographer was to perceive these without passing judgment on them.

The concept of friction enabled what Tsing (2005) came to call an "ethnography of global connection," alert to the generativity and unpredictability of global capitalism's world-changing effects in the places where it landed and on the people on whom it landed. She found that the destabilization of traditional lifeways combined with the arrival of new characters, commodities, and information generated a great deal of imaginative, future-oriented world-making activity, sometimes on a grand scale. Without denying harm, loss, and disaster, the world-making approach enables a fuller, truer account of this critical turning point in the human and planetary condition. World-making activity, says anthropologist Dorinne Kondo, "links structures of power, labor processes, and performances of gendered, national, and racialized subjectivities, in historically and culturally specific settings" (2018, 6). Feminist political economists J. K. Gibson-Graham take a related approach in *A Postcapitalist Politics* (2006), as does literary and cultural studies scholar Doris Sommer (2005) through her concept of cultural agency. Imaginative, future-oriented world-making likewise describes the extraordinarily rich outpouring of Indigenous thought that has accompanied the millennium, from locations across the planet (see below and chapter 5). Far from speaking for and about themselves, Indigenous thinkers today address all humanity, exhorting non-Indigenous and Indigenous people to remake their place on the planet and in the cosmos and aiming to show them how.

This turn toward what I am calling *world-making* shifts the understanding of cultural continuity. Continuity is defined not by the collective maintenance of practices, stories, and beliefs over time but by the shared work of world-making conducted by the group over time. Practices, stories, and beliefs play a fundamental role in this work, but they are not the work itself. This reconceived continuity appears to be one of the epistemic shifts that mark the millennium.[6] The emergence of planetarity as an analytical frame marks another such shift.

Planetarity

Some readers of this book may find it hard to remember when the idea of planetarity was not around. But in the 1990s, by and large, it wasn't. And then after the millennium, it was. The landmark comic series *Planetary* started in 1999, introducing a superhero team that called themselves Archaeologists of the Impossible, who operated in a space called the Wildstorm Universe (Ellis and Cassaday 2014). The term *multiverse* seems to have got its start in *Planetary*. In literary studies Gayatri Chakravorty Spivak began speaking of planetarity in the late 1990s and headlined the concept in her 2003 manifesto for comparative literature, *Death of a Discipline*, as a way to delink from capitalist-humanist globality and "render our home uncanny" (2003, 74). In her account, too, the term registers the millennial crisis of agency and futurity: humans must reimagine themselves as "planetary subjects" rather than "global agents." Critic Masao Miyoshi called for a similar "turn to the planet" in a 2001 essay where he sees the climate crisis as requiring the restoration of a sense of totality against the disaggregation wrought by the 1980s and '90s (Miyoshi 2001). When I used the term *planetarity* to title an essay written in 2004 (Pratt 2005), I recall being struck when French president Jacques Chirac called that same year for a "réponse planétaire" to AIDS. No one, I thought, would have used that phrase a decade earlier. In 2003 a landmark *réponse planétaire* took place in response to the threat of a US invasion of Iraq. As some readers will remember, on February 14 of that year, an integrated, planetarized demonstration took place across the world's towns and cities, held together by cell phones, aimed at heading off the invasion before it happened. Not surprisingly, Alfa y Omega participated, planetarily, posting the message: "No to war! Because this planet, this humanity, needs voices and arguments that fight for peace, to unite all peoples in a single common cause to definitively eradicate injustice, hunger and sickness for they are the origin of much hatred and violence, and feed terrorism."[7] The planetary imagination flourished. In October 2010 the Great Solar TV ruled as people across the planet watched in real time the theatrical rescue of thirty-three Chilean miners trapped for weeks in the depths of, well, the planet. It was the finale of a two-month melodrama that included an idealized, planetarized performance of international cooperation of the kind Miyoshi longed for. Planetarity is in part a product of the communications revolution. As a concept, planetarity resonates above all with what I have been calling the crisis of futurity linked to climate change and the impending ecological catastrophe. I recently came across an email I received in late 2000 from a colleague in Chile who evoked in a desperate tone the *infierno* (hell) humans were constructing on the planet, the mass pauperization, extinction, and imaginable futures that awaited our species. Its planetary, trans species, apocalyptic world-making seemed so powerful and striking then that I printed it out and kept it. Two decades on, it's a commonplace. The box of oat milk on my counter invites me to "Join Planet Oat"; I am already a member of Planet Fitness. Yet our home remains uncanny. Repairing what has been damaged or restoring what has been destroyed no longer defines the world-making project. As Elizabeth Kolbert (2021, 137) puts it, "The choice is not between what is and what was, but between what is and what will be."

Along with planetarity, the geotemporal concept of the Anthropocene appeared, to mark, in Povinelli's words, "the moment when human existence became the determinate form of planetary existence—and a malignant form at that" (2016, 9). *Geo-* replaces *post-* as the prefix of preference. I found myself writing about geolinguistics, while the geographers invented geohumanities and geoaesthetics (Elias and Moran 2015).[8] Planetarity shifted the focus toward ecological standpoints that conjugated the human with the nonhuman, the living with the nonliving. Povinelli proposed the concepts of geontology and geontopower to ground an inquiry into forms of power where "the living and the nonliving co-compose to produce singular modes of existence and forms of power—and empowerment" (2016, 5). World-making is reconceived as a joint enterprise among all existents, as many aboriginal peoples had imagined it all along.

The essays in part I of the book reflect on this millennial and epochal transition. The opening essay examines the expansionist discourse of modernity, whose world-making powers lost their purchase at the end of the century. It lays out in particular the critique of modernity developed by Latin American theorists in the 1990s. The next three chapters draw on materials from Latin America to trace the anxieties of the 1990s in vernacular culture, literature, and social analysis. As always, I find it fruitful to think through the lens of mobility and travel. Chapter 2 shows how older forms of travel writing were repurposed in the 1990s to capture the escalation of human migrancy and the way popular culture addressed the life-destroying forces of globalization as invading monsters. Chapter 3 rethinks human mobility as a relation between people who move and people who stay in place and uses that framing to reflect on contemporary mobility and placedness. Chapter 4 examines how novels of the 1990s allegorize civic breakdown and the crisis of futurity. Chapter 5 looks at how indigeneity acquired planetary force at the end of the twentieth century and how that process continues to unfold. Turning to the 2000s, chapters 6–8 discuss the postmillennial moment, marking the new conditions of knowledge making linked to the ecological imperative. These chapters explore the term Anthropocene, review mutations of the concept of the contact zone, and reflect on intersections of ecology, militarism, and tourism. Thinking across the millennial divide, chapter 9 juxtaposes the current wave of authoritarianism, including Trumpism, with that of the 1970s and 1980s in Latin America, exemplified by the dictatorship of Augusto Pinochet in Chile.

Longing

The work of world-making is driven by desire and will and by the force of life itself seeking to project into the future. This is part of what I attempt to capture with the word *longings* in my title. The term carries a particular poignancy in relation to the predicament at the millennium. All life-forms, including humans, face a new configuration of certainty and uncertainty, namely, the certainty that everything is going to change drastically, the certainty that these changes will be impossible to anticipate or control and will produce increasingly hostile conditions of existence. It is impossible not to long for this to be otherwise. Some propose planetarity as a new field of imagination and agency that escapes the exhaustion and dead-endedness of the *post-*, a prefix that came to attach itself to just about everything. In this frame, utopian longings spring forth, like those expressed in a 2015 volume called *The Planetary Turn*, where the turn arcs toward the promise to "move beyond the limits of globalization, cosmopolitanism, environmentalism" toward a "multi-centric and pluralizing, actually existing worldly structure of relatedness, critically keyed to non-totality, non-homogeneity, and anti-hegemonic operations typically and polemically subtended by an eco-logic" (Elias and Moraru 2015, xxiii). This idealized futurology flowers in the context of a "subtending eco-logic" that with utter clarity anticipates dystopia on the same range and scale. In the existing eco-logic, moreover, the available human response is anything but sublime: it can only be managerial. Conserving pluridiversity and relationality boils down to the work of counting, tagging, and tracking endangered species (cougars, bald eagles, blue frogs, . . .) and staging their survival and reproduction, perhaps in captivity. In the midst of such arduous micromanagement, the ideal of the multicentric totality inhabits the sphere of longing. Planetarity at most offers a lifeboat.

Concepts

Throughout this book my thinking has been guided by the work of Australian feminist philosopher Elizabeth Grosz, in particular the theory of the concept of her 2011 book, *Becoming Undone: Darwinian Reflections on Life, Politics, and Art*, notably in a chapter tellingly titled "The Future of Feminist Theory: Dreams for New Knowledges" (74–88). Grosz's approach builds on Gilles Deleuze and Félix Guattari's claim that "all concepts are connected to problems without which they would have no meaning, and which can themselves only be isolated or understood as their solution emerges" (1994, 16). So, for example, I treat planetarity as a concept linked to the crisis of futurity and agency posed in particular by climate change and impending ecological catastrophe. Concepts, Grosz elaborates, "emerge, have value and function only through the impact of problems generated from outside" (2011, 80). Concepts, however, are not solutions to problems. Rather, they enable the search for solutions by opening up alternatives to the present, by enabling the imagining of possibilities. They do so by "transforming the givenness of chaos, the pressing problem, into various forms of order, into possibilities for being otherwise" (78). Concepts are not propositional, not capable of being true or false. We need concepts, Grosz says, to "think our way in a world of forces that we do not control," the more so because the solutions to our pressing problems inevitably lie "beyond the horizon of the given real" (82). This last point is critical. The solutions lie beyond our horizon because the real in which "we" (whoever the "we" is) are living is the real created by the pressing problem. So, for example, the concept of patriarchy identifies a pressing problem and enables the search for solutions to the problem. But no one living in patriarchy can fully imagine what a nonpatriarchal society would actually look or feel like, because we are imagining such a society from within patriarchy. We are required to work toward an outcome we cannot know. The concept enables that work through its power to "add ideality to the world" (79).

Grosz's vision holds for many of the concepts that animate this book—planetarity, Anthropocene, contact zone, coloniality, indigeneity, decolonization, and others. In different chapters I discuss these concepts in her terms. All arise in connection with pressing problems and enable thinking beyond immediate events and horizons. At the same time, Grosz emphasizes, concepts are completely worldly. They are anchored in real events, experiences, and materialities and in this sense are not abstract. They generate agencies of all kinds—ambitious world-making activity, Tsing would say. The changes they enable will also be real events, experiences, and materialities. For Grosz, these worldly, problem-related, and future-generating dimensions of concepts make them "indispensable to movements seeking radical change. . . . Theory is one means by which we invent radical and unforeseen futures" (82–84).

Though concepts cannot be judged as true or false, they can and must be judged both for the futures they enable or disable and for their successes at doing so. The ethical dimension is always present. They have life spans—concepts appear, give what they have to give, subside, and are replaced by others. Humanists will remember a moment in the early 2000s when the concept of cosmopolitanism appeared to have the potential to define a revitalized project for global humanity (perhaps as a replacement for modernity). A flurry of books appeared, but then the idea exhausted its promise and faded away. That was another millennial moment. In chapter 15 I approach political independence as a concept, arguing that colonial leaders struggling for independence in the nineteenth century did not and could not know in advance, or even imagine, what it would actually look like. I then show it did indeed engender radically different futures.

Coloniality

Cuzco is also a pivot point for part II of this book as well, which centers on the dynamics of coloniality, recolonization, survivance, and decolonization in contemporary and historical contexts. Indeed, two of the chapters take place in and around Cuzco. Formerly the capital of the Inca Empire, under Spanish colonialism Cuzco was, and today remains, a place defined and energized by the intersecting dynamics of empire, coloniality, indigeneity, and decolonization. It is an unparalleled place from which to think about those planetary longings.

Just as ecological crisis demands new kinds of knowledge making, so did colonialism when it became a serious object of study in the late 1970s. It would be hard to exaggerate the impact of this development on knowledge making in the academy. For those who did not live the change, it can be hard, maybe impossible, to imagine how little the workings of empire and colonialism were thought about or understood in the metropole in the 1970s, or how thoroughly, as Edward Said put it, "the literary-cultural establishment" had "declared the serious study of imperialism and culture off limits" (1994, 21). As one who did live that change, let me illustrate it with a small anecdote.

In 1977, not long after I arrived as an assistant professor at a prestigious American university, I was invited by colleagues in comparative literature to give a talk about my research. I presented a paper on André Gide's novel *L'Immoraliste* (*The Immoralist*; 1902) and Albert Camus's short story collection *L'Éxil et le royaume* (*Exile and the Kingdom*; 1957). Using my training in close reading, I discussed the two works as explorations of Franco–North African colonial relations and the colonial imagination, at different points in the trajectory of French colonialism in North Africa. I read Camus's story "La femme adultère" ("The Adulterous Woman") as an attempt to rewrite and partially decolonize Gide's novel, while at the same time reconfirming European superiority and whiteness (Pratt 1979). The reception surprised me. The scholars who studied European literature understood what I was saying but simply did not find it credible. To them it just made no sense to see these French works as in any way about colonialism or North Africa. They were existential parables about the homelessness of modern man; they could not be illuminated in any way by the history of French imperialism in North Africa. The real or historical Africa had no relevance at all to the interpretation of either work. Misled perhaps by my interest in language, I had simply failed to grasp the philosophical nature of the texts.

That, dear reader, was the pre-postcolonial moment.[9] The omnipresence of empire and coloniality woven throughout the European literary canon was invisible and unthinkable because no one yet knew how to think about it. Nor did many want to think about the complicity of European systems of knowledge and artistic traditions with Europe's imperial and colonial enterprises. The writings of anticolonial and anti-imperial thinkers—C. L. R. James, Frantz Fanon, Aimé Césaire, Albert Memmi, Walter Rodney, Amílcar Cabral, Kwame Nkrumah, Eduardo Galeano, Guillermo O'Donnell, Chinua Achebe, Samir Amin, Immanuel Wallerstein, Conor Cruise O'Brien, and so many others—were out there and easily available in 1977 (see chapter 16), but they still lay beyond the horizons of mainstream literary scholarship. They inhabited a faraway space then called the third world. Scholars studying the third world did come into contact with these thinkers, as I had through the study of Latin America, where literature and revolution were joined at the hip. (Chilean revolutionary poet Pablo Neruda was awarded the Nobel Prize in Literature in 1971.)

Things were about to change. A book called *Orientalism* (Said 1978) was in press at the very moment I was giving my talk., and it would change the landscape of literary studies forever.[10] Today few readers would find it implausible to read *The Immoralist* and *Exile and the Kingdom* as about colonialism. In fact, it is impossible now to read them any other way. It is now normative to find the West unthinkable apart from its imperial enterprises. In this respect we have lived a knowledge revolution. Said called it a "huge and remarkable adjustment in perspective and understanding" (1993, 243).

In the 1980s, empire and imperialism were core concepts for this new critical project, not colonialism or the postcolonial.[11] As I argue in chapter 16, postcolonialism displaced the initial anti-imperialist frame. In a telling moment in *Culture and Imperialism* (1993), Said attempted to weld the two terminologies together: "The real potential of post-colonial liberation," he said, "is the liberation of all mankind from imperialism" and the "reconceiving of human experience in nonimperial terms" (274, 276). For me, this is still the point.

Decolonizing Postcolonialism

Postcolonial inquiry took shape through a series of exclusions that enabled its rich conversations but limited its scope. Four in particular stand out. First, postcolonial inquiry bracketed out the so-called first wave of European imperial expansion, that is, the Spanish, Portuguese, British, and French colonial enterprises of the fifteenth through eighteenth centuries, all over the planet but most conspicuously in the Americas. Postcolonial inquiry began with the so-called second wave of European incursions, which for some was inaugurated by Napoleon in 1800 and for others by the scramble for Africa in the 1880s, ending with post–World War II independences in Africa and Asia.[12] Second, postcolonialism bypassed noncolonial forms of empire, such as the militarized control exercised by the United States under the Monroe Doctrine (1823) and the Platt Amendment (1901), or the economic domination France and Britain exercised over Spanish America after it became independent from Spain. This latter form of domination came to be called *neocolonialism*, meaning the continuing exercise of imperial power in economic form after colonies became politically independent (Nkrumah 1964, 1965). The separation is artificial and misleading, for colonial, noncolonial, and neocolonial forms of empire ran in parallel and worked hand in hand. In the nineteenth century, Britain and France were simultaneously colonizing powers in Africa and Asia and equally aggressive neocolonizers in Spanish America. Indeed, they helped Spanish Americans gain independence from Spain in order to gain access to their markets and resources themselves. Joseph Conrad's *Heart of Darkness* (1899), one of postcolonialism's sacred texts, needs to be read alongside his remarkable novel *Nostromo* (1904), which depicts British neocolonialism in South America. And both should be read alongside another of their contemporaries, the Philippine novelist José Rizal, whose novels penetratingly deconstruct waning Spanish colonialism and rising nationalism in the Philippines (see chapter 16).

Third, postcolonial studies focused its attention on the Afro-Eurasian landmass, to the exclusion of Oceania and, above all, the Americas. This certainly avoided some inconvenient complications. Chronologically, Spanish America became postcolonial in the 1820s and the United States in 1776. How does the term apply to them? For a long time, neither postcolonial scholars nor Americanists showed much interest in exploring that question. Interesting parallels were lost in the process. Americanists eventually zeroed in on the term *settler colonialism* to remake the study of US history, society, and culture. Today this term is the framework for a huge scholarly reassessment (see, for example, Grandin 2019).

Fourth, and finally, postcolonialism's elision of the Americas went hand in hand with an elision of indigeneity, one of the most consequential formations arising from the colonial encounter. Postcolonial scholarship rarely addresses Indigenous agency and has not found Indigenous thought a source of insight into the colonial or ex-colonial condition nor into the work of decolonization. To be fair, the disinterest has been mutual. Indigenous scholars have argued that postcolonialism's foundational concepts of hybridity and mimicry disavow indigeneity altogether (Grande 2015) and that with respect to Indigenous and other subordinated peoples, the postcolonial project is a mutation of colonial power itself, an act of recolonization that keeps Indigenous ways of knowing in a place of otherness or invisibility (Rivera Cusicanqui 2020). Below I suggest that, among other things, different strategies of decolonization are at work in the two formations.

Indigeneity

As the millennium turned and the search for new knowledges and possibilities for being intensified, postcolonialism waned, and Indigenous knowledge making began to flourish in a new, extroverted way (see chapter 5). In the time of planetarity, Indigenous people see plainly that their futures depend on compelling non-Indigenous people to change their ways of world-making and that many of those people are searching for guidance as to how to do so. This is another development in the millennial intellectual landscape that would not have been predicted in the 1970s or 1980s. Numerous examples are found throughout the book. Chapter 5 reviews the geopolitical conditions that globalized and planetarized Indigenous agency at the end of the twentieth century.

The first thing to underscore about indigeneity is that it is nobody's primary identity. To be Indigenous is to be a member of a people, tribe, or nation that has its own unique name and self-identity—one is Maori, Cree, Navajo, Mapuche, or a combination of such, before one is Indigenous. And that name invokes a continuity that goes back to the time before the colonial encounter, when indigeneity did not (yet) exist. Indigenous power, identity, and being arise from this continuous, collective making/becoming, what Australian anthropologist Genevieve Bell has called the "undelible continuity" from precolonial through colonial and then ex-colonial times.[13] Autochthonous or tribal names designate an arc of being and becoming that exists independent of the colonial invader. Language, ceremony, clothing, music, story, and dance are among its formal enactments today. When Indigenous groups disappear, it is because that arc of collective becoming has ended, often through death or disbursal.

In an important book that appeared at the turn of the millennium, Anishinaabe (Chippewa) theorist Gerald Vizenor introduced the term *survivance* to name this process of living Indigenous being/becoming. *Survivance* denotes much more than *survival* and is intended to correct that pathos-laden term. Survivance is "an active sense of presence," sustained by stories that "renounce domination, tragedy and victimry" (Vizenor 1999, vii). It is carried out by world-making practices of retention and refusal. Indigenous subjectivity is grounded in place (though not necessarily ancestral place), where political sovereignty and the sacred both dwell. In *Decolonizing Methodology* (1999), Maori theorist Linda Tuhiwai Smith explains that acquiring or inheriting a collective name is where indigeneity begins, not ends. Indigeneity for Smith names an ongoing, nonteleological process of self-invention, the living out of a collective's being in time and place. That being is both autonomous and relational, and both affirmative and oppositional or contestatory.

The focus on self-creation is critical, because unlike tribal names, the term *indigeneity* is relational, a product of the colonial encounter. The colonial labels for the colonized—*Indigenous, First Nations, pueblos originarios* (original people), *autochtones* (autochthonous), *aboriginal, native*—all refer to anteriority in time and place; that is, they evoke an other who was there first, before someone else arrived. The arrival is what creates the before-and-after moment—you become Indigenous only when somebody else shows up uninvited. Thus, the term *indigeneity* names a relation, not a condition. It inaugurates what I call the *colonial divide* (chapter 14) and usually sets in motion a narrative of invasion, struggle, displacement, dispossession, otherness, and survivance (or extinction). It creates an Indigenous we that is a historical agent, and a historical debt that the colonizer can never repay.

Indigeneity is thus energized from two sources: the self-making energies of precolonial being and the struggles surrounding the unresolved (and seemingly unresolvable) colonizer-colonized relationship as it unfolds in time. I have found it fruitful to imagine indigeneity today not as a condition but, as already suggested, as a force. I see indigeneity as a force that generates agency wherever it comes into play. It has the power to make things happen, but what it will make happen is not systemic or predictable. This force can operate on any range or scale, in any register, using any materials. Indigeneity today can generate a land occupation, a United Nations bureaucracy, a poetry anthology, a beauty contest, international travel, academic programs, tax law, dance and theater, court battles, alternative legal systems, medical tourism, gambling tourism, hairstyles, education experiments, insurgencies, archaeology, cosmovisions.[14] As I discuss in chapter 14, when colonial optics represent Indigenous people as historically inert, they deny Indigenous people the dynamic, innovative agencies that colonial power itself forces on them. In just about any context you can think of, indigeneity has the potential to generate actions, events, meanings, feelings, intentions, decisions, relationships, outcomes. Powerful cultural constructs operate in this unbounded, generative manner, and that is the source of their power. At the same time, many Indigenous communities today inhabit conditions more precarious than ever. States and corporations have found ways to use recognition against them. Everywhere, Indigenous people face powers greater than their own. As a concept, in Elizabeth Grosz's sense, indigeneity arises in connection with the "pressing problem" of colonial injustice, which continues to operate and renew itself. The struggle for decolonization continues.

Perhaps now it is clearer why postcoloniality and indigeneity have not been friends. Postcolonialism's foundational intervention was to deconstruct and supersede the binary oppositions of colonizer/colonized, refusing to regard these parties as inhabiting separate and opposing realities. The postcolonial project grasped the colonial condition as collusion, entanglement, mediation, and interpenetration of subjects positioned in multiple, shifting ways with respect to the colonizer/colonized divide. Hybridity, impurity, mimicry, ambiguity, mobility, and ambivalence are the ingredients of the colonial relations and experiences it explores. An important goal was to complicate the militant stance of anticolonial thought, which condemned colonialism unequivocally and saw the colonized as victims (see chapter 16).

Indigeneity, by contrast, decolonizes by sustaining and developing ways of being, knowing, and doing that contest the dominant ways of the colonizers and correct their weaknesses and errors. From this perspective, Quechua-American theorist Sandy Grande argues that "the concepts of *mestizaje*, hybridity, and border subjectivity dear to both critical pedagogy and post-colonial studies cannot be models for Indigenous subjectivity" (2014, 117). They are, Grande finds, "part of the fundamental lexicon of Western imperialism" (117). These terms come into play only after colonialism's foundational act of dispossession has occurred and colonial society has taken shape. Rather than addressing the colonial encounter, hybridity and *mestizaje* presuppose it. The postcolonial optic thus cannot be a model for Indigenous emancipation. This does not mean that Indigenous being cannot recognize or inhabit hybridity, entanglement, ambivalence, and the rest. It means Indigenous emancipatory projects do not begin there. Perhaps this is why the postcolonial paradigm treated them as irrelevant. In the time of planetarity, however, they have taken on an extroverted, even didactic authority, offering possibilities for being and futures in the face of impending doom.

Decolonization

As I suggested earlier, it has been a tremendous achievement to come to know what we now know about how empire and colonialism work; how they generate knowledge, orchestrate desires, and execute power; how they produce subjects, aesthetics, tastes, pleasures, and plenitudes; how they can enchant the world. We learned to observe the projection onto others of beloved things Europe was destroying in itself and of despised things Europe could not confront in itself. We learned to discover the deep moral unrest writhing at the heart of it all and surfacing from time to time in horrible forms.

We also learned that the colonial story is not over. As Spivak (1999) has observed, Eurocentrism, ethnocentrism, and colonialist thinking cannot simply be set aside; they must be worked through, even as they persist around us in continuously mutating forms. The work of decolonization is this continuous, unending process of working through, a collective making and unmaking that is arduous and decisive for the future of all beings.

In the twenty-first century, the concept of coloniality has emerged to advance this work. The term originated in Spanish in the concept of *colonialidad del poder* (coloniality of power), proposed in the 1990s by Peruvian sociologist Aníbal Quijano to observe that though Spanish colonial rule was 150 years in the past, power of all kinds and at all levels in Peru continued to operate along colonial lines (Quijano 2000). It is interesting to note that this concept emerged in Quijano's work at the end of the millennium, after decades devoted to analyzing Peruvian society from a Marxist perspective. Quijano's felicitous term entered the English academic lexicon in the late 1990s, introduced by US-based Argentine theorist Walter Mignolo (2011). *Coloniality* names a force. It introduces a fruitful way to contemplate the long, evolving afterlives of colonial world-making, its reiterations, mutations, and renewals in the present and into the future, as I do in part II of this book.

This persistence is the "pressing problem" (Grosz 2011) that the concept of coloniality enables us to see, as a step in the search for alternative futures. As with indigeneity, it is fruitful to think of coloniality not as a condition but as a generative force that is able, wherever it comes into play, to create agency and make things happen. Coloniality, too, has powers of self-creation and self-renewal. Coloniality can be clever and sly, for colonialism itself has been delegitimated. Historians note that often measures presented as removing colonial domination actually reassert it in a new form, as when slavery is abolished and replaced by indentured servitude or when colonial rule is replaced by neocolonial economic domination. One of the painful lessons the millennium has brought is that white supremacy remains alive and well in the world, reanimated and relegitimized on a mass scale. As a force, coloniality can operate in any arena—a free-trade agreement transforms domestic small farming into export monoculture; a scholar in the Global South is required to publish in Europe or North America to keep her job; a white scholar's attack on an Indigenous intellectual becomes international news (chapter 11); white northerners spend their winters in all-inclusive resorts staffed by underpaid workers and sustained by local resources (chapter 8); a mining company is allowed to ruin the water supply of multiple Indigenous communities; markets in replacement organs run from south to north; planeloads of deportees run from north to south, along with the winter tourists. Coloniality is commodified and marketed all the time in nearly any zone of consumption—films (from *Out of Africa* to *Indiana Jones*), fashion (endless leopard print), food, travel, and so on. Such commodifications reanimate colonial values. No wonder today we hear calls to "decolonize everything!"

The list of watershed books that appeared in 1999 includes Emma Pérez's *The Decolonial Imaginary*. A Chicana feminist theorist, Pérez introduced the adjective *decolonial* in contrast with *postcolonial* to inaugurate an intellectual/political project focused on decolonizing knowledge, historiography, imaginations, selves. She proposes a decolonial imaginary that operates in a space between the colonial and the postcolonial, a zone of creative transformation where the decolonizing subject makes its home and does its world-making work (Pérez 1999, 5–6). This is a space where decolonization names not a political process but a wholesale transformation of subjectivities and ways of being and knowing, one in which decolonizing people are empowered actors.[15] In the past decade, promoted by Mignolo, the concept of the decolonial has become a keyword enabling scholars and educators across the Americas to engage with coloniality (including their own) in a way postcolonial and anticolonial thought did not.[16] Critics lament the term's easy detachment from political agency and from the grounded institutional, political, and educational struggles for decolonization (Rivera Cusicanqui 2010).

The essays in part II of *Planetary Longings* are all studies in coloniality, past and present. The first three take up late twentieth- and early twenty-first-century cases where coloniality is in play, generating what I like to call traffic in meaning. Using examples from a range of times and places, chapter 10 examines ethnography's debt to the colonial travel archive and some of the attempts in the 1990s to decolonize it. Chapter 11 analyzes the epistemic panic generated by Guatemalan Indigenous writer and activist Rigoberta Menchú, culminating in David Stoll's 1999 book-length attack on her truthfulness. Moving into the new millennium, chapter 12 takes up Spanish director Icíar Bollaín's ironized reenactment of Spanish colonialism in her film *También la lluvia* (*Even the Rain*; 2010). Revisiting the colonial archive, chapter 13 offers a critical reflection on the concept of cultural translation by bringing contemporary translation theories to bear on an eighteenth-century Andean judicial text that sentences an Indigenous rebel leader to death. Chapter 14 takes up the concept of coloniality to juxtapose two eighteenth- and nineteenth-century female figures in the southern Andes. Chapter 15 explores mutations in the concepts of independence and decolonization between Spanish America and the Philippines. Chapter 16 recalls the broad current of third-world anticolonial, anti-imperial thought that got sidelined by postcolonialism.

How Did You Get Here? Why Did You Come?

That visit to Cuzco in 2002 was pivotal in yet another way. Almost to the day, it marked thirty years since my first visit there in the summer of 1972. That visit was part of a life-defining experience that underlies this book. A fellow Stanford graduate student and I (she in anthropology and I in comparative literature) received National Defense Education Act funds to spend our summer learning Portuguese. We had two options: enroll in an intensive course at the University of Texas or come up with enough additional money to get us to Rio de Janeiro, where we would audit classes at the public university. What a no-brainer! Neither of us could afford both round-trip plane fare and three months living in Rio. But what if we traveled overland and spent half the summer getting there? We would still have time to fulfill our language-learning obligation and fly back just in time for classes. And we would get to travel through South America, where neither of us had ever been (though we had both spent time in Mexico and Spain). I already knew and loved South American literature. This was my chance to see where it came from.

So we did. From California we got a free ride to Guatemala with two rich Salvadoran students taking home new BMWs. Not till we were in line at the

El Paso border did they tell us we were there as decoys, to distract the border guards from the automatic rifles hidden behind the back seat of their cars. For what? "Pa' matar campesinos," they said ("to kill campesinos"). Popular insurgency was already underway in El Salvador, and they were on the other side. Trapped, we did our decoy job and stuck to buses and trains after that. In Latin America, wherever there is a road, there is some form of commercial transportation—a bus, a van, a truck, or even, at one river, a platform on a pulley. Few people own cars. We followed the Pan-American Highway south through Colombia, Ecuador, and Peru down to Lima, then headed inland and upward, into the southern Andes—Huancayo, Ayacucho, Cuzco, through Puno and across Lake Titicaca into Bolivia, then south into Argentina, across the northern pampa into Paraguay, and from there across the Friendship Bridge (with police on our heels) into Brazil. Two months of hard travel through unforgettable geographies and adventures got us to Rio. There was no tourism in that part of the world in 1972, just a handful of travelers who kept crossing paths at hostels and bus depots along the way. Only one travel guide to South America existed, and we all used it. Over and over again, people asked us, "How did you get here?" and, almost as often, "Why did you come? Why would anyone come here?" The trip cemented my lifelong engagement with all things Latin American—geography, people, politics, art, popular culture, music, language. The Andean region, which turns up repeatedly in this book, grabbed me and has never let go. So in 2002 I honored that original trip by repeating, with the help of that vegetarian son, the climb to the top of Huayna Picchu to retake a photograph from thirty years before and register my gratitude.

Generation

For my generation of scholars, the last three decades of the twentieth century were a time of astonishing transformation and innovation in the work of knowledge making. Every discipline underwent a methodological revolution. Disciplinary boundaries were challenged at every turn; new objects of study bounded into view, called forth by new concepts and methods. Cold War preoccupations created area studies, geographically framed spaces of inquiry that marshaled expertise from multiple disciplines (and gave defense money to comparative literature students). The transgressive, insurgent energies galvanized by 1960s uprisings eventually took up residence in university departments. The democratization of higher education demanded new subject matters and fields of inquiry. Objects of study appeared that were impossible to house in existing disciplines—things like ideology, hegemony, everyday life, subjectivity, gender, ethnicity, modernity, sexuality, *mestizaje*, the social imagination, dependency, madness, the state. Methodologies traveled and trespassed. Humanists brought interpretive methods to bear on domains beyond literature, religion, and the arts, especially domains otherwise deeded to the social sciences. In those disciplines, empiricism and formalism had left large uncultivated spaces ripe for trespass, and knowledge makers trespassed. Literary scholars extended the tools of close reading to any form of text, and textuality expanded its purview from writing to any complex object. Textuality became not a feature of an object but a lens for looking at objects and discerning their text-ures. Fruitful divisions of labor developed between disciplines and transdisciplinary inquiries. Feminism challenged literary canons and at the same time refreshed and reanimated them. The archives gave up new treasures. Experts and trespassers became complementary, each benefiting the other.

For individual scholars, these methodological revolutions were enormously liberating. You could be a scholar and teacher without necessarily housing yourself in a discipline or a single department. You could rove and belong to multiple conversations. You could cultivate the arts of trespass. Where there were fences, you could climb them, bearing gifts. You could look for commonalities and continuities across contrasting or opposing domains. You could show, as I sometimes do here, that what high culture is doing, popular culture is doing too, maybe better or sooner. I was trained in textual analysis and have loved its revelatory powers when deployed in discursive regimes that fail to reflect on themselves (like ethnography in chapter 10 or a sentencing document in chapter 13). What an exhilarating experience. Introducing *Keywords*, Raymond Williams wrote "The work which this book records has been done in an area where several disciplines converge but in general do not meet" (1976, 2). Today, because of Williams and many other innovative theorists, many of the disciplines do meet in postdisciplinary spaces with names that end with the word *studies*. The work that this book records is the result of having lived that knowledge-making revolution, lived the change. Those three decades of intellectual dynamics were the gift of a lifetime. My debts are too many to name.

These revolutions in knowledge making were animated to a significant degree by social justice and liberation struggles that also shaped the generation of scholars and teachers who grew up in the 1950s and entered universities in the 1960s and early 1970s. These struggles have been the driving force of our work. We learned to think surrounded by anti-imperial, anticolonial, antiracist, antipatriarchal, antiauthoritarian struggles—for independence all over Africa, for sexual liberation and gender equality, for desegregation in South Africa and the United States, against Soviet takeovers in Eastern Europe and US imperialism in Southeast Asia and Latin America.

Location

For each of us, the particularities of our locations and experiences channeled the ways these engagements took shape in our lives. I grew up in a small farm town in English Canada in the 1950s, in a world steeped in coloniality, though not monopolized by it. In Listowel, Ontario, we were British subjects and members of the British Commonwealth. We studied, worked, and played beneath portraits of the Queen of England. We sang to God to save her every morning—and look, as of this writing, she is still alive. The back of our school rulers listed the English monarchs in chronological order so we could learn to recite them by heart. People kept scrapbooks of the royal family. My aunts and uncles fought proudly for England in World War II, my grandfathers and great-uncles in World War I. Every winter the town put on a Gilbert and Sullivan operetta along with the skating carnival and of course hockey. (Once, unforgettably, a hypnotist came through.) We had good schooling, but it taught us that everything that was important happened somewhere else. We lived outdoors, spending summers at cottages on lakes and winters on backyard rinks. We were taught Canadian history but did not learn that it mattered, even to us. We learned to sing through English folk songs—"Sir Eglamore that Valiant Knight, fa la daffy down dilly"—and in church choirs that sang English hymns. We wouldn't have been able to imagine Canadian hymns. We devoured British children's literature—Enid Blyton, Albert Payson Terhune, A. A. Milne—though we also read and loved the *Little Women* books, L. M. Montogmery's classic *Anne of Green Gables* series, and endless tales of the Far North, usually involving heroic sled dogs. In high school we were taught to write well, using English essayists as models. To this day, I write like an essayist. The empire made geography important. Every year each student received an atlas, Commonwealth countries in red. We belonged to this immense planetary constellation—the empire closed us off from ourselves but opened the planet to us. My love of geography, both maps and land, began there and has never left me. The moment I learned to read, *Great Wonders of the World*, given to me by my grandmother, became my favorite book. That's where I want to live, I thought. Out there.

Anticolonialism was in the mix too. After all, we were a colony, populated by those who left the motherland by choice or force. The town's name was

Irish, brought by refugees from the potato famine in the 1840s. Our grandmother, Annie MacGillivray, made sure we knew what the English had done to the Highland Scots: Bonnie Prince Charlie's exile, the routing of the clans, the Battle of Culloden (1746). That defeat had brought the highland MacGillivrays to Canada. She read us Bobby Burns, played the piano, and sang "Bonnie Charlie's nu awa'" from a songbook stored in the piano bench. Our aunts flung the highland fling at Christmas. Like many families in the town, the MacGillivrays had a tartan and a family crest that defiantly said, "Touch not the cat / bot with a glove." From early on I knew colonial violence existed, anticolonialism too, with music, poetry, and dance to go with it.

We were colonizers, too, settler colonialists, but unforgivably we did not know ourselves well that way. Indian myths, symbols, and token objects were all around us, but as children we had no idea our Native age-mates were being taken from their parents and sent to harsh, faraway residential schools where some of them died. Most of us did not fully grasp that devastating reality till decades later when, in a millennial breakthrough, Canada's Truth and Reconciliation Commission did its work (2008–15).

Our parents were ambitious for their six children, two sons and four daughters. These ambitions had different implications for the two genders. In the minds of the adults, the sons had knowable futures. The eldest would take over the father's profession (in this case, a law practice, which he did); the younger would seek another path (in this case, it was to be medicine, which he didn't). For them, the difficult thing was escaping this fate should they want to. The girls, in contrast, faced a futurity gap. Our mother, a feminist raised in Toronto, was athletic and university educated. She taught English at the town high school. She wanted bigger things for her daughters . . . but what were they? In the 1950s and early 1960s, nobody seemed to know. The adults could not tell us what was possible for young women of our generation. The world was clearly changing, but no one around us seemed able to discern what we might aspire to. We would certainly go to university (our mother wanted all smart girls to go to university), but to study what? What for? For the daughters, the future was a journey without a map. I faced a particular challenge, for I had been born into a cruel injustice: a large deep port-wine stain covered one side of my face. I was a freak. This catastrophe placed me among the wretched of the earth, for life. It made my possibilities particularly hard to imagine. When I asked my mother one day if she thought anyone would ever give me a job, she answered, "I don't know." I had no idea whether I would be able to build a life I would want to live. There's a crisis of futurity for you.

At the same time, in that little town, the empire had left us surrounded by single women who had built lives outside marriage and family. World War I had left a cadre of educated, independent spinsters whose male counterparts had died. They were nicknamed the Senate and had the status of community elders. They prided themselves on being cultured and cosmopolitan. They read, painted, dressed well, traveled, taught school, played golf and bridge, ran clubs, held teas, confronted straying husbands. They seemed to have little use for men; often they lived with their sisters. Passing by at church, they would ask what I was reading and give advice like, "Remember, always have your own money." As the Queen does.

Listowel was a small but not isolated place. We heard what was going on in the world. Refugees arrived from Hungary, South Africa, and later Vietnam. I first heard the word *fascist* from a Sunday school teacher who had fled apartheid. The couple who owned the scrap metal business had numbers tattooed on their arms. They had met in Bergen-Belsen; he later became our mayor. Listowel had one Black family, a Chinese restaurateur, and, somehow, a family of Japanese farmers whose son became student body president. Were there racism and anti-Semitism? Yes, of course. But the primal everyday prejudice was anti-Catholicism. The town of three thousand had thirteen Protestant churches and a single Catholic one, located just outside the town limits. Intermarriage, to many, was catastrophic.

Eventually we got TV. The day John F. Kennedy was assassinated, our high school history teacher, a Finnish socialist from a northern mining town, announced it on the public-address system, weeping, and we were all sent home. I mourned for months, made a scrapbook. But Canada was roiling, too, in a drama of decolonization. That same year, 1963, the Front de Liberation du Québec formed in Quebec, a Marxist-based revolutionary guerrilla group with the goal of liberating its homeland from Anglo-Saxon domination. It aimed to found a sovereign nation on socialist principles and worker justice. The model was Cuba. The group's manifesto was titled *Nègres blancs d'Amérique* (White Negroes of America) (Vallières 1968). The rest of the decade was punctuated by bombings, kidnappings, hijackings, even killings, and horrible uncertainty about whether the country could hold together, or wanted to. It did, but to this day the political wing of the sovereignty movement, the Parti Québecois, founded in 1967, remains a player in Canadian politics. Our father had been prescient. Though he had been taught to hate the Catholic French, he saw that bilingualism was the country's only path forward. One by one, he sent us to Quebec for long summers working on our French.

Even as separatism threatened, Canada decolonized. 1967 was a year of nationalist delirium, as the country celebrated the centennial of its founding. It acquired its own flag and hosted the world's fair in Montreal. It was a massive, ecstatic ritual of (white) emancipation that all of my generation remember. In its aftermath, programs in Canadian studies began to appear in universities. But I was already on my way to find the Great Wonders of the World.

Futurology, Independence

The four sisters had to forge their own paths, and all did. It took courage, risk, and hard work. One became a nurse, married a doctor, divorced him, and became a gifted surgeon. One studied history, played varsity ice hockey, taught school in Lesotho, landed a reporting job at a small-town weekly, and wound up as managing editor and expert political writer at a major Canadian newspaper. One studied English in Canada and Oxford, became a competitive gymnast and rower, got an entry-level position at the Canadian Broadcasting Corporation, and became a prizewinning documentary TV writer and director who worked all over the world. For my part, I had figured out early on that academic achievement would be my path, my "shot," as the hero of *Hamilton* put it. Books were always my salvation; they took me elsewhere. In high school I was discovered to have "a gift for languages" and was able to study French, Latin, and German. This, I realized, was my ticket to "out there."

So it was that in September 1966, I stood before a registration desk at the University of Toronto to sign up for the honors BA in modern languages and literatures. I was unprepared for urban university life, a gifted and hardworking student from a farm town who scored high on provincial exams and won a scholarship but had no idea what was possible. The degree involved reading the canons of three European literatures from the Middle Ages to the present in the original languages. That did not sound hard to me. I loved the *desdoblamiento*, the multiplying of the self that multilingualism enabled. I read grammars for fun. "Which three languages do you plan to work in?" the clerk asked. I hadn't thought about it. French and English, certainly, and then, without a second's hesitation, I jumped over German, Russian, and Italian and chose Spanish. Did I already know that those three languages, and later Portuguese, would open exit doors from Anglocentrism and Eurocentrism, two well-worn paths that I desperately wanted to escape? I think so. Did I already understand that I was connected to Spanish not through Spain but through the Americas, where we were all living out the long, overlapping afterlives of empire? Probably, in some inchoate way. Without yet having read a page of Latin American or African literature, did I already suspect I would find in them, among so many things, geographies from and in which to think more richly, creatively, ethically, and deeply? Besides English and French, I chose the only other imperial language on the list, that is, the only one that governed worlds outside of Europe as well as in Europe. The great preoccupations of this book, futurity, coloniality and "the re-conceiving of human experience in non-imperial terms," as Said noted (1994, 276), came together in that choice that made all the sense in the world, though at that moment I might not have been able to say why.

Conclusion

"The political alternatives to present domination," says Elizabeth Grosz, "are not there waiting to be chosen, possible but not yet real. These alternatives . . . are not alternatives, not possibilities until they are brought into existence. . . . Only if the present presents itself as fractured, cracked by the interventions of the past and the promise of the future, can the new be invented, welcomed, and affirmed" (2004, 261). Our Great Solar TVs have for some time now been showing signs of the planetary crisis of futurity. The Anthropocenic threat was well underway in 1966 when I stood at the registrar's desk in Toronto. Some people knew it, but most people didn't know it or know how to know it. In *The Great Derangement* (2016), Amitav Ghosh argues that one of the central problems facing the West is the way industrial capitalism has miseducated and disabled the imaginations of its subjects, rendering them unable to imagine forces and transformations on the vast scale now required. Realism has taught them to treasure specificity in storytelling, the local, the empirical, the concrete. They can grasp, to take a recent example, the last living northern white rhino but not mass extinction, can comprehend illness but not a pandemic. This is surely one of the foremost, most robust elements of the present that must be fractured or cracked as we humans figure out how to live the living and dying that lies before us. This is a daunting and riveting challenge.

PART I |

FUTURE TENSIONS

MODERNITY'S FALSE PROMISES

When the term *postmodern* began circulating the planet in the 1980s, two reactions prevailed among Latin American colleagues, both of them ironic. One was, "Dammit, we haven't even got to modernity yet, and they're calling it off!" and the other, "Fragmentation? Decenteredness? Coexistence of incommensurate realities?—if that's it, we've always been postmodern. *They're catching up to us*." This is by way of saying, as Argentinean critic Graciela Montaldo so lucidly put it, "In general, postmodernism serves in Latin America primarily as a way of thinking about the scope of our modernity" (1997, 628). This, she argued, was the case in Europe and the United States as well. She was right. The 1980s and 1990s saw a rich and interesting rethinking of modernity by scholars in many parts of the world. In Europe and North America, the reflection began, I believe, with Marshall Berman's 1982 classic *All That Is Solid Melts into Air* and culminated, I think, with Arjun Appadurai's groundbreaking *Modernity at Large* (1996). In Latin America, it began with Beatriz Sarlo's watershed *Una modernidad periférica* (A peripheral modernity; 1988) and the groundbreaking volume *Imágenes desconocidas: La modernidad en la encrucijada posmoderna* (Unknown images: modernity and the postmodern crossroads; Calderón 1988b) and culminated, arguably, in Montaldo's "Strategies at the End of the Century" (1997). In Europe and North America, scholars often upheld what I here call the standard account of modernity and tried to address its internal inconsistencies. In Latin America and the Caribbean, the discussion was shaped by more skeptical, decolonizing energies. Scholars began reanalyzing modernity in global and relational terms. Indeed, the argument is made that the process of decolonizing knowledge was one factor giving rise to the *post* in *postmodernity*, because it made modernity into an object of critical reflection, viewed from its own periphery. But what made modernity available in that way was the fact that it had outlived its usefulness. Its ability, in Elizabeth Grosz's terms, to enable possibilities of being otherwise in the face of the chaos and pressing problems of the present (Grosz 2011, 78) was collapsing. It had resulted in a world it was no longer able to explain or direct. In particular, it was clear that the futurology it bore at its heart—that one day the whole world would be fully and equally modern—was a myth. The self-interested and self-deluding mythologies of modernity that prevailed in the Eurocentric intellectual commons, what I will call the standard account, came into question, notably from the global, relational perspectives newly coming into play in the 1990s. These perspectives made visible that coloniality was built into the concept of modernity and its futures.

This chapter does two things. First, it reviews the Eurocentric standard account with an eye to how it worked as a kind of endlessly generative meaning machine. Second, it maps out some key aspects of the global and relational account, especially as articulated by thinkers from Latin America. Section I examines how modernity talked about itself at the metropolitan center from which it saw itself as emanating, and how it became an identitarian discourse. It then looks at the subjugating strategies the standard account used to encode those it defined as its others. Section II, the second half of the essay, considers how those others characterized modernity from their positioning both inside and outside it. One goal of this chapter is to identify some of the contours of a global and relational account of modernity. Another is to suggest that the opacity and incoherence of the standard account derived to a significant degree from its denial of the fact that European modernity was a product of its interactions with other parts of the world. The standard account imagines northern Europe as a civilizational center where modernity arises sui generis, and the rest of the planet as a recipient to which modernity, as a superior civilizational model, will inevitably spread. Many people on the periphery, especially intellectuals, found this story meaningful and convincing and devoted themselves to making it come true.

I | Modernity at Its Center. The Standard Account

How has modernity described itself to itself? In the vast corpus of writings that make up the standard account, four characteristics stand out.[1]

1 Standard accounts are marked by an effort to establish an *array of features* that define modernity. Their presence can be taken as the indicators of its presence. Different accounts name different features; the list of candidates is quite vast. All of the following have been proposed:

   – democracy, the nation-state, class formation
   – industrialization and industrial divisions of labor
   – the high-/low-culture distinction in the cultural sphere
   – urbanization, mass culture, mass society, mass education
   – expansion of markets and wild capitalist growth
   – the hegemonization of instrumental rationality, bureaucratization of society
   – the rise of science as a truth-seeking discourse
   – the privileging of reason as the path to true knowledge
   – the rise of the individual and the idea of his [*sic*] freedom
   – idea of progress, progressive time
   – change as an inherently positive value

   The specific items on the list are less important than the fact that the standard account assumes there should be such a list. At the same time, as the compilation above makes clear, the array of possible defining features seems potentially infinite and not at all coherent. As I suggest below, such inconsistency was necessary for the standard account to work.

2 The standard account requires a *narrative of origin* for modernity. At the same time, it has never settled on one, nor really tried to. Rather, the literature offers a widely varying array of narratives of origin. For example, there is an argument that starts modernity in 1436 with Johannes Gutenberg. Another locates the starting point in the late 1400s with Portuguese maritime expansion. Often accounts start specifically in 1492. Another cites the "long 16th century"—1450–1640 (Touraine 1992). Others, such as Stephen Toulmin (1990), mark 1637, the year of

René Descartes's *Discourse on Method*. For others, Gottfried Leibniz is the key figure. Another widespread version places the starting point at the mid-eighteenth century with the rise of science. Another places it at the end of the eighteenth century with the French Revolution (though not the Haitian and Andean revolutions that occurred at the same time). Some philosophers start modernity in 1800 with the publication of G. W. F. Hegel's *Phenomenology of Spirit*. The first decades of the nineteenth century provide yet another starting point, marked by industrialization, urbanization, and the rise of the nation-state. Other accounts place the starting point at the beginning of the twentieth century with the rise of mass communications, mass society, and modernist aesthetic projects. This was a common position in Latin America. In the ex-colonial world, modernity is often seen as beginning in 1945. That year marked the point at which center-periphery relations were redefined by the paradigm of development versus underdevelopment. It was also the point at which, according to Immanuel Wallerstein (1979), it began to be impossible to think of Europe as the center of the world. In the 1990s the president of El Salvador observed that now that the guerrilla uprising had been defeated, modernity could at last begin in Central America. José Joaquín Brunner and others made similar claims for postdictatorship Chile. Matei Calinescu, in his monumental *Five Faces of Modernity* ([1977] 1987), if anything, vexes all these accounts by telling us that the Latin word *modernus* in its modern sense dates from the sixth century AD (not a date that figures in any standard account) and that in English *modernity* was first used in 1622 (confirming one account), while in French *modernité* turns up only two hundred years later, in 1849 (confirming another account).

What kind of a thing can modernity be if it has so many beginnings? What kind of a concept both needs a moment of beginning and yet constructs a multiplicity of beginnings spanning centuries? Any beginning can be invoked, depending on the argument one wants it to support and the futures one wants it to enable. Why has this state of explanatory excess not been more troubling? More on these questions below.

3 Every standard account defines modernity with respect to a civilizational other. There has to be another. But as with essential features and narratives of origin, a great many such others have been invoked. Modernity's civilizational others have included feudalism, absolutism, the primitive (tribal or subsistence societies), the traditional (peasant and

rural societies), the irrational (animals, non-Westerners, and women), and the underdeveloped or backward (the colonial/ex-colonial world). What remains constant is that in every account, there has to be an other. The borders with these others have been policed and reproduced by the modern academic disciplines institutionalized at the center in the second half of the nineteenth century. Anthropology produces and enforces the category of the primitive; economics, those of backwardness and underdevelopment. Political science administers the distinctions between state and nonstate, simple and complex societies; philosophy, the distinction between the rational and the irrational; literary studies and art history that between high culture and popular or vernacular culture. History administers the concept of progressive time and determines who occupies it and who does not. Sander Gilman has traced the way images of Africans defined the borders of Western aesthetics in the work of Hegel, Arthur Schopenhauer, and Friedrich Nietzsche (Gilman 1982, discussed in Gilroy 1993, 8). In social theory, the vague term *tribal societies* turns up freely when the boundaries of the modern need to be marked in the sand.

In 1998 at the University of Guadalajara, Mexico, Hungarian philosopher Agnes Heller gave a series of lectures on the question, "What is modernity?" Over several days, her richly elaborated account required continuous reference to a contrasting entity called "premodern societies," which by the end of the series had acquired the following characteristics:

- stable social orders
- fixed and absolute norms of goodness, truth, and beauty (as examples, Heller cited the art of Egypt and Mesoamerica, which, she stated, remained unchanged for thousands of years)
- a pyramidal social structure with a male at the top
- the life of the subject is completely determined at birth by its place in the pyramid. There is neither mobility nor the desire for mobility.
- subjects do not question their place in the order, nor desire change
- the ancient is sacred
- the dominant worldview is supplied by religion and founded on absolutes
- what the subject perceives as its needs are given at birth and correspond to its place in the order. Needs are assigned qualitatively.
- domestic violence exists in normalized forms

- sex is obligatory on the woman's part
- passions and emotions are expressed more freely
- happiness exists not as a subjective state but as an objective condition determined by concrete criteria.

It is easy to reconstruct for each item on this list what feature of modernity was being established by means of the contrast (see also Heller, 1999 and Grumley 1999). But the standard account does not require this list to be bounded, coherent, or empirically verifiable. Did the philosopher really believe those items were general attributes of societies outside European modernity? For its part, the Mexican audience wanted to know where the Catholic Church fit in the schema.

So, for a third time, the question arises. What is the rationale for requiring a fixed other and generating a range of them to choose from, again according to the argument one wants to make and the futures one wants to enable? Why has this infinity of content been a feature of, rather than a problem for, the discourse on modernity? In the standard account, essential features, a unified other, and a narrative of origin are the mechanisms for establishing an object of study. At the same time, since a multiplicity of features, others, and narratives of origin are generated, the object of study can be established, centered, and re-centered in an infinity of ways. An infinity of arguments can be made, an infinity of stories told.

4   Finally, the standard account depends on a form of interpretive power I have come to call the monopolistic use of categories. I use this phrase to refer to an interpretive logic whereby if A is a symptom of B, then every instance of A *may be read as* an instance of B. Thus, if rationality is a criterial feature of modernity, then wherever the interpreter encounters rationality, *if they choose to do so*, they may identify it as indicating the presence of modernity. By the same token, all instances of irrationality may be read, *if the interpreter chooses*, as signifying the presence of the non- or premodern. This structure of possibilities grants the interpreter a huge capacity for absorbing or creating otherness, according to the argument they want to make and the futures they want to enable. I focus here on the phrase "if the interpreter chooses" to stress that this is a form of *interpretive power* on whose workings it is essential to reflect. Who, we may inquire, has access to the power to do such choosing and assign such meanings? Where is this power handed out, and to whom? How is access to it constructed and enforced? What

happens when an unauthorized party contests this power or lays claim to it and proposes an alternative account? Investigating the possibility of "alternative modernities," in *The Black Atlantic*, Paul Gilroy remarked on "the ease and speed with which European particularisms are still [in 1993] being translated into absolute universal standards for human achievement, norms and aspirations" (1993, 7–8). This monopolistic interpretive power is an important dimension of the standard account. Modernity sees itself as owning the characteristics it uses to identify itself and entitled, indeed, called on, to export them to others.

MODERNITY AS IDENTITY

I have been considering so far the way modernity represents itself to itself in the standard account, the way it brings itself into being, the way it lines up a geographic, epochal, civilizational concept of modernity with a range of entirely real historical processes and events, adding, as Grosz puts it, "ideality to the world, transforming the givenness of chaos, the pressing problem into various forms of order" (2011, 78). The concept of modernity, I suggest, was one of the chief mechanisms through which Europe constructed itself and its future as a center, as *the* center, with the rest of the planet as a—its— periphery. The pressing problem was how to establish and sustain global hegemony, what Wallerstein (1979) famously called the modern world system.

This identity-creating force is what Homi Bhabha alludes to when he says the story of modernity is "about the historical construction of a specific position of historical enunciation and address" (1994, 201). Note that this characterization is outer directed, involving address. Modernity is (or was) an extroverted, *diffusionist* project that seeks to interpellate others from a center. It wants to spread—that is its futurology. One of its prime tasks was to make particular kinds of sense of, and give particular kinds of direction to, Europe's interactions with other parts of the world. I have thus found it quite helpful to think about modernity as an identity discourse, as Europe's (or perhaps the white world's) identity discourse as it sought global dominance—as it became the first world. The need for narratives of origins, distinctive features, reified others, and the policing of boundaries combined with the slippery capacity to create and erase otherness at will—these are hallmarks of identity discourses. In this sense, the centrism of modernity is in part ethnocentrism. The standard account does not identify it in this manner, though white supremacist discourse does. The monopolistic use of categories I mentioned earlier is here an ethnocentric practice. Though Euro-, ethno-, and androcentrism are not normally found on that list of features by which modernity characterizes itself, they come into view when modernity's others gain the interpretive power to question the monopolistic use of categories. This is the import of Gilroy's call for an "ethnohistorical reading of western modernity" (1993, 8) and of Enrique Dussel's charge that modernity is constituted by a "eurocentric fallacy." It is, Dussel says, "a European phenomenon constructed in a dialectical relation with a non-European alterity which is its ultimate content" (1993, 65).

Dussel's formulation points to an axis of tension that has little visibility or importance in standard Eurocentric accounts but that is extremely significant elsewhere: the contradiction between modernity's need for fixed others, on the one hand, and its diffusionist, subject-producing ambitions, on the other. Its identitarianism is at odds with its futurology. Frederick Buell (1994, 335) speaks of the incompatibility between modernity's will to produce subjects outside its borders and its need to maintain its alterity in order to define itself. Put another way, the need to establish fixed others in order to define itself is at odds with the ambition to modernize others through processes of diffusion. This internal contradiction intersects with another: modernity's concept of individual liberty requires the subordination of others. In classic liberal theory, liberty consists in the possibilities individuals have to develop their capacities and follow their desires and interests (Held 1983). This self-realizing concept of the individual presupposes a division of labor in which reproduction and care work are carried out by others. Liberty thus conceived depends on the existence of population sectors who by definition are unfree, charged with the reproductive, dependent, custodial, and tutelary labor that enables the free individual. These conflicting dynamics explain much about the ways the standard account encodes its periphery, to which I now turn.

MODERNITY'S OTHERS. FROM CENTER TO PERIPHERY

How does the center encode the periphery from within modernity? Postcolonial criticism has reflected richly on this question. Two key terms have surfaced: *outside* and *behind* (but not, it appears, *below*). Terms like *primitive* and *tribal* mark what is outside modernity; terms like *backward* and *underdeveloped* mark what it is behind. *Feudal* and *traditional* mark things as simultaneously outside and behind. Again, note the centralizing, monopolistic use of these categories: given the interpretive power, the interpreter can choose to read anything that fails to correspond to preconception as an instance of either outsideness or behindness—rather than, say, as an instance of alternative, emergent, diasporic, or contestatory forms of modernity. Nor can the schema recognize phenomena that participate simultaneously in modernity and some other matrix, like postconquest Indigenous social formations in the Americas, for example.

It is important to observe that in the semantics of this spatialized conceptual language, the normative positions of "insideness" and "infrontness" are assigned exclusively to the imagined center from which modernity emanates. In other words, the presence or absence of modernity anywhere can be determined only from that one site. There is no room, say, for the very plausible story that those "in front" are there because they are pushed or propped up by those "behind," or that those "in front" are trapped looking ahead and therefore cannot see what is going on "behind." In other words, the historical agency of the periphery in creating modernity remains systematically invisible to the center. So does what is actually going on in the places modernity is diffusing to. Those binaries of inside/outside and in front/behind obscure the fascinating and variegated global phenomenon of what Beatriz Sarlo (1988) called "peripheral modernity." Likewise, those "in front" and "inside" can easily ignore the degree to which modernity is a product of the periphery's interactions with the center through interfaces like colonialism, neocolonialism, or commerce, for example. Today these phenomena no longer appear to scholars as "outside" or "behind" the modern. They are understood now as within it. Researching and theorizing their role has been one of the central empirical and conceptual tasks in producing a global and relational account of modernity.

As Sarlo observes, to be marginal or peripheral is not to be disconnected from a center but to be intimately connected to it in particular, highly meaningful ways. These connections on the periphery are local, not in the sense that one cannot see the whole picture, but in the sense that one sees the whole picture from a particular epistemic location that is not a center. For similar reasons, gender is a powerful deconstructive category. As ethnographer Anna Lowenhaupt Tsing (1993) reminds us, precisely because women are systematically trivialized and marginalized by modernity, women's knowledges have developed—globally—with a degree of autonomy and distance from both the assimilationist and the othering mechanisms of modernity. The product of forms of agency and meaning making invisible to modernity, women's knowledges systematically offer alternative conceptualizations of the global relations and states of affairs that the centrist lenses of modernity misidentify. Tsing's concepts of marginality and gender are points of entry to a global, relational account of modernity.

II | Modernity on the Periphery

Beyond the center, which is to say, across most of the planet, the roster of features, narratives of origin, and relations of otherness that make up the standard account routinely fail to describe the world. Mexico City is not Paris. Within the standard account, these divergences all have the same explanation: backwardness, the time lag. The periphery is simply behind and will in time catch up. At a particular point in the future, all will be fully and equally modern. That positivist telos made it possible to posit modernity's universals as universals—they will indeed correspond universally when everyone has caught up. The process just has to unfold.

As soon as the time lag is revealed as a lie, however, that futurology fails. The teleology of catching up breaks down, and center-periphery relations come into view as a structure of inequality that creates or constitutes the center. Though scholars today take this structure of inequality as a given, a world system (Wallerstein), in fact, the teleology of catching up lost its credibility only quite recently—in the 1970s, when import-substitution policies broke down and produced a global debt crisis. Only then were modernization and progress called seriously into question. That breakdown was key in making peripheral modernities an object of study. It is the context for the rich body of discussion on which this essay draws. Nevertheless, the futurology of modernization—conveniently treated as synonymous with *modernity*—continues to exert enormous power in the world. It rationalizes invasion under false narratives of diffusing democracy and obscures the torrential flow of profit from the third world to the first.

The epistemology of backwardness and the teleology of progress also have long histories among non-European intellectuals, as meaningful, indeed compelling, interpretive frameworks. They have underwritten great senses of optimism and confidence in ex-colonial societies. They also generated negative diagnostics of failure and lack. *Truncated, partial, incomplete, fragmented*—these are the terms used to describe Latin American modernity in two important Latin American volumes dedicated to rethinking modernity in the late 1980s (Calderón 1988; and a 1987 special issue of the Argentine journal *David y Goliat*). While for many Latin American thinkers this incompleteness was an obvious fact, others questioned the interpretive authority that enabled the center to project reductive and negative self-definitions on others. "Among us," said José Joaquín Brunner, "cultural unease does not come from the exhaustion of modernity, but from exasperation with it" (1987, 39). In a landmark essay titled "Brazilian Culture:

Nationalism by Elimination," Brazilian critic Roberto Schwarz (1992) speaks eloquently of the painful existential conditions that the diffusionist force of modernity creates for intellectuals. The center calls on them constantly to embrace trends and vocabularies arriving one after another from abroad, produced in reference to alien sociocultural contexts and epistemological dilemmas. On the receiving end, these become what Schwarz calls "idéias fora do lugar" (ideas out of place). Ideas, of course, can be adapted in new places—it is no accident that the theory of transculturation originated in Latin America—but, argues Schwarz, a deeper problem remains. The exports come in such rapid sequence that there is never time to domesticate each one or follow it through before the next one arrives. This pacing is not an accident but a dynamic of colonizing power. Schwarz speaks eloquently of the psychic, human, and social cost of this condition of forced receptivity, which deprives the society of the chance to create its own forms of self-understanding and its own futurologies, grounded in its own reality, history, and pressing problems. In particular, Schwarz foregrounds the self-alienation that results when accepting a diagnosis of backwardness and incompleteness as the price of admission to a club (the modern world) in which membership is necessary. On the periphery, according to Schwarz and others, the price of embracing modernity has been to live one's own reality in terms of lack, fragmentation, partiality, imitativeness, and unfulfillment—while plenitude and wholeness are seen as existing elsewhere. This is one of modernity's most powerful planetary fictions.

While Schwarz denounces the epistemic violence of the center's diffusionism, other thinkers claim the epistemic privilege of the periphery, its power to unmask the standard account and reveal the center as it cannot reveal itself. Schwarz's compatriot Silviano Santiago exemplifies this position. For him, peripheral intellectuals occupy "o entre-lugar" ("the space between"), a site from which they can reflect back to the center images of itself that the center could never generate itself but from which it has much to learn. The periphery's powers include the ironic task of enlightening the center about itself.

Santiago does not seem to deny the painful existential conditions Schwarz identifies, however. He simply notes there is a payoff, not for the nation (Schwarz's domain of concern), but for a human field held in common by center and periphery. Santiago's argument has a historical dimension. He argues that to the extent modernity has a self-critical, self-interrogating capability, it is the result of the long-term presence of voices from the periphery. René Antonio Mayorgal makes a similar point. The periphery is a source of insight for the center because the "insufficiencies" of modernity are displayed there (Larraín Ibañez 1996, 139). This also makes the periphery a source of solutions that cannot be generated at the center.

As the texts to which I have been referring attest, since the 1980s more and more writers have laid claim to the periphery's power to describe and define itself, offering empirical and conceptual alternatives to the centrist imagery of backwardness and lack. A rich and suggestive literature has resulted to which Latin American thinkers have been important contributors. Rejecting the center's account, which treats global diffusion as a kind of natural by-product of modernity, this critical literature explores a variety of conceptual relationships between center and periphery. This literature has been an important force in undermining the hegemony of modernity and its mythologies. In these final pages, I illustrate three of these relational parameters: contradiction, complementarity, and differentiation.

1—CONTRADICTION

The power structure of center-periphery is in open contradiction with the emancipatory, democratizing project of modernity. Intellectuals in the Americas have been pointing this out for five hundred years. In the very export of its ideas, in other words, modernity stands in contradiction with itself, though this is systematically invisible at the center. Thus, Homi Bhabha asks, "What is modernity in those colonial conditions where its imposition is itself the denial of historical freedom, civic autonomy, and the ethical choice of re-fashioning?" (1988, 198). For Bhabha, the history of the colonial and ex-colonial world generates an alternative futurology, an alternative narrative of emancipation: freedom and agency are not given by modernity. Rather, they have to be fought for within it. From this standpoint, modernity appears not as an agent that grants freedom but as an agent that sets in motion certain conflicts and that is itself constituted by those conflicts.

2—COMPLEMENTARITY

As observed earlier, the standard account of modernity includes a futurological narrative of diffusion. Modernity emanates outward from its center and does so naturally by virtue of its civilizational superiority. This supposition defines the center as a center. And from that center, the actual content of the diffusion—the specifics of what gets diffused, when, how, and to whom—is of no particular interest. It is unproblematic and inconsequential—nothing about it could alter the conception of what modernity is. Far from being a constitutive feature of modernity, or an aspect of a global division of labor, diffusion is a side effect. On the receiving end, however, it is highly con-sequential. Diffusion translates into processes of reception, transcultura-tion, resistance, adaptation, and so on. On the receiving end, the content and character of processes of diffusion create reality. For example, in the standard Eurocentric account of modernity, European out-migration and African slavery do not appear as events. Europe's displaced peasantries sim-ply disappear from history the moment they board ship, while captured Africans do not come into view at all. But in the Americas, both groups are crucial historical actors without whom the history of modernity in the Americas cannot be told. The "backward" peasantries displaced by mod-ernization in Europe are invited to the Americas as a modernizing force to overcome "backward" Indigenous and mestizo peoples. (What would Eu-ropean modernity have looked like if those displaced peasantries had not departed? Would Italy and Ireland have had agrarian revolutions as Mexico and Russia did?) Paul Gilroy (1993), Roberto Schwarz (1992), Sidney Mintz (1985), and others insist that slavery be located firmly within the modern. Gilroy demands we "look more deeply into the relationship of racial terror and subordination to the inner character of modernity" (1993, 70–71). Gil-roy's The Black Atlantic (1993) makes one of the first comprehensive inter-ventions to set terms for a transatlantic account of modernity, particularly with respect to culture. He insists on the idea of countercultures within modernity, and cultural formations that live simultaneously inside and out-side modernity's borders.

When uncontested, the standard account assumes a transparent and un-problematic assimilation of modernity's gifts on the reception end. Noth-ing in the standard account requires questioning this assumption. On the reception end, however, the idea of assimilation explains little or nothing. Filling that explanatory gap is surely one of the main reasons that the theory of transculturation arose in Latin America and that concepts like hybridity, mestizaje, and créolité became the bases for powerful analyses of cultural dynamics in the Americas (more on this below).

3—DIFFERENTIATION

I spoke above of the interpretive monopoly that prevails in the standard ac-count. To challenge that interpretive monopoly, non-Eurocentric thinkers assert difference against false claims of sameness. For instance, the standard account tends to assume that progress on the periphery has the same referen-tial meaning as progress at the center. On the periphery, however, it becomes glaringly apparent that progress there is not the same at all. The difference is futurological. In the center, progress can refer to futurities like "bettering the human condition" or "moving toward greater human plenitude." But on the periphery, where modernity is imagined as arriving by diffusion, progress means a futurity of "catching up" or "imitating what has already happened elsewhere." That teleology, as many critics point out, imposes a permanent identity crisis in which, as Bhabha put it, whatever one does is "not quite" enough (1994, 88).

In the colonial and ex-colonial places to which modernity gets exported, modernity and modernization tend to differentiate sharply. They crack apart so completely that thinkers often see modernization as actually displacing modernity. Reflection on this question in Latin America has been rich and diverse. Gino Germani (1969) argued that modernization worked as much against modernity as for it. For Aníbal Quijano (1988), after World War II, modernization eclipsed all other aspects of modernity. For him, the two are completely incommensurate. While Latin America became a passive recipient of modernization from the late nineteenth century on, Quijano argues that it has been an active producer of modernity since 1492. The history of modernity is unthinkable without the Americas. Quijano blames British capitalism for bringing modernization without modernity to Latin America. Alain Touraine (1988) rejects any equation of modernity and modernization and, in fact, any fixed relation between the two. What needs to be grasped, he argues, is the way any particular social formation combines modernity with some particular form of modernization. Norbert Lechner (1990) posits an irreducible tension between the two. Lechner defines *modernization* as the unfolding of instrumental rationality, and *modernity* as the unfolding of a normative rationality leading toward autonomy and self-determination. In the Latin American context, the first is destructive of the second. Thinking about Peru, anthropologist Rodrigo Montoya (1992) makes a similar argument, defining *modernity* as self-determination and autonomy, while *modernization* refers to capitalist development and the Western civilizing project. On the neocolonial periphery, Montoya argues, it is impossible to achieve modernity by means of modernization. This is the basis for his proposal to create a distinct modernity using Andean Indigenous principles.

Other theorists, including José Joaquín Brunner (1994), Néstor García Canclini (1989), and Frederick Buell (1994), sometimes use *modernity* and *modernization* interchangeably. This has the effect for the most part of reducing modernity to modernization. Perhaps this reduction registers the impact of postmodern and post–Cold War thought, which tends to see modernity's

CHAPTER ONE |

grand emancipatory projects as a thing of the past, replaced by a new form of citizenship anchored in consumption.

CONDITIONS OF PERIPHERAL MODERNITY

I have been exploring the outlines of a global and relational account of modernity. Beyond the center, I have argued, on the receiving end of modernity's diffusion, what modernity becomes will, among other things, contradict, complement, and differentiate itself from the standard account. In the Americas, two existential and epistemic realities, both colonial, seem key in shaping what modernity becomes and what becomes of it. These two realities are (1) a condition of *imposed receptivity* based on unequal power and (2) the *copresence of modernity's "selves" and "others."* These final pages develop these two observations.

By *imposed receptivity*, I refer to the circumstances, lamented by Roberto Schwarz, of being on the receiving end of an asymmetrical relation of diffusion. Gabriel García Márquez's invented town of Macondo in *One Hundred Years of Solitude* vividly captures the colonial dynamic whereby things descend on the periphery unpredictably from places unknown. The receiving community has power to determine how these new elements are received but not whether they are received.

By *copresence of modern selves and others*, I refer to historical situations in which the disciples of modernity face the task of founding societies that integrate both themselves and their nonmodern others.

These two dimensions of ex-colonial reality turn up repeatedly when scholars trace the historical and cultural dynamics of modernity in the Americas. A few examples illustrate the point. As discussed in chapter 15, imagining independence from Spain, Latin American thinkers envisioned a future in which enlightened, European-descended elites governed unenlightened multiracial masses. Those masses were what "held things back," it was understood (Rama 1984). More recent analyses, however, argue the opposite. Among elites, the new historians say, modernity's diffusion often ended up preventing progress by fortifying existing colonial hierarchies. In particular, in the heterogeneous societies of the Americas, modernity's need for well-defined others actually sharpened distinctions between elites (seen as governed by modernity) and masses (seen as governed by tradition, tribalism, or barbarism). In the core imaginary of modernity, Indigenous peoples and mestizo masses existed outside the very history the enlightened elites were assigned to make. Peruvian sociologist Guillermo Nugent makes this interesting argument in *El laberinto de la choledad* (The labyrinth of cholitude; 1992). In the nineteenth century, Nugent argues, Peru's Indig-enous majority was rapidly "expulsados del tiempo" (expelled from time). They were no longer seen as players in the creation of the Peruvian nation.[2] Modernity polarized. As Nugent puts it, "los señores se hicieron más señores y los indios más indios" (the oligarchs became more oligarchical and the Indians became more Indian; 71; translations mine). The othering mecha-nisms of modernity legitimized, and indeed imposed, what in modernity's own terms was an antimodern social regression. There was no space in the standard account for the heterogeneous social formations that emerged wherever European imperialism left its mark. In Argentina the modern lib-eral project not only expelled Indigenous people from time but unleashed a full-fledged campaign of genocide, set in motion by President Domingo Faustino Sarmiento, one of the most cosmopolitan, modern intellectuals in the hemisphere at the time. On the periphery, eradicating the Indigenous population and importing displaced European peasants were complemen-tary, not contradictory, strategies.

In Peru, Nugent argues, the elites created what he calls a *countermoder-nity*, in which aspects of modernity were used to bolster a colonial social order that the center would have regarded as archaic. This resulted, says Nu-gent (1992, 73), from a selective reception of modernity, which landed elites saw as essentially foreign to themselves. This is quite different from the way the standard account imagines modernity's diffusion. Yet what I'm calling the condition of imposed receptivity makes such selective reception inevi-table. The option of simply rejecting modernity outright did not exist, nor did the option of ignoring it.

But why would Peru's elites experience modernity as "essentially for-eign"? Often this is taken as evidence of their backwardness. But another ex-planation suggests itself, namely, the copresence of the self and the other, the ex-colonial condition. In Peru the lived realities of an Indigenous majority and three centuries of colonial cohabitation were more than enough to make modernity foreign. The standard account does not allow for the type of so-cial formation that the elites on the periphery were charged with modern-izing. This is another key insight of a global and relational account.

Schwarz elaborates a somewhat similar argument with respect to Brazil. "When Brazil became an independent state," he says, "a permanent collabo-ration was established between the forms of life characteristic of colonial oppression and the innovations of bourgeois progress" (1992, 14). That Brazil remained a slaveholding society, for example, shaped the idea of freedom that developed there. To be free in Brazil was to be unenslaved. Schwarz argues that in Brazil the concept of "free" individuals developed not around the Rousseauian idea of personal freedom defined in the standard account but around the idea of patronage, or (in Portuguese) *favor*, a form of bondage distinct from slavery. In this system, free (i.e., unenslaved) persons survive by making themselves dependent on the favor of individuals of wealth and power. Such a system obviously is at odds with modern individualism and liberalism. Yet it was sustained—and even imposed—by modern categories of freedom and autonomy projected from the center onto a slave society. The result, argues Schwarz, is a form of peripheral modernity peculiar to Brazil. The *favor* system, Schwarz argues, shaped Brazil's modern institutions, its bureaucracies, and its system of justice, all of which, "though ruled by *favor*, affirmed the forms and theories of the modern bourgeois state" (24). Schwarz underscores the "extraordinary dissonance that results when modern culture is used to this purpose" (24).

Again, to the standard account, the *favor* system signals backwardness, a failure to absorb modern democratic ideals. But Schwarz insists: How could it be otherwise? The reality was that, as in Peru, liberal ideas could be neither rejected nor implemented in Brazil in the nineteenth century. Imposed receptivity made it impossible to reject modernity's prescriptions; the copresence of modernity's others made it impossible to implement them. Again, the futurology fails. Under no circumstances does Schwarz accept a diagnosis of backwardness to account for such situations. "Modern" centers and "backward" peripheries, he insists, belong to the same order of things and are products of the same historical conditions. Slavery in Brazil (and throughout the Americas) was not an archaic, premodern holdover. It was fully integrated into the historical project of the republic. The conditions upholding slavery in Brazil (which lasted until 1888) are as modern as those governing the mode of production at the center. In fact, they are irremediably entangled. What possible futures can be imagined that contain them both?

This is the global, relational problem that the standard account systematically obscures. In that account, the *process* of diffusion/reception of modernity abroad is at most a spontaneous and collateral effect, which can reveal nothing important about the nature of modernity itself. Modernity's norms do not appear as generating an international division of labor, for example, or webs of global relations. On the reception end, however, the diffusionist force of modernity becomes a powerful determinant of reality in all its dimensions. Its empirical particularities are very consequential, in everything from clothing to constitutions. This is a truism to which metropolitan theorizing on modernity remains remarkably immune—Marshall Berman, Stephen Toulmin, Agnes Heller, and their interlocutors took no notice of it, for instance, in otherwise comprehensive treatises. Their Euro-centered intellectual spheres did not call on them to do so.

I cannot resist adding a resonant anecdote from the history of modernity on another periphery, northern Africa. In a fascinating study of French colonial cities, anthropologist Paul Rabinow (1989, 277) argues that "France's first comprehensive experience in urban planning" took place not in France but in Morocco. Early twentieth-century French urban planners, he shows, despised France because it was so bound by tradition that it could not truly be modernized. At the turn of the twentieth century, they saw the colonial frontier as the place where experimental modern urbanism could truly develop. Colonial power was a help: everything could be done by fiat. Negotiation with tradition was not required. Working by colonial fiat, the French architects designed new ultramodern cities that were also colonial cities: racial hierarchy and the copresence of the other were built into the design, in the form of urban segregation. One of the priorities was to arrange the permanent cohabitation of French and Muslim populations in segregated, adjacent, aesthetically pleasing spaces where each group could sustain its own world. So here the colonial frontier becomes not the site of backwardness but the vanguard of modernity. Morocco was an opportunity to create a modern urban social formation, sustained by the violence of colonial power. Rabinow's aim was to revindicate the early twentieth-century French planners by noting that they worked out of a deep respect for cultural differences. This tolerance, he argues, was replaced later by homogenizing, technocratic attitudes. One cannot help but observe, however, that in the designs the copresence of the other is taken into account through segregation, a practice that enforces and reinforces the categories of otherness that are key to modernity's self-definition. Do such formations on the periphery represent a dissonant deployment of modernity, to use Schwarz's term? Are they instances of countermodernity, to use Nugent's term? Or the pseudo-modernity lamented by Octavio Paz (Brunner 1988, 96)? Or are they alternative realizations of modern plenitude, as Paul Gilroy might say?

PERIPHERY AND PLENITUDE

The first decades of the twentieth century are often seen as the moment at which modernity erupted in Latin America. Political participation democratized, and urban middle classes emerged along with consumer markets, industrialization, the technological transformation of daily life, and modern oppositional movements: unions, feminism, Marxism, anarchism. Cities grew and acquired influence over the landed gentry. In the arts, radio, photography, cinema, and avant-garde movements flourished. What happens if we examine this consolidation of modernity through the lenses I have been proposing here? Let me offer just a few examples from the domain of literature and aesthetics.

In the arts, the standard account identifies modernity with urbanization and urban aesthetics, from Charles Baudelaire's flaneur in Paris in the 1860s to Walter Benjamin's study of Baudelaire in the 1930s. The aesthetic projects of the European avant-gardes originated in the city. In the standard account, the city is the vanguard of modern civilization, its cutting edge, its most dramatic creation. In the absence of the city, modernity is absent also. The rural becomes synonymous with backwardness, modernity's other. From the point of this urban norm, how would one view a novel like *Don Segundo Sombra* (1926), an Argentine classic by Ricardo Güiraldes? It is a nostalgic bildungsroman about the Argentine pampa that narrates the relationship between a young gentleman and an old gaucho or cowboy. Within metropolitan norms, it is scarcely imaginable that such a folkloric pastoral appeared in the years between, say, Virginia Woolf's two experimental masterpieces *Mrs Dalloway* (1923) and *To the Lighthouse* (1927). Viewed from there, Güiraldes's novel seems a clear case of anachronism.

But the fact is that in the Americas, North as well as South, modernity produced a flourishing of experiments in nonurban aesthetics, artistic projects anchored not in the city but in the countryside, the jungle, the mountains, border regions, and the heterogeneous ex-colonial social order.[3] The avant-garde movement in Brazil, for example, was launched in 1928 by an outrageous document called the "Anthropophagist Manifesto" (*anthropophagist* means "cannibal"), by the poet and cultural activist Oswald de Andrade. The aesthetic program it proposes, with seriousness and irony, embraces the decidedly nonmodern figure of the cannibal as the touchstone for a modern Brazilian cultural practice. Anthropophagist aesthetics resignified the relation of imposed receptivity. What comes to us from abroad, it said, we will neither imitate nor obey; rather, we will devour it, defecate what is not of use to us, and absorb the rest into our own flesh. What a dramatic reimagining of diffusionism! Critic Silviano Santiago lays out the futurology: the "co-existence of castration and liberation" in anthropophagist thought both "evokes a condition of cultural dependency" and posits the possibility of "an original third-world culture that necessarily participated in the European ethnocentric tradition, at the same time as it questioned it"

(1996, 177). The other central figure of Brazilian modernism, Mário de Andrade, was a cosmopolitan poet, novelist, ethnographer, musicologist, photographer, pedagogue, and autodidact who never left Brazil. He wrote the canonical novel of Brazilian modernism, *Macunaíma* (1928), a comic prose fantasy whose hero is a Tupi Indian who, like a picaresque trickster, travels throughout the territory of Brazil causing trouble. Mario de Andrade also wrote one of the great urban poems of all time, the *Paulicéia Desvairada* (in English titled *Hallucinated City*), a book-length avant-garde paean to the city of São Paulo. The poem appeared in 1922, the same year James Joyce published *Ulysses*. My point here is that for the modern artists of the Americas, both country and city were privileged terrains.

The same would be said of a contemporary of the Brazilians, the Guatemalan novelist Miguel Ángel Asturias, winner of the Nobel Prize in Literature in 1967. Asturias wrote a famous experimental urban novel about dictatorship (*El señor presidente*, 1938) and the equally famous experimental rural novel *Hombres de maiz* (1949). The first of these inaugurates the dictator novel, which would become an important subgenre in Latin American literature. The second is a unique experiment in which the author tries to construct a Guatemalan national imaginary by recuperating and resignifying Maya mythology. Asturias exemplifies concretely the anthropophagic image of the Brazilians. His contact with Maya mythology did not and could not have taken place in a modernizing Guatemala, which in the 1920s did not value its Indigenous pasts. Rather, it happened in France at the Sorbonne, where Asturias was sent to study law and escape dictatorship. Modern Mexican literature includes many modern and modernist writers who experimented in rural aesthetics. Examples include Nelly Campobello, Agustín Yañez, and Juan Rulfo. Parallel figures in Brazil include José Lins do Rego, Gracilian Ramos, Jorge Amado, and Raquel de Queiroz. Campobello and Queiroz exemplify a wave of modern women's writing that includes Gabriela Mistral and Marta Brunet (Chile) and Teresa de la Parra (Venezuela). Mistral, who received the Nobel Prize in Literature in 1942, wrote a vast, posthumously published text titled *Poema de Chile* in which a woman poet traverses the territory of her nation in the company of an Indigenous child. In this exercise of freedom, the city is nowhere in sight. For modern Latin American women writers, the city often represented a descent into immobilization and unfreedom. In modern European literature, it is difficult to encounter anything like these kinds of nonurban aesthetic experiments; in North America, however, one does.

Yet another series of modernist literary experiments takes place in what could be called *frontier aesthetics*, in which such writers as Horacio Quiroga (Uruguay), José Eustacio Rivera (Colombia), and Rómulo Gallegos (Venezuela) use South American geographies to allegorize the borders of modernity and the vexed relations between modernity, coloniality, and capitalist modernization.[4] Read against European psychological fiction of the time, these geographic allegorizations easily appear anachronistic. Read against the contradictions of peripheral society, however, the anachronism disappears (Lechner 1990). The novels capture the modern condition. The corpus also includes a modern project that is both impossible and unnecessary in Europe. Works of what might be called *ethnographic aesthetics* address that singular predicament of ex-colonial states: the coexistence of modernity's selves and its others. From folklore collections to works of social realism and indigenism, this corpus often exhibits the polarizing racism Nugent describes.

Such projects in rural, frontier, and ethnographic aesthetics reflect important dimensions of modernity in the Americas. They also laid the groundwork for the so-called boom of Latin American narrative in the 1960s. It is not often observed that the classic novels that make up the boom are overwhelmingly nonurban, from Alejo Carpentier's *Los pasos perididos* (*The Lost Steps*; Cuba, 1956) through José María Arguedas's *Los rios profundos* (*Deep Rivers*; Peru, 1958), Carlos Fuentes's *La muerte de Artemio Cruz* (*The Death of Artemio Cruz*; Mexico, 1962), Mario Vargas Llosa's *La casa verde* (*The Green House*; Peru, 1966), and Darcy Ribeiro's *Maira* (1972). When in his masterpiece *Grande Sertão: Veredas* (*The Devil to Pay in the Backlands*; 1956) the Brazilian João Guimarães Rosa wanted to imitate James Joyce, he substituted the city of Dublin with the vast interior plains of Brazil. It worked.

One cannot help but be fascinated by the dynamism of these projects. In the terms under discussion here, they often involve reversals in which the periphery reclaims the center. Equally striking is the degree to which they are anchored in the copresence of self and other, the ex- and neocolonial condition. These were creative engagements with reality, history, and futurity in terms not laid down by the center. To return to the relational categories introduced above, they are peripheral modernisms standing in relations of contradiction, complementarity, and differentiation with those of the metropolis. Their emancipatory power, as critics have often noted, lies chiefly in refusing the self-alienated position of imposed receptivity, as Roberto Schwarz would have it, or in using that position as a site of creative authenticity, as Silviano Santiago would say.

The "magic" of Latin American magic realism, as Jean Franco (1967, 1978) pointed out, derives from another feature alien to the metropole: an engagement by writers with the popular. In the standard account of modernity, popular and vernacular cultures have little place. If anything, they are perceived as forms of otherness ("tradition," for example). But as a number of researchers have shown, one of the most conspicuous characteristics of Latin American modernities is the interaction between currents imported or imposed from the center and the deep, heterogeneous cultural formations developed among the racially, ethnically, and regionally diverse popular classes. Research on this subject, by such figures as Jesús Martín-Barbero, Néstor García Canclini, Jean Franco, Ángel Rama, William Rowe, and Vivian Schelling, among others, shows the complexity of how cultural diffusion has worked within modernity. Emphatically rejecting the centrist idea of a diffusion that displaces what preexisted it, these scholars argue that even that which is imposed must enter *through* what is already there. This point was argued at length in an influential book by Rowe and Schelling, *Memory and Modernity* (1991). "In Latin America," they insist, "modernity rises through the popular" (3). Like the theorists of heterogeneity, hybridity, and *créolité* mentioned earlier, Rowe and Schelling are theorizing the reception end of a diffusion that the center sees as unproblematic and inconsequential. Even what is imposed, they argue, must enter through what is already there, through everything that is already there—which means modernity enters through the very things that the center defines as what it is not: religion, the traditional, the tribal, the non-Western, the unlettered, the unenlightened. How could it be otherwise? In example after example, Rowe and Schelling look at how popular mythology, local drama, and ritual encode the history of modernity; how popular religion with its feasts, saints, ritual calendars, art forms, and cosmologies engages and is engaged by modernity (see chapter 2). They observe how vernacular culture generates its own cast of character types—the *malandro*, the *cholo*, the *chola*—codifying forms of subaltern agency within modernity.[5] They discuss sports, crafts, forms of urbanization, social movements, and the impact of oral tradition on electronic media. The obvious conclusion is that in its dynamic, mobile engagement with modernity, popular culture cannot be contained by the modernist geography of outsideness or behindness, nor by Raymond Williams's concepts of the emergent and residual (Williams 1976), nor, one suspects, by Néstor García Canclini's vision of subjects "entering and leaving modernity" (García Canclini 1990), or Eduardo Galeano's idea of an American "modernidad barroca" (baroque modernity) distinct from Europe's "modernidad ilustrada" (enlightened modernity) (Larraín Ibañez 1996, 173; see also Echeverría 1991).

The thinkers of the 1980s and 1990s whose work I have reviewed here made huge advances in retheorizing modernity on a planetary scale. This retheorizing is the most consequential achievement of the critical analytical work that came to be called postmodernism. The exhaustion of one concept opens the door for others attuned to the events, experiences, and pressing problems of the present.

WHY THE VIRGIN
OF ZAPOPAN WENT TO LOS ANGELES

Every October in Guadalajara, Mexico, a city of five million in the western state of Jalisco, and the second-largest city in Mexico, close to two million people converge on the city center to accompany the Virgin of Zapopan on her annual journey from the cathedral of Guadalajara to her home in the basilica of Zapopan, eight kilometers away. For hours following a predawn mass, a huge river of people moves steadily up the long avenue, accompanied by the drums, flutes, and metal clogs of nearly two hundred teams of young *danzantes* from pueblos and barrios throughout the region, costumed in one way or another as Indians. They have practiced their routines for months. Near the end of the procession comes the Virgin herself, a rather plain-looking, doll-like figure about a foot high in a large glass case atop a flower-festooned car. It must be a new (virgin) car, one whose engine has never been started. It is pulled along by ropes gripped by hundreds of her devotees and an official guard dressed in Spanish colonial costumes. Behind her come huge castle-like birdcages full of songbirds to entertain her as she makes the

2.1 — Popular image of the Virgin of Zapopan. SOURCE: ERIC BONDOC.

journey. After the Virgin of Guadalupe, she is the most powerful virgin in Mexico. She is just over five hundred years old, and she has her own website.

The Virgin of Zapopan came into being in the 1530s during the process of evangelization of the local Indigenous population, merging, according to some accounts, with a local deity named Tepozintl, whose shrine she took over. She began developing divine powers, especially around matters concerning water—droughts, floods, and the epidemics that came with them—and later around disasters of all sorts. In 1653 the church officially declared her *milagrosa*, capable of miracles, raising her credibility with the non-Indigenous population of Spaniards, mestizos, and criollos. By the 1730s, as she entered her second century of life, the demands on her powers had become so great that she created a second version of herself called *la peregrina*, the pilgrim. *La peregrina*'s job was, and still is, to move around. She spends the rainy season rotating among the many parishes of Guadalajara, helping to prevent flooding, a constant problem in its lowland location. She

2.2 — Catholic faithful accompany the image of the Virgin of Zapopan, during the annual pilgrimage to the Basilica of Zapopan, in Zapopan, state of Jalisco, Mexico, on October 12, 2019. The annual pilgrimage has been recently added to UNESCO's Intangible Cultural Heritage of Humanity. PHOTO BY ULISES RUIZ / AFP. SOURCE: GETTY IMAGES.

also supports the ecological movement trying to save the rapidly shrinking Lake Chapala (familiar to readers of D. H. Lawrence's *The Plumed Serpent*). Elaborate processions, decorations, and fiestas accompany her from parish to parish, where hosting her is an honor and a serious obligation.

So since 1734 there have been two of her, *la original* (the original), who remains at home in Zapopan, and *la peregrina* (the pilgrim), who travels. These practices distinguish the Virgin of Zapopan from most other virgins, who do not travel themselves in their physical incarnations but rather appear as images in secular spaces like the walls of a house or the trunk of a tree. (Mexican anthropologist Renée de la Torre [2008] reports that in the 1990s these appearances began occurring in spaces of transit, such as freeway underpasses and airports, what she calls *no-lugares* [nonplaces].) Over five centuries, the mutations of the Virgin of Zapopan trace the regional consolidation that from the 1500s led toward Mexico's self-definition as a rural-based, pluri-ethnic nation-state with strong regional cultures, today marked by migration.

I invoke the Virgin of Zapopan not for divine protection (though I wouldn't say no), but because she subsumes themes I propose to take up in these pages: mobility, modernity, and citizenship as they play themselves out in the late twentieth and early twenty-first centuries. I join those who are reflecting on what is being called globality by thinking through mobility. Particularly intriguing in this respect is the Virgin of Zapopan's strategy of self-duplication, *desdoblamiento* in Spanish, which enables her to be in more than one place at once and to both go and stay at the same time. Though she exists as a statue, this ability to move and self-multiply makes her a kind of anti-monument, a genuine roving signifier—which may be why, though no icon could be more profoundly and complexly Mexican, the Virgin of Zapopan has never been incorporated into Mexico's official iconography or patrimony. She is part of local, popular, vernacular religiosity and, for many generations, has been repressed or unwillingly tolerated by the official church. My title promises that we will get the Virgin of Zapopan to Los Angeles, and so we will. But I propose to get there, thinking through mobility, by considering some of the ways in which unofficial or vernacular imaginaries render the processes that official parlance subsumes as globalization.

Thinking through Mobility. Recycled Archives

One of the things that made people want to call the world *postmodern*—and post almost everything else—is the dramatically altered patterns and scale of human mobility that developed in the closing decades of the twentieth century. Mass labor migration and mass tourism are two of the most conspicuous, with climate-caused displacement likely to catch up. Tourism became the largest industry in the world after the drug trade. Labor migration continues to run along colonial pathways, with large-scale movement of ex-colonial subjects into the metropoles. At the close of the twentieth century in the United States, one person in ten had been born in another country, and another one in ten had a parent who was. In California half the children entering school spoke languages other than English (a fact educators stupidly viewed as a handicap rather than a resource). There were seventy-five thousand Russians in Sacramento. Every city in Europe and North America has sizable diasporic communities from multiple parts of the globe, and these have impacted every aspect of institutional and everyday life. Fifteen percent of the population of Guyana lives in New York City; nearly half of Suriname is in the Netherlands.

The metropole is a self-interested host to these reversed diasporas but not necessarily a hospitable one. As a scholar of travel literature, I found it truly fascinating to observe, beginning in the 1990s, the reappearance of vernacular narrative genres that thrived three hundred years ago as travelers came back to Europe from faraway shores with tales of suffering and survival, monsters and marvels, shipwrecks and strandings. Toward the end of the 1990s, such stories began reappearing daily in news media. But the events they told were not happening in faraway places but at the metropole's own borders. There was the shipwreck story of the nine hundred Kurds who in the spring of 1999 ran aground on the coast of southern France. Stowaway stories had a rebirth, telling not of the English boy hiding under the deck and heading for the South Seas but of a young African man found frozen to death in the wheel casings of a jet in a European airport (Ferguson 2002), or of Eastern European families clinging under trains in the Chunnel. In 1998 the castaway tale was revived in the widely publicized drama of Elián González, the Cuban child who washed up on a beach in Florida and became a cause célèbre among Cuban Americans. It was not Polynesians but Floridians who decided the child was a reincarnation of the baby Jesus, helped ashore by dolphins. Today pirates again cruise off the coasts of Africa and gangs of thieves descend on migrants as they walk. Death and rescue tales are back, reaching us daily from the shores of Greece and the Arizona desert, like that of the infant miraculously rescued from the arms of its dead mother, a young Salvadoran trying to cross into the United States in the summer of 2000. In past centuries the rescuers would have been passing Bedouins; today they are the Border Patrol, whose chief role is to hunt such people down. Captivity narratives surface today in Beverly Hills, where Asian domestic workers tell of indentured servitude and forced confinement, and in sweatshops and brothels in cities across the globe. New forms of captivity have emerged, like the mass detention camps where migrants are confined in wretched conditions while they wait for their futures to be decided.

The suffocating nightmare of the slave ship resurged in 1999 in the port of San Francisco, where eighteen Chinese laborers emerged mad with suffering from the depths of a freighter. They had traveled in a cargo container, where seven companions had died. The following spring, England was shaken by the story of forty-three Chinese men who perished from carbon monoxide poisoning in the back of a truck smuggling them from the Netherlands. In April 2001 reports of white-on-black lynchings reappeared, not from the archives of Alabama, but from the southern coast of Spain. At the same time, US newspapers waxed smug about what was billed as the rescue of the Lost Boys of Sudan. Of some twelve thousand orphaned Dinka survivors of civil war in Sudan, a handful were brought to communities in the United States. The boys were rescued from slavery, which was discovered to have made a comeback in parts of Africa owing to falling commodity prices and the undermining of traditional agriculture—signature effects of globalization.[1] Meanwhile, the Ivory Coast had become a global center for child labor and child trafficking (US Department of Labor 2004). In the fall of 2001, Europe discovered itself host to thousands of captive female sex slaves, many of them Russian and Eastern European. In turn, abolitionism dusted itself off and came down from the shelf, led, as it was in 1800, by the British Anti-slavery Society, now known as Anti-Slavery International.[2] This is surely not what anyone expected to be doing at the turn of the new millennium.

Since the 1990s, the metropole's borders have become theaters, and as with the death and survival literature of the past, the dramas recounted in our news media every day have been doing the work of staging the new planetary order, a newly mutating imperial order, creating its subjects, creating us as its subjects. In one important way, this contemporary recycling of the seventeenth- and eighteenth-century travel archive turns the old one inside out, for its prevailing focus is not the living but the dead. The earlier genres—tales of captivity, shipwrecks, castaways, and the like—were almost always produced by the survivors themselves, those who providentially (a key term) lived to tell the tale. By definition, there was always a happy ending that affirmed the viability of an emergent metropolitan global, often imperial, subject. Today's recyclings of these genres are chiefly about nonsurvivors. They depict not dramas of triumphal homecoming but tragedies of no return. Now (and how clear this became after September 11, 2001) it seems to be death dramas that grip and resonate, though many success stories can be told.

If anything, the necropathy has intensified over time. In the 1990s and early 2000s, children were exceptions to the death cult. They often appeared as survivors, rescued from piles of adult corpses, the most famous case being Elián González, who washed up on the shores of Florida. A decade later, beginning with the 2012 photos of three-year-old Syrian Kurdish child Alan Kurdi washed up on a beach in Turkey, images of child corpses became a painful new hallmark of the grinding cruelty and desperation of the south-to-north migration system.[3] On both sides of the Atlantic, migration stories mutated from individual to a group or even mass scale—overloaded boats in the Mediterranean, overland caravans of thousands in Central America and Mexico. In both instances, migration itself had changed, partly through the elaboration of hugely profitable infrastructures able to move people in large

2.3 — Mexican popular *calavera* (skull) art depicting the selling of bones to pay the national debt, 2002. SOURCE: ERIC BONDOC.

numbers, partly through political and environmental deterioration in home countries.

What is the work of this literature of suffering and loss? Is it a mirror in which, in a key of pain and guilt, metropolitans contemplate themselves as a kind of fortress sustained by violent exclusion and assailed by desperate people no less deserving than themselves? Is it displaying to itself its intensifying legitimation crisis? Or is the effect rather to remind those on the inside of the fortress how lucky they are and how threatened in a world so deeply divided between "us" and "them"? Either way, the dramas of death and despair establish an alternative register to the dehumanized narratives of globalization that occupy the economic literature and business pages.

Against Flow

Late twentieth-century mobility was driven by processes of decolonization set in motion after World War II but also by imperatives and possibilities created by technological advances, the communications revolution, and above all neoliberalism or late capitalism, the new and ruthless phase of the empire that we are now living. This was not as obvious in the early 1990s as it is now. In the early 1990s, among scholars across the ideological spectrum, the academic talk on globalization had an outright utopian character. In one early anthology on the topic (Featherstone 1990), the authors spoke of a new "cosmopolitan ideal" of a "dream of a secular ecumene," "the crystallization of the entire world as a single place," and the "emergence of a global human condition" (Robertson 1990, 28) and a "world culture" that is an "organization of diversity" (Hannerz 1990, 237). "Humankind," said Ulf Hannerz in that heady moment, "has finally bid farewell to the world which could with some credibility be seen as a cultural mosaic" (237). Today it is hard not to hear in these joyous phrases a revised, eternally innocent imperial narrative and a failure on the part of metropolitan scholars to seek correctives to the inevitable blindness of privilege.

Early on, the metropolitan discourse on globalization established its preferred metaphor, an image of mobility and innocence that is still very much with us: the metaphor of *flow*. Flow evokes a planet traversed by continuous, multidirectional, frictionless movement of people, goods, money, information, languages, ideas, art, images. If one is in the "local," the aim is to find ways to tap into the flow, through an assembly plant, say, or maybe a new cash crop, a tourist attraction, a workforce sent abroad, or at the very least a satellite dish, a boom box, a downloaded CD, and now of course a cell phone. But, thinking through mobility, the asphyxiated Chinese workers in the back of the truck in England were not flowing. The Rio Grande flows but not the men, women, and children who drowned trying to cross it. As the Brazilian scholar Teresa Caldeira (2001) reminded us early on, the wealthy do not flow either. They increasingly retreat behind the walls of gated, guarded communities; abroad, they wall themselves up in resort enclaves designed to give the illusion of place. (Even Pope John Paul II, in a statement issued for World Tourism Day in 2001, condemned the proliferation of "sophisticated holiday resorts that are cut off from any real contact with the host country" [John Paul II 2001].) Given the ubiquity of the flow metaphor, it is perhaps worth spelling out some of the confusions and evasions that follow from it— if only because that metaphor is surely worth preserving for some purposes:

1 Flow doesn't distinguish between one kind of movement and another— between, say, the migration of domestic laborers from the Philippines to the Middle East, on the one hand, and the travels of sex tourists from Europe or Japan to Thailand or Cuba, on the other. Tourists, as

tourists, must return to their countries of origin, while transplanted workers often must not because home depends on their earnings. The Philippines is one of a number of countries, including most of those in Central America, in which remittances from workers abroad are the chief source of external revenue.

2 Flow bypasses the question of directionality. American TV series are widely seen in South Africa, but South Africa's fascinating multiracial, multilingual soap operas do not reach North America. Half of Mexico's hydroelectric power flows north out of Chiapas, while much of the resident population there has no electricity. Money, we are told, changes hands one hundred times more often than goods do, but that flow in the end also has a direction. In 2003 the secretary general of the United Nations, Kofi Annan, told the General Assembly that when all forms of exchange were taken into account, there had been a net flow of $200 billion from poor countries to rich ones the previous year (UN News 2003). To put this into perspective, the entire US foreign aid budget in 2000 was a mere $22 billion, a fraction of what Argentina alone paid the United States in debt service that same year. In 2001 debt service payments to rich countries were taking up fully half of Ecuador's national budget—hence the outward "flow" of 14 percent of Ecuador's population in ten years.[4]

3 Flow naturalizes. It makes it easy to ignore the state policies, transnational arrangements, and structured institutions that create these possibilities and impossibilities of movement—known institutional villains like the World Bank and International Monetary Fund but also the expanding kleptocratic national business classes empowered in the name of the free market. The spread of Hollywood films across the planet is not a natural dispersion of culture. It is a business proposition aimed at undermining other national cinemas, authorized by trade deals imposed by rich countries on poorer ones. The result early on was that cinema shrank worldwide. Fewer films were being made and distributed, and many fewer people in the world had access to cinema at all because local movie houses had disappeared. Over time, transnational collaboration revived filmmaking, but national cinema all but disappeared.

4 Flow obliterates human agency and intentionality. It's an intransitive verb: things flow; nobody flows them. This is very handy. To depict

money as flowing obscures that it is sent and received. People who flow are people who have *decided* to go or return, who have been *sent* or *sent for* by others as part of a considered strategy. By obliterating agency, flow takes the existential dimensions of human movement off the table, from the excruciating choices forced on people to the emancipatory possibilities to which mobility gives rise.

5 Flow perversely suggests a natural, gravity-driven process that will automatically reach a tranquil horizontal equilibrium. Markets are imagined as levelers, inherently democratizing access. As early as the late 1990s, however, the world of unfettered neoliberalism has seemed to have no gravity. Its forces have proven to be resolutely vertical, and top and bottom seem to recede before our eyes as wealth concentrates in some places, and immiseration proliferates in others. Thanks to the North American Free Trade Agreement (NAFTA), in 1999 workers in Mexico were calculated to have one-seventh the earning power they had in 1970, and their wages were half what they were in 1980. At least a third of the 100 million *mexicanos* possessed virtually nothing at all; people were shorter on average than they had been thirty years before. As in other countries whose agricultural systems were devastated by multinational food producers, hunger in Mexico was eventually replaced by another form of malnutrition, an obesity epidemic, as high-calorie processed foods replaced traditional diets.[5]

The rich countries experienced verticalization too. We hear the statistics over and over: in the United States, the Federal Reserve reports, the top 1 percent of the population controls 40 percent of the country's wealth; the top 10 percent controls 77 percent. It is difficult not to see in the attack on the twin towers an assault on this verticality.

Flow exemplifies the official, legitimating language of globalization. It is not a value-neutral term but a positively charged one detached from any ethical dimension. This is language with no top or bottom, as when doubled working hours, child labor, reduced food intake, infanticide, or scavenging in dumps and dumpsters (as recommended once by the Oregon Welfare Department) become "coping strategies" (González de la Rocha, 2000). Or when jobless immiseration is called the "informal economy." Or when any interaction can be described as an "exchange" regardless of how asymmetrical, unequal, or forced it might be. It is surely the task of humanists to denounce such language, to insist on an ecology of public discourse and an ethical component in policy talk. If not us, then who?

The Return of the Monsters

In imaginative literature, at least in Latin American fiction, this newly predatory world registered as the opposite of flow. As discussed in chapter 4, novelists in the 1990s began producing narratives of isolated survivors trying to create meaningful spheres of action in claustrophobic indoor spaces to which they had withdrawn to escape a social world that had become a holocaust. Others depicted violent delinquency, in which the absence of a livable future meant nobody had anything to lose.[6] In vernacular culture, it registered the way it did in previous predatory stages of empire, by the appearance of monsters. In the 1980s, for example, the migratory diaspora from the Global South into the United States did not yet register directly in the national imagination. But it turned up indirectly, in the drama of the killer bees. As readers familiar with Michael Moore's 2002 film *Bowling for Columbine* may know, these were a species of bee transported from Africa to Brazil as part of a breeding experiment. After some were released by mistake from a Brazilian laboratory, they began to spread. The bees acquired their killer label when they turned out to be much more aggressive than the resident species, which had originated in Europe. As the bees spread throughout the Americas, their movement was read from the United States as a relentless northward-directed invasion, the same terms in which human migration from South and Central America would later be coded. In the 1980s, as the United States moved into the largest wave of immigration in its history, the approach of the killer bees became a national obsession for years. Moore associated the killer bee story with the rise of a culture of fear in the United States. The killer bees were the template for the paranoid narrative frame that resurged in the spring of 2018 with the advance of immigrant caravans from Central America.

When the bees actually arrived in the early to mid-1990s, as the story played out, they did what immigrants to the United States have always been supposed to do. They assimilated. Interbreeding with the local bees, they produced new strains resistant to the mites that were destroying local bee populations. Within a decade it became difficult to tell them apart.

In the mid-1990s in the wake of NAFTA, Mexico and the Caribbean witnessed the appearance of the *chupacabras*, or goatsucker. This was a large winged, batlike creature about four feet tall that came out at night and attacked the corrals of goats throughout rural Mexico. Humans and other domestic animals were also vulnerable to attack. Newspapers published pictures of women with neck wounds and corrals apparently strewn with goat corpses. Hypothetical drawings of the creature appeared first in newspapers

2.4 — *Chupacabras.*
This comic lead
figurine links the
monster to NAFTA,
2002. SOURCE: ERIC
BONDOC.

and then on T-shirts; the inevitable *corridos* (Mexican ballads) turned up, and the *chupacabras* made a few cameo appearances on the television show *The X-Files.* The goatsucker, so the story unfolded, originated in a secret laboratory on a US military base in Puerto Rico, where the creature was produced by a failed genetic engineering experiment. This origin story would carry forward to the COVID-19 virus in 2020.

The *chupacabras* seemed to comment richly on the assault on rural and agricultural life signified by NAFTA in 1994. Collective landholdings (*ejidos*) were forced to privatize. Subsistence agriculture was told to disappear; goats and corn should be replaced by export crops like kiwis, snow peas, or avocados. Farmers were under enormous pressure to use genetically altered crop strains that would require them to use Monsanto seeds, and even then it was obvious that US agribusiness was going to suck the blood out of small-scale farming in Mexico. Why goats? The monster targeted the noncommodified relations between people and their animals that lay at the heart of rural life. In rural Mexico, stewed goat—*birria*—is the standard ritual food at weddings. By the spring of 2001, the *chupacabras* acquired a new resonance. It seemed to prophesy the wholesale holocaust of farm animals imposed in Britain in response to an epidemic of foot-and-mouth disease caused by the profit-driven transporting of livestock by transnational agribusiness. As with the killer bees, popular culture anticipated the events in something like an allegorized form.

Popular culture did similar work in rural Peru and Bolivia, incarnating new forces of destruction in monster forms. The 1980s and 1990s saw a resurgence of the *pishtako*, a monster who first appeared among Indigenous Andeans in the sixteenth century during the violence of the Spanish invasion. *Pishtakos* are creatures who put people to sleep with magic powders, then suck the fat out of their bodies so that they waste away. In the late 1980s, while the killer bees pressed northward, the *pishtako* made a series of appearances in the Andes, driven by globalization (Wachtel 1994). This time it was seeking human fat for export to the United States to lubricate machines—cars, planes, computers. Traffickers were also understood to be selling human flesh to fancy restaurants in Lima. Originally the *pishtako* was sometimes depicted wearing a sackcloth tunic reminiscent of Spanish friars. Anthropologists reported a widespread panic in 1987 when a story circulated that an army of five thousand *pishtakos* wearing lab coats had been sent to Ayacucho province in Peru to collect human fat to be sold to pay off Peru's national debt. The debt, thanks to the global lending machine, was real—the Andeans were not out of the loop. The episode captured with impressive exactitude the nature of the forces bearing down on them. Indeed, readers tempted to think of the *pishtako* in exclusively mythical terms might want to ponder its relation to the metropolitan practice of liposuction, which also emerged in those years. Why not pay off Peru's debt with the abundant excess fat of Americans instead of Peruvians? But American fat *is* Peru's debt, the ripped-off resources converted into cheap processed food and northern hyperconsumption.[7]

Around the same time the *pishtako* was abroad in the Andes, in the neighborhoods of Lima rumors spread about the *sacaojos* (*sacar* = remove; *ojos* = eyes), predators who kidnapped children, stole their eyes for export, and returned them blind. The *sacaojos* was just one of a multitude of stories of organ theft, which in the 1980s and 1990s became powerfully meaningful in places where global capitalism was threatening the integrity and continuity of communities and identities. By the mid-1990s, these stories had become widespread enough that the US Information Agency set up a website to disclaim them. One of the most common was the tale of the stolen kidney. In its best-known version, which many readers will have heard, a man in a bar is seduced by an attractive woman, with whom he goes to a hotel, awaking the next day to find he has been drugged and one of his kidneys removed for sale in Europe or the United States. The story had many variants, but its frequency and distribution were astonishing. Again stemming from a place of fear and vulnerability, the story registered the permutations of the global order quite precisely, particularly new forms of industrial production that assemble things out of parts made anywhere in the world. As with the *sacaojos*, third-world bodies become manufacturers of parts to be exported and inserted into wealthy first-world bodies in need of repair. Communities fragment, forced to sell pieces of themselves abroad, lodged in the belly of the beast. North American versions of the stolen-kidney story, which spread among truckers, for example, likewise registered new forms of vulnerability. Globalization has created a legal international market in organs, including kidneys (it might be legal, but one can surely ask: Is it legitimate for a poor person to finance a child's education by selling a kidney?). The global reach of the organ-theft story derives from its psychic and symbolic resonance.

The resurgence of monsters and dismemberments was not a third-world phenomenon. In the United States, the resurgence took place in film and television, most notably in the highly successful TV series *The X-Files*, whose ninth and last television season ended in 2002. Most of the monsters mentioned above made appearances on the program, which drew heavily on referents harking back to the Cold War, including 1950s fears of nuclear contamination and invasion from outer space. Updating these referents in the 1990s helped create the subject of the new post–Cold War global order, a subject that saw itself at the mercy of unknown and possibly state-sponsored predatory forces.

Demodernization. From Grids to Nodes

The recycling of death and survival tales, and the resurgence of monsters and dismemberments, suggests, I think, the operation of a process one might call *demodernization*. Let me explain what I mean. Commentators regularly note the "Dickensian" quality of changes brought by free-market economics, like impossibly low wages or the resurgence of child labor and slavery. Ex-colonial countries found themselves economically recolonized by former mother countries as international finance organisms forced them to turn over their resources to private corporations. As James Ferguson (1999) observed in a telling study, by the 1990s Zambia's copper industry was back in the hands of the company that owned it in colonial times, a sale forced on it by international lenders who controlled balance-of-payments support.

In Indonesia the tribal Dayaks revived headhunting in the context of an invading lumber industry that brought ecological destruction and a foreign labor pool. Parts of the western United States, the *New York Times* reported in May 2001, seemed to be turning back into the frontier: Euro-Americans were migrating out, and the land was reverting to an uncultivated state. Buffalo were making a comeback. This withdrawal might have been called a *decolonization*, but if so, it was taking the form not of increased modernization but of something more like its opposite—a reversal; hence my term *demodernization*. To take another example, the erosion of public health-care systems brought tuberculosis back, and air travel sent it round the globe. The privatizations relentlessly promoted by free-trade neoliberalism after 1980 inevitably reversed liberalism's equalizing work, generating demodernizing throwbacks to earlier scenarios. Ferguson (1999) posits the emergence of a global subject for whom the "expectation of modernity" exists as a thing of the past.

These reversals of liberalism can often be grasped as a shift from grids to nodes. In the imaginary of modern liberalism, health care, for example, is one of a range of apparatuses that was supposed to take the form of a *grid* blanketing national territories, intended to reach and include all citizens. Electricity was perhaps the modern grid par excellence, along with rail and road transportation, the postal service, the telegraph, telephone and television, education, electoral and judicial systems, and now the internet. When grids fail, that is, when the trunk lines are not sustained, these grid formations become nodal, that is, noninclusive.[8] The territories between nodes are bypassed. So cell phones (nodes) replace unsustained or nonexistent national phone grids; it can become easier in highland Peru to call Florence or New York than the next village over—provided you have a cell phone. In many countries the state's failure to maintain transportation grids leaves cultivators and artisans with no way to get products to market. Meanwhile, their products are replaced by imports from abroad, which arrive easily through a center-to-center nodal system. As Ferguson (1999) describes, Zambia, an agricultural country, today imports corn, unbelievable as it seems, from the United States and South Africa. The demise of passable roads—a state responsibility—left Zambian farmers unable to sell what they grew to anyone at all. Educational grids suffer similar fates. In 1991 the Zambian government spent sixty dollars a year on each primary-school pupil; in 2000 it was fifteen dollars, and 20 percent fewer children were enrolled (Ferguson 1999). Rich countries are hardly immune to the effects of the erosion of the regulatory, redistributive, and custodial functions that liberal states and international apparatuses used to perform. The corporate aggression that drives agricultural prices down in Zambia does the same in North America, making all but large-scale farmers superfluous.[9]

Telling the Story Otherwise

J. K. Gibson-Graham, the conjoined authors of two important and far-reaching treatises on global capitalism, *The End of Capitalism (As We Knew It)* (1996) and *A Postcapitalist Politics* (2006), have a warning for us, however. They argue against accounts of globalization, laudatory or critical, that reduce everything to the same thing and ignore the economic heterogeneity of the world, especially "the prevalence and diversity of noncapitalist economic activity worldwide" (2006, ix). They warn against explanations that give capitalism an interpretive monopoly, "subordinating local subjects to the discourse of globalization," thereby reproducing the "received wisdom of capitalist dominance" (xix). Such accounts, they caution, will seem coherent and plausible but will remain oblivious to all the things that cannot be subsumed into the narrative of neoliberalism or late capitalism. Grasping how the world really works economically, they argue, requires that we reinvent our economic imaginaries, and their book seeks to do so. Three key insights stand out. First, within capitalist societies, noncapitalist modes of production persist and flourish, and capitalism would not work without them.[10] Second, the operations of capitalism produce all kinds of unintended consequences that capitalism itself cannot explain or subsume into its narrative. Third, the operations of emancipation processes like Zapatismo or worldwide women's movements create conditions and practices that cannot be incorporated into a capitalist account of capitalism. Chapter 3 analyzes several examples.

Gibson-Graham outline a practice, often counterintuitive for critical intellectuals, of consciously seeking ways to tell the story of capitalism otherwise, by attending to disharmonies, unintended consequences, and emancipatory processes, however trivial they might seem. Indeed, an appearance of triviality may be an effect of the workings of the dominant narrative in the analyst. Intellectuals, Gibson-Graham argue, are accountable for creating worlds as well as describing them. Their interventions have consequences; their responsibilities should include identifying in existing worlds elements of the world they would like to come into being. They are accountable to the future as well as the present (a theme that recurs throughout this book).

For example (it is my example, not theirs), in the imaginary of globalization there is a tendency to see the global consumer order as a grid—a planetary blanket of Starbucks, Nikes, McDonald's, and 7-Elevens. But this imagined picture is radically oversimplified. Consumption, and the ability to consume, is heavily nodal. Markets have no need to be grid-like or inclusive—a market does not care who is doing the consuming as long as enough of it is going on to generate the desired level of profit. Indeed, if consumption is concentrated in a node, overhead goes down. The economic polarization produced by globalized capitalism means there are enormous stretches of people and places—whole regions and countries—that, far from being integrated into a planetary Walmart, are and know themselves to be entirely dispensable with respect to what is seen as the global economic and political order; they know themselves to be nonparticipants in the futures that that order invites people to imagine for themselves. This is particularly true of small-scale agricultural societies, whose lifeways are being decimated everywhere.[11] The neoliberal order creates not necessarily the conditions for its own demise (those are probably ecological) but certainly conditions it can't make sense of in its own terms: vast sectors of organized humanity who have minimal access to either cash or consumption and whose challenge is to make livable, meaningful lives by other means. By what means do people in the marginal places of the postprogress world—delinked rural areas or the huge improvised subsistence neighborhoods that ring many global cities—make life viable and worth living? What succeeds, and what does not? If people lack even the prospect of economic security, a job, or the chance to build a family, what alternative sense of futurity can be found or created? And if none, what forms of meaningfulness and transcendence can be achieved in the present? Global hip-hop culture tills this terrain.

Lifeways geared to ecological balance and continuity are not functional for late capitalism, which operates by a kind of roving flexibility: the assembly plant is here today, gone tomorrow. Avocados are profitable; then they are not. Roving capital is hostile to the cosmos in the sense of an integrative universe where meaning is anchored in practice and place. Such formations require continuity and interconnectedness and produce them. They "get it together." So it is that in the presence of capitalism's disaggregating momentum, formations that produce continuity and interconnectedness persist and find new ways to install themselves. In the 1990s, tales of organ theft, for example, were countered by stories in which new access to information and mobility was used to reassemble bodies and recover stolen body parts, ancestral remains, and commoditized sacred objects. In 1999 the brain of Ishi, the famed last member of the Yahi tribe in California, was recovered from a storeroom of the Smithsonian Institution (Clifford 2013). The bones of the native Greenlanders whom Franz Boas brought to New York a century ago were recovered in 1993 by their descendants for reburial (Harper 2000). By 1990 such decolonizing recovery processes had become common enough for the US Congress to pass the Native American Graves Protection and Repatriation Act. In these processes of reassembling, getting it together, the acts of recovery affirmed the power of communities to seek wholeness or fullness in a place. Of course, as Gibson-Graham would remind us, we interpreters have the power to decide that such processes are insignificant, but we are accountable for that choice and for the futures it calls forth.

Why the Virgin of Zapopan Went to Los Angeles

Apparently, getting it together is what brought the Virgin of Zapopan to Los Angeles. Around 1995 the Virgin multiplied herself again, this time in response to calls from migrant devotees living in Southern California. This third self, the migrant one, is called *la viajera*, the traveler, who now visits annually at a parish in Los Angeles. So now there are three of her, *la original, la peregrina, la viajera*. In the globalizing 1990s, the Virgin's powers of mobility and *desdoblamiento* were called on to bring her into the orbit of her diasporic community, whose members, owing to the tightening of policing at the border under President Bill Clinton, were less and less able to make annual visits home. In this context the Virgin's strategy of *desdoblamiento* parallels the new forms of identity, belonging, and citizenship being worked out by mobile workforces and social movements all over the planet. As most readers will know, it became common for pueblos in Mexico and Central America to have full-fledged satellite communities in the United States. Roger Rouse's (1991) pioneering study showed that part of Redwood City, California, was a satellite of Apatzingán, Michoacán. Maya ethnographer Victor Montejo (1999) reported on Tzotzuhil-speaking communities in Florida, as well as apartment buildings reorganized according to Mesoamerican sociospatial relations. In the post-NAFTA years, the Mixteco of Oaxaca developed a transnational network extending from Puerto Escondido to Anchorage, and from Fresno to New Jersey. All over rural Mexico, towns and villages rescheduled and redesigned local fiestas to accommodate their migrant populations (a pattern that, incidentally, reemphasized religious calendars over national holidays). In recent years, such activities were curtailed by increased policing at the border. But the main point remains: as transnational economics increasingly pushes and pulls people into migrancy, immense creativity and commitment go into making and sustaining connections to family, community, and place—keeping it together. The figure of the immigrant eager to leave their origins behind coexists alongside this other immigrant story whose project is sustaining connectedness, often through processes of self-duplication like those of the Virgin of Zapopan. Working abroad to sustain home often implies dual citizenship in both the literal sense (more and more countries are allowing it) and the existential sense of a kind of doubling of the self into parallel identities in one place and the other. This can be both a fragmenting and an empowering experience.

In economic terms, you could say that with the demise of the mechanisms that used to redistribute wealth from north to south—national development programs, protection of local markets, international aid—migrating workers are redistributing it "by hand." (According to the Pew Center, Latin American and Caribbean workers sent $74.3 billion home from abroad in 2016 [Budiman and Connor 2018].) This function was recognized by President George W. Bush in 2001 when, following the disastrous earthquakes in El Salvador, he gave permission for 150,000 undocumented Salvadorans to remain in the United States, earning money to send back to help their families recover. In 2019 they were still here but fighting deportation. Though the economic motivations for the remittance system are obvious, Gibson-Graham would tell us to look at the ways this doubling, this mobilization of the self here to sustain others there, this project of keeping it together across the gulf of migrancy, is in other respects not functional for capitalism. The remittance system does not obey the dictates of acquisitive consumerism or the self-maximizing individual. In important respects it is life by other means. Fears of nostalgia should not prevent us from attending to the mechanisms people are using to get it together and keep it together in the face of the intensified disaggregations that are functional for capitalism. The current hero of this story, and not just in the metropole but in places like highland Guatemala, too, is the cell phone. But the mobile virgins are important too. They can show up to offset the monsters.

The inability of neoliberalism to create belonging, collectivity, and a believable sense of futurity produces, among other things, crises of existence and meaning that are being sorted through by the nonconsumers and consumers of the world alike, in ways neoliberal ideology neither predicts nor controls. The roving virgins are its symptoms and its inscrutable agents.

MOBILITY AND THE POLITICS OF BELONGING

> Being the third son of the family, and not bred to any trade, my head began to fill very early with rambling thoughts.—DANIEL DEFOE, *Robinson Crusoe* (1719)

In March 2002, Argentina was in the midst of a legendary financial meltdown. In December 2001 it had defaulted on its foreign debt, the largest such default in the world at that time. Banks were closed; business stopped; unemployment and underemployment surged to 40 percent (McDevitt 2009; see also Epstein and Pion-Berlin 2006). Commerce was next to impossible—no one could get cash, and those who had it could not know from one day to the next what it would buy. Everyday life was completely taken over by the crisis. People responded in all kinds of ways. There were marches, pot-banging demonstrations, and graffiti protests. And there was an extraordinary wave of invention. In the absence of money, elaborate barter systems developed. Jungian analysts traded therapy for plumbing or dental work. Alternative currencies appeared. Private cars became impromptu taxis. Neighborhoods formed mutual-aid networks to share food and other resources. Women in

3.1 — Argentine gaucho. SOURCE: FLICKR PHOTO BY JMAGE.

fur coats sold their jewelry in the street to pay for food. People held on to the remains of normalcy. Stores opened; shoppers came and went, looked at wares; clerks gave prices, though all knew no sale would take place. One man undertook a more ambitious exercise to inspire his suffering nation. Dressed in the iconic Argentine poncho and sombrero (see figure 3.1), he mounted on horseback and set out to ride around the entire periphery of the country, depending for his subsistence on the hospitality of his fellow citizens. The nineteenth-century national iconography (man, horse, poncho, sombrero) left no doubt that this experiment in mobility aimed to reaffirm an ideal of nationhood in the face of a catastrophe induced by dependence on the International Monetary Fund and other international lenders.

In *The Practice of Everyday Life*, Michel de Certeau famously subsumed travel writing into a larger body of "narrative that interminably labors to compose spaces, to verify, collate, and displace their frontiers," "an immense travel literature concerned with actions organizing more or less extensive social, cultural areas" (1984, 123). The *Argentino*'s mobility experiment, in de Certeau's terms, would "compose" the space of the nation, "verify" and "collate" its frontiers as a bounded whole, reenact it as a grid of hospitality, a gift economy separable from commerce, debt, and money. The newspaper story itself, complete with an image, affirmed the affirmation. The ride itself would perform it, reenacting the nation as territory and collectivity in the flesh of the man, the horse, *and their hosts.*

I emphasize the role of the hosts because that "immense travel literature" de Certeau talks about defines itself overwhelmingly around the agency of the traveler. It obscures or elides the fact that acts of moving are almost always constituted in relation to acts of staying. Host-guest relations play a constitutive role in travel. Journeys are organized as movement between points of hospitality, that is, points where movers are received by stayers, people in place. The presence and hosting capacity of the stayers (or their hostility, for that matter) usually determine the traveler's route. Host-guest relations are essential not only to the logistics of the Argentine horseman's project but to its meaning. Pilgrimage, travel as a sacred act, is habitually imagined as an act carried out by the pilgrim, but anyone who has participated in a pilgrimage knows it involves a serial enactment of relations between pilgrims and others who sustain them as they go. This support is often also a sacred act. Such interaction is not incidental to a pilgrimage but constitutive of it as a logistical exercise and sacred act.

So we may pose a general question: Where and in what ways is it illuminating to reflect on travel not as the moving of a body or set of bodies but as the enactment or unfolding of relations between bodies in place (stayers) and dis-placed bodies (movers)? What can one learn by recognizing such relations in the architecture of mobility? More specifically, thinking of the Argentine horseman, what roles do going and staying have in the performance of selfhood, citizenship, and belonging?

As de Certeau reminds us, there are a great many practices of everyday life in which rhythms of going and staying organize "more or less extensive social, cultural areas," to invoke his words. Visiting, for example, involves an organized arrangement of bodies that move and bodies that remain in place. For a visit to take place, someone must be at home when someone else comes by—a social division of labor with high potential for reciprocity. My small-town grandmother lived at the end of the era when bourgeois ladies used calling card to announce their at-home hours and their visits. Visiting enacts host-guest relations, which belong to the gift economy and are valued for being noncommercial (or for pretending to be such, as in the hospitality industry). The private, reciprocal practice of visiting has the status of a public good. In that same small town, the weekly newspaper announced in print who had visited whom each week, often on Sundays. People reported their visits and visitors. Among families and communities, visiting embodies collective life in dances of moving and staying.

Commerce also takes this form. As an embodied interaction between buyers and sellers, commerce is also executed as an organized choreography of movers and stayers. In market and store shopping, vendors stay with the wares, and buyers circulate among them, examining the goods, enacting their freedom to choose. In traveling sales—the ice cream truck, the stadium popcorn vendor, the world's millions of *ambulantes* (street vendors; literally, walkers)—vendors move among customers who are in place. The choreography changes when money is not involved, as the inhabitants of a town in Morelos, Mexico, discovered in the early 2000s. Responding to a scarcity of cash, the community set up a market based on barter alongside its regular outdoor cash market. In order to work, the cash market required that the moving buyers greatly outnumber the immobile vendors.[1] In a barter system, the organizers discovered, everyone is both a buyer and a seller, so it required equal numbers of sitters and walkers. Each participant had to be assigned one role or the other. The contrasting arrangements literally embodied the contrast between profit-oriented and reciprocal exchange.

War is also narrativized in the frame of those who leave and those who stay behind. Warriors go off to war; the nonwarriors—women, children, and elders—remain in place. Such framing distorts by identifying the warrior as the sole agent of warfare, ignoring the essential participation of those who stay home (or "behind"). Yet those stayers make war possible by assuming the functions that the departing warriors no longer fulfill and, in addition, producing enough surplus to supply the warriors as they engage in the high-consumption activity of war making. War is performed relationally by those who go and those who remain. But here again, the activity is typically imagined from the point of view of the party who goes, not the ones who stay. Many novels of empire build on another relation of going and staying: the younger son who must go out to make his way in the world, while the eldest son stays in place and inherits the father's property, titles, profession, or trade. Robinson Crusoe, quoted in the epigraph, is one of many imperial protagonists set in motion by this relation.

Mobility generates stories because it counts as a state of exception. The normative geosocial ordering of the world attaches people to places; placedness forms the basis for community and belonging. Only territorial entities can make people citizens. This chapter reflects on the interplay of placedness and mobility in relation to modernity, indigeneity, and globality.

Moving, Staying, Knowing

The tendency to privilege moving over staying in the "immense travel literature" that de Certeau evokes has shaped the study of travel and travel writing. (I should know.) It, too, is built overwhelmingly around the agency of the traveler. When Western scholars study travel and travel writing, unless they make a deliberate effort to the contrary, they automatically read and think from the point of view of the travelers, looking over their shoulders even when criticizing their discourse or acts. The alignment of analyst with traveler is so habitual and entrenched that it is difficult to perceive or to perceive as consequential. This means that the critical literature on travel writing has operated within the conventions of the genre it studies, in a kind of critical mimesis. To the extent that this critical mimesis prevails (it is not a methodological necessity), the study of travel writing reproduces the often imperial and statist lines of power that generate metropolitan travel and travel writing themselves. This is the case even when those lines of power are being critiqued. This configuration limits critics' ability to "displace modernist myths of travel," as Caren Kaplan (1990, 9) puts it. This convention must be deliberately disrupted for the study of travel writing to fulfill its critical potential.

The alignment of scholar with traveler is held in place, I think, by authority. In the modern Western imagination, mobility is the privileged figure both for freedom and for knowing. The traveler is the figure par excellence of the self-possessed autonomous subject defined by a set of inalienable rights that attach to its body, wherever it may be located. Mobility is the proof and performance of that subject's liberated, rights-possessing state, which transcends place. Mobility in turn is the figure for modern knowing. This sentient subject pursues knowledge of the world by moving through it, from place to place, topos to topos, idea to idea, exploring, following leads, tracking things down. Discovery is tied to voyage. The freedom and authority of the scholar align with those of the traveler and travel writer. As Indigenous scholar Sandy Grande (2014) astutely points out, postmodern approaches if anything intensify the modernist paradigm by privileging a mobile, transgressive, ungrounded hybrid subject as the new agent of critical knowledge. Emancipated from the trammels of bounded identities, this subject transcends boundedness and comprehends from a position one theorist described as "resplendent placelessness" (Grande 2014, 239). This is the point at which, Grande argues, Indigenous perspectives provide a means of interruption. From an Indigenous point of view, to put it crudely, that untrammeled mobile traveler-knower is an ominous and all-too-familiar figure—he arrives uninvited, on horseback, carrying a rifle. (That is my image, not hers.) In Grande's words, thinking from indigeneity, "the seemingly liberatory constructs of fluidity, mobility, and transgression are perceived *not only as the language of critical subjectivity but also as part of the fundamental lexicon of Western imperialism.* . . . The concepts of mestizaje, hybridity and border subjectivity dear to both critical pedagogy and postcolonial studies" cannot be models for Indigenous subjectivity. Their "deplaced," ungrounded subject "masks colonial power" (240, emphasis mine). As discussed in the introduction, the concept of indigeneity itself is born out of the unsolicited encounter between an arriving subject and those it finds already there.

One way to disrupt the equation of mobility with freedom is simply to ask: Where is mobility an enactment or figure of unfreedom? Does the imperial lexicon enter here too? Chattel slavery comes immediately to mind, along with the multiplied and accelerated forms of forced displacement that, as discussed in chapter 2 and throughout this book, have been the hallmarks of neoliberal globalization: economically compelled migration, the rout of rural and forest-dwelling peoples, slavery and other forms of human trafficking, kidnapping, deportation, "rendition," internment, expulsion, flight.[2] The United Nations High Commissioner for Refugees calculates there were nearly 80 million displaced people in the world in 2020, more than ever before. Of these, 3.6 million are displaced Venezuelans—in Latin America *desplazado* (displaced) is now a formal demographic category. As argued in chapter 2, it is a painful irony that flow has been the privileged metaphor for globalization's powers of redirection, obscuring the difference between movement as freedom and unfreedom. Forced mobility has long been a privileged weapon for assaults on collective life, and it has operated in this way on an unprecedented scale since the 1990s. What place should this observation have in the critical study of going and staying?

We should also pose the complementary general question. When does staying in place become a figure for freedom? In the modern Western literary canon, the examples that come to mind are eccentric or perverse: Herman Melville's Bartleby the scrivener, who "prefers not" to leave the office; André Gide's *immoraliste*, mesmerized in an Algerian oasis, unable to rouse himself to action (Gide 1902); Walden Pond as Henry David Thoreau's experiment in staying; radical introvert Emily Dickinson housebound in Amherst; Franz Kafka's cockroach man and Fyodor Dostoyevsky's underground man.

In these canonical texts, the choice to remain in place counts as a radical act of individualism, narcissism, or existential breakdown, an act of refusal. Such examples seem to confirm the claim that in Western modernity, mobility is the normative figure for freedom, knowledge, and self-realization. A more forceful disruption of such identifications arises among the other inhabitant of the imperial landscape, the Indigenous.

El derecho a no migrar

In 2003 the Mixteco, one of Mexico's largest and most influential Indigenous groups, took a stand against migration. At a gathering of leaders in Oaxaca, they demanded recognition of a new human right: *el derecho a no migrar* (the right to not migrate). It was striking that this demand came from the Mixteco, known for their resourcefulness and ingenuity in sustaining their collective forms of organization and social reproduction in Oaxaca even after state neglect and NAFTA (the North American Free Trade Agreement) forced them into the northward migrant stream.[3] The Mixteco were among the founding models of transnational community, exemplars of the ongoing shifts in the way human belonging was organized across the planet. Yet now they were claiming the right to stay or, rather, the right to choose to stay.

El derecho a no migrar implies a revised relation between citizen and state, a new entitlement: the right not to be forced into the migrant stream, the right to a genuine choice. It was new mostly because in modern states, such an entitlement used to be taken for granted. Citizenship in a nation-state meant territorial belonging; staying was the expected case (though millions of Irish, Italian, and German immigrants to the Americas knew otherwise). The norm changed as states came to depend on pushing their citizens into the migrant stream. The Mixteco's claim stands out also because the new human right is collective, not individual. The Mixtecos, as a people and an aggregate of territorialized communities, demand not to be compelled to *collectively* undergo the effects of dislocation and disruption. The dislocations of migration were suffered communally by those who went and by those who stayed.

Migrancy in this conception is not the individual experience of the migrant. Not at all. The demand for a *derecho a no migrar* calls on the state to recognize migration as a mass imposition, not an individual choice. It calls on the state to recognize its complicity in forced migration. The reorganization of the global economic landscape in the interests of multinational corporations produced many national economies dependent on large-scale out-migration of their labor forces. This mass mobility is functional for states in two ways: (1) out-migrants' basic needs are met elsewhere (or not at all), and (2) migrants send back money to support those who stay in place. By the early 2000s, *remesas* (remittances) had become the largest or second-largest source of foreign exchange for a whole set of countries and regions, including the Philippines, Mexico, Central America, Ecuador, and the Caribbean. If you are a migrant, the state does not want you back but does want you to keep sending money, to exercise your citizenship and belonging cost-effectively from elsewhere. Today migrant labor is the main mechanism of north-south economic redistribution, a redistribution carried out by hand at Western Union offices and similar venues. In upholding such relations, even tacitly, states are extending their reach beyond their own borders.

El derecho a no migrar raises a challenge to rights discourse, which, as Grande notes, normally attaches rights to individual bodies in a way that is intrinsically unplaced. With respect to rights, people are interchangeable. The Mixteco demand assumes placedness; it assumes individuals are members of collectivities where they are irreplaceable in community structures, rituals, kinship networks, generational relationships, and reproductive units. Each departure creates, among those who stay, an absence that cannot be filled; communities and families become a fabric full of holes; social reproduction becomes impossible. A Mexican anthropologist, researching migration in rural communities, commented on the sadness surrounding the unwanted departure of yet another group of ever-younger sons and brothers:

> Ahora que migran tan jóvenes, claro, ya pasaron sus 5 años básicos de vida en su rancho pero todavía están madurando muchas cosas a los 14, 15 y 16 años! Ahora ni siquiera se van con la familia! Qué pasará con su identidad de indios, campesinos, pobres, etc.?[4]

> Now that they migrate so young—they've spent their 5 basic years on the rancho, but many things are still maturing at the age of 14, 15, 16! And now they aren't even leaving with their families! What will become of their identities as Indians, peasants, poor people, etc.?

The *Devocionario del migrante* (Migrant's prayer book; 1997), published by the Archdiocese of San Juan de los Lagos in western Mexico, addresses this experience of involuntary mobility as a state of unfreedom. It includes a prayer for migrants to use as they board the bus:

> Tú [Jesucristo] que conociste la amargura del destierro cuando con María y José tuviste que buscar refugio en tierra extranjera, comprendes que a

3.2 — Mexican popular *calavera* (skull) art depicting the killing of migrants at the Arizona border, 2002. SOURCE: ERIC BONDOC.

mí también el alma se me destroza de amargura al dejar a mis seres queridos. Cuídalos, Señor. Haz que nunca se olviden de mí y que nunca los olvide yo, a pesar de la lejanía. Te pido, ahora, que este viaje llegue a buen término. Líbrame de todo accidente y que en todo me vaya bien. Virgen Santísima, Madre de Jesús, guía mis pasos y dame la fuerza necesaria para superar todas las dificultades del camino. Señor, yo te entrego mi fe, para que siempre me encuentre firme frente a los peligros que me puedan hacer dudar de tu amor.

You who knew the bitterness of exile when with Mary and Joseph you had to seek refuge in a foreign land, you understand that bitterness tears up my soul, too, as I leave my loved ones. Care for them, Lord. Make sure they never forget me and I never forget them, despite the distance. I pray to you now that this voyage may turn out well. May you keep me free of accidents and may things go well for me. Holy Virgin, Mother of Jesus, guide my steps and give me the strength to overcome the difficulties of the road. Lord, I give my faith to you so that I may stay firm in the face of dangers that could make me doubt your love.

Here travel equates with grief and loss: *refugio, destierro, amargura, leja-nia, necesidad, peligro, destrozar, dejar, olvidar, dudar,* as it does in the slave narratives of the eighteenth and nineteenth centuries and in the literatures of exile birthed by modern states.

This is not to say that all migrants or all Indigenous migrants experience migrancy in this way. Migration is often an effective response by communities, families, and individuals to the extremely uneven distribution of economic and social opportunity across the globe. For individuals oppressed by the norms of their cultures, departure can indeed be a path to liberation and self-realization. The overall point is that the scale of today's displacements, voluntary, involuntary, or anywhere in between, marks a significant shift in human geography. Climate change is accelerating it. New geographers will be required to map the planet as reconfigured by the new phase of global capitalism and its accompanying climate catastrophe. The Mixteco are among those new geographers. Their claim of a *derecho a no migrar* marks the state of staying in place as no longer normative. It has become an entitlement, in need of a label. Their claim bears out Grande's argument that indigeneity both calls for and points toward differently defined emancipatory projects framed not by "Western conceptions of democracy and justice that presume a 'liberated' self" but by "a construct that is also geographically rooted and historically placed" (2000, 240). I return to this subject in chapter 5.

Mobility, Placedness, and Indigeneity

Indigeneity today has become a planetary discourse affirming and demanding the freedom to remain in place, to be placed, to be entitled to remain, entitled not to be compelled by some external agent to move (Dirlik 1999; Starn and de la Cadena 2007). As discussed in the introduction, indigeneity as a concept refers not to a quality that characterizes a group of people but to a historically constructed relationship between subjects who inhabit a place and subjects who arrive(d) there uninvited from elsewhere, between displaced subjects who arrive and the placed subjects they find already there. As both history and myth, indigeneity unfolds in time and place from this unsolicited encounter. Put succinctly, no one is Indigenous until somebody else shows up. This is both an old story and a vital contemporary one. In the final pages of this chapter on mobility and the politics of belonging, I examine one instance of each. I turn first to a haunting literary tale about indigeneity, encounter, and place from mid-nineteenth-century Peru. I end the chapter with the ambitious experiments

CHAPTER THREE |

in citizenship and mobility launched by the Zapatista movement in late twentieth-century Mexico.

"Si Haces Mal No Esperes Bien"

In 1861 Argentine writer Juana Manuela Gorriti published a serial tale called "Si haces mal no esperes bien" (He who does evil should expect no good) in a Peruvian magazine (see Gorriti 1907). Gorriti, who had long lived in Peru, was its most famous woman writer, a feminist, and the host of Lima's most celebrated literary salon. In this story Gorriti spells out the colonial underpinnings of Peruvian modernity, using the alignment of whiteness with movement and arrival, and the alignment of indigeneity with unsolicited encounter and anchoring in place. The mythic story hinges on a specific spot on the well-traveled road from Lima up into the Andes to the province of Jauja, where a series of unsolicited encounters occur. In the first, a white soldier rapes an Andean girl who is herding animals at this spot by the road. (Rape is a founding trope of colonialism and a paradigm for unsolicited encounter between he who arrives and she who was already there.) The second encounter occurs five years later, when the same young woman returns to the spot, again herding animals and now accompanied by the daughter born of the rape. In search of flowers, the child strays to the roadside, into the path of a military convoy whose officer orders his men to snatch the child as a gift for his mistress in Lima. The mother recognizes him as the man who raped her and fathered her child; the officer does not realize he has just kidnapped his own daughter.

Torn from her place, the child becomes a cipher, passing from one colonial, patriarchal script to another. With ingenious literary architecture, Gorriti uses the serial geography of the road to invoke, one after the other, the mobile regimes of power defining this neocolonial Peruvian modernity. (Related theoretical discussion of Peruvian modernity can be found in chapter 14.) The officer hands the child off to his muleteers with orders to take her to Lima. They are ambushed by bandits who abandon her by the roadside along with other objects not worth stealing. A French naturalist passing on horseback rescues her, making her part of his collection ("Traigo en mi maleta el reino vegetal y el mineral. He aquí el animal. ¡A Francia, pues!"; I have the vegetable and mineral kingdoms in my case, and now here is the animal. To France, then!; 158), and takes her back to France to become a surrogate for a daughter who died. She grows up there, and as a young French woman, she marries a young Peruvian student, who brings her home with him to Lima. He has fallen in love with her because she reminds him of his beloved sister. Once there, she becomes sickly and disturbed, haunted by feelings she cannot explain. With her life in peril, doctors send her to the mountains for fresh air, accompanied by her husband and father-in-law.

Thus ensues the third encounter. When they reach the same fatal spot in the road, the young woman begins to weep, and "en ese momento una figura extraña, una mujer envuelta en una manta negra, pálida como espectro, se alzó detras de un peñasco gritando con lúgubre acento: ¿Quién llora aquí?'" (At that moment a strange figure, a woman wrapped in a black shawl, pale as a ghost, rose from behind an outcropping shouting in a grim tone, "Who weeps here?"). Recognizing the officer, she attacks him: "¡Por fin te encuentro! ¡Ladrón de honras, ladrón de niños, en vano te ocultas!" ("At last I found you! Thief of honor, robber of children, in vain you hide!") The muleteers dismiss her as "la loca de Huairos" (the crazy woman of Huairos), but the reader knows, of course, that it is the Indigenous mother still there, fixed at the founding point of colonial violence (167). That night, she enters the *tambo* (hostel) where the travelers are lodged, and the young woman asks her to tell her story. She does, and the young woman realizes that this is her mother—and that she is married to her half brother. Colonial rape has set the stage for neocolonial incest, circuited, like all things modern, through Paris.

Gorriti's story hinges on indigeneity understood as a colonial relation between movers and stayers, between colonizers who arrive, pass through, police, surveil, and plunder and the colonized who stay, endure, haunt, and wait for justice. It is important to notice that the Indigenous woman is not fixed in place by ancestral belonging, the usual ideology of indigeneity, but by the colonial script: unsolicited encounter, violence, dispossession, moral debt.[5] That script also keeps bringing the officer back to the same place. His mobility is not an enactment of freedom, though it seems so to him. Rather, his mobility brings him back to the site of the founding assault over and over again because there is only one road here. There is no future at the end of Gorriti's story. The daughter dies, the son enters a monastery, and only the Indigenous mother remains, haunting her daughter's grave—the one who stays.[6]

Decolonizing Mobility

It would be misleading to leave the colonial script in place, however, for contemporary Indigenous people and movements are rewriting it. They are doing so not by abandoning values of place and placedness but by appropriating both the powers of movement and the powers of hosting for their own purposes in solicited rather than unsolicited encounters. They are decolonizing

3.3 — Zapatista march. SOURCE: MOYSÉS ZUÑIGA SANTIAGO. FROM THE AUTHOR'S COLLECTION.

relations of going and staying. In 2016 the Standing Rock Sioux in North Dakota issued a general invitation for people to join them in an occupation to oppose an oil pipeline that endangered their water supply. Thousands arrived, invited this time, and joined a tent city that lasted for nine months, sustained by donations from all over the world. Some fifteen thousand people participated in person, and millions from afar. In Bolivia, Peru, and Colombia, Indigenous people have for several decades now used long marches from the lowland tropics to capital cities as a way of making demands on national governments.

Experiments in going and staying, in mobility and placedness have been a hallmark of the Zapatista movement and one of its chief decolonizing strategies.[7] Right from their beginning in 1994, the Zapatistas defined themselves in terms of a place: the Lacandon jungle of Chiapas. This was not an ancestral home for the Zapatista base but a place to which they had been displaced by hydroelectric and other projects that had invaded their former land bases. From this place, they deployed a string of experiments in extroversion. They became hosts and travelers. Some readers may recall the blanket invitation they issued to the world in 1996, to a summit on neoliberalism hosted by them, in San Cristóbal de las Casas in Chiapas. They launched a gigantic, unprecedented act of hospitality, a vast solicited rather than unsolicited encounter. As at Standing Rock, a global cast of thousands attended, and out of that gathering, according to David Graeber (2011), came the activist network that went on to organize the groundbreaking antiglobalization demonstrations in Seattle in the spring of 1999. From the place and placedness of indigeneity, the Zapatistas superseded the colonial script by soliciting encounter and making themselves the agents of contact. This is what decolonization looks like.

Three years later, in the spring of 1999, they took another bold step in an experiment reminiscent of the Argentine horseman with whom this chapter began. Hemmed in and harassed by the Mexican army, the Zapatistas announced a nationwide *consulta ciudadana* (citizens' consultation). Delegations of one man and one woman, members of the Zapatista popular movement, would travel to each of Mexico's 2,500 electoral districts (*municipios*), where they would spend a week meeting with anyone open to dialogue with them. A call went out for local host committees to form in each of the 2,500 districts to organize the visits and raise funds. Miraculously, this happened. There were Zapatista supporters everywhere. So it was that in March 1999 five thousand Indigenous adults from Chiapas, plus another thousand or so children, became the ones to travel. Their fellow Mexican citizens became their hosts. The vast majority of the travelers had never before left their home districts; many, particularly the women, spoke no Spanish. Most of their hosts—chambers of commerce, students, teachers, unions, community groups—had never listened to an Indigenous language or sat across a table from an Indigenous person. The *consulta* produced innumerable first encounters.

In this experiment the Zapatistas set out to travel not from margin to center (that is, from Chiapas to Mexico City, which they later did) but from one place (Chiapas) to *all of the others* (the national electoral grid). Like the Argentine horseman's ride, this strategy identified the nation as the totality of its inhabitants (the electorate) and not its government (the elected representatives). By sending male-female pairs, the Zapatistas intercepted the sexual scripts of both colonialism and patriarchal hospitality, which grants male visitors sexual access to the (male) host's women.[8]

The Zapatistas have developed many strategies of decolonization. Among these, their experiments in remaking relations of going and staying, sending and receiving, stand out. Reconjugating the colonial matrix of mobility, placedness, and indigeneity, they assert indigeneity as a force of full-fledged, extroverted engagement with the West's dominant traditions and epistemologies. In the Zapatista imaginary, the counterimage to remaining in place is not nomadism but crossing: "El zapatismo," says one of their communiqués, "no es, no existe. Solo sirve, como sirven los puentes, para cruzar de un lado a otro. Por tanto, en el zapatismo caben todos los que quieran cruzar de uno a otro lado" (Zapatismo does not exist. It only serves, the way bridges serve, to cross from one side to another. Therefore, zapatismo embraces all those who wish to cross from one side to another side).[9] Let that be the image of mobility and decolonization with which I leave you.

CHAPTER FOUR

FIRE, WATER, AND WANDERING WOMEN

This chapter examines some distinctive narrative configurations that emerged in Latin American fiction in the 1990s in the context of the large-scale reconfiguring of economic, social, and citizen-state relations that we have been discussing throughout this book. I examine five novelistic experiments, all published between 1994 and 1997. All of them, I argue, capture the end-of-the-century crisis of citizenship and social connection through brilliant allegorical fictions that register civilizational crisis and peer ahead to futures that cannot yet be deciphered.

Literary experiments always play with genre. In the five novels discussed here, the authors twist the conventions of the novel to create a sense of extreme pathology around the fictional worlds they create. Patterns of mobility and entrapment, going and staying, are particularly pathologized, often on gendered lines. The social and sexual contracts (Pateman 1988) are breaking down. The people in these novels, mostly men, are trapped in confined spaces; others, often women, are unable to find shelter. Male and female bodies prove unable to occupy the same space and the same story. Women

4.1 — *The Two Fridas*: Self-portraits of gay activist-artists Pedro Lemebel and Francisco Casas, known as the Mares of the Apocalypse, Chile, 1989, restaging Frida Kahlo's painting of the same name. SOURCE: "COLECTIVO DE ARTE YEGUAS DEL APOCALIPSIS." PHOTO BY PEDRO MARINELLO.

tend to wander off or be expelled from the plot. Fire and water appear repeatedly in their mythic role as purifying forces of apocalypse. The real world is not absent. In one novel, the apocalypse is species extinction; in another, the out-of-control violence of the drug trade; in another, the AIDS crisis; in another, patriarchal authoritarianism. Attempts at alternative world-making fail. These are novels of civilizational crisis. At the same time, their depictions of both women and homosexuality register the explosion of feminist and gay activism in the 1990s in Latin America, along with a number of what came to be called new social movements.[1]

My corpus includes Fernando Vallejo's La virgen de los sicarios (Colombia, 1994; Our Lady of the Assassins, 2001), Mayra Montero's Tú, la oscuridad (Puerto Rico, 1995; In the Palm of Darkness, 1997), Mario Bellatin's Salón de belleza (Mexico, 1994; Beauty Salon, 1997), Ricardo Piglia's Plata quemada (Argentina, 1997; Money to Burn, 2003), and Diamela Eltit's Los vigilantes (Chile, 1994; Custody of the Eyes, 2005). Many others could have been added to the corpus.

Fernando Vallejo's partially autobiographical La virgen de los sicarios is a performance of extreme cynicism. The novel is set in the city of Medellín, formerly the center of the Colombian drug trade. The narrator-protagonist, Fernando, is a middle-aged man of letters who returns to his home city after an absence of thirty years. Following a proud Colombian tradition, he has been trained as a grammarian. A gay man, he forms a couple with a young sicario, or professional assassin, who is facing unemployment owing to the collapse of the Medellín drug cartel. Like a pair of flaneurs, the two experience what appears to be an endless excursion winding through the streets of the city. Alexis, the young sicario, returns to his assassin's trade, now as a form of entertainment or social activism, depending on how one chooses to interpret his actions (remember, I mentioned cynicism). One after another, while Fernando looks on, Alexis randomly kills fellow citizens who cause irritation or inconvenience—a hippie neighbor whose music offends him, a woman whose children are screeching on the bus, a taxi driver who refuses to turn down the radio, a waitress who serves badly. Events unfold until the inevitable denouement: Alexis is assassinated by another sicario who is avenging the death of his brother, killed by Alexis. The whole story is narrated in an ironic, acerbic, cynically amused tone that canonized Vallejo as the voice of an apocalyptic millennium:

¿Cómo puede matar uno o hacerse matar por unos tenis? preguntará usted que es extranjero. Mon cher ami, no es por los tenis: es por un principio de Justicia en el que todos creemos. Aquel a quien se los van a robar cree que es injusto que se los quiten puesto que él los pagó; y aquel que se los va a robar cree que es más injusto no tenerlos. Y van los ladridos de los perros de terraza en terraza gritándose a voz en cuello que son mejores que nosotros. (Vallejo 1994, 59)

How can someone kill or be killed for a pair of trainers? you who are a stranger to these parts will ask. *Mon cher ami*, it's not for the trainers: it's for a principle of justice we all believe in. The guy from whom they're going to rob them thinks it's unjust that they take them off him, seeing that he paid for them; and the guy who's going to rob them off him thinks it's more unjust for him not to have them. And the barking of the dogs travels from level to level yowling to us they're better than we are. (Vallejo 2001, 61–62)

Fernando and Alexis share the urban space of the city with women. Women appear in the streets, in stores, on buses, in houses and public spaces, but the two men do not live or interact with them. Fernando expresses an intense dislike toward women and female bodies, especially reproductive bodies, "porque ¿cuál es la ley de este mundo sino que de una pareja de pobres nazcan cinco o diez?" (Vallejo 1994, 68) ("because what is the law of this world if not that from a couple of poor people five or ten more are born?"; Vallejo 2001, 72). Far from needing women, the couple creates a male world in which women seem to be completely superfluous.[2] As we shall see, this all-male world-making, carried out in social spaces given over to violence and death, is a recurring trope in the 1990s.

Like many novels of the 1990s, *La virgen de los sicarios* presents a world in which the social contract is collapsing. The most visible evidence is the arbitrary, uncontrolled, yet legitimized violence that governs relations among citizens. Fraternal, civic bonds do not exist. And the sexual contract? In Vallejo's novel, the sexual contract has transferred onto male bodies, to the exclusion of female ones. It is a homo- or monosexual rather than heterosexual arrangement. Between Alexis and the grammarian, the sexual contract maintains its hierarchical, subordinating power. The narrator's antisentimentalism makes the relation appear mainly transactional. Financed by Fernando, the young *sicario* takes on a number of functions stereotypically associated with the subordinated bourgeois feminine: consumerism, ignorance, passivity, idleness, economic dependency, triviality, physical beauty, sexual availability. The narrator occupies the masculine roles of provider and sexual partner. Violence, however, is Alexis's work, a kind of reverse reproduction. In this civilizational meltdown, the male couple generates dead people, not live ones. Alexis cannot die like young romantic heroines in childbirth, but he dies by its double in this violent parallel universe: murder. What makes the situation perverse is not homosexuality but violence and misogyny, the homicidal and suicidal male world the men have made. Though it is monosexual, this male order is not purely masculine, for Alexis embodies many qualities of the feminine, and that is part of the sexual contract between the two men. The feminine remains; women and female bodies have become superfluous. This configuration, as we shall see, recurs in other novels in the corpus.

The new all-male world-making that goes on in these novels is suicidal as well as homicidal. The characters are self-condemned to annihilation. Alexis, like the young *sicarios* who appear in Víctor Gaviria's courageous films of the 1990s, *Rodrigo D: No futuro* (*Rodrigo D: No Future*, 1990) and *La vendedora de rosas* (*The Rose Seller*, 1998), knows he is going to die young. His death is marked in the novel by an apocalyptic rainstorm that floods the city: "cuando a Medellín le da por llover es como cuando le da por matar; sin términos medio, con todas las de la ley y la conciencia" (Vallejo 1994, 87) ("when it decides to rain in Medellín it's like when they take it into their heads to kill someone with no half measures, but completely and conscientiously"; Vallejo 2001, 94). In the other four texts analyzed here, apocalypse comes as both flood and fire.

Plata quemada (1997)

Ricardo Piglia's documentary novel *Plata quemada*, published in 1997, has several elements in common with *La virgen de los sicarios*. The protagonists in *Plata quemada* also create a closed all-male world in which women are redundant, indeed absent. Here, too, violence is the narrative motor in a society that is breaking down, and the plot marches inexorably toward an apocalyptic ending that is simultaneously homicidal and suicidal. As in *La virgen de los sicarios*, the family is present as an old order, associated with a rural or provincial past and evoked with nostalgia. In contrast with Vallejo's novel, however, the homosexual love relationship here is fraternal, not patriarchal. It does not simulate the heterosexual contract; rather, it sexualizes the fraternal bond.

Based on real events that took place in 1965, *Plata quemada* narrates a criminal adventure in which a group of Argentinean thieves rob a bank truck in Buenos Aires and flee to Montevideo in Uruguay. It culminates in a prolonged confrontation between the thieves and the police. The thieves commandeer an apartment where they plan to defend themselves and negotiate their escape in exchange for returning the money. They have weapons and drugs. Outside in the street, the civic order gathers—police, a detective, a journalist, a radio operator, a few female witnesses. These civic actors are almost exclusively male, and the narrator shows them thinking about their families—wives, mothers, sisters, and children, even in the moment of confronting death. With one exception, the few female characters who appear in *Plata quemada* serve as accomplices to the men. They are in their place.

Inside the commandeered apartment, the brothers-in-crime embark on their suicidal trajectory. Trapped by the authorities, the thieves make the dramatic decision to set fire to the stolen money that has set the whole story in motion. Flaming bills begin to rain down on the crowd outside. Burning the money, their means of exchange, marks a break with the civic order more serious than the theft itself. Their fellow citizens find the act unbearable:

> Indignados, los ciudadanos que observaban la escena daban gritos de horror y de odio, como en un aquelarre del medioevo (según los diarios), no podían soportar que ante sus ojos se quemaran cerca de quinientos mil dólares . . . quemar dinero inocente es un acto de canibalismo. (Piglia 1997, 190–91)

> Filled with indignation, the citizens gather to observe the scene, offering shouts of horror and loathing, looking like something from a witches' sabbath straight out of the Middle Ages (according to the papers), they couldn't bear the prospect of 500,000 dollars being burned before their very eyes. . . . "Burning innocent money is an act of cannibalism." (Piglia 2003, 157–58)

With the burning of the money, the thieves enter a new, apocalyptic state of transcendence ("drugged up, flying high") that culminates in the scene of Franco Brignone's death in the arms of his lover, the Blond Gaucho. The scene is described as the holy image of a pietà: "El Nene le sonrió y el Gaucho Rubio lo mantuvo en sus brazos como quien sostiene a un Cristo. . . . Estuvieron un momento inmóviles, la sangre corría entre los dos. Un absoluto silencio reinaba en el departamento" (Piglia 1997, 218) ("The kid smiled at him and the Blond Gaucho held him up in his arms like an image of the deposition of Christ. . . . They remained motionless for some moments, the blood coursing between the two of them. Total silence reigned in the apartment"; Piglia 2003, 181). The civic order wins a Pyrrhic victory. On the one hand, it wins the confrontation because it controls public space, the flow of information, and the instruments of state violence. But on the other hand, it loses on the ethical and the affective side, the side of love.

In Piglia's novel, the focus on male relationships raises an interesting question: Are the men rejecting women, or are they rejecting their claims over them? With its apocalyptic overtones, is *Plata quemada* contemplating a world without women or a world in which men have no claim over women, leaving women free to wander and protagonize their own stories? Can men renounce their sexual privilege? How? What would that look like? What would women do? Piglia offers a bare glimpse of an answer. The criminal group initially includes one female character, a fifteen-year-old adolescent who has fled her home and joined the delinquents. She disappears, however, the moment the thieves' escape gets underway. In a fascinating touch, the young woman re-appears in the novel's epilogue, some months after the whole debacle. Piglia encounters her on a train heading from Argentina to Bolivia, fleeing arrest. They strike up a conversation, and she tells him the story of the heist. (The anecdote appears to be true.) Piglia wonders at the fact that the story survives in one of those superfluous wandering female bodies. In the last lines of his book, he evokes "la muchacha que se va en el tren a Bolivia y asoma su cara por la ventanilla y me mira seria, sin un gesto de saludo, quieta, mientras yo la veo alejarse, parado en el andén de la estación vacía" (Piglia 1997, 252) ("the young girl travelling on the train to Bolivia, leaning out of the window with a serious expression on her face, tranquil and without any parting gesture, while I, standing on the empty station platform, watch her recede into the distance"; Piglia 2003, 209). Indeed, having told him the story, she is again superfluous, *super-fluous*, flowing away as the sexes separate once again. The *alterity* of the female body remains—now an absolute alterity, opaque and indecipherable.

Tú, la oscuridad (1995)

In *Tú, la oscuridad* (1995), by Cuban–Puerto Rican novelist Mayra Montero, the gesture of rejecting sexual privilege is made explicit. Like *La virgen de los sicarios* and *Plata quemada,* this text, too, inaugurates an all-male order through a violent drama in which male-female relations break down, in both the animal and human orders. The apocalyptic finale results not only in death but in extinction. *Tú, la oscuridad* tells a transspecies story set in Haiti. It unfolds around the expedition of an urban herpetologist to the Haitian mountains, accompanied by a local guide, in search of an endangered species of frog, the *grenouille de sang* (blood frog). The narration alternates between the voices of the two men, the Haitian guide and the herpetologist. As a prelude to the search for the frog, the guide tells of another search he undertook in the same mountains in his youth, whose object was a fleeing woman. He was hired by a German traveler to search for his wife, who had escaped into the hills. He received orders to bring her back, dead or alive (the sexual contract is firm and in force). Finally, at night, the young man finds the woman, nude, crazed, and refusing to return. She, too, is trying to wander and survive. By brute force the young man brings her down from the hills and returns her to her husband, who shoves her into a car and beats her until she is unconscious or perhaps dead. This flashback, which has strong allegorical overtones, condemns the heterosexual contract as violent, criminal, and above all Western, white, and foreign. The otherness of Haiti offers a site to imagine things otherwise.

This new male pair, the herpetologist and his guide, set off to this same mountainside. Like Vallejo's Medellín, this jungle is a space of death governed by smugglers and drug traffickers. Civil order no longer exists. After arduous work, the two men find a living specimen of the *grenouille de sang*. It turns out to be an aged male who, lacking a female mate, will be the last of the species:

> Se trataba de un macho adulto, bastante viejo por lo que deduje de la piel de las patas y de la cabeza, desorientado entonces por los años. Tuve la sensación de que me hallaba frente a un ejemplar longevo, una criatura que se olvidó de morir. (Montero 1995, 228)

> It was an adult male, fairly old judging by the skin on his feet and head, disoriented by age. I felt as if I were holding an ancient survivor, a creature that had forgotten to die.

With pure delight, I cannot help but see this solitary aged male as yet another allegorized instance of the collapsed sexual and social contract. Species extinction has deprived him of any companion of either gender. Here, too, the plot marches inexorably toward death, in this case, extinction. The novel's apocalyptic denouement confirms the reading. It comes, as in Vallejo's novel, by water. The boat carrying the male trio—the scientist, his guide, and the frog—shipwrecks in a storm, and they all drown. Erzulie, the Haitian goddess of the water, is responsible for the accident.

Tú, la oscuridad is the only novel in my corpus that ties the crisis of the human sociosexual order explicitly to the ecological crisis of the planet. Montero specifically evokes the rapid extinction of amphibians that surged suddenly worldwide in the 1990s. This process, according to the experts Montero cites in the novel, remains mysterious and inexplicable. Haitian mythology suggests a possible collective animal suicide:

> -Ya empezó la gran huida—recalcó-. Ustedes se inventan excusas: la lluvia ácida, los herbidicas, la deforestación. Pero las ranas desaparecen de lugares donde no ha habido nada de eso. (Montero 1995, 132)

"The great flight has begun," he repeated. "You people invent excuses: acid rain, herbicides, deforestation. But the frogs are disappearing from places where none of that has happened."

It is worth underscoring the allegorical mode in which civilizational breakdown is imagined in these novels. Few Latin American novels of the 1990s seem to offer realist portrayals of the economic and geopolitical forces eroding social relations. Perhaps the *testimonio* had taken over the space of realism. In any case, novelists opted for allegorical and speculative modes. *Plata quemada* would seem to be an exception, because it is a documentary novel about a real episode that took place in the 1960s. But it is a documentary novel about an earlier era now gone. Piglia had tried to write the story in its own time, the 1960s, but found the story untellable then. He states in his epilogue: "Siempre serán misteriosas para mí las razones por las que algunas historias se resisten durante años a ser contadas y exigen un tiempo propio" (1997, 251) ("It will always remain a mystery to me why some stories resist being told for years on end, demanding their own moment"; Piglia 2003, 209). The gay movement, along with Argentina's catastrophic turn-of-the-century moment, opened an imaginative space where the tale could resonate.

The strange absence of realism in these novels and their suicidal, apocalyptic denouements offer no way out of the civilizational crisis. None proposes returning to the past. None proposes incorporating women into the male fraternal order. In *Plata quemada*, there are no female police or female thieves; in *La virgen de los sicarios*, there are no female assassins; in *Tú, la oscuridad*, there is one female scientist, who chooses a violent death. In all these novels, women are present but outside the story. Absent the sexual contract, female bodies enter a zone of semantic and ideological instability, which could also be freedom. What might these bodies now mean, to themselves and to men? What agency and alterity can be assigned to them? In Montero's novel, a series of marginal female characters suggest possibilities for an autonomous and free existence. They are all irrelevant to the story line, but they are there.

Salón de belleza (1994)

I turn now to two novels of world-making whose protagonists retreat to enclosed spaces where they make heroic efforts to inaugurate alternative sociosexual orders in the face of civilizational breakdown. Again, both are allegorical, apocalyptic, and suicidal. In both, the world-making efforts fail. The two novels are *Salón de belleza*, by the Peruvian novelist Mario Bellatin, and

Los vigilantes, by the Chilean Diamela Eltit, both published in 1994. Their publication date, their literary quality, and the fact that by coincidence they were both written in Mexico City are among a number of elements these novels have in common.

In *Salón de belleza*, the all-male social configuration arises not through crime or violence but through sickness. Narrated by an urban transvestite hairstylist, the novel relates the gradual transformation of his beauty salon into *el Moridero* (the Terminal), a hospice for men dying from an unnamed plague clearly identified with AIDS. The beauty salon, an extroverted, creative, feminized space, gradually mutates into an introverted, regimented, masculine space, sealed off by the rupture of the social contract in the society at large. The transformation begins when the hairstylist and his two partners offer shelter to a close friend whose "única alternativa habría sido morir bajo uno de los puentes del río que corre por la ciudad" (Bellatin 1994, 49) ("only option was to die under one of the bridges by the river that runs parallel to the city"; Bellatin 2009, 37). From that point on, growing numbers of dying men with no place else to go arrive, one after the other. The aesthetic and pleasurable function of the beauty salon is replaced by the ethical and compassionate function of a refuge for the dying. The partners acquire different equipment, selling "las secadoras, así como los sillones reclinables para el lavado del cabello . . . para comprar . . . colchones de paja, catres de hierro, grandes ollas y una cocina de querosén" (Bellatin 1994, 21) ("the hair dryers and the reclining armchairs I used to wash hair in order to obtain . . . mattresses, iron cots and a kerosene cooker"; Bellatin 2009, 11). In almost obsessive detail, the narrator explains how he developed this new institution, revealing that at the moment he is telling the story, he, too, has reached an advanced stage of the illness and is facing death. In fact, the nearness of death apparently motivates the narration, not because the protagonist wishes to leave a record of his heroic story but because he experiences a paternal anxiety regarding his project: "Me preocupa mucho saber quien va a hacerse cargo del salón cuando la enfermedad se desencadene con fuerza en todo mi cuerpo" (Bellatin 1994, 24) ("I worry about who will take care of the beauty salon when the disease spreads inside me"; Bellatin 2009, 12).

Like all good allegory, *Salón de belleza* makes concepts concrete. The story registers with precision the processes of privatization, impoverishment, and erosion of the state's custodial function, all associated with the neoliberal regimes of the 1990s. The scarcity of public resources and the lack of rights to basic sustenance and health care condemn those who are ill to a cruel death to which the state is indifferent. The hairdresser's response is personal and altruistic. It consists not in a collective demand on the state but rather in a private, individual, and fiercely autonomous initiative. In fact, the Terminal raises privacy and autonomy to the level of constitutive principles. It is supported, the narrator tells us, by money donated by relatives of the sick men. Families are prohibited from contributing anything else except bedding and sweets. The narrator/owner takes charge on his own of all of the work of the place, with a simple and highly perfected routine he describes in detail. The space is closed off: the sick men are not allowed to leave, and no one may enter, neither visitors, nor doctors, nor representatives of charitable organizations. Those latter two, doctors and charities, are objects of a special sort of disdain on the narrator's part because they are guided by humanist principles that end up prolonging suffering and delaying the inevitable outcome: "No sé donde nos han enseñado que socorrer al desvalido equivale a apartarlo de las garras de la muerte a cualquier precio" (Bellatin 1994, 50) ("I don't know where we got the idea that helping sick people means keeping them away from the jaws of death at all costs"; Bellatin 2009, 38).

And, above all else, women are excluded from the Terminal, no matter how sick or desperate they may be. Here again, the feminine work of nursing and caretaking is taken on by male bodies, while female bodies are in this case expelled from the story into a semantic vacuum. The narrator's logic is cruel and misogynist:

El salón en algún tiempo había embellecido hasta la saciedad a las mujeres, no iba pues a echar por la borda tantos años de trabajo sacrificado. Nunca acepté a nadie que no fuera de sexo masculino. (Bellatin 1994, 34)

The beauty salon had once been dedicated to beautifying women and I wasn't willing to sacrifice so many years of work. Which is why I never accepted anyone that wasn't a man. (Bellatin 2009, 23–24)

Female corporeality, detached from the work of beautification, cannot be integrated here.

While awakening the reader's solidarity with the victims of the plague, the narrator also reveals a dark side of his project, which transforms the narrator from benevolent angel into nothing less than . . . a *manager*. The pragmatism that leads him to prohibit any medicine or care that would prolong life gradually extends to all affect and desire. When he falls in love with a beautiful young patient, the narrator begins to neglect the others, which leads him to forbid himself any affective relationship in the future: "Aún no había perfeccionado del todo mi técnica" (Bellatin 1994, 43) ("I still had not yet perfected my technique"; Bellatin 2009, 31). The withholding of affection acquires a practical function: it promotes more rapid death.

> He llegado a un estado tal que todos son iguales para mí. Al principio les reconocía e incluso llegué a encariñarme con alguno. Pero ahora todos no son más que cuerpos en trance de desaparición. (Bellatin 1994, 25)

> It's come to a point where they're all the same to me. At first, I would get to know them, I even got close to some of them on occasion. Now, however, they are nothing more to me than bodies on the verge of disappearing. (Bellatin 2009, 15)

Like women, emotion remains out in the street: the sick men's inconsolable lovers appear at night, overwhelmed with grief and the desire to see their loved ones. Prohibited from entering, they are left howling on the sidewalk while the narrator asks himself, "qué podía mover a esos seres a buscar a alguno de los huéspedes" (Bellatin 1994, 63) ("What could move these people to come looking for sick guests"; Bellatin 2009, 52).

It is impossible to point to a specific moment when the narrator's altruism mutates into violence, inflicted and self-inflicted. The narration is nonlinear and confessional, a spiral that takes on first monstrous, then pathetic, dimensions; the narrative voice, always impassive (the novel is a stylistic tour de force), becomes increasingly infiltrated by managerial, instrumental, and corporate-like speech. Aesthetics, forced out in the salon's conversion, returns in a fascist mode. Now the narrator finds beauty in order, efficiency, seriality, abstinence. This transformation is ritualized in an apocalyptic moment, by fire, as in *Plata quemada*. Forced by his own sickness to withdraw from his transvestite nightlife, the narrator piles up all of his feminine attire—"los vestidos, las plumas y las lentejuelas" (Bellatin 1994, 54) ("the dresses, the feathers and the sequins"; Bellatin 2009, 42)—on the patio and sets it alight, singing and dancing madly around the pyre, with the intention of sacrificing himself as well. As with the burning of money, this purifying, exorcizing ritual marks the rupture with the civic world outside and opens up a path not to transcendence but to a suicidal register. In the text's last lines, the narrator questions this surrender in terms that show he does not yet understand it:

> Cuando vino todo ese asunto de la transformación del salón se produjo un cambio. Por ejemplo, siempre pienso dos veces antes de hacer algo. Luego analizo las posibles consecuencias. Antes no me habría preocupado el futuro del Moridero tras mi desaparición. Habría dejado que los

huéspedes se las arreglaran solos. Ahora, sólo puedo pedir que respeten la soledad que se aproxima. (Bellatin 1994, 73)

When the place was transformed, though, I changed. Now, for example, I always think before I do anything and then I analyze the possible consequences. For example, in the past I wouldn't have worried about the future of the Terminal when I'm gone, I would have let the guests work it out as best they could. Now the only thing I ask is that they respect the loneliness to come. (Bellatin 2009, 62–63)

Allegorically, the epidemic in *Salón de belleza* is not just AIDS but also a rationalist, bureaucratic, anti-ludic, fascist mentality that is like a virus that turns desire into repression, debauchery into chastity, freedom into egocentrism, egalitarianism into fascism, pleasure into sadomasochism, mobility into self-incarceration. There's no need for a state to repress and rationalize: once citizens are infected, they will do it themselves. In other words, there is a civilizational crisis. The Terminal is a failed project. It has no future, and there is no escape from it. The terminal settings in *Plata quemada* and *Tú, la oscuridad* could be described in the same way.

Los vigilantes (1994)

Strangely enough, the combination of a failed foundational project, expelled women, purifying fire, abandoned poor people, altruism, and internalized authoritarianism reappears in *Los vigilantes* by Chilean novelist Diamela Eltit. In its national context, this novel is associated with the disillusionment and despair of the Chilean transition of the 1990s (see chapter 9). This was the decade in which Chile's triumphal return to democracy faded into disappointment as the neoliberal policies of the dictatorship continued. Within the corpus we are examining here, *Los vigilantes* is the only text with a female protagonist. As in *Salón de belleza*, the protagonist makes a heroic attempt to define an autonomous space and establish an ethical, authentic project in the face of a harsh, violent, degenerating society. The protagonist of Eltit's novel is a woman with a young child. Separated from the child's father, she rejects the society that surrounds her and seeks to live apart. She wants to educate her son as she wishes and practice her own form of maternity. Her adversaries include the boy's father, his grandmother, and the neighbors who monitor the mother's conduct. The novel consists almost entirely of letters from the protagonist to her son's father, defending her behavior. As in Bellatin's novel, the heartless civic order is marked by the presence of homeless people who appear in the streets, dying of cold and begging for shelter. The citizens condemn any altruistic actions toward these desperate people. Again, we are witnessing a civilizational crisis.

As in Bellatin's novel, *Los vigilantes* proposes a social world in which protection and redistribution no longer form part of the social contract. Like the sick men in *Salón de belleza*, the homeless people in Eltit's novel are the product of an unequal society that does not recognize collective responsibility. In the social world of *Los vigilantes*, altruism signifies a betrayal of the social contract. Halfway through the book, we learn why the protagonist is under scrutiny. She has committed an unforgivable wrong: on a freezing winter night, she gave shelter in her house to a homeless family that would otherwise have died in the cold. For her neighbors, this gesture was an intolerable transgression for which they seek to expel her from the neighborhood. At the end of the book, despite the narrator's fierce self-defense, they succeed. Just as in Bellatin's text, the citizenry comes together only to punish their neighbor for following a benevolent concept of civic responsibility. As in Bellatin's work, what motivates the protagonist to turn her personal world upside down is the specter of her fellow citizens dying in the streets. That powerful recurring image sums up the erosion of the liberal social contract that became so acutely evident in the 1990s.

Los vigilantes dissolves the liberal social map organized around distinctions between public and private spaces, state and civil society. The protagonist's interlocutor/accuser is simultaneously her ex-husband, the father of her child, a judge, and a defender of occidental values, the West.[3] The neighbors take on the surveillance role of the state. These configurations echo the vicissitudes of the postdictatorship experience in Chile. As Eltit and many other intellectuals observed, the long-awaited restoration of electoral democracy brought only a continuing neoliberal order in which radical inequality was considered natural and irreversible, and citizens internalized the normative and repressive functions of the authoritarian state. The intense surveillance imposed on Eltit's female protagonist by her neighbors is an obvious variant of the state surveillance leveled at suspected dissidents that condemned individuals to an interminable process of self-defense. The ex-husband, after all, is also a judge.

Eltit addresses the collapse of the social and the sexual contract as simultaneous processes, intimately linked. In her novel, both have become instruments of policing, surveillance, vigilantism. *Los vigilantes* stands in a complementary relationship with the other four novels examined here. It focuses on the relationships (parenting, marriage) that those novels discard. As in the other novels, the protagonist of *Los vigilantes* occupies a delimited space within which to establish an alternate sociosexual order. In an overdetermined way, the new order here complements the all-male fraternities discussed above. The central relationship, mother and son, is one of radical alterity. The female protagonist, subordinated to the sexual contract, has no option but to operate from within it, from within the law. Her alternative civilizational project fails owing to her lack of power and her subordinated statuses as mother/wife/daughter-in-law. In contrast to Bellatin's hairstylist, for example, Eltit's female protagonist does not have the right to close her door to her mother-in-law's inspections or the neighbors sent by her husband. While the hairstylist is free to develop his "technique" in the Terminal, the protagonist of *Los vigilantes* is obliged to respond to constant questioning. She inhabits a discursive regime interrogated simultaneously by the sexual contract (husband) and the social contract (judge). She can defend herself only within this regime, or against it through lies and secrecy, the weapons of the weak. Her letters show her as heroic and resistant, neurotic and dissembling, alternatively defiant and abject. For her, violence means not power but defeat:

> Adoptaste conmigo los antiguos hábitos porque estás a la espera de mi levantamiento en donde mi insurrección se enfrente con la tuya y me obligues, de una vez y para siempre, a medir nuestras fuerzas. Pero no te otorgaré ese placer, porque yo sé que no sabes cuáles son las fuerzas que me mueven, con qué fuerzas, que no sean las tuyas, me mantengo a pesar de la hostilidad de todos los climas y eso te exaspera. (Eltit 1994, 46)

> You took up the ancient ways with me because you are hoping I will rise up to the point where my insurrection confronts yours and you can oblige me, once and for all, to match forces. But I shall not grant you that pleasure, because I know you don't know what forces move me, with what forces, which aren't yours, I maintain myself in spite of any and every climate's hostility. And that exasperates you. (Eltit 2005, 37)

To avoid violence, she opts for abjection, apologizing for her transgression with the destitute family and begging for the father to save her from a custody suit filed by his mother against her.

Just like those of the hairstylist, the bank robbers, the assassins, and the herpetologists, the woman's world-making project fails. In the cruel patriarchal-neoliberal context, her maternal project turns out to be just as suicidal as that of Piglia's thieves or Vallejo's *sicario*. Condemned for having given shelter, she is expelled from her house with her son. She becomes one of the disposable women who inhabit the edges of all these novels. Starving and frozen, she and her son drag themselves at night to the bonfires lit by homeless people by the river. Like the burning of money in Piglia's novel and of feminine finery in Bellatin's, the scene is apocalyptic and transcendent. Beside the bonfires, the mother-son pair ends up "fijos, hipnóticos, inmóviles como perros AUUUU AUUUU AAUUU aullando a la luna" (Eltit 1994, 130) ("fixed, hypnotized, motionless, like dogs HOOOW, HOOOW, HOOOW, howling at the moon"; Eltit 2005, 104).

Indecipherable Alternatives

Among the many elements shared by Eltit's and Bellatin's novels, one is particularly fascinating. As I mentioned at the beginning of the chapter, in both novels, inside the claustrophobic enclosed space there exists a parallel order of meanings that is understood to be significant but indecipherable. In *Salón de belleza*, this alternative order unfolds inside a set of large aquariums filled with tropical fish that once decorated the beauty salon and that remain in the Terminal. The narrator gives detailed commentary on these alternative lifeworlds:

> Todo iba bien en los acuarios que mantenía antes de la muerte de las Monjitas [especie de pez tropical], hasta que de un dia para otro comenzaron a aparecer hongos en unos Escalares que habían continuado con vida desde los tiempos de prosperidad. . . . Finalmente todos los cuerpos fueron contagiados y los Escalares se fueron al fondo un par de días antes de morir. No estoy seguro, pero creo que para aminorar la impresión encontré rapidamente los Guppys que hasta hoy dia me acompañan. (Bellatin 1994, 41)

> Everything seemed to be going well in the two aquariums that still had life in them until one day fungus appeared on some angelfish that had survived from the early, better days. . . . In the end, all the fish became infected and the angelfish sank to the bottom of the tank and died a few days later. I'm not quite sure why, perhaps to lessen the impact of seeing them like that, but I quickly bought more guppies, ones that are still with me. (Bellatin 2009, 28–29)

While they parallel the enclosed human world of the Terminal, the aquariums represent alternative spaces of world-making that neither the narrator nor the reader can decipher. Of special interest to the narrator is the function of violence within the fish tanks. Some of it is feminine. Mothers unpredictably eat their young or kill the father. As the aquariums deteriorate, the narrator notes the fishes' stubborn effort to survive. This is allegory within allegory.

In *Los vigilantes*, the alternative order of meaning is invented and maintained by the child, a preverbal boy who plays all day with a set of containers that he organizes and reorganizes in obviously meaningful ways that seem to be related to the main narrative but again are indecipherable to the protagonist:

> Cuando las contempla, se ríe y yo siento como si quisiera romperlas con sus carcajadas. . . . Las vasijas están rigurosamente dispuestas en el centro de su cuarto formando una figura de la cual no entiendo su principio ni menos su final. (Eltit 1994, 76)

> When he contemplates them, he laughs and I feel as though he would like to smash them with his horselaughs. . . . The vessels are strictly arranged at the center of his room, forming a figure whose principle I fail to understand, much less its purpose. (Eltit 2005, 59–60)

Here again, we have allegory within allegory. The son ends up achieving, it would seem, the world-making power his mother is denied. He, too, makes her superfluous:

> Tu hijo ahora se arrastra por el piso de manera circular alrededor de sus vasijas. . . . En el círculo que va configurando, es posible comprobar que su propósito se acaba de cerrar sobre si mismo. En el centro de su perfecta circunvalación se empieza a perfilar un mundo que tiene sus partes perfectamente unidas para formar un todo. (Eltit 1994, 113)

> Your son is now dragging himself across the floor, circling his vessels. . . . From the circle he's fashioning it's possible to see that his scheme ends by closing in on him. At the center of his perfect circumnavigation there begins to be described a world with its parts perfectly joined in order to form a whole. (Eltit 2005, 88–89)

Might this child, allegorically, be the new new man, the architect of an alternative future that cannot be known from within the given real? New futures, says Elizabeth Grosz (2004, 261), are not there to be discovered; rather, they must be "brought into existence." "This space, and time, for invention, for the creation of the new, can come about only through a dislocation of and dissociation with the present rather than simply its critique. Only if the present presents itself as fractured, cracked by the interventions of the past and the promise of the future, can the new be invented, welcomed, and affirmed" (261). In these lucid, pessimistic, critical, suicidal novels at the turn of the past century, new civilizational possibilities appear but only as lateral configurations that humans can see but not understand.

CHAPTER FIVE |

PLANETARIZED INDIGENEITY

The neoliberal era brought many surprises. When Ronald Reagan and Margaret Thatcher came to power in 1980, nobody (not even the two of them) would have predicted that their free-market reforms would bring slavery, piracy, child labor, and human trafficking back to the global stage as they did (see chapter 2). Likewise, I doubt many foresaw the surge of Indigenous politics, activism, thought, art, and institution building that has unfolded across the planet since the turn of the millennium. As discussed in the introduction, I find it fruitful to think about indigeneity not as a social category or a program but as a force, a force often engaged in the imaginative, future-oriented world-making activity I spoke of in the introduction. Examples of this activity are interspersed throughout this book (chapters 3, 11–14, for example). In this brief chapter, I review the conditions that galvanized and empowered indigeneity and Indigenous people on a planetary scale in the last decade of the twentieth century and the beginning of the twenty-first.

The End of Assimilationism

By the 1920s, throughout the Americas as well as in Australia and New Zealand, forces across the political spectrum believed the modern future of Indigenous peoples, those who had survived conquest, dispossession, and genocide, lay in their assimilation into Western modernity as class and civic subjects. It was expected that native peoples would dissolve willingly, or at least unavoidably, into a clearly superior modern civilization. For an energetic, democratizing modernity, Indians qua Indians were a problem in need of a solution. In Latin America, where several countries had Indigenous majorities (and still do), left and progressive class politics recoded native people as campesinos (peasants). The term *indio* belonged to the racist language of oligarchic paternalism. The Mexican government made this deindigenizing move after the revolution of 1910–20, even as it gave Mexico's Indigenous past a central place in the new nationalist cultural matrix. In Mexico that assimilationist erasure changed in the 1990s when the Zapatista movement reclaimed indigeneity as a revolutionary force.[1]

Similarly, in Peru in the 1920s, José Carlos Mariátegui, who founded the Peruvian Communist Party, famously declared, "In Peru the problem of the Indian is a problem not of race but of land" (Mariátegui 2009, 38). The pressing problem in his view was the semifeudal hacienda system, which needed to be eradicated. Indigeneity had no place in that modernizing future. Land redistribution finally came to Peru in 1968, when a left-wing military dictatorship took over through a coup. Again, the neglected Indigenous majority were declared campesinos in hopes of eradicating the derogatory category of *indio* and the colonial prejudices that went with it. The erasure of Andean indigeneity became a dogma for the Shining Path guerrilla movement that erupted in Peru in the 1980s and 1990s.[2]

In North America, official assimilation/eradication policies likewise prevailed. From the 1920s to the 1970s and beyond, the United States and Canada (as well as Australia) imposed residential school systems that aimed to eradicate Indigenous societies and incorporate their young into the capitalist labor force. The cruelty, violence, and damage these programs inflicted on native people and their communities is now known, thanks to the work of many scholars and activists.[3] At the time, however, white authorities argued that assimilation was the progressive option.[4] In the 1930s the US government "granted" native people US citizenship, a move that purportedly offered equality but simultaneously aimed to eliminate tribal and treaty rights. In the 1960s Canada's Liberal icon, Prime Minister Pierre Elliott Trudeau, also upheld the assimilationist vision for native peoples. Today his son, Justin Trudeau, also prime minister, presides over a far-reaching national effort to rectify past and present injustices to Canada's native peoples. It is one of his top political priorities. A lot changed between these two generations.

Indigenous people brought their struggles to the international arena as soon as that arena took shape after World War I. In 1923 Haudenosaunee (Iroquois) Chief Deskaheh (also named Levi General) and Maori religious leader T. W. Ratana traveled to Geneva, hoping to defend Indigenous rights before the League of Nations. Neither was allowed to speak. Things began to shift after World War II. In 1957 the first internationalization of the Indigenous cause took place. The International Labour Organization (ILO) passed Convention 107, the Indigenous and Tribal Populations Convention, which called for the protection of Indigenous and tribal peoples across the world. Even so, the ILO declaration maintained the assumption that it was addressing a "problem" that "would disappear with the gradual integration of these peoples into the societies in which they lived" (ILO 1957). By 1989, however, the terms had completely changed. The ILO replaced Convention 107 with a new Indigenous and Tribal Populations Convention (Convention 169), which remains an important basis for Indigenous demands today. Far from assuming assimilation, Convention 169 calls for the full participation of Indigenous groups in the national life of their countries as autonomous, self-identified collectivities (ILO 1989). What happened between 1957 and 1989?

Indigenous activism grew in the 1960s and 1970s alongside civil rights, feminist, desegregation, antiapartheid, antiracist, and anticolonial struggles in many parts of the globe. In the United States, the militant American Indian Movement (AIM) was founded in 1968. This period marked a significant democratization of politics and power in many sectors. In the context of such developments, in 1982 the United Nations (UN) founded a Working Group on Indigenous Populations within its human rights sector. As discussed further below, the UN's commitment to Indigenous issues expanded out from there. From the late 1980s on, a number of ex-colonial states with large Indigenous populations, including Nicaragua (1987), Colombia (1991), Paraguay (1992), and Venezuela (1999), rewrote their constitutions to describe themselves as multiethnic, multicultural states, marking an end to official policies of assimilation. In 1991 the Canadian government converted half of its vast Northwest Territories into the territory of Nunavut, placed under Inuit governance.

In Spanish America, the Columbus Quincentenary of 1992 mobilized Indigenous groups on a continental scale for the first time, in response to the

Spanish government's propaganda campaign to celebrate the conquest as a benign *encuentro de dos culturas* (encounter of two cultures). Groups from over a dozen countries launched a countercampaign called "500 Years of Resistance." In Quito in July 1990, 120 representatives attended the Primer Encuentro Continental de Pueblos Indios (First Continental Meeting of Indigenous Peoples) and produced the "Declaración de Quito" (2000), whose opening paragraphs recognize that "the struggles of our people have acquired a new quality in recent times. This struggle is less and less isolated and more and more organized." Ten years later, a second "Declaración" was centered on the ecological question. Its opening resolution called for recognition that "Indigenous people historically have played and continue to play an important role in conserving forests and biological diversity, and maintaining natural ecosystems" ("Declaración de Quito" 2000).

The Neoliberal Catalyst

The biggest catalyst for global Indigenous activism was the new phase of capitalist expansion facilitated by free-trade agreements that favored multinational corporations and intensified extractive industry, especially in the Global South. The neoliberal restructuring of the global economy changed the game for Indigenous, tribal, and land-based peoples everywhere by placing their land bases in new jeopardy and weakening the ability of states to defend them against encroachment. Governments were pressured, bribed, and forced to open their national territories to multinational corporations that rapidly intensified the exploitation of forest, mineral, petroleum, and agricultural resources all over the planet. Overriding existing agreements and balances of power between states and tribal peoples, the multinationals invaded areas inhabited by forest dwellers and land-based communities in new rounds of dispossession. Willingly or otherwise, states disregarded protective arrangements with Indigenous and tribal peoples and peasants, leaving them vulnerable to forces, both legal and illegal, with which they had no possibility of negotiating on an equal footing, if at all. Weakened states thus failed to make good on the promises of those new pluri-ethnic constitutions. Indeed, sometimes they cynically used constitutional recognition against Indigenous interests by creating state-sponsored Indigenous representatives who were obliged to negotiate with the state on its terms rather than their own. Such apparently legitimizing tactics disarmed the other forms of resistance by which Indigenous peoples had defended themselves in the past. The result has been a worldwide erosion of Indigenous and tribal lands, communities, economies, cultures, and languages. On the other hand, it created new alliances with environmental movements rising everywhere in response to the same conditions (Tsing 2004).

At the same time, governments and corporations have faced intense resistance and ambitious demands whose scale was truly unanticipated. New forms of Indigenous identity and activism have taken shape. Contemporary indigeneity is both rural and urban, at times majority urban. The continuing displacement of rural people into towns and cities since the 1970s has created growing urban Indigenous populations, who, though poor and marginalized, have access to communications technology, education, bilingualism, and mainstream skills. In Chile, for example, the urban Mapuche population outnumbers the rural population by two to one. In Bolivia during the 1990s, the Aymara community living in El Alto, the plain directly above La Paz, grew into a city of a million people. Its inhabitants retain ties to their communities of origin in the countryside. El Alto has its own schools and universities, speech, dress styles, architecture, rappers, and media. Because it straddles the highway between La Paz and its airport, El Alto holds the power to shut down transnational flows in and out of Bolivia. As voters, candidates, and party members, the people of El Alto are a decisive force in Bolivian elections.

As discussed in chapter 3, the assault on rural and forest life has also pushed Indigenous people in significant numbers into international labor migration circuits, forming communities and networks abroad that support resistance on the land. The North American Free Trade Agreement (NAFTA) sent large numbers of Indigenous Mexicans from Oaxaca into labor circuits in California and from the state of Puebla to New York. Spain received large numbers of Quichua migrants from Ecuador and of Quechuas and Aymaras from Bolivia. Since 2015 failing harvests resulting from climate change have driven hundreds of thousands of rural Mayans out of Guatemala toward the US border.

So it was that through the 1990s, even as traditional class-based forms of resistance to capitalism—trade unions, left political parties, guerrilla fronts, communist states, national liberation fronts—experienced defeats, new and revitalized Indigenous identifications, alliances, and political possibilities emerged. This occurred even in places where indigeneity had not previously been part of the equation, like southern Africa, the Philippines, India, and Taiwan.[5]

Often such activism was encouraged by UN involvement. In Botswana the San began defending their land base and their survival by demanding rights as an Indigenous people. San groups who had concealed themselves as Zulus began reclaiming their San identity (Tomaselli, Dyll, and Francis 2008, 349). In a wry historic twist, South African Afrikaners, the white founders of apartheid, also applied to the UN for Indigenous status after they were expelled from power in 1994 (the UN declined). Tribal peoples in rural India began claiming Indigenous priority in disputes with other peasants over farmland. In 2005 in Taiwan, an aboriginal group thought to have disappeared a hundred years ago reappeared, much in the way Indigenous Salvadorans resurfaced after 1992 when the shooting in its civil war finally stopped. They had gone underground in the 1930s after thirty-five thousand of them were massacred by the army. The Mapuche in southern Chile were also a largely forgotten population until they got in the way of the development projects of Augusto Pinochet's dictatorship in the 1980s. Today they are a permanent part of Chile's political and cultural landscape. Their economic, cultural, artistic, and ecological initiatives are debated every day in Chilean media. In sum, in the words of Aymara sociologist Pablo Mamani, "Indigenous peoples have become strategic populations for catalyzing the attack on the neoliberal model" (2005, 7). Wherever postcolonial melancholia abides, it's not here.

Indigeneity as Planetary Force

The evolution of Indigenous issues at the UN indexes the consolidation of indigeneity as a planetary construct and a force. As already mentioned, in 1982 the UN founded a Working Group on Indigenous Populations within its human rights sector, and in 1985 that group began drafting a Declaration of Indigenous Rights. They declared 1994–2004 as the International Decade of the World's Indigenous Peoples. In 2002 the UN established a Permanent Forum on Indigenous Issues and appointed a designated rapporteur to monitor the circumstances of Indigenous people worldwide. If anything, resistance to the rights declaration grew as Indigenous power increased. Not until September 2007, after more than twenty years of negotiation, revision, and compromise, did the General Assembly ratify the Declaration on the Rights of Indigenous Peoples. By then, the stakes in the declaration had grown. Some countries, especially in Africa, argued that Indigenous rights promoted a divisiveness that could undermine long habits of cooperation and make ethnically diverse countries ungovernable. Others claimed the declaration imperiled the territorial integrity of existing states. One hundred and forty-three countries voted in favor of the declaration, but four negative votes weighed heavily: New Zealand, Australia, Canada, and the United States, all rich countries with large, highly visible Indigenous populations and long histories of engagement between states and aboriginal peoples. All four have since signed the declaration.

Why would those four states feel threatened? Between 1983, when work on the declaration began, and its passage in 2007, much had happened. In Latin America the Columbus Quincentenary had mobilized a pan-Indigenous movement. The Zapatista movement that burst forth in 1994 in Mexico marked a dramatic turning point (chapter 3). In Guatemala, when the UN declaration passed, Maya activist Rigoberta Menchú was running for president, as had her compatriot Rigoberto K'emé Chay in 2003. In Bolivia the UN declaration was inserted whole into its new 2008 constitution, which completely restructured national governance and established a Ministry of Decolonization.

Such examples, I hope, make clear why I conceive indigeneity today as a generative force that is able to create agency and make things happen in any situation in which it comes into play—be it a mining claim, a UN forum, a beauty contest, or an urban uprising. On an increasingly planetary scale, indigeneity creates and is created by the friction that Tsing (2004) identifies as the stuff of global connection. For example, in the early 2000s, anthropologist Renato Rosaldo received word that the Ilongots, the Philippine hill tribe among whom he had done fieldwork in the 1960s and early 1970s, had reconstituted themselves as the Ilongot Tribes of the Philippines, headed by an overall chieftain. No entity called Ilongot Tribes of the Philippines existed in the 1970s or even the 1990s. The idea of an overall chieftain was not only new but very much at odds with the decentered, antihierarchical Ilongot social organization Rosaldo had studied.

The Ilongots, it appeared, were becoming Indigenous. "Find out what's happening where they live," I told him. "I'll bet there's a mining or a logging company involved." It appeared I was right but not in a way I would have predicted. Internet searches revealed that a large gold deposit had been found in a mountainous region that had once been Ilongot territory. They had been displaced by Ifugao farmers, a far larger and more powerful group. The Philippine government had been encouraging foreign-financed mining projects, and an Australian company was seeking permission to exploit the gold. But the Philippines had also passed an Indigenous Peoples' Rights Act (1997), which allowed groups to defend their ancestral domains against unwanted encroachments. That's where the Indigenous twist came in. The current Ifugao inhabitants could not claim Indigenous rights over the territory because the Ilongots had lived there before them. Only the Ilongots could claim ancestral Indigenous rights there (Kenny 2006, Hunt 2006). But if the Ilongots successfully reclaimed the land, would they give it back to the Ifugao, who had dispossessed them and still held them in contempt? Or would the Ilongots opt for sweet revenge? Uninvited, the force of indigeneity had entered their world and given them power. At the same time, according to Ifugao activist J. P. Alipio, the Philippine government had been using the Indigenous Peoples' Rights Act to help mining companies get certificates of Indigenous consent. "The communities can say 'no' a hundred times," the activist said in an interview, "and they keep coming back to different community leaders until they say 'yes' just once, and that's it" (Hunt 2006). The activist was in Australia promoting a campaign there against the mining company.

Indigenous people are by no means winning victories or taking power wherever they assert themselves; indeed, on the whole, their power remains fragile, though real triumphs do occur.[6] For many groups, today's activism is a response to the direst perils and vulnerabilities they have ever faced. As dynamic and inventive as it is, Indigenous activism today continues to battle colonialism, racism, social marginalization, poverty, and vulnerability, often realized in exacerbated, sometimes apocalyptic, forms. In the contemporary geopolitical terrain, becoming Indigenous, as the Ilongots did, entails transformation and risk. Subjects enter new relationships within and among themselves as well as with outside entities. You can't know where you're going to end up, and there's no going back. Nor should this force be idealized, despite its grounding in legitimate demands for justice. Like any force, indigeneity has destructive potentials too. It, too, has the power to create exclusions. Where it comes newly into play, its effects can undo longstanding balances of power. Speaking of central Africa, for example, Cameroonian scholar Francis Nyamnjoh (2007) argues that the relation of nonequivalence between Indigenous and non-Indigenous obstructs the working out of differences on an equal footing, generating conflicts that cannot be solved except by domination of winners over losers.

Remaking the Intellectual Commons

The turn of the twenty-first century has seen an extraordinary surge of Indigenous and Indigenous-inspired thought that marks a significant change in intellectual landscapes worldwide. From Australia to Amazonia to Alberta, Indigenous and Indigenous-descended scholars are carrying out intellectual work that is stunning in its quality, range and diversity, and methodological experimentalism. Here, too, indigeneity has expanded its presence and planetarized. This explosion of ambitious, innovative intellectual work is another of the defining characteristics of indigeneity today. In geographically distant places Indigenous thinkers are laying out transformative civilizational projects, entering voids left by collapsed narratives of progress and bringing newer speculative spaces into being by challenges to what Ghanaian scholar Molefi Kete Asante calls "the European monopoly on human ideas" (2006, 153).

Bolivia is one vivid instance. There, the Indigenous and popular mobilization that culminated in the 2004 revolution was accompanied by an explosion of intellectual work that continues today. Works by Patzi (2004), Mamani (2005), Yurja Mamani (2005), Paredes (2008), and Rivera Cusicanqui (2008) exemplify the extraordinary diversity of this large and growing body of work. In English-language scholarship, methodological inquiry holds a significant place, as Indigenous knowledge makers develop ways of theorizing and conducting research grounded in their own geographies and histories, and geared to their interests and ways of knowing (Tuhiwai Smith 1999; Denzin, Lincoln, and Tuhiwai Smith 2008; Native Critics Collective 2008, Barker 2017, Huaman and Martin 2020). Philosophical and theoretical works are another central focus of millennial Indigenous activism and creativity, as Indigenous thinkers reach out to the world and non-Indigenous people look for alternatives to the catastrophic course of the present.[7]

One distinctive aspect of this expanding global corpus is its extroverted nature. At the millennial turn, Indigenous thinkers are addressing all humankind about how to inhabit the planet. It is by definition futurological; it directly addresses the crisis of futurity. The Indigenous has become a generative space for noncapitalist and anticapitalist civilizational thinking and a source for the more radical visions needed to respond to the unfolding environmental catastrophe. Even as it aims at sustaining Indigenous life, this stream of extroverted thought claims a place in a global intellectual, political, and cultural commons, actively recruiting new audiences, Indigenous and non-Indigenous—with ideas meant to travel, to reach all humankind. While speaking as members of specific groups with specific historical and cultural coordinates, Indigenous intellectuals, some of whom have passed through universities and some of whom have not, address simultaneously their own groups, a pan-Indigenous public (that is, the open-ended network of people and peoples that the term *Indigenous* now interpellates), and non-Indigenous readerships whom they call on to indigenize their ways of thinking, being, and doing. Ultimately, the scope of care and concern in these writings is planetary and cosmic. What is at stake is the future of the earth and all its beings.

This outpouring of extroverted Indigenous thought is of considerable interest to scholars who are convinced that the intellectual monopoly of the West is in urgent need of being liberated from its own limitations. Indigenous thought remakes the intellectual commons. Like indigeneity itself, it is relational. Its driving force is the prolonged, active rejection of Western normativity that underwrites Indigenous survivance. The result is scholarship that engages that normativity to both transform and displace it. Indigenous thinkers seek alternatives to the liberal tradition, and an expanded and reshaped intellectual commons. Much more than an indictment of Western critical theory or an idealization of alternatives, contemporary Indigenous thinkers use the intersection and clashes between Indigenous and Euro-American critical thought to reveal new insights, imperatives, and possibilities. They make serious proposals for the self-reinvention of the West, at a time when such reinvention has proven as unattainable as it is urgent.

ANTHROPOCENE AS CONCEPT
AND CHRONOTOPE

Coined in the 1980s by a Great Lakes biologist from Michigan named Eugene Stoermer, the term Anthropocene was popularized around 2000 by the Nobel Prize–winning atmospheric chemist Paul Crutzen from the Netherlands. It proposed, as Elizabeth Povinelli writes in *Geontologies*, to "mark a geologically defined moment when the forces of human existence began to overwhelm all other biological, geological, and meteorological forms and forces and displace the Holocene. It marks the moment when human existence became the determinate form of planetary existence—and [she adds] a malignant form at that" (2016, 10). Anthropocene contains a morality tale, taken up by Anna Lowenhaupt Tsing and colleagues in their strikingly titled collection *Arts of Living on a Damaged Planet* (2017). The coauthors describe Anthropocene as "the proposed name for a geologic epoch in which humans have become the major force in determining the continued livability of the earth. . . . The enormity of our dilemma leaves scientists, writers, artists, and scholars in shock. . . . How can we best use our research to stem the tide of ruination?" (Gan et al. 2017, 11). Dipesh Chakrabarty put it bluntly in his now classic essay "The Climate of History": "Humans have become geological agents, changing the most basic physical processes of the earth" (Chakrabarty 2009, 38).

Whether or not the stratigraphic authorities authorize the term, the concept is out there.[1] It has triggered lively debate, not about the -cene side of the term but about the anthropo-. If, as Tim Mitchell argues in Carbon Democracy (2011), it's really about carbon, and specifically about the industrial revolution driven first by large-scale coal mining and then by oil, then it's not about humans in any blanket way; it's about industrial capitalism. Hence, Jason Moore (2018) prefers Capitalocene. There's a lot to be said for this choice. One could certainly argue that everybody and everything now lives the way capitalism allows them to live and dies the way capitalism allows them to die. But Anthropocene has stuck, probably for some bad reasons, like the comfort of its humanism or the way it bypasses actual responsibility by allowing geological time to displace historical time (Bonneuil and Fressoz 2016). Anthropocene now appears as shorthand for climate catastrophe in general.

The 2001 Amsterdam Declaration on Earth System Science offered its own term for the planetary turning point. Earth, the scientists said, now operates in a "no-analogue state": "The Earth System has moved well outside the range of the natural variability exhibited over the last half million years at least. The nature of changes now occurring simultaneously in the Earth System, their magnitude and rates of change are unprecedented. . . . The Earth is currently operating in a no-analogue state" (International Geosphere-Biosphere Programme 2001).[2]

Whatever this new -cene gets called, it differs in a fundamental way from previous geological-era markers. Up through the Holocene, such markers are retrospective. They look back at deep planetary time. The Holocene, proposed in 1833 and adopted in 1885, came into view as a bounded era probably because it was ending. Anthropocene and its alternates, by contrast, look mainly ahead, to deep time in the future. They inaugurate exercises in futurology. Anthropocene requires a radical rereading of the near past—the past two or three centuries—to grasp what forces and failures brought things to this pass (Mitchell's Carbon Democracy in 2011 is one important example). But the future is what's really at stake. Anthropocene announces a future that is unprecedented and therefore unpredictable in both the everyday and scientific senses of the term. Yet at the same time it predicts with absolute certainty catastrophic changes that will make the planet increasingly uninhabitable for carbon-based life. A tangle of predictability and unpredictability hums at its heart. Is it just an irony that the Anthropocene addresses simultaneously (a) the certainty that purposeful human activity has overwhelmed all other forces/agents and (b) the certainty that human activity is going to be overwhelmed by the forces/agents it has unleashed? Is it an irony or a predicament that the imperative to predict, anticipate, and prepare coincides with the increased impossibility of predicting and preparing on many fronts? Irony or no, the climate crisis is a crisis of the imagination (Ghosh 2016, 9).

Anthropocene as Concept

Its futurological character and its attachment to a pressing problem define Anthropocene as a concept in the sense in which, guided by Elizabeth Grosz (2011), we are using the term in this book (see the introduction). The value of Anthropocene as a concept lies not in its ability to accurately identify a geological boundary but in its ability to address a problem, to make order out of chaos. Grosz's definition of a problem as "a conjunction of forces that requires some kind of response under peril of danger" (79) is a pretty good description of Anthropocene's concern: the recognition that humanity has created the conditions for its own demise or that capitalist development is on track to make the planet uninhabitable for carbon-based life. The ability of concepts to point you toward futures that "lie beyond the horizon" is surely helpful when you're in a no-analogue state.

What's striking about Anthropocene as a concept is that the ideality it adds to the world seems to be an ideality of death, of end-time. In Grosz's terms, Anthropocene transforms the chaotic givenness of environmental catastrophe and mass extinction into an imagined order of being otherwise, in which the geological planet continue to be and unfold but humans and other carbon-based life are gone. That's the "revolutionary transformation" that lies beyond the horizons we can see.

Anthropocene as Chronotope

The problem, though, is how this transformation will unfold. How will humans and other life-forms live out what Nils Bubandt describes as "an increasingly given fate of ruination and extinction" (2017, G136)? How will all we living species live the dying—our own and that of the life-forms around us? What material, ethical, political, aesthetic, and affective choices will earth beings be called on to make? What will be possible? Anthropocene demands the meaning machines and desiring machines through which the dramatic, unknowable trajectory of catastrophe can become a story and be lived. Hence, it is also illuminating to think of Anthropocene as what narrative theorist Mikhail Bakhtin called a *chronotope*, a particular configuration of time and space that generates stories through which a society can examine itself. Bakhtin studied novels. "In the literary artistic chronotope," said Bakhtin, "spatial and temporal indicators are fused into one carefully thought-out, concrete whole. Time, as it were, thickens, takes on flesh, becomes artistically visible; likewise, space becomes charged and responsible to the movements of time, plot, and history. The intersection of axes and fusion of indicators characterizes the artistic chronotope" (1981, 84). The frontier, for instance, is one of the United States' most enduring artistic chronotopes, a foundational time-space configuration that saturates American literature and film, generating plot after plot around settler colonialism and gendered whiteness.

New chronotopes, Bakhtin said, create "previously nonexistent meanings." Old ones "continue stubbornly to exist" even after they have "lost any meaning that was productive in actuality or adequate to later historical situations" (85). The frontier chronotope continues stubbornly to exist, recycled yet again, for example, in Alejandro Iñárritu's 2015 film *The Revenant*. The film recounts the gruesome endurance-and-survival story of a nineteenth-century white fur trader in the Far North. The movie itself is a revenant, a ghost, recycling an exhausted frontier fantasy in an ecology that today is rapidly dissolving as the planet warms.[3]

Anthropocene is a new chronotope that tries to organize previously nonexistent meanings. It is distinguished by a unique time-space configuration that is multipolar. Anthropocene posits a human subject in the present (you and I, dear reader) who imagines a future subject who, long after humans are gone, reconstructs the present era through what it will have left behind. Our detritus, to some hypothetical future nonhuman geologist, will reveal a world that became, as Bubandt puts it, increasingly "shaped by human activity but . . . also increasingly outside human control" (2017, G134). Franklin Schaffner's classic film *Planet of the Apes* (1968) offered something like a first draft of such a chronotope. After nearly four thousand years in space, a crew of American astronauts lands on a planet where humans are despised and enslaved by a highly developed (English-speaking) society of apes. Most viewers remember the film's climactic moment when, on a beach in the "Forbidden Zone," Charlton Heston, playing one of the astronauts, encounters the half-buried remains of the Statue of Liberty and realizes he is on Earth in the long aftermath of nuclear holocaust. The film even includes an archaeologist, the ape Cornelius, who is conducting a dig in the Forbidden Zone. Cornelius is puzzled because the more deeply he digs, the more highly developed the civilizational remains become. Time seems to run backward. He has found the Anthropocene, the futurology of catastrophe in its 1960s incarnation as nuclear war. A nonhuman intelligence looks back on and tries to reconstruct what we, but not they, know as a tale of arrogance and hubris wrought on a planetary scale by the architects of a supposedly advanced civilization. Fifty years later, Schaffner's plotline resonates anew. It is no accident that the film was remade (by director Tim Burton) at the turn of the millennium, appearing in 2001 followed by multiple reboot series since 2011.

In its twenty-first-century incarnation, the Anthropocene chronotope becomes a mechanism and a demand for human subjects to "call forth previously nonexistent meanings" by reimagining and remaking themselves in the space-time-matter of the planet and its beings. Bakhtin would not be surprised that this quest is as much about writing as doing. It requires experiments in thought and action, as well as in storytelling, language, and genre. What new narrative and expressive forms will express this radically transformed relationship of humans with the planet and the future? Experiments are underway. In the 2017 collection *Arts of Living on a Damaged Planet* (Tsing et al. 2017), for example, many writers experiment with the genre of nature writing, reorienting it to capture damaged, debris-strewn, non-Edenic places populated by afterlives of human activity now enmeshed into the landscape's own generativity. Efforts to erase the divide between human and nonhuman agencies abound in the emergent Anthropocenic tropology. Interspecies entanglements are among the new plot elements and objects of study (see chapter 7). Nonhuman, even nonanimate, beings come into view as agents and protagonists.[4] In fiction, the Anthropocenic chronotope has given rise to the subgenre of climate fiction, storytelling projected into futures in which the reality the reader inhabits has been devastated and transformed.

Novelist and essayist Amitav Ghosh has argued that experiments like these fall far short of developing the radically different expressive resources needed to capture the enormity of the climate challenge. In his important 2016 book *The Great Derangement*, Ghosh argues that "an imaginative and cultural failure lies at the heart of the climate crisis" (8), which must be overcome. The cultural matrices, the forms of storytelling that developed with carbon democracy, Ghosh argues, are constitutively unable to grasp the pace, scale, unknowability, and unpredictability of what is happening. Indeed, those matrices have concealed such things, "disabling" people's imaginations. Carbon democracy's privileged literary form, Ghosh claims, is the realist novel—storytelling

6.1 — Eroding shoreline along Alaska's coast. SOURCE: BRUCE RICHMOND/ANN GIBBS, UNITED STATES GEOLOGICAL SURVEY.

anchored in the everyday, in democracy's everyman, in the unfolding of individual lives (characters) in environments that remain constant (settings). Phenomena such as mass extinctions, biblical-style floods, polar vortices, melting glaciers, continent-scale fires and species invasions, viral plagues that planetarize in a matter of weeks, massive population displacements—such phenomena are not at home in realist novels. They do, however, inhabit what are called premodern imaginaries that modernity overcame (Ghosh 2016, 22). Realist storytelling, Ghosh says, turns away from the kind of gigantic, unheard-of events that people must learn to grasp in order to respond to climate catastrophe. Realism operates by verisimilitude, a quality that unprecedented events lack. They are, as we say, unbelievable. To return to the frontier myth, realism, for example, boils the expansive myth of manifest destiny down to the family quotidian of Laura Ingalls Wilder's *Little House on the Prairie* series. That is its democratizing, civilizing job. In the modern literary system and its miseducated imaginations, the cosmic, the superhuman, the supernatural, the uncanny, the cataclysmic, the miraculous, the monstrous, the sublime live in minor genres—science fiction, horror, fantasy, children's literature (where the animals have been sent)—and in poetry. But imagining the Anthropocene cannot mean simply rehabilitating those genres. In addition to multipolar temporality, *longue durée* futurology, aerial photography, and satellite-scaled geography, the Anthropocenic chronotope requires a unique causality in which humans' own actions return to haunt them *in forms they utterly failed to anticipate*. The uncanny will be the Anthropocene's verisimilitude.

At the present moment, these properties seem more achievable in visual media than in verbal expression. In the hands of Canadian visual artist Edward Burtynsky, aerial photography has become a medium of choice for grasping the uncanny reality of humans impacting the planet on a scale far beyond their own ability to anticipate it (see Burtynsky, n.d.). His painstakingly crafted photographs reach for the sublime, that combination of grandeur, beauty, and terror—an entire river basin turned a vivid orange by mine tailings; an actual mountain of used tires simultaneously expressing abundance and catastrophic waste; a cavernous industrial space where row upon row of identically uniformed electronics workers extend as far as the eye can see; the gorgeous arabesques of a dying Colorado River traced on the smooth canvas of the desert. To my eyes, Burtynsky's aesthetic suggests that at this immense, far-greater-than-human scale, extractivist capitalism has become a machine that is running itself. Humans work for it and not it for them. This machine creates the subjects it needs in order to deploy its endless expansionism. It structures their desires, dictates their intentions, mobilizes their talents as it needs them. There is no need for more cell phones, but the cell phone–producing machine needs to feed itself. Humans have become the sorcerer's apprentices. What can fracture this present so that alternative futures can be brought into being?

Anthropocenic thought often looks to non-Western knowledges for alternatives to modern capitalist thinking about how to inhabit the world. Ethnographers are conducting bold collaborative writing experiments, such as Marisol de la Cadena's *Earth Beings* (2015) and Davi Kopenawa and Bruce Albert's *The Falling Sky* (2013), that pull metropolitan readers deep into Indigenous cosmovisions, rather than transposing those cosmovisions into familiar terms. Indigenous knowledges are valued for their cosmic scale and for the aliveness, agency, and sentience they find in nonhuman beings, animate or not. As discussed in chapter 5, Indigenous thought has become a key element in twenty-first-century futurology.

Yet in a way, as Burtynsky's powerful photographs also suggest, nothing enlivens the world more than capitalism. For capitalism, everything that exists or can be imagined carries the potential to be transformed into something that generates profit. Nothing is inert. Everything has the ability to inspire some process of extraction, invention, manufacture, the adding of value. How possible will it be to force these exhilarating powers into retreat or to repurpose them in undamaging ways?

Conclusion

"This space, and time, for invention, for the creation of the new, can come about only through a dislocation and dissociation with the present rather than simply its critique" (Grosz 2004, 261). Anthropocene is doing the enabling work of both concept and chronotope. It is setting useful inquiries in motion, organizing intellectual energies, pushing imaginations to retrain. Yet even as Anthropocene brings the forces of the present into view, it has not yet shown signs of being able to "transform them into new and different forces that act in the future" (Grosz 2011, 80). The fatal limitation of Anthropocene is surely that, unlike Burtynsky's photography, it leaves the anthropo- in its place. It remains compatible with the man/nature dichotomy and the narrative machine of man acting on nature. So far, it offers mainly a story, a structure of desire, whereby humankind undertakes to redeem itself by acting on nature in different ways than it has in the past, thus rescuing both nature and itself. But tell that to Hurricane Maria or the coronavirus or the mountain pine beetle. That rescue story is long gone—this is a no-analogue state.

Like most commentators, Ghosh suggests that pessimism means inaction and muteness, that in order to move forward, we have to find some way to be optimistic. I wonder whether that is true. In ecological discussions, optimism operates like an etiquette, papering over the ruthlessness and cruelty of the forces in play. There's no point in applauding optimism for the sake of optimism, nor in ignoring the creative and inspiring dimensions of the pessimist account. Even if you accept that it's too late for carbon-based life to survive on Earth, there is still a rich creative challenge in thinking about how to live this ending, how to organize life around it, how to engage the other life-forms that will share the experience, what kinds of aesthetics, ethics, poetics, politics, psychic engagement, and intimacy can be created to navigate the experience. The pessimist standpoint has a futurity, too, the possibility of a *buen vivir* (living well) unfolding toward extinction.

CHAPTER SEVEN

MUTATIONS OF THE CONTACT ZONE

From Human to More-Than-Human

The well-known essay "Arts of the Contact Zone," which I wrote thirty years ago (Pratt 1991), began as a keynote for a conference on literacy co-organized by the Modern Language Association and the AFL-CIO. Not surprisingly, it was first taken up by writing teachers and began appearing in Freshman Composition readers all over the United States.[1] For the next twenty years or so, every fall, I received emails from students in these classes. "Dear Mrs. Pratt," they always began (their heads were still in high school), "I have to write a paper about the contact zone for class tomorrow. Could you please tell me what it is?" Or "I read your paper about the contact zone, and I was just wondering, what did you mean?" Or "I think my church might be a contact zone. Is that possible?" Or "Can a family be a contact zone?" These emails come rarely now, perhaps because students, and even their teachers, doubt the author of something written so long ago could still be in possession of their faculties—or perhaps because the concept is less of a mystery to students today.

I answered those emails religiously. They offered me an opportunity to show first-term college students that their curiosity was a good thing, their intellectual development mattered, and they should take it seriously. I never set down "what I meant," of course, and was careful not to provide prose that could make it into the paper that was due the next day. But I tried to encourage each writer down some productive path. I confirmed that churches and families absolutely can be contact zones, but the point was not whether they were or not; it was what insights emerged from thinking about them that way—in Elizabeth Grosz's terms, what alternative futures or possibilities of being otherwise might appear on the horizon (Grosz 2011, 78).

The *contact zone* was born out of an act of reimagining. The aim was to move the study of empire from the European imperial center and recenter it at the sites of imperial intervention, in effect to decenter Europe. Before the 1960s, European analysts of empire, even its critics, spoke and thought from the center of imperial power outward. Scholarly imaginations operated, in other words, within the diffusionist paradigm of imperialism itself (see chapter 1). Scholarly authority thus aligned with imperial authority; analysts looked over the shoulders of the imperialists. The third-world decolonization movements and anticolonial thinkers discussed in chapter 16 called attention to the mythologies by which empire represented itself to itself and its subjects. Scholars began retheorizing imperialism in relation to the "pressing problem" (Grosz 2011, 78) of decolonization. To New World scholars like me, this certainly made sense. To grasp how imperial power worked, it was necessary to move the position of analysis from the imperial center to the places where exploration, invasion, and colonization were unfolding, which I named the *contact zone*. This required reeducating scholarly imaginations, developing new research methods, seeking out archival sources (such as, in my case, travel writing), and learning to read them (Wolff 2002). Educating imaginations has always seemed to me the central work of scholarship and teaching, especially in the humanities. The concept of the contact zone also offered a way of undoing Eurocentrism in education, curriculum, and pedagogy, by rereading imperial literary canons, for example, and bringing to bear materials that challenged their authority. Countries born out of colonial processes, like those of the Americas, had their own internal decolonizing to do, while former colonial powers found their former colonies surging back on them through immigration, in a kind of implosion of empire.

Concepts in Grosz's theorization (see the introduction) are about futures and in their very conception aim to be generative. They are, across geographies and disciplinary boundaries, ideas meant to travel, and travel they do. They slide out of the hands of their creators, who do not own them and should not want to. Once they start enabling people to think about being otherwise, they typically get drawn into a widening range of contexts as long as they continue to generate insights. It is impossible to predict where traveling ideas will land and bloom and what new futures they will generate. The contact zone has been a traveling idea because the pressing problems it addresses cross the global geopolitical order, as do the ethical, decolonizing energies that animate it. In the new millennium, it began turning up in a range of new domains where speculative world-making was going on.

The Concept at Large

In December 2002 the following email message appeared on my screen, from a young Canadian teaching English composition in Blagoevgrad, Bulgaria.

Dear Dr. Pratt,

I just thought you might like to know:
I assigned your "Contact Zone" piece from *Ways of Reading* to students here at the American University in Bulgaria. AUBG was established here after the fall of communism with the aim of teaching critical thinking and leadership on the model of an American liberal arts college. About 75% of the students are Bulgarian, and the rest come, mostly on scholarship from countries ranging from Croatia to Mongolia. In a first-year composition course I asked students to write an essay making suggestions for a course on Balkan Civilization. I got a wide range of responses.

1. Most students stressed the study of history, suggesting that students compare school textbook accounts of single events in the history of the region, and work carefully toward consensus on what actually happened. Not one student thinks this consensus would actually be achieved, but most think it would be worthwhile to push the discussion as far as can be done. One student suggested the perhaps dangerous technique of showing a highly nationalist anti-Turkish Bulgarian historical film as a center for discussion.

2. One student suggested interviews with students of other nationalities to find out what ethnic jokes are being told about one's own ethnicity.

3. One student suggested that the issue of religion should be approached through its place in daily life rather than through theology or general principles, saying people would find it easier to sympathize across confessional lines that way.

4. Serbian students without exception blasted their previous education as corrupted by nationalism. The war has had a deep effect on them, and the quandary of being a Serb in 2002 is a significant concern for them. Kosovar Albanians, in contrast, are not especially preoccupied with the issues of the war.

5. Several students thought the study of linguistics would help a class like this. Some Bulgarian students thought that it might be scientifically proven that Macedonian is really a kind of Bulgarian. Other students thought that the incontrovertible presence of foreign, especially Turkish, words in each language would help to dismantle myths of national purity.

6. Students stressed the demands on the professor in a class like this, saying that principles would be less important than social skills in context. All who mentioned the issue expressed a preference for an outsider rather than a person of Balkan nationality.

7. A few Bulgarian students devoted parts of their essays to reaffirming their belief in nationalist Bulgarian views of Balkan history: "500 years of the Ottoman yoke," etc.

8. Some students came to realize that they knew more about France than about the country next door.

9. A cohesive group took issue with you on the issue of nation, saying the idea of "imagined community" doesn't do justice to nation as they experience it.

So, your paper at the MLA years ago is still echoing here in Blagoevgrad.

Exported educational models are often problematic. Nevertheless, I found the message moving. Here was a teacher putting a piece of writing to work across time, distance, and difference to enable reflection on an unprecedented and traumatized present, on the pasts that made it, on possible futures, and on learning itself. The nine points the class passed on had the makings of a book of wisdom on how to construct shared knowledge in contact zones fractured by conflict. Let me offer a little exegesis.

Point 1 specifies the importance of rewriting history. It describes the exercise of creating provisional communities across lines of difference through a pursuit of consensus. The pursuit need not actually produce consensus in order to succeed in enacting a provisional community and mediating differences.

Point 2 specifies the power of converting difference into reciprocity, that is, of enacting or performing difference as reciprocity. Point 3 calls for privileging the lived experience of differences over knowledge, beliefs, and ideologies. At the level of belief, differences readily translate into clashes. But differences are lived as the copresence of bodies in spaces, where the uneasy arts of the contact zone thrive.

Points 4 and 5 indict essentialisms and the instruments that produce them, and identify language as an instrument to mitigate them. Point 7, however, shows how difficult this can be. The Bulgarians reasserted a subaltern identity linked to claims for redress. Once articulated, essentialisms anchored in claims to superiority or redress do not simply go away. They have to be worked through.

Point 6 highlights the position of the mediator. In this case the role is held by a subject I like to call the Committed Outsider. In this teacher's classroom, his displacement and distance, combined with his serious commitment to being where he is, enable him to create the space for the intercultural dialogue. However, the teacher's outsider status is useful only insofar as he is familiar with the insider knowledge and experience of those whose dialogue he is sponsoring. The fact that the search for understanding was going on in a lingua franca (English) that was nobody's national tongue was probably valuable. Point 8 identifies the role of sanctioned ignorance in producing marginality, and point 9 shows the need for marginal subjects to critique and reconceive concepts (like "imagined communities").

The teacher's account reveals two features that usually characterize the building of contact zone dialogues: performativity and improvisation. By *performativity*, I mean that the power of the dialogue consists not only, or even principally, in content or meanings produced but in the fact of its taking place as an embodied event. *Improvisation* refers to the obvious fact that where relations of mutuality and reciprocity have not been present, have broken down, or have detonated into violence, new relationships have to be made up out of what is there in the embodied moment. Performativity and improvisation imply a third term: *imperfection*.

In his class the teacher was seeking to address the thing for which his location has provided the master metaphor: balkanization. Boldly, he chose a head-on approach: reclaiming that very term by having students imagine a course on Balkan civilization. He proposed an imagined object whose contours were to be drawn through a collective pursuit of truth and understanding in which all the participants are seen as having a stake. It was a risky choice, perhaps, to engage the group in the civilizational thinking that so readily produces essentialisms. Notice, however, that the imagined object was a course on Balkan civilization and not Balkan civilization itself.

The travels expanded as the millennium unfolded. In 2016 a high school teacher from Patagonia wrote me to say teachers there had organized their annual conference around the contact zone in an effort to create a new curriculum that addressed the demographic makeup of their region, especially its Indigenous and immigrant components. They were working on a Spanish translation of the essay. In Europe the dual challenges of European integration and increased immigration from the Global South brought the contact zone into play decades after its conception. In 2015 a research group in France adopted the concept to think a French society both internally diverse and transformed by immigration. In 2017 a history and anthropology institute in Germany held a conference called Contact Zones and Border Regions, focused on the area where Germany, Poland, and Czechoslovakia meet and overlap.[2] In China in 2018, a group used the contact zone to frame a historical study of European minorities in China. That same year, Chung-Ang University in Seoul, South Korea, established a research center on Reconciliation and Coexistence in Contact Zones. Sponsored by the Korean Ministry of Education and the Korean Research Foundation, its central concerns include, of course, the North Korea–South Korea relationship.[3] In all these instances, the concept's work was not to be true or false but to enable groups of people to think toward alternative futures in a world of forces that they do not control and that surround them with real events and experiences.

Ideas have lives of their own; their inventors don't own them. There is one common use of the contact zone concept that I find misguided. Sometimes, in liberal thought, the contact zone gets articulated not as a device for imagining situations of heterogeneity, inequality, and conflict but as the name of a solution for these challenges. It becomes an ideal to be aspired to—an Edenic, harmonious place where people separated by deep historical differences successfully collaborate, cooperate, and resolve their differences, each side responsive to the others' needs and interests. Often this vision is offered as a predefined future, a programmatic agenda. Contact becomes the alternative to conflict. Such a normative use of the contact zone is ideologically coherent; that is, it makes sense. But it denies the concept's critical force, jumps over the necessary step of thinking through the chaotic, uncontrollable energies that are in play. Such an acritical use of the concept cannot explain, for example, how, as in Rwanda and Yugoslavia, peaceful contact zones can erupt into genocidal violence with the strike of a match. Human mobility is the great creator of contact zones, but idealizing them ignores the geopolitical variety of the contact zone's forms: tourism, migration in all its forms, trafficking, expulsion, exploration, flight. These cannot simply be folded together in an idealized scenario.

The Interspecies Contact Zone

The contact zone began a new journey in the 2010s when environmental geographers called on the concept to help them study multispecies interaction and more-than-human encounters. They asked, Can the contact zone usefully jump the wall between the human and the not human? Can it usefully address the "pressing problem" of the threat of environmental breakdown and mass extinction? Can it create possibilities of being otherwise for beings that are not human? What interesting questions! In 2017 a group of young animal geographers organized a symposium The Contact Zone: Where Species Meet.[4] Where, I wondered, would this intersect with the study of empire?

The contact zone's original act of decentering required transferring the center of analysis from Europe to the sites of interaction among Europeans and the peoples they landed on. The geographers applied this paradigm to interactions among humans and more-than-human entities. What gets decentered is the human. The contact zone helps displace anthropocentrism, as it did Eurocentrism in its original context. You shift the center of analysis to the sites of engagement, interaction, and entanglement between humans and nonhuman entities. The call in each case is *not* for analysts to stop being European or human, which is, after all, not possible if that is what one is, but for the analyst to stop being Eurocentric or anthropocentric. The pressing problem here is the unfolding catastrophe of mass extinction of nonhuman life-forms owing to the impact of humans on their habitats. The move to the multispecies contact zone requires knowledge seekers to purposefully redefine the contours of their sphere of attention, observation, engagement, and care. It requires reengineering affect and that structure of desire that we call curiosity.

In a straightforward, flattened sense, no being is ever *not* in a multispecies contact zone; no human is ever not coexisting with more-than-human beings. No being is ever not participating in a multispecies ecology and food chain. Life-forms, plant or animal, all exist in coexistence and interdependence, at the very least because they are each other's food. No species lives on its own kind. In this transspecies register, the contact zone enables efforts to transcend the normative tradition of species-specific science and center on those modes of coexistence and codependence. What possibilities for being otherwise might this experiment produce?

The geographers sought to keep their work connected to the problem of human domination and the ends of power. In this register the imperial contact zone and the environmental contact zone are linked by more than analogy.

They are reflexes of each other, ruled by many of the same myths. The hier-archized European/non-European and human/nature dichotomies are both ideological foundations of capitalist modernity. They are both engines built to drive the creation of wealth through ever-intensifying extraction and to make that trajectory meaningful, inevitable, and good. Contemporary environmental thought inhabits the political and ecological landscapes created by imperial plunder, settler colonialism, neocolonial industrialization, and neoliberal extractivism (Gómez-Barris 2017). In addition to considering how humans and other species interact, the geographers also ask how imperial legacies and mythologies shape those interactions and assign them meaning. What forms of power are in play, what alternative affects and agencies can be found or imagined, and what might be the limits on human domination?

In the papers published from the symposium (Isaacs and Otruba 2019), one writer, for example, studied *Blue Planet*, the BBC's television masterpiece on oceans (Wilson 2019). She showed how this enormously successful series redeployed an imperial tool kit. She posed the question whether its power to move people could nevertheless do some ecological good. Another shadowed an urban cow in India for days, watching how this legally protected animal living among humans enacted the freedom given to her by law and religion. It enabled her, among other things, to mobilize human labor for her own purposes. A third scholar studied conservationism as an interspecies enactment of power through the hands-on example of an annual gathering of conservationists and migrating seabirds on a New Jersey beach (Isaacs 2019). Another studied relations among marine life, water turbines, humans, and the gigantic tides of the Bay of Fundy in Nova Scotia (Fredriksen 2019). All these elements were engaged in a struggle over possible futures. Another scholar explored how human institutions in the North American West interact and negotiate with forest fires (Sutherland 2019). This work raised the interesting question of the analytical status of fire, a life- and death-giving force that is not animate but impinges on animate life-forms at every turn.

In these interspecies studies, the concept of the contact zone produced a more complex and textured picture of human domination of nature by recovering the agency and unpredictability of more-than-human agents. The scenarios are never simply about humans acting on other species. *Blue Planet*, for example, includes footage of the exhausting efforts humans make to "capture" the images they want animals to give them. Shilpa, the urban cow in India, knows how to get humans to do all kinds of things for her, including taking care of her children while she forages. Dedicated and impassioned as they are, the shorebird conservationists are limited in what they can accomplish. They cannot ensure that migrating shorebirds arrive, nor influence where they go next or what happens to them. The birds decide these things. Banding and tracking are the main forms of agency by which the conservationists can enact their care and love. In the Bay of Fundy, none of the humans know or can know how sea creatures or tides will respond to turbines if they do arrive. The contact zone is a zone of hazard and unpredictability. But the goal is not to enable futures that eliminate these, surely.

In multispecies contact zones, humans' main form of agency is often the ability to influence other humans. In the geographers' work, interactions in interspecies contact zones often turned out to involve contests among different human agents around different ways of knowing and living with fellow beings, different ways of being human. The makers of *Blue Planet*, for example, erased and subalternized the expert knowledge and accumulated experience of people who made their lives in the places being filmed, even as they exploited that knowledge to do their work. In the Bay of Fundy study, a three-way contest appears among three parties: Indigenous fishers, whose extractive activities are organized by Mi'kmaq tradition; white fishers, whose knowledge comes from generations extracting food from the waters at a commercial scale; and scientists, who construct their knowledge mainly through electronic tracking devices. The study of western wildfires centered on a conflict between provincial managers, who see their task as preventing and eradicating fires, and federal managers, who prioritize controlled burning. In the shorebirds' case, the tension is between the human leisure users of the beach and the ethical and affective imperative that drives the conservationists. The empowered Indian cow is the product of a struggle over the role of religion in Indian nation building, which religion won. At stake in these contact zones, then, are competing forms of human intervention and interaction. There is no unmanaged, untouched habitat to retreat to or recover or leave alone. Apparently, the future is management-by-humans. Radically different possibilities are in play, however, attached to different ways of being human.

Beyond Management

And yet contact zone analysis reveals the limitations on humans' ability to manage what other creatures do or think. One serious challenge in describing multispecies contact zones is how to express the actions and agency of more-than-human beings. When the contact dramas under study involve humans, logocentrism can do its work. Humans have language. They can verbalize their intentions, demands, fears, misapprehensions. They can explain themselves; they can use interpreters. In human contact zones, language establishes a degree of equivalence among parties, even when radical inequalities are present. All participants have "voice." For humans, perhaps the most powerful impact of multispecies interaction is learning to engage without language. Animals and plants certainly interact, communicate, and express desires and intentions within and between species, including humans. A tree blooms wildly to attract the insect that will pollinate it; a screeching bird fakes an injury to attract a possible predator away from its nest; one tree warns another of an invasive blight or passes it nutrients it lacks (Wohlleben 2016). Logos is obviously irrelevant, but voice is everywhere, and messaging abounds—songs, dances, decorations, aromas, gestures, changes of color, texture, body stance, the releasing of toxins, warning pricks, underground networks. There are myriad ways in which life-forms communicate within and across species, including with humans. From dance to painting, all human forms of aesthetic expression are shared with, and learned from, nonhuman life-forms. And so we can ask, What role do roses play in their symbolization of sexual love among humans? How did the great white whale create Moby Dick? How did the reindeer create Rudolph and Santa Claus?

In the interspecies contact zone, language moves to the margins. Yet intimacies thrive. Relations of companionship, cooperation, competition, enmity, enslavement, suspicion, love, dependency, and avoidance unfold. They are everywhere; there are no single-species ecologies. The New York subway system, one of my habitats, is a multispecies contact zone where rats and humans carry on a permanent negotiated relation of cohabitation and mutual avoidance. Both are extremely numerous. People do not want to see rats, and the rats know it; rats do not want to see people, and the people know it. The rats cannot get rid of the people, and the people cannot get rid of the rats, and both know it. We have negotiated a voiceless, symmetrical relationship. When rat-human encounters occur, they involve terror and flight for the rat and disgust and recoil for the humans. This is a common interspecies contract between urban life-forms that have been verminized. Life-forms that are not verminized have different contracts. Look around you. Talk to an urban beekeeper or the person who feeds squirrels.

In another of my habitats, a small rural community of lake dwellers in central Canada, multispecies contact is the stuff of life. People come here, as I have for decades, because they want to inhabit the more-than-human. Interspecies encounters are a constant in conversation. The local newspaper publishes columns devoted to bird and animal sightings and plant bloomings. People pay attention to other species and limit their own footprint so that other life-forms will continue to accompany them. People struggle to make their lives here so they won't have to leave. If they do, many return to grow old.

From Contact Zone to Force Field

Multispecies interaction is one thing, but more-than-human encounters bring nonanimate, nonliving actors into play as well. How to conceptualize more-than-human agents that are not animate life-forms? Agents like earth, air, fire, and water; darkness and light; heat and cold. All life-forms interact continuously with these nonanimate forces in ways big and small. These non-animate actors determine the conditions for life and death of all living things, but they themselves are not reproductive cellular or viral entities, though in many cultures they are considered sentient and alive (de la Cadena 2015). In the geographers' terminology, such forces belong in the category of the more-than-human but not in the multispecies frame. At the same time, we language makers easily incorporate such forces into our vocabularies of agency, expressivity, desire, beauty, awe. We absorb them into managerial vocabularies of containment and control and into the affective vocabularies of love and fear. Surely fires want to burn and spread, we think as we watch western North America in flames. You can see fire reaching out for the next log, jumping across roads, grabbing rooftops. Surely one is negotiating with the wind when one seeks shelter from a hurricane. We give them names. How can lakes, rivers, and seas that rise, fall, flow, sustain, and destroy be imagined as inert?

The more-than-human category makes me wonder whether when it comes to the agency of these powerful noncellular, noncorporeal actors, we might do better talking about force fields instead of contact zones. Here again, I use *force* to refer to the ability to make things happen, to trigger chains, combinations, and arrays of events. Imagine the Bay of Fundy tides, for example, as a force field that compels all kinds of entities into play—sea life, fishnets, energy companies, artists, birds, sensors, turbines, graduate students—in chains and combinations that cannot reliably be predicted. The wildfires that are becoming an increasingly powerful planetary actor compel chains of actions and responses from every existing thing that is present. In the summer of 2018, a wildfire in northern Manitoba caused the community of Little Grand Rapids to be evacuated by plane hundreds of miles south to Winnipeg. Avalanches of events followed. The fire interrupted electricity in the community, causing the supplies of moose meat and fish stored in freezers to spoil and ruining the freezers. Without this access to cold storage, the community's food system did not work. They could return to their dwelling place only when the Red Cross offered to supply them with new refrigerators. Think of how many other chains of events that fire set in motion without necessarily causing them. That is what I mean by a *force field*.

Environmentalist thought, bulwarking against environmental devastation and mass extinctions, leans toward futures that foster life and its flourishing. It is driven by an affect I have come to call the love of the world. Yet, as the geographers well know, the big geoforces of fire, water, wind, darkness and light, and heat and cold deal in death and destruction as readily as in life-giving. They are not life-forms; they do not desire life or seek it; they do not face extinction. In many places, they are deities. As humans seek ways of being otherwise with them, they will find other ways of being with us. What concepts can take us to possible futures to be built from there?

IS THIS GITMO OR CLUB MED?

They're living in the tropics, they're well fed,
they've got everything they could possibly want.
—DICK CHENEY on prisoners at Guantánamo,
interview with Wolf Blitzer, CNN, June 23, 2005

If you type "Vieques" into a search engine nowadays, you will be bombarded by travel ads, first from big commercial tourism sites like Tripadvisor or BookingBuddy, followed by a long string of vacation guides, hotel guides, island guides, beach guides, spa guides, and a bank of aerial shots of turquoise waters and curved sun-drenched beaches with nary a soul in sight. Those empty, uncommercialized beaches are there because until 2003 two-thirds of the island of Vieques was owned by the US Navy, which used it for sixty years as a training site for aerial bombing, amphibious landings, ship-to-shore gunfighting, and ground warfare (Torres Rivers 2003). In Vieques, tourism is layered on top of the detritus of Cold War militarism, just one of the ways these two imperial enterprises, militarism and tourism, intersect on the planet's tropical islands. Vieques shares this history of convergence with Hawaii, Guam, the Marshall Islands, the Philippines, and many other places.

8.1 — Island of Vieques. SOURCE: EDGAR TORRES.

Vieques is a small island of fifty-two square miles that lies a few miles east of Puerto Rico, to which it was annexed in 1854. It's been an imperial playing field for five centuries. Claimed by Spain in the 1490s, it became a base for Taíno resistance to the Spanish invasion. For three hundred years after the Taíno were crushed, Vieques was left unsettled and became a haven for piracy, contraband, and accompanying forms of frontier anarchy. Spain fended off attempts by France, Britain, Denmark, and Scotland to take it over and colonize it. In the early 1800s, the colonial governor of Puerto Rico finally decided to settle Vieques. Sugar plantations were established, attracting laborers, slave and free, from all over the Caribbean. Sugar was gold in the nineteenth century (Mintz 1985). In 1898, following Spain's defeat in the Spanish-American War, Vieques was annexed to the expanding US empire, along with the Philippines, the rest of Puerto Rico, and another potential but as yet unrealized resort site, Guantánamo Bay in Cuba. The island's economy was in deep decline when in 1941, in the middle of World War II, the US Navy expropriated the plantations, paid off the landowners, threw out the sugar workers, and turned two-thirds of the island—twenty-

CHAPTER EIGHT |

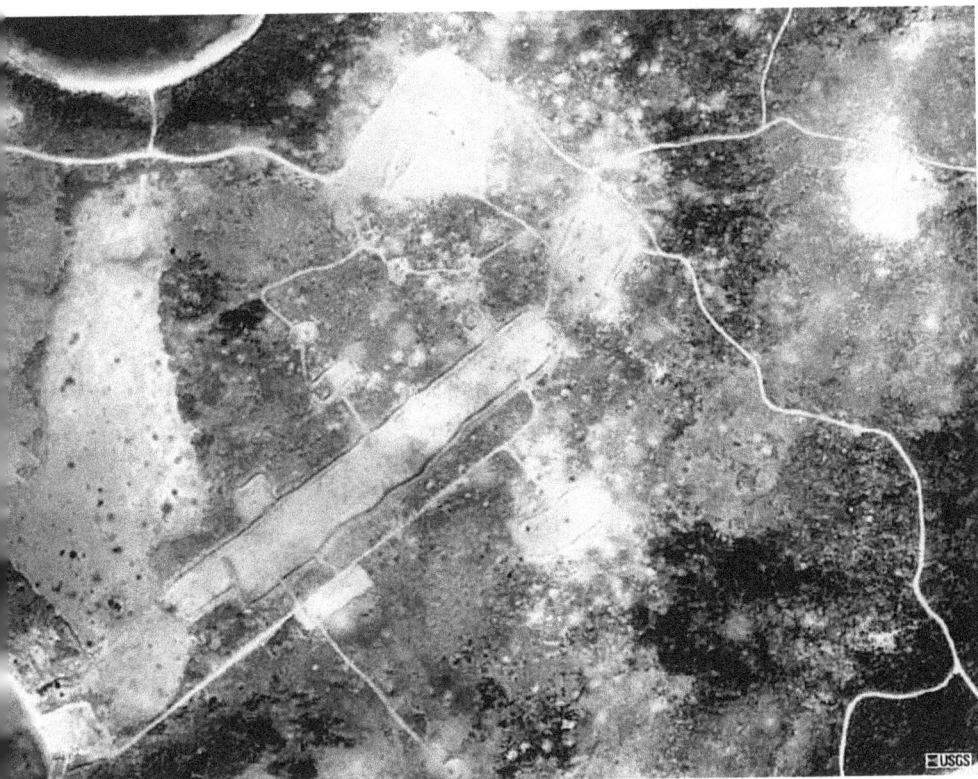

8.2 — Map of bombing ranges, Vieques. SOURCE: UNITED STATES GEOLOGICAL
SURVEY.

six thousand acres—into a training base, firing range, and military waste
dump. For the inhabitants, by then fewer than ten thousand, it was a military
occupation. For the next sixty years, Vieques and its surrounding waters
were bombed an average of 180 days a year, by an estimated 5 million pounds
of ordnance *per year*, some of it live and much of it not.

Its waste dump received an estimated 22 million pounds of military
and industrial waste over the course of the navy's occupation (McCaffrey
2002, 2006). The occupation generated almost no jobs for the local economy, which depended mainly on subsistence agriculture and fishing. Today
43 percent of Viequenses live below the poverty line.

Anticolonial politics flourished in Puerto Rico from the moment of its
annexation by the United States. Efforts to expel the navy from Vieques,
led by the Puerto Rican Independence Party, were continuous, but they got
traction only in 1999, when a Puerto Rican worker was accidentally killed

in a practice bombing (Murillo 2001). The death made Vieques into a cause célèbre for Americans opposing the rightward shift of US politics. A string of celebrity activists joined an occupation of the island—from Jesse Jackson and Robert F. Kennedy Jr. to singers Ricky Martin and Willie Colón, actors Edward James Olmos and Jimmy Smits, Nobel Peace Prize winner Rigoberta Menchú, writers Ana Lydia Vega and Gianni Braschi, and baseball star Carlos Delgado. Some of them, most memorably Reverend Al Sharpton, went to jail for months.

In 2003 the protesters won. The navy ended all its military operations in Vieques and began what was to become its largest cleanup operation ever. Under the guidance of the Environmental Protection Agency and the Department of the Interior, the navy was charged with demilitarizing the landscape and making Vieques safe for tourism (Fox 2012; Navarro 2009). In a strategic move, the federal government turned over most of the navy's lands to the US Fish and Wildlife Service, which declared the former bombing range a wildlife refuge. This move cleverly closed the most damaged area of the island off from economic development and human settlement. Both of these would have required a nearly impossible cleanup. Within the wildlife refuge, the irremediably contaminated live ammunition range, where no effective cleanup was possible, became a wilderness area, closed off entirely from humans. This region of Vieques is probably the only spot in the United States that is both a wilderness area and an Environmental Protection Agency Superfund site. That doubling is possible because cleanup standards refer only to the health of humans and are indifferent to the well-being of any other life-forms. In empire's hinterlands, wilderness and wasteland, refuge and death trap, can become one. While more than 800,000 tons of explosives have been removed from Vieques so far (Bearden 2005), debate continues as to whether enough has been done for human inhabitants and potential visitors (Bearden 2005; Fox 2012). No other stakes are recognized.

In Vieques, US militarism snatched a Caribbean island out of the narrative of development that swamped the Global South after Bretton Woods. Sixty years later, rehabilitated and demilitarized, the island was reinserted into that narrative under a new guise. The time warp greatly enhanced its value as a tourist destination. Vieques, the travel sites crow, has not a single stoplight, golf course, or McDonald's (the lack of a hospital goes unmentioned).

The story of Vieques is not the story of Latin America as a whole, however. In the bigger picture, militarism and tourism, though both forms of occupation, are not always BookingBuddies. In the Monroe Doctrine (1823), the United States declared Latin America its exclusive geopolitical sphere of influence, a relation summed up in the colloquial image of the *patio de atrás*, or backyard. It has conducted over fifty military interventions there since 1898 (M. Becker n.d.). Many of them, including the 1954 coup in Guatemala, the 1973 coup in Chile, the 1980s Contra invasion in Nicaragua, the 1983 invasion of Granada, and the 2009 coup in Honduras, were motivated by unacceptably democratic election outcomes in those countries. US militarism in Latin America has been almost exclusively concerned with making the hemisphere safe for American capitalism and unsafe for communism, socialism, labor rights, and economic redistribution. Apart from direct interventions, the United States during the Cold War invested enormous resources in militarizing Latin America through networks of schools and training programs for militaries and police, some publicly known and many not (Franco 2013). Latin American militarism, which gave us the dictatorships and torture regimes of the 1970s and 1980s, was to a significant degree a creation and an extension of US militarism.

Where do these militarized geopolitics converge with tourism? For the most part, they don't. Overall, tourism has developed in Latin America in rather limited ways. For the moneyed elites of the region, tourism does not compete with industrial agriculture, extractive industry, and the drug trade for profitability. In both its urban (Rio de Janeiro, Mexico City) and nonurban (Cancún, Machu Picchu, Galápagos Islands) forms, tourism requires a great deal of infrastructure, usually supported by concentrated, multifaceted state investment. Mexico, Costa Rica, and Cuba have made such an investment. On the whole, other countries have not. Chile, Peru, Argentina, Colombia, Venezuela, Ecuador, Guatemala, Honduras, Nicaragua, Uruguay, Brazil—these are all countries with enormous unrealized potential for tourism. The Peruvian highlands are peppered with archaeological sites and natural wonders, yet powerful economic monopolies funnel the first world's curious hordes down a single railroad track to Machu Picchu. Ecuador does the same in the Galápagos. The Chilean state invests almost nothing in tourism along its 2,650 miles of stunning coastline. The United Nations World Tourism Organization's 2015 list of the ten top tourist destinations in the world includes only one Latin American country, Mexico, in last place (UN World Tourism Organization 2015).

Is the industry insufficiently profitable? Is an expanded presence of first-world foreigners unappealing to places where states and oligarchs hold power by withholding education, health care, and environmental and economic security from their inhabitants? The hinterlands and out-of-the-way places where tourism thrives are often also the places where labor exploitation and resource plunder thrive (Patagonia or the Amazon, for instance). The ecological and human depredations of mining, lumber, and agrarian mono-culture do not naturally line up with the orchestrated, aestheticized desires of the tourist industry. For the state of Nicaragua and its business class, no tourist development could approach the profit-making potential of a pro-posed artificial waterway across the middle of the country, an alternative to the Panama Canal. The project, should it be realized, will destroy the inland lakes and forests that are Nicaragua's main potential for tourism. For the government of Néstor Kirchner in Argentina, mountaintop-removal mining in Patagonia far exceeded the potential of tourism to generate the wealth it sought in order to reduce inequality. The mountain climbers will have to go elsewhere. For Brazil, the value of the Amazon River system as a source of hydroelectric energy renders trivial its value as an ecosystem, a human habi-tat, or a tourist destination. Dozens of dams are planned and underway. It's no accident that the new left-leaning governments in Brazil, Bolivia, and Ec-uador in the early 2000s all pushed to allow resource extraction in the huge national parks they themselves created under the banner of conservation. Conservation operates, as it has in the United States, as an instrument for taking hinterlands out of the control of their inhabitants and placing them at the disposal of whatever the state defines as the national interest. Even in Mexico, if it came down to a faceoff between tourism and the drug trade, the latter would win hands down. Tourism is one of the biggest industries in the world (E. Becker 2013), but in capitalist Latin America, while it thrives in some sites, it does not compete with other profit machines.

But there is more to say about this. Dick Cheney's astoundingly perverse remark quoted as my epigraph may offer a more suggestive point of entry into our topic. What do military bases and tourist resorts have in common? Even for militarism gone mad, how can Gitmo be imagined as Club Med? Well, both are all-inclusive occupation machines designed to keep you on the premises and satisfy your wants and needs there. Both are enclaves on foreign soil, carrying out the extroverted work of empire. Both command local resources, including sex industries; both require negotiated acceptance by host societies. Tourism and militarism unfold in geographies organized by empires and the afterlives of empire. Both are heirs and instruments of these geohistorical forces. The rifle of Teddy Roosevelt, the big-game hunter in Africa, is the same as the rifle of Roosevelt, the Indian killer in the South-west, and Roosevelt the Rough Rider in Cuba. Military bases and tourist resorts are enclaves that enact the us-them scripts through which empire unfolds and mutates over time. Soldiers and tourists, the mobile bodies in this game, have to be taught these scripts, its rules. So do the societies that host and service these enclaves. Local labor has to be instructed on how to perform its subaltern status in exercises of hosting; tourists and soldiers must be taught how to honor and obey the structure of privilege. All must be trained to organize their appetites, aspirations, and expectations in line with specifications. All must be told why they are here and what the mission is. All must be policed all the time (tourism and policing go hand in hand—start with *A Passage to India*). In 1867 *Blackwood's Magazine* commented on the unfreedom of the tourist: "Perhaps one ought to pity this class of beings, for they are docile and obedient, and, indeed, their offensiveness comes less of any self-willed viciousness, than of a subjection to certain established regulations" (quoted in Buzard 1993, 94). Sounds a bit like the army, doesn't it? Or Gitmo. Or Disneyland.

But here we must distinguish between tourism and tourists, and between militarism and soldiers. In each of these dyads, it's easy to demonize the latter in the name of the former. But tourists are not tourism. If tourists must be taught to be tourists, and soldiers to be soldiers, it's because they are other things prior and in addition to those roles. Outposts of empire attract people in search of displacement, renewal or escape, adventure, experiences unavailable at home. For as long as the United States has been an imperial power, young people of limited means have joined the military to *get away*, to see the world, to see the ocean, to act on their knowledge that other places are not like here. For decades, the landlocked desert states of New Mexico and Arizona have fed a stream of young Chicanos and Native Americans into the navy for reasons like these. (New Mexico has monuments to both the Bataan Death March and the Rough Riders, enterprises to which it contributed a disproportionate number of men.) Tourists are people with the means to seek out experiences different or absent from their daily lives. Leisure tourism is shaped around providing things corporate work culture withholds, including such basics as sleep, sunlight, music and dance, physical exercise, relief from stress, and a break from surveillance and clock time, from the double day and the culture of busyness, from the myriad mechanisms of social discipline that dehumanize and despiritualize metropolitan life. How to quarrel with such a list? The quest for such desiderata is compatible with everything we denounce about tourism and militarism—enclave mentalities, superficial engagement, exploitation of others, the exercise of white supremacy, excessive consumption of resources, and destructive intervention in other people's worlds. These things coexist, but they are not simply the same thing.

CHAPTER NINE

AUTHORITARIANISM 2020

Lessons from Chile

On October 25, 2020, in a national plebiscite, Chileans voted overwhelmingly to rewrite the constitution put in place in 1980 by the military dictatorship of Augusto Pinochet. The dictatorship itself ended in 1990, through an earlier plebiscite (discussed further below). When democratic governance was restored in 1990, many expected the despised constitution to be replaced quickly. (Pinochet died in exile in 2006.) Instead, it took thirty long years of effort, seven years of continuous protest, and a year of unrelenting daily demonstrations that faced a campaign of police brutality to force the government to call the vote. Turnout was enormous, and nearly 80 percent voted in favor of writing a new constitution.[1]

It was easy to understand why. The 1980 constitution built into the fabric of the country both military power and the neoliberal economic and social reforms that the Pinochet regime, supported by the US government, was installed to impose. The so-called Chicago Boys, economists trained by Milton Friedman, had designated Chile as a laboratory for their free-market economic philosophy. The 1980 constitution established minimal state intervention, allowing private sectors to control public services. "It facilitated the privatisation of public sectors such as health, pensions and education, helping Chile become one of Latin America's richest but most unequal countries. Poverty rates were slashed, but the country's growing middle class lived hand-to-mouth, saddled by debt and reliant on credit payments" (McGowan 2020).

The final year of protest was sparked by an increase in public transportation fares in November 2019. This was the equivalent of a crushing new tax on working people, who relied overwhelmingly on public transport to get to and from work every day. It quickly evolved into a protest against economic inequality in general, and from there it zeroed in on the constitution, which enshrined that inequality in the fabric of the nation. People had demanded change for decades, but the rich would not give up neoliberalism's gifts willingly.

Nine days after Chile's plebiscite, US voters also went to the polls, in an election all agreed was the most important in a generation, perhaps ever. It, too, was a plebiscite on authoritarianism, economic inequality, and private versus public power. Donald Trump's first term fully displayed his autocratic, antidemocratic tendencies; intolerance of dissent; and taste for cruelty and violence. Like Chileans, in the summer of 2020, Americans, too, were in the streets en masse, protesting the continuing string of police murders of Black citizens. As in Chile, these protests faced campaigns of police brutality directed and encouraged by the president. Some were reminded of Chile. In July 2020, when Trump dispatched squads of unidentified armed federal agents to Portland using antiterrorist powers established after 9/11, one Twitter user declared, "The Pinochetization of America cometh."[2] Indeed, the news photos from the two countries that month were nearly indistinguishable. A month earlier, US-based political journalist Masha Gessen had published a powerful book analyzing Trumpism based on her years living in Vladimir Putin's Russia (Gessen 2020b). As the "Pinochetization of America" tweet suggested, there were lessons to be learned from Chile as well.

In this chapter I discuss some key features of the Pinochet dictatorship, in particular its discourses and public performances of authoritarianism, echoed in the Trump regime. I then look at how Chilean activists and artists challenged them, focusing in particular on the work of the brilliant experimental writer Diamela Eltit. I then discuss the expressive means used by the 1988 media campaign to unseat the dictatorship. At the end, I offer a few observations on how these Chilean experiences resonate with the workings of Trumpism and efforts to dismantle democratic rule in the United States. Readers will hear echoes throughout.

9.1 — Chilean dictator Augusto Pinochet. SOURCE: MINISTERIO DE RELACIONES EXTERIORES DE CHILE.

The Language of Dictatorship

About eight months after the coup of September 11, 1973, General Augusto Pinochet gave a speech to a new state entity, the National Secretariat for Women (Secretaría Nacional de la Mujer), established by the ruling military junta and headed by Lucía Hiriart de Pinochet, the general's wife.[3] To a select audience, Pinochet proposed to "lay out the thought of the authorities with respect to the role corresponding to women in the plans of the government over which I preside, and the new state that it proposes to install in the future" (Pinochet Ugarte 1976b, 5).[4]

It takes little more than this opening sentence to grasp the raw authoritarianism that characterized the military regime, still in its early triumphal and extremely violent period (Munizaga 1983). People have roles that "correspond" to them; "thought" is in the hands of the authorities; these, it is understood, do not include women. Citizenship consists, as Pinochet liked to say, in ordering or obeying, and only those who do one or the other well are useful to the state. "In Chile," the speech continues, women have always been "active and effective collaborators in the lives of men"(11)—so the dictator codes the role that women played in bringing him to power.[5] The women of Chile, he explains (subsuming them all under those who supported the coup), "sought the shelter of a strict authority that would reestablish order and public morality in our country" (7). The authority of the authorities, apparently, includes command over the assignment of motives and desires. Women's needs are defined by the leader; their actions are assigned a meaning and even an epistemology: "In her feminine instinct," the Chilean woman "saw clearly that what was being defined in those dramatic days [leading up to the coup] was not simply a game of political parties; it was the life or death of the nation" (7). Pinochet speaks of the "clairvoyance" (*clarividencia*) of this generic *mujer chilena* (Chilean woman) in seeing past party politics—which the regime abolished the moment it took power.

Obviously, I am not quoting this rhetoric for its subtlety. As the speech continues, in keeping with an ideology of domesticity established in the previous century, women are told that following the traditions of "the West" (*el occidente*), their "mission as women and mothers" has been and remains to defend and transmit spiritual values, serve as a moderating element (against the warlike impulses of men, it seems), educate and instill consciousness and conscience, and serve as repositories of national traditions (8). While acknowledging women's right to a profession, the general calls for greater recognition of the work that "corresponds" to them, which is, of course, child-rearing. Equality of rights and opportunity is undisputed, he says, but woman's "authentic participation" must "be exercised in relation to her characteristics" (11).

The constant, explicit interpellation of women was a hallmark of the Pinochet regime. One of the tragic ironies in Chile is that the dictatorship took advantage of the near vacuum in Chilean political discourse as regards women. Political parties, from right to left, were all bastions of male privilege. They had never put women into the picture; Pinochet rarely left them out—not because the regime particularly cared about women but because patriarchal values were the key to the one thing it could not dictate for itself: legitimacy. As Jean Franco (1992) observed, one of the regime's tactics was to mobilize in its favor masculinist gender ideologies that held across classes and across the political spectrum. As the speech makes clear, the aim was not to empower women but to win their loyalty and reassure men by constantly showing women their place. The tactic won him a solid bloc of female supporters, but it also backfired. In his seventeen years in power, Pinochet presided over a social and political mobilization of women unprecedented in Chile, and probably in Latin America. This mobilization had everything to do with the general's eventual demise. At the same time, the patriarchal ideologies he propagated influenced the way women were seen and saw themselves (Corradi, Fagen, and Garretón 1992).

The paternalism and authoritarianism heard in Pinochet's pronouncements were by no means reserved for women. They characterized his rhetoric across the board. Scholars have repeatedly commented on the homogenizing, monoglossic, prescriptive, and abstract rhetoric of the Southern Cone dictatorships.[6] They sought not to replace public discourse with an imposed silence but to simulate it with a relentless drone that apparently interpellated all citizens yet actively singled out and made a target out of anyone they chose. Like the martial music played on the radio during a coup, this drone erased the idea of culture or the social as the site of conflict, heterogeneity, and negotiation of difference. As Priscilla Archibald observed, the absence of argument or evidence was key. Pinochet's was a discourse of pure statement, in which the words *thus* and *therefore*, if they occur at all, refer not to facts or reasons but to essences and eternal laws.[7] Against the drone of abstraction, essentialism, and declaration, the literary practice of *testimonio* acquired force as a form of resistance. Circulating clandestinely, people's *testimonios* of experiences at the hands of the dictatorship laid bare the regime's practices of concealment, represented what was concealed, and, as discussed in chapter 11, reasserted the languages of evidence, bodily experience, and truth, as well as the value of the distinction between truth and untruth, which the regime overrode.[8]

Parody the Patriarch

Another powerful weapon of resistance was parody. Ten years into the dictatorship, the experimental writer and video and performance artist Diamela Eltit undertook a risky experiment. Walking the streets of Santiago, she had encountered a homeless man whose demented ramblings performed a remarkable simulation of the dictatorship's endless monologue. Living in a vacant lot, he called himself "El Padre Mío" (My Father). Eltit recorded, transcribed, and edited the man's monologues and, in the face of the censorship regime, published them in a book titled *El Padre Mío* (1989). In book form, El Padre Mío's monologues became scrambled parodies of the dictator's voice, which by now lived in every Chilean's head. El Padre Mío uncannily reproduced many dimensions of the reality that had become common to all Chileans: paranoia, uncertainty, an omnipresent sense of victimization and death, and a crisis of language in which words seem unattached to referents. At the same time, his ravings reproduced the megalomania and paranoia of the dictatorship itself. Here is a sample of El Padre Mío's verbal performance:

> You're taking me for a ride with this plan. How would I not know that? I'm the man who is going to give the orders here, me. I am going to give the orders in the country. Because I have no commitments either to them or to King George, who has been giving the orders lately and has that rank. El Padre Mío gives the illegal orders in the country. For many years he has been living off illegal bank deposits, from the money that belongs to the concession of the personnel of the administration. He is the accomplice of El Padre Mío in these matters. I would like to do you a service in exchange for the sale of your rights. Because I was asked to take up these tasks, not El Padre Mío, nor Mr. Colvin, who is Mr. Luengo, who is a congressman and a senator. (Eltit 1989, 23)

Under the military regime, the book implies, only the madman in the street can speak freely, and he has something truthful to say. Alternatively, the only man in the street who is speaking freely is mad. Like the *testimonio*, *El Padre Mío* affirms marginality as a critical source of insight in any hegemonic structure. Its speaker seems to appropriate the disembodied oratory of the dictatorship and reflect it back in a form that censorship authorities cannot recognize but that citizens can.

A New Institutionality

El Padre Mío parodies in particular the abstraction of the dictator's rhetoric, which created an unbridgeable, tectonic gap between what the regime said and what its citizens were experiencing. What Pinochet called the "plans of the government and the new institutionality it proposes to establish in the future" was underway. The Pinochet regime had what Giselle Munizaga (1983, 1993) called a foundational project. It is common to think that military dictatorships aim simply to impose order, suppress opposition, and uphold established hierarchies. But Pinochet, a highly educated man, had much greater ambitions. Crippling the militant left was only one small part of it (accomplished with extreme violence in a matter of weeks). When he spoke, as he did all the time, of "the new institutionality" ("la nueva institucionalidad"), he meant a wholesale transformation of state and civil society, no fooling (see Catalán and Munizaga 1986). He made Chile into a poster child for free-market capitalism.

In terms of political economy, the foundational project was to interrupt the post–World War II trajectory of national development in Chile by redirecting industrial production from national markets, driven by rising wages, to global markets, facilitated by substantial wage cuts (Frank 1976, 1981; Larsen 1983). As Hernán Vidal succinctly put it, "Pinochet's job was to offer a cheap workforce to the world" (1983, 47). By 1975 wages had dropped by 30 to 50 percent, leaving a huge proportion of the population destitute. This rapid, drastic immiseration mobilized Chilean women, who collectivized domestic life in every way they could. In vast impoverished neighborhoods, shopping, cooking, eating, sewing, child care, medical care, laundry, and artisanal production moved out of private houses into circles, clubs, and cooperatives, with support especially from the Catholic Church, the only oppositional force the regime was obliged to tolerate. In the face of such extreme circumstances, the regime's pious rhetoric about women's roles became an insult.

Economic intervention was accompanied by a shutting down of civil society and its interfaces with the state. Political parties were abolished; a press blackout was followed by draconian censorship; curfews were imposed; public assembly was prohibited; universities were purged; presses were shut down; the judiciary was suspended; the opposition was annihilated; and a regime of terror based on torture and disappearance was installed. To understand how drastic this rupture was, one needs to recall the acute politicization of Chilean society at the time of the coup. The dramatic struggle between the Unidad Popular (Popular Unity) government and its opposition had played out in daily demonstrations in streets and plazas, particularly in the central plaza in front of La Moneda Palace, the seat of the presidency.[9] The Chilean military shredded that script in the very staging of the coup: La Moneda, a pivotal site of political expression, was bombed by the air force—an extraordinary self-inflicted wound. The national soccer stadium, a pivotal site of national citizenship, was taken over and transformed into a detention and torture center where, among other horrors, the revered singer-guitarist Víctor Jara was tortured and killed. The stadium became a fortress and a theater of cruelty (as the US southern border did under Trump). It is hard to exaggerate the symbolic and psychic force of the militarization of this arena that had been built for the exercise of a secular, civilian, masculine nationality. (It is no accident that in 1989, when elections were restored, the new president, Patricio Aylwin Azócar, gave his acceptance speech there.)

Defying Fortress Chile

The repurposing of the stadium epitomizes the reimagining of the nation itself that followed the coup. Chile became Fortress Chile, its entrances and exits fiercely guarded, its dissidents expelled, the order of the seen and unseen reconfigured. Hence, the powerful impact of another experiment in witnessing that took place in 1985. It was memorialized in print by Gabriel García Márquez in *La aventura de Miguel Littín, clandestino en Chile* (*Clandestine in Chile: The Adventures of Miguel Littín*; 1986). Miguel Littín was a prominent leftist filmmaker who had been exiled by the dictatorship and absolutely prohibited from returning to Chile. In 1985, using a disguise and a false passport and supported by extensive collaboration with the underground resistance, Littín slipped back into Chile accompanied by no fewer than three European film crews. In defiance of the regime, they traveled the length and breadth of Chile under false pretenses, filming what became *Acta General de Chile* (General survey of Chile; Littín 1986), an extraordinary portrait of the country under the dictatorship.[10] A straightforward documentary, almost a travelogue, the film follows the exile as he recovers place and the embodied experience of home. It includes generous footage of walks through city streets and of the beloved Chilean landscape viewed from the windows of moving trains. On multiple occasions, Littín narrowly escapes capture. The whole production was an audacious and high-risk prank. The film, and García Márquez's narrative account, made a mockery of Fortress Chile. It affirmed the omnipresence of the clandestine opposition despite years of repression. More important, like *El Padre Mío*, it demonstrated that the dictatorship, with eyes everywhere, lacked the competence to know what it was seeing. Time and again, Littín escapes the police unrecognized. The film crews, who hid their intentions, even penetrated La Moneda Palace. As Eltit dramatized in *El Padre Mío*, Littín's hoax showed that the regime's claim to interpretive power could be contradicted openly. The heroic infiltration seized agency, refused the culture of fear, and appropriated—or intercepted—the tools of deception.

Littín's adventure worked within the masculinist construct of power that the dictatorship mobilized in its own acts of penetration, whether nocturnal invasions of homes, sexual torture, or university purges. (Indeed, within a year of Littín's visit, opposition movements were crushed again following an assassination attempt against Pinochet.) But by the time Littín slipped inside the fortress walls, other forms of resistance had been put into play, with great effectiveness, by dozens of oppositional groups overwhelmingly composed of women (see, for example, Palestro 1991). These groups likewise intercepted and redeployed the dynamics of the secret, the seen, and the unseen. The international community became familiar with images of demonstrating women parading photos of the disappeared, who were thus made to reappear. Startlingly original acts of political theater were staged on national days of protest, which occurred monthly during a period of intense opposition between 1983 and 1986. In Santiago, for instance, a mock election was held to remind people of the act of voting. Ballot boxes mysteriously appeared on street corners, and people were invited to cast votes. From inside houses, women banged pots at an appointed hour each day, appropriating a strategy once used against the government of Salvador Allende Gossens. Appearing out of nowhere, teams from the Colectivo Acciones de Arte (Art Actions Collective) painted murals on buildings and photographed them, knowing they would soon be erased. Resistance thrived in the literary sphere as well, despite shutdowns of bookstores and presses. Clandestine writers' workshops flourished and experimented. Fiction writer Pía Barros in her workshops responded to censorship by developing a new form of publication: the "book-object" (*libro-objeto*), which disseminated short prose texts disguised as other consumer objects such as boxes of stationery or concealed in little burlap bags. The book-object pointed a parodic finger both at censorship and at the consumerism that neoliberal economics had brought to Chile.

Flames in the Night. Two Scenarios

Such practices counteracted the authoritarian reorganization of citizenship that the Pinochet regime imposed in the most everyday ways. Rearranging and resymbolizing public spaces were among the dictatorship's principal physical and psychic weapons. A propaganda pamphlet that appeared in 1976 offers a detailed example. Translated into English as *Chile Lights the Freedom Torch*, the pamphlet reproduces the public speech Pinochet made on September 11, 1975, the second anniversary of the coup. An anonymous foreword describes in fervent detail the solemn, daylong public celebration that culminated in the speech (Pinochet 1976). Its detailed description of the spectacle offers a window on the authoritarian and, in this instance, fascist imagination. As described in the pamphlet, the day's festivities began in the military garrisons, where "solemn religious services were held" (5). The day culminated in an evening rally held in a large public plaza in Santiago. Here, to the light of thousands of torches "giving to the night an unforgettable appearance," the four-man ruling junta took its place at a high podium backed by a gigantic map of Chile (7). A gigantic national flag was raised in the center of the square, and then, as the translation (hilariously) reads, "President Pinochet addressed to all Chileans a brief harangue." Following the speech, "four anonymous civilians representing women, youth, rural workers and urban workers" approached the podium and lit four torches (7). These were handed off to four cadets, representing the four branches of the armed forces, who in turn took them up to the podium and handed them off to the four members of the junta. Together, they lit an enormous freedom torch that, based on the photos, formed a ring the size of a large auditorium. At the end of September, the "month of the fatherland," this torch was moved "in a somber ceremony" to the hilltop where in 1541 the Spaniard Pedro de Valdivia had founded Santiago de Chile. "There it will remain forever as a symbol to a country that wants to be true to its [white, European] origins" (9).

An intriguing aspect of the ritual is the foursome chosen to represent civilian society—women, youth, and rural and urban workers. The list elides the sector that, under civilian rule, constitutes the core of national citizenries: the adult men of property. This is the group who in classical state theory attend the assembly and vote. In the dictatorship's ritual schema, the youth, the women, and the workers seem grouped around this absent center (there are no slots for teachers, intellectuals, or businesspeople in this ritual). What replaces that classic civilian core is the military, whose vertical relations are reproduced as the torches move up the podium. *Enlightenment* here refers to flames in the night.[11]

Nocturnal flames also burn in a text that stands in fascinating counterpoint with the dictatorship's spectacle. I refer to Diamela Eltit's brilliant avant-garde poetic fiction *Lumpérica* (1983), a text that deploys many of the elements of the fascist spectacle but uses them to plumb the depths of the dictatorship's damage and claw a way toward rebirth. Like *El Padre Mío*, *Lumpérica* challenges the dictatorship in its own terms.

Lumpérica is likewise set at night in a Santiago plaza that is presided over by a gigantic figure called "El Luminoso" (The Luminous One [masculine]).[12] El Luminoso turns out to be a flashing neon sign (cf. Pinochet's illuminated map) that projects light and words onto the bodies of those below. This is a potent image for the authoritarian state: light/power/language emanating in darkness from an unseen source above. Eltit's protagonist is a woman named "L. Iluminada" (The Illuminated One [feminine]) who, defying curfew, spends a long, hallucinated night bathed in the cold light of El Luminoso, engaged in what seems to be an epic struggle to achieve a convergence of selfhood, agency, language, body, citizenship, and meaning. Like Littín's return, it is an exercise in regrounding the self. The obvious blank in L. Iluminada's name where the *a* of the article *La* should appear is reminiscent of a neon sign in which one letter has gone dark. The absent *a* suggests what is there to be recovered: a marker of gender and also of being—"the-ness"—itself. The new convergence of selfhood and agency must be found (or created) in the cold night of the plaza under the relentless semantic projections of El Luminoso. There is no elsewhere. The process the reader accompanies as the text unfolds is arduous and full of agony and desire. The book is a masterpiece.

L. Iluminada's struggle is witnessed by another social group that made no appearance at Pinochet's ceremony, the lumpen of Santiago, referred to as "the pale ones" (*los pálidos*). These are the street people who trickle into the plaza, curfew or no, with nowhere else to go. (Eltit says that the idea for the book came to her late one night when she had permission to be out after curfew and drove past the empty plazas of Santiago, indicators of the interruption of public life that had taken place.) In the opening scene, L. Iluminada lies on her back on the cold cement at the center of the plaza. She writhes in pain and desire as El Luminoso baptizes her with "the name of her citizenship" (su identificación ciudadana), the label that "corresponds to her" (an echo of Pinochet's words on women [Eltit 1983, 7]). It is, we are told, a "desolate citizenship" that stamps labels on her and the pale ones "like commercial products" (8). The question then becomes what sorts of agency and consciousness are left for her under El Luminoso's imprint. The delirious 150 pages that follow are an odyssey of mind and body in search of an answer. The elements of fascism, dismembered into fragments, are scattered throughout the text.

Baptized by El Luminoso, L. Iluminada rebaptizes herself by sticking her hand into the bonfire around which she and the pale ones are sitting for warmth. "Just for the sake of giving herself a new identity," the narrator remarks derisively, "she turns to tradition like a quote" (29). The hand in the fire is a cliché. Self-mutilation pays off, however: "New damage has been done, and a new circle opened in literature" (29). It is hard to miss the scene's medieval resonance, apparently substituting the medievalism of Pinochet's priestly ritual with the equally medieval counterculture of witchcraft. The hand in the fire was once the test of truth for those accused of witchcraft. Inflicted on herself, the test gives L. Iluminada, as she tells us, the "power to disorganize language" (30). Bringing her burned hand to her mouth, she utters the sentence "I am thirsty" ("Tengo sed") and ritually "deconstructs the phrase, word by word, syllable by syllable" (30). What gets deconstructed is not only the figure of Christ thirsting on the cross and asking for water but also more vividly the scene of torture, which the phrase "I am thirsty" irrevocably evokes in the vocabulary of this period in Chile. The message seems to be that physical pain itself must be reclaimed if citizenship is to be restored. Within the national security state, self-harm challenges the "secret" of state violence.[13] Indeed, the "I am thirsty" episode is followed immediately by an interrogation, in which the interrogator asks, "What are the uses of a public square?" (37). This is a question about citizenship. It juxtaposes the abstract, verticalized plaza of Pinochet/El Luminoso with the horizontal relations on the ground among L. Iluminada and the pale ones.

As the novel unfolds, almost ritualistically, L. Iluminada takes the reader through a series of hallucinated and hellish metamorphoses, in an infernal descent through which the female subject repossesses herself and the power of the word. Autoeroticism and self-mutilation are key routes to the power of the word, to a hell of writing. The journey culminates in fifteen vignettes, called "cuts" (cortes), referring simultaneously to filmic or textual excerpts and to self-inflicted wounds. The section is introduced by a photo of a woman, probably the author, with her arms bound in bandages. The fifteen cuts take L. Iluminada through descending states of madness, from which she emerges at dawn, lucid, serene, and alone in the light of El Luminoso, who seems now to be transmitting signals only for her. She recognizes herself as irrevocably vulnerable to his messages but able, by moving her body, to determine which letters strike her and where. El Luminoso is limited by his "estatismo," a pun on "static-ness" and "statism."

As the text draws to a close, L. Iluminada ambiguously recodes her own body. From a paper bag she takes out a mirror, a pair of scissors, and a necklace. She cuts off her hair, puts on the necklace over the gray dress that links her with the gray cement of the plaza, and prepares to exit. Evidently, this is the new self-possessed citizen-woman. The reader is not sure what exactly has been won, but the message seems clear: after a decade under the light of El Luminoso, the road back to self-possession, agency, and freedom involves great struggle, not least within ourselves.

Saying Yes to No

L. Iluminada's quest prophesied the struggle that took place five years later, through which Chileans did recover their citizenship. In 1988, as prescribed by his 1980 constitution, Pinochet called a referendum on the continuation of his regime. A yes vote would give Pinochet another eight years in power. A no vote would mean that presidential and parliamentary elections would be held within a year. It was a fight over the future. Pinochet envisioned the plebiscite as a pro forma reauthorization that he had no real chance of losing, perhaps not realizing that the international community, the Chilean business class, and even some members of the junta were ready for a return to legitimate government. And lose he did, largely because of a brilliant television campaign that won the battle of futurity by transforming exhaustion and hopelessness into political energy. A group of political parties allied to promote the no vote. The government and a smaller number of parties supported the yes vote. In a first in Chilean politics, the sides agreed that during the final month before the vote, each side would have a fifteen-minute slot on national television each night to make its case to the public. Futurologists were recruited. The regime hired an Argentine public relations firm. The no side set up a team of US and Chilean advertising experts (including some former supporters of Allende).

The Campaña del No (Campaign of the No), as it was called, faced the challenge of undoing fifteen years of "desolate citizenship" under Pinochet(Arriaga 1989). Millions of adult citizens had never experienced voting; for millions more, it was a distant memory. Through focus groups, the Campaña del No found that most Chileans did not want the dictatorship to continue but lacked confidence that the referendum would make any difference. After fifteen years of dictatorship, moreover, the idea of saying no to a dictator who demanded acquiescence and punished dissent was daunting for many. As *Lumpérica* prophesied, a recovery of selfhood, desire, agency, and civic identity was needed. The no campaign saw that its mission was to make saying no in public desirable, maybe even fun. They adopted a blatantly futuristic theme "La alegría ya viene" (Here comes joy), with a lively, memorable theme song that still echoes in people's heads. In television segments, the song is accompanied by a cornucopia of images of cheery Chileans of all ages and ethnicities acting in motion in public outdoor spaces and in daylight. One amusing skit after another made it fun to say no. The word *no* was repeated by smiling faces dozens of times in each segment. Music, play, comedy, art making, dance, and sports were everywhere. The goal was to recover the experience of freedom and agency and the pleasures of collective civic life and to project them into a possible future. In staged street interviews, citizens matter-of-factly affirmed their intention to vote no. The principles of advertising were at work: associate the object you are promoting with positive feelings and experiences. Chilean and international celebrities supported the campaign, and some, including Richard Dreyfuss, Christopher Reeve, and Jane Fonda, made cameo appearances. At the same time, survivors of state violence appeared, recounting their experiences and urging the no vote, while other scenes showed the poverty many faced, especially the elderly.

This hopeful register seems the opposite of *Lumpérica*'s drama of anguish and slashed, burned flesh. Yet in both Eltit's novel and the Campaña del No, the recovery of freedom and citizenship is brought about through physical motion and embodied self-expression in public spaces: "What are the uses of a public square?"

The yes campaign was far less successful technically, affectively, and artistically. It offered no pleasure or play and no renewal. In authoritarian fashion, its segments often presented white patriarchal authority figures monologuing from behind a desk, archival footage of violent confrontations during the Allende period, or images of Chile's prosperous industries, which thrived by impoverishing workers. Martial music accompanied appearances by the generals. Such was the promised future. In the latter days of the campaign, it tried to alter its tactics, but it was too late. The no vote won, 55 percent to 44 percent. Pinochet, in good authoritarian fashion, assembled his generals to reject the result and retake the state by force. The generals refused. Elections were scheduled, and Patricio Aylwin Azócar became president in 1990.

The Campaña del No made saying no the vehicle for an imagined return to joy and to the normal civic and social life that people wanted. The instrument of victory was television, which the Pinochet regime itself had deliberately spread throughout the country so its propaganda could penetrate every home. The return to joy did not fully materialize. The transition from dictatorship to democracy proved far more difficult, fraught, and disappointing than many had hoped.[14] One of the main obstacles was the 1980 constitution, which subsequent governments modified but repeatedly refused to replace. It ensured the dictator a permanent place in the government and removed the military from government control. The dictator and his henchmen, in other words, were already inserted into whatever future was forged.

The other impediment was the neoliberal economic restructuring that remained in place, creating a crisis of futurity that was probably most intense among the young, for whom even the prospect of founding a household often remained out of reach. In a postdictatorship novel titled *Mano de obra* (Workforce; 2002), Eltit explored these continuing conditions and their potential for fomenting a return to authoritarianism. The novel's protagonists are a group of young people who live together and work for low wages at a supermarket. In pitiless, often clinical language, the novel evokes the despair, dehumanization, ruthless exploitation, obscene excesses, and scarcities that accompany life under unfettered commodity capitalism. In the supermarket we witness the mercantilization of the social contract. The idea of rationality as a principle in opposition to chaos becomes a joke. In the sphere of their home life, the characters struggle to create humane collective living arrangements despite their poverty and vulnerability. Their efforts dissolve into cruelty, isolation, and psychological breakdown. The characters are incapacitated by the levels of submission their economic insecurity imposes. They become incapable of generating alternative possibilities. At the end they lose their jobs, are evicted from their rented house, and enter the semantic vacuum of the street. Futureless, expelled even from exploitation and abjection, they end up reaffirming the magic power of white male authoritarianism—a denouement with horrible resonance in postdictatorship Chile. They can be made superfluous (and superfluid); they cannot, however, be made to disappear. This story resonates in the United States as well, as even two full-time minimum-wage jobs do not bring in enough to found a household, a fact linked here, too, with a turn to authoritarianism and white rule. Here the novel is a prophecy, as *Lumpérica* was for Chile in 1983. This difficult transition out of dictatorship is what L. Iluminada was about to face as she donned her necklace and cut her hair before leaving the plaza. She was preparing for battle, not a ball. In 1983 *Lumpérica* was prophetic of a future that was still playing itself out in the fall of 2020.

For those living in the United States in 2020, *Lumpérica* offers a warning. Read it as futurology. If the attempt to consolidate authoritarian rule in the United States is allowed to succeed, its impact will be profound and prolonged. Whether you support or oppose it, it will penetrate deep into your psyche and impose a "desolate citizenship" from which you will have to struggle long and hard to recover. At the same time, if the "Pinochetization of America" proceeds, Eltit and the many other Chilean writers, artists, activists, and scholars will have much to teach Americans about how to contest it, how to keep a grip on reality, and how to empower creativity and trespass in the midst of repression and fear.

Coda. New and Old Authoritarians

In *Strongmen*, a study of twentieth-century authoritarian rulers across the world, Ruth Ben-Ghiat (2020) distinguishes among three generations of strongmen: the fascist dictators of 1900–1940, the military dictators of 1945–1990 (including Pinochet), and the post-1990 "new authoritarians," a growing contemporary list that includes Rodrigo Duterte (Philippines), Recep Erdogan (Turkey), Vladimir Putin (Russia), Jair Bolsonaro (Brazil), Narendra Modi (India), Viktor Orbán (Hungary), and Donald Trump (United States).

Unlike the two earlier groups, the new authoritarians come into power through elections, often by means of media-rich populist campaigns. Once elected, they seek to remain in power either as dictatorships or as illiberal democracies with token elections. Refusing to accept electoral defeats is a common maneuver these new strongmen attempt in hopes of advancing from what Masha Gessen (2020a) calls an "autocratic attempt" to an "autocratic breakthrough."[15] As I wrote these words in December 2020, such an attempt was unfolding in the United States, culminating on January 6, 2021, in the violent takeover of Congress by several hundred insurgent Trump supporters in an attempt to halt certification of the election. The new authoritarians use their elected terms, as Trump did, to put in place elements intended to facilitate an authoritarian breakthrough. These include undermining judicial neutrality, weakening electoral processes and opposition parties, placing loyalists in positions intended to be apolitical, increasing executive power, and so forth.[16] The playbook is now familiar. After surveying all three generations of authoritarian regimes (fascist, military, and new), Ben-Ghiat identifies a set of commonalities, all of which survivors of Trumpism will recognize. Authoritarians all rule in a personalist fashion and always in the name of a project of national renewal ("I alone can fix it"). They share a set of essential "tools of rule," Ben-Ghiat says: propaganda, virility, violence, corruption.

Across the divide between new and old authoritarianisms, readers of this chapter may have noticed commonalities between the Pinochet and Trump regimes, despite sharp contrasts in style and length of rule. Both leaders, for example, liked outdoor mass gatherings in which they received their followers' adulation. Pinochet's gathering described above was a structured, solemn, ritualistic occasion following purely fascist aesthetics. Freedom torches marked the rigid hierarchy in a classic expression of what Gessen calls the "vertical of vassalage" (2020a, 3). Trump's rallies were boisterous populist entertainments full of transgressive boorishness and mockery. Here the autocrat stood surrounded by his followers, distanced but not above them, the focal point on which their adoration converged. In Trumpism the polarities seemed reversed: the insurgent, countercultural energies were on his side, while liberals and progressives stood for institutionality and the rule of law. The flaming freedom torches appeared in the hands of white supremacists threatening order, not upholding it.

Both leaders created theaters of violence where their virile cruelty and ruthlessness were on display, inflicted on targeted groups. In Pinochet's case, the targets were the left, rounded up, imprisoned, and tortured in centers

9.2 — US-Mexico border detention center, McAllen, Texas. SOURCE: DEPARTMENT OF HOMELAND SECURITY.

known to all. Today many of those centers are memory sites. Trump's regime targeted undocumented immigrants and asylum seekers, who were detained, dehumanized, and subjected to physical and psychological torment in a vast network of detention centers that one day will also be memory sites.

Both leaders interpellated women in their traditional reproductive, domestic, and sexual subordination, though again their styles of masculinity contrasted sharply. Both enjoyed speaking in public, and both used the language of declaration, absolutism, and abstraction, disdaining evidence and argument. Both routinely overrode the distinction between truth and untruth, soliciting belief in whatever they claimed. Both subscribed to white supremacy and an idea of northern European superiority (Trump admired Russia; Pinochet revered Prussia). Both strongmen generated a steady stream of propaganda intended to install their voice in every household and every brain in the nation. Pinochet did so through television and radio, with the help of a censorship program that silenced other voices; Trump used those media and added his nonstop Twitter output and the force field of social media. Both took power in periods of liberalization that created anxiety and desire for order. Like all authoritarians, both men ruled in the name of law and order but thrived on creating chaos in ways that were indifferent to the public good. Both held in contempt the masses whose loyalty they solicited. Both built a cocoon of sycophants around themselves and were therefore shocked at being voted out of office. Both were loved and lionized by large swaths of their populations—a third or more of Chileans fervently supported Pinochet throughout his presidency and beyond. In the 2020 US elections, 73 million out of 153 million voters supported Trump.

The playbooks of resistance also show points of convergence. Both strongmen inspired nonstop streams of parody, in Chile in a proliferation of underground literature, in the United States on the internet and television. Alec Baldwin's famed impersonation led the way. The mimetic ravings of El Padre Mío were paralleled by Sarah Cooper's brilliant lip-synched re-enactments of Trumpian rants. In Chile ephemeral public art was another rich medium for creative dissent. The murals of the Colectivo Acciones de Arte in Santiago were paralleled in the United States by Robin Bell's ingenious light projections. And of course, in both cases, the bodies marching en masse in the streets of both countries in the summer and fall of 2020 were necessary, if not sufficient, for ending authoritarian rule, whether in an incipient phase, as in the United States, or long into its afterlife, as in Chile.

COLONIALITY,
INDIGENEITY, AND
THE TRAFFIC IN
MEANING

THE ETHNOGRAPHER'S ARRIVAL

In his introduction to *Argonauts of the Western Pacific* ([1922] 1961), Broni-slaw Malinowski celebrates the advent of professional, scientific ethnogra-phy: "The time when we could tolerate accounts presenting us the native as a distorted, childish caricature of a human being are gone," he declares. "This picture is false, and like many other falsehoods, it has been killed by Sci-ence" (11). The statement is symptomatic of a well-established habit among ethnographers of defining ethnographic writing over and against older, less specialized genres, such as travel books, memoirs, journalism, and accounts by missionaries, settlers, colonial officials, and the like. Although it will not supplant these genres altogether, professional ethnography, it is understood, will usurp their authority and correct their errors. In almost any ethnogra-phy, dull-witted figures called "mere travelers" or "the casual observer" show up from time to time, only to have their superficial perceptions either cor-rected or corroborated by the serious scientist.

This strategy of defining itself by contrast to adjacent and antecedent dis-courses limits ethnography's ability to explain or examine itself as a kind of writing. To the extent that it legitimates itself by opposition to other kinds of writing, ethnography blinds itself to the fact that its own discursive practices were often inherited from these other genres and are still shared with them today. In a former life or an earlier phase of capitalist expansion, Malinowski might have been a traveler or an explorer. The amateur observers dismissed at the outset of ethnographies often turn up a hundred pages later as corroborating witnesses (as they do in Edward Evans-Pritchard's *The Nuer* [1940], for example). The convention of dismissing previous travelers is itself inherited from travel writing.

At times one still hears expressed as an ideal for ethnography a transparent, tropeless discourse that would render other realities "exactly as they are," not filtered through an observer's values and interpretive schema. For the most part, however, that wild goose is no longer being chased, and it is possible to suggest that ethnographic writing is as trope governed as any other discursive formation. This recognition is obviously fundamental for those who are interested in changing or enriching ethnographic writing or simply in increasing the discipline's self-understanding and accountability. In this essay I examine some key tropes of classic ethnographic writing and show how they derive from earlier discursive traditions. In particular, I focus on the vexed but important relationship between personal narrative and objectivist description in ethnographic writing and its history in travel writing.

A controversy that took place in the flagship journal *American Anthropologist* in the 1980s illustrates the difficulties ethnography has had in establishing its relations to adjacent discourses. The controversy surrounded Florinda Donner's *Shabono: A True Adventure in the Remote and Magical Heart of the South American Jungle* (1982). The book is a personal account of the experience of a graduate student in anthropology who, while doing fieldwork in Venezuela, is chosen by members of a remote group of Yanomamo to live with them and learn their lifeways. The book was a commercial success. On the cover of the paperback, Carlos Castañeda hails it as "at once art, magic and superb social science"; a Queens College anthropologist calls it "a rare and beautiful book . . . [that] illuminates the world of the Yanomamo Indians [and] conveys a sense of the mystery and power still to be found in ritual"; *Newsweek* praises it for going "way beyond anthropological questions and categories into the far reaches of a fascinating alien culture."

Controversy about *Shabono* broke out when the September 1983 issue of the *American Anthropologist* published a comment accusing Donner of plagiarism and fraud. "Frankly," said reviewer Rebecca De Holmes, "I find it hard to believe that Donner spent any length of time with the Yanomamo".

Donner's ethnographic data, she suggests, were "rather expertly borrowed from other sources and assembled in a kind of melange of fact and fantasy for which Castañeda is so famous" (De Holmes 1983, 665). De Holmes's most serious accusation is that much of Donner's borrowing was outright pla-giarism from another remarkable book, a modern captivity narrative called *Yanoáma: The Narrative of a White Girl Kidnapped by Amazonian Indians*, which appeared in Italian in 1965 and in English translation in 1969 (Biocca and Valero 1969). This book, whose authenticity is not in doubt, presents the life story of a Brazilian, Helena Valero, who lived from childhood to adult-hood with a group of Yanomamo who kept her following an attack on her family.[1]

De Holmes supported her charge of plagiarism with a series of sample passages from the two books and a sizable list of what she called "parallel accounts of the same events, plus similar or identical time sequences" (666). The anthropologists with whom I spoke had found this evidence immedi-ately convincing. They agreed with De Holmes that Donner's book must be a fabrication and that Donner had probably never lived with the Yanomamo.

As a literary scholar, I was surprised both by how quickly people rushed to this extreme conclusion and by how schematic the terms were in which the issue was discussed. Donner's book, anthropologists felt, was either true or false, meaning, apparently, that she had either lived with the Yanomamo or had not, and nothing more was at issue. I was also a little suspicious of their eagerness to settle the matter quickly and at Donner's expense, even though many anthropologists had apparently read and appreciated Don-ner's book and found it credible. *Shabono*, it looked to me, was being "killed by science," in Malinowski's words, without much in the way of a trial. The case threatened some delicate disciplinary boundaries. Most pointedly, it brought to the surface the anguished, messy tangle of contradictions and uncertainties surrounding the interrelations of personal experience, per-sonal narrative, scientism, and professionalism in ethnographic writing. By way of explanation, let me develop the example a little further.

To a nonanthropologist, one of the most interesting puzzles in the debate on *Shabono* was that the book's factual accuracy did not seem to be in ques-tion. De Holmes's meticulous scrutiny had produced only a single ethno-graphic error in three hundred pages (a reference to running between *rows* of manioc; the Yanomamo do not plant in rows). It was accepted implicitly that given enough secondary material, one could, in fact, construct a vivid, con-vincing, ethnographically accurate account of life in another culture *without personal experience in the field.* Why, I wondered, would ethnographers be so willing to concede such a thing? And if it were so, exactly what sort of damage would Donner's (alleged) deception cause?

What was at issue was not ethnographic accuracy but a set of problematic links among ethnographic authority, personal experience, scientism, and originality of expression. If Donner really did live with the Yanomamo, why would her text so resemble Valero's? But by the standards of ethnography, the opposite question also arises: How could her account *not* resemble Valero's if they are both accurately describing the same people? The allegedly plagiarized passages De Holmes cites are indeed very similar to Valero's text, though never exact repetitions. The first five instances listed include (a) a Nabrushi club fight between men, (b) women's fishing techniques, (c) a girl's coming-of-age confinement and subsequent presentation to the group as a woman, (d) preparation of curare and testing on a monkey, and (e) an invitation to a feast (De Holmes 1983, 665). Of these, one describes a generalized practice (fishing techniques), and the other four are rituals—events anthropologists have always specialized in treating as codifiable, repeatable forms. If Donner's account of these rituals had *not* coincided in detail with Valero's, she could also be suspected of deception. But what was being argued was the exact opposite.

In the end, for De Holmes, the authority of the ethnographic text derived directly from the writer's personal experience, in turn confirmed by originality of expression: "If Donner's *Shabono is* to be called 'superb social science,' as Castañeda claims, it must be shown that the ethnographic data on which she bases her story was actually gathered personally by her while living among the Yanomama and not rewritten from previously published works" (667).

By contrast, for Debra Picchi, who reviewed the book in the same journal, *Shabono's* failure to be science arises rather from its "narcissistic focus" on Donner's "personal growth in the field." "To confine anthropology to the personal experiences of specific anthropologists is to deny its status as a social science" and "renders the discipline trivial and inconsequential" (Picchi 1983, 674). Donner fails to display what for Picchi is the distinguishing characteristic of anthropology's project, namely, a "commitment to the documentation of relationships between behavioral variables on a cross-cultural basis" (674). For Picchi, the idea of borrowing from other sources is not the problem. Since Donner rejected formal field methods, destroying her notebooks early in the game, "one assumes," Picchi says, "that the standard anthropological information included in the book is the result of the reconstruction from memory or research of the now extensive literature on the Yanomamo Indians" (675). Picchi takes the book to be a bona fide "ethnography of the Yanomamo Indians . . . based on 12 months of fieldwork" (675) and recommends it to teachers of introductory anthropology.

What happens here to Donner's fairly explicit claims *not* to be writing a work of anthropology or social science? How did her claims become irrelevant to this discussion? What placed her personal narrative within anthropology's purview? And once there, why was there such confusion about how it should be evaluated?

For some reason, it all made me think of a minor being dragged into a bar in order to be thrown out and turned over to the police—that'll teach her. So "disciplining" is often done, if not in bars, then certainly in academies. What Donner clearly did was use her anthropological training to write an infuriatingly ambiguous book, which may or may not be "true," is and is not ethnography, is and is not an autobiography, does and does not claim professional and academic authority, is and is not based on fieldwork, and so on. An ungrateful apprentice can do no worse. If Donner did fabricate much of her story (as she may have), she has disgraced the profession by lying, and lying so well no one could tell. If she did not fabricate her story, she scored one of the anthropological scoops of the century. For her experience, as she recounts it, is, in many respects, an ethnographer's dream. She is *invited* by the group to study their lifeways; instead of sessions in which she interviews them, it is they who sit down to teach her. She is spared the anguish and guilt of paying her way by distributing Western goods; the group has chosen to stay so remote that it is a near-first encounter. To realize this ethnographer's dream and then to refuse to convert it into the currency of the discipline that made it all possible, this indeed might seem a monumental betrayal.

I have dwelt on the case of *Shabono* because it illustrates some of the confusion and ambiguity that personal narrative, not having been killed by science, raises in the discursive space of ethnography. Personal accounts of field experience are not unknown within academic anthropology. Indeed, they form a recognizable anthropological subgenre, but they are always paired with a formal ethnography, the book Donner did not write. Famous examples include David Maybury-Lewis's *The Savage and the Innocent* (1965), following his *Akwē-Shavante Society* (1967); Jean-Paul Dumont's *Under the Rainbow* (1976) and *The Headman and I* (1978); Napoleon Chagnon's *Yanomamo: The Fierce People* (1968) and *Studying the Yanomamo* (1974); and Paul Rabinow's *Symbolic Domination: Cultural Form and Historical Change in Morocco* (1975) and *Reflections on Fieldwork in Morocco* (1977). Earlier examples include the writings of Clyde Kluckhohn and Roy Franklin Barton. This personal subgenre is also the conventional space into which Malinowski's diaries were published. Of these pairs of books, the formal ethnography counts as professional capital and authoritative representation; the personal narratives are often deemed self-indulgent, trivial, or heretical in other ways. Despite such disciplining, they have kept appearing, kept being read, and above all kept being taught within the borders of the discipline, for what one must assume are powerful reasons.

Even in the absence of a separate autobiographical volume, personal narrative is a conventional component of ethnographies. It turns up almost invariably, for example, in introductions or first chapters, where opening narratives commonly recount the writer's arrival at the field site and the initial reception by the inhabitants, then reviews the slow, agonizing process of learning the language and overcoming rejection; the anguish and loss at leaving. These conventional opening narratives are not trivial. They play the crucial role of anchoring that ethnographic description in the authority-giving experience of fieldwork. They often turn out to be the most memorable segments of an ethnographic work—nobody forgets the frustration-ridden introduction to Evans-Pritchard's *The Nuer* (1940). Opening narratives are responsible for setting up the initial positionings of the participants in the ethnographic enterprise: the ethnographer, the natives, and the reader.

I think personal narrative persists alongside objectifying description in ethnographic writing because it mediates a contradiction within the discipline between personal and scientific authority, one that has become especially acute since the advent of fieldwork as a methodological norm. James Clifford refers to "the discipline's impossible attempt to fuse objective and subjective practices" (1986, 109). Fieldwork produces an authority anchored to a large extent in subjective, embodied experience. One experiences the indigenous environment and lifeways for oneself, sees with one's own eyes, and participates in the daily life of the community. But the expert text resulting from such an encounter is supposed to conform to scientific norms where authority resides in the absolute effacement of the speaking and experiencing subject and the potential replicability of results.

In terms of its own metaphors, the scientific position of speech is that of an observer fixed on the edge of a space, looking in and/or down on what is other. Subjective experience, in contrast, is spoken from a moving position already inside or down in the middle of things, looking and being looked at, talking and being talked at. The terms *observational* and *experiential* also capture the contrast. To convert fieldwork, through the mediation of field notes, into formal ethnography requires a tremendously difficult shift from the latter to the former. Much must be left behind in the process. Johannes Fabian characterizes the temporal aspect of this contradiction when he speaks of "an aporetic split between recognition of coevalness in some ethnographic research and denial of coevalness in most anthropological theorizing and writing" (1983, 36). There are strong reasons why field ethnographers so often lament that their ethnographic writings leave out or hopelessly impoverish some of the most important knowledge they have achieved (including self-knowledge). The main evidence of a problem is the fact that ethnographic writing tends to be so dry and boring. How, one asks constantly, could such interesting people doing such interesting things produce such dull books? What did they have to do to themselves? In the preface to *Argonauts*, Malinowski describes the process as an arduous journey: "In Ethnography the distance is often enormous between the brute material of information ... and the final authoritative presentation of the results. The Ethnographer has to traverse this distance in the laborious years between the moment when he sets foot upon a native beach ... and the time where he writes down the final version of his results" ([1922] 1961, ii).

Personal narrative mitigates this contradiction between the embodied engagement called for in fieldwork and the self-effacement called for in formal ethnographic description. It recuperates at least a few shreds of what was exorcised in the conversion from the face-to-face field encounter to objectified description. As it turns out, though, this discursive division of labor has a long history.

Ancestral Ethnography

The practice of distinguishing between personal narrative and objectified description, and switching between them, is not the invention of modern ethnography. It has a long history in those kinds of writing from which ethnography has traditionally distinguished itself. By the early sixteenth century, it was conventional for European travel accounts to consist of a juxtaposition of first-person narration, recounting one's trip, and descriptions of the flora and fauna of regions passed through and the manners and customs of the inhabitants. These two discourses were quite clearly distinguished in travel books, with narrative predominating over description. The descriptive portions were sometimes seen as dumping grounds for surplus data that could not be fitted into the narrative.

To give a classic example, a book called *The Captivity of Hans Stade of Hesse in* A.D. *1547–1555 among the Wild Tribes of Eastern Brazil*, first published in Germany in 1557, achieved a wide readership in sixteenth- and seventeenth-century Europe, not least because it dealt with cannibalism, a topic of heated debate at the time (Staden [1557] 2008). Staden's remarkably vivid account is divided into two parts. The first, some hundred pages long, recounts his captivity among the Tupi Nambas, and the second, some fifty pages long, offers a "veritable and short account of all the by me experienced manners and customs of the Tuppin-Imbas, whose prisoner I was" (117). Staden's descriptive agenda in the second section has much in common with modern ethnography, including chapters on "what their dwellings are like," "how they make fire," "the places wherein they sleep," "how skillful they are in shooting wild animals and fish with arrows," "how they cook their food," "what kind of regimen and order they have in government and laws," "what they believe in," "how many wives each of them has, and how he manages them," "how they are betrothed," "how they make their beverages wherewith they drink themselves drunk, and how they order their drinking," and so forth. Indeed Staden's descriptions truly resemble those of modern ethnography in their specificity, their search for neutrality and evenhandedness, and their linkage of social and material orders. Here is his description of a house, where spatial organization is seen as determined by social relations:

> They prefer erecting their dwellings in spots where they are not far from wood and water, nor from game and fish. After they have destroyed all in one district, they migrate to other places; and when they want to build their huts, a chief among them assembles a party of men and women (some forty couples), or as many as he can get, and these live together as friends and relations.
>
> They build a kind of hut, which is about fourteen feet wide, and perhaps a hundred and fifty feet long, according to their number. The tenements are about two fathoms high, and round at the top like a vaulted cellar, they thatch them thickly with palm leaves, so that it may not rain therein, and the hut is all open inside. No one has his specially-prepared chamber; each couple, man and woman, has a space of twelve feet on one side; whilst on the other, in the same manner, lives another pair. Thus their huts are full, and each couple has its own fire. The chief of the huts has also his lodging within the dwelling. They all have commonly three entrances, one on each side, and one in the middle; these are low, so that they must stoop when they go in and out. Few of their villages have more than seven huts. (125)

I use this sixteenth-century example to underscore that the discursive division of labor I am talking about, between experiential and objectivist discourse, is not the product of an erudite tradition nor of the rise of modern science, despite its continued existence in contemporary ethnography. Staden was a ship's gunner with little formal education, and his book was a popular vernacular publication. It predates the rise of natural history in the eighteenth century by over two hundred years.

Even further back in the annals of travel writing, one finds that objectivist description is older than personal narrative. Two other popular classics, Marco Polo's *Travels* (1298) and *The Travels of John Mandeville* (late 1300s), are written almost entirely in descriptive mode with no first-person voice. Storytelling is completely absent. In other words, the most direct antecedent for scientific ethnography appears to be the descriptions of manners, customs, places, and flora and fauna that have been a staple of popular European travel writing for a good seven centuries.

In some instances in travel writing, description is found enmeshed in narrative, as illustrated by this excerpt from another travel classic, Mungo Park's *Travels in the Interior Districts of Africa* ([1799] 1860):

> We stopped a little at a village called Dangali; and in the evening arrived at Dalli. We saw upon the road two large herds of camels feeding. When the Moors turn their camels to feed, they tie up one of their fore legs, to prevent their straying. . . . The people were dancing before the Dooty's house. But when they were informed that a white man was come into the town, they left off dancing and came to the place where I lodged, walking in regular order, two and two, with the music before them. They play upon a sort of flute; but instead of blowing into a hole in the side, they blow obliquely over the end. (46)

Though interwoven, particularized narrative and generalized description remain distinguishable here, and shifts from one to the other are clear, the most conspicuous signs being, of course, the shift from past tense to present tense and from specific persons to tribal labels. (As I illustrate below, this configuration turns up in the work of Malinowski and Raymond Firth.)

In its various guises, the narration-description duality has remained remarkably stable in modern travel writing right down to the present, as has the conventional ordering—narration first, description second, or narration superordinate, description subordinate. By the late nineteenth century, however, the two modes often had about equal weight in travel books, and it became common for a trip to result in two separate volumes, such as Mary Kingsley's masterpiece *Travels in West Africa* (1897) and *West African Studies* (1899). Richard Burton's *The Lake Regions of Central Africa* ([1868] 1961) alternates chapters of narration with chapters describing the "geography and ethnology" of each region passed through.

Modern ethnography obviously lies in direct continuity with this tradition, despite the disciplinary boundary by which it separates itself off from travel writing. It is no surprise to find that the conventional opening narratives in ethnographies display clear continuities with travel writing. For instance, Raymond Firth, in his classic *We, the Tikopia* (1936), introduces himself via the trope of the Polynesian arrival scene, which became a commonplace in the literature of the South Sea explorations of James Cook, Louis Antoine de Bougainville, and others in the 1760s and 1770s. Firth's is a memorable passage, to which Clifford Geertz (1983c) also turned his attention:

> In the cool of the early morning, just before sunrise, the bow of the Southern Cross headed towards the eastern horizon, on which a tiny dark blue outline was faintly visible. Slowly it grew into a rugged mountain mass, standing up sheer from the ocean. . . . In an hour or so we were close inshore, and could see canoes coming round from the south, outside the reef, on which the tide was low. The outrigger-fitted craft drew near, the men in them bare to the waist, girdled with bark-cloth, large fans stuck in the backs of their belts, tortoise-shell rings or rolls of leaf in the earlobes and nose, bearded, and with long hair flowing loosely over their shoulders. Some plied the rough heavy paddles, some had finely plaited pandanus-leaf mats resting on the thwarts beside them, some had large clubs or spears in their hands. The ship anchored on a short cable in the open bay off the coral reef. Almost before the chain was down the natives began to scramble aboard, coming over the side by any means that offered, shouting fiercely to each other and to us in a tongue of which not a word was understood by the Mota-speaking folk of the mission vessel. I wondered how such turbulent human material could ever be induced to submit to scientific study.

Finally the visitors are able to come ashore, and a familiar ritual follows:

> At last the long wade ended, we climbed up the steeply shelving beach, crossed the soft, dry sand strewn with the brown needles of the Casuarina trees—a home-like touch; it was like a pine avenue—and were led to an old chief clad with great dignity in a white coat and a loin-cloth, who awaited us on his stool under a large shady tree. (Firth 1936, 1–2)

Firth reproduces in a remarkably straightforward way a utopian scene of first contact that acquired mythic status in the eighteenth century and continues with us today in the popular mythology of South Sea tourism. Far from being taken for suspicious aliens, the European visitors are welcomed like royalty by a trusting populace and taken to meet their leader. For instance, compare Bougainville's arrival in Tahiti in 1767:

> We run with all sails set towards the land, standing to windward of this bay, when we perceived a pariagua coming from the offing, and standing for the land, and making use of her sail and paddles. She passed athwart us, and joined a number of others, which sailed ahead of us, from all parts of the island. One of them went before all the rest; it was manned by twelve naked men, who presented us with branches of bananas; and their demonstrations signified that this was their olive branch. We answered them with all the signs of friendship we could imagine; and they then came along side of our ship, and one of them, remarkable for his prodigious growth of hair, which stood like bristles divergent on his head, offered us, together with his branch of peace, a little pig, and a cluster of bananas. . . .
>
> The two ships were soon surrounded with more than an hundred periaguas of different sizes, all which had outriggers. They were laden with cocoa-nuts, bananas, and other fruits of the country. The exchange of these fruits, which were delicious to us, was made very honestly for all sorts of trifles. (Bougainville [1771] 1967, 213)

Bougainville has a lot more trouble than Firth getting his ship anchored, but once he does, the same script resumes:

> When we were moored, I went on shore with several officers, to survey the watering-place. An immense crowd of men and women received us there, and could not be tired with looking at us; the boldest came to touch us; they even pushed aside our clothes with their hands, in order to see whether we were made exactly like them: none of them wore any arms, not so much as a stick. They sufficiently expressed their joy at our arrival. The chief of this district conducted and introduced us into his house, in which we found five or six women, and a venerable old man. (220)

The similarities between the two scenes are obvious, and there are some interesting differences too. Bougainville's version of the arrival scene uses one trope Firth does not reproduce, the scene in which the natives try to undress the foreigners to establish their humanity and symbolically level the difference between them. Firth stays dressed, like the king he is about to meet. Bougainville carefully mentions the material relationship immediately established between the Europeans and the natives, an exchange of gifts whose spontaneous equality he stresses. In Firth, this opening exchange is present but dematerialized, an exchange of "smiles, in lieu of anything more intelligible or tangible at the moment" (1936, 5), leaving it unclear (as ethnographers do) what his material relation to these people is going to be. At the same time, Firth demystifies the utopian egalitarianism of the trope with his ironic question about how all this "human material could ever be induced to submit to scientific study." Indeed, his irony here lightly marks the royal arrival trope as a trope and as part of a language of conquest. Firth tacitly acknowledges that his own project is also an assertion of domination. Firth's opening self-presentation suggests the unfolding story of his ethnographic monopoly on Tikopia and its inhabitants (Firth 1936 1).

Malinowski in *Argonauts of the Western Pacific* ([1922] 1961) deploys a different trope, also from the annals of travel writing. His opening narrative, a "brief outline of an Ethnographer's tribulations," opens with the now-famous line: "Imagine yourself suddenly set down surrounded by your gear, alone on a tropical beach close to a native village while the launch or dinghy which has brought you sails away out of sight" (4). This is unmistakably the image of an old-fashioned castaway. That it turns up here is especially apt since it corresponds to Malinowski's own situation at the time. An Austrian citizen living in Australia, he had been sent to sit out World War I in the Trobriand Islands rather than risk reprisals or deportation.

There are many reasons the castaway is an evocative and utopian self-image for the ethnographer. For one thing, a direct historical connection joins them. In the Spanish Empire, the first fieldworkers were castaways. In the early phases of contact, the Spanish Crown developed a practice of offering convicts their freedom in exchange for agreeing to be left ashore somewhere in the Americas to make contact with local populations and learn their languages and lifeways. Two years later, if they survived, they would be picked up and given work as interpreters and cultural mediators.[2]

We may prefer not to dwell on the image of the convict. There are other ways in which, as the figures of Valero, Donner, and Staden suggest, castaways and captives realize the ideal of the participant-observer. The authority of the ethnographer over the "mere traveler" rests chiefly on the idea that the traveler just passes through, whereas the ethnographer lives with the group under study and learns the language, as captives and castaways also do. In some aspects, the experience of captivity resonates a lot with the experience of fieldwork—the sense of dependency, the lack of control, the vulnerability to being both isolated completely and never left alone. Then again, castaway and ethnographer differ fundamentally in their material relation to the Indigenous host. Castaways take up a place within the host social and economic organization; that is how they survive—if, indeed, they do, for captivity is a higher-risk business than grant-funded fieldwork. Anthropologists customarily establish a relationship of exchange with the group based on Western commodities or cash. That is how they survive and try to make their relations with informants nonexploitive. But of course, such strategies are enormously problematic, for they make anthropologists constant contributors to what they themselves regard as damage to their object of study. The captive or castaway, by contrast, is innocent, and one can see why it would be a compelling image to the contradiction-ridden ethnographer. We should note, however, that actually going native, as captives often do, is taboo among anthropologists.

Firth and Malinowski, in their opening anecdotes, both invoke well-established images from travel literature to situate the ethnographer. The bodies of both their ethnographies deploy narrative and descriptive discourse, as travel writing does. Both writers move freely and fluidly between the two, introducing anecdotes constantly to illustrate or elaborate on the ethnographic generalizations. In a way somewhat reminiscent of Mungo Park's text cited above, Firth is full of complex passages like this one, where ethnographic generalizations, eyewitness anecdotes, and personal irony interweave:

> Relatives by marriage do occasionally get in sly digs at each other without absolutely transgressing the bounds of good manners. Pa Ranifuri told me with great glee of how the Ariki Taumako spoke to him of his classificatory son-in-law Pa-Panisi as *"Matua i te sosipani"*—*sosipani* being the native pronunciation *of saucepan*, of which sooty vessel this man was as far as I recollect the only possessor in the island. As a dark-skinned foreigner he was slightly sneered at (behind his back) by the Tikopia. Scolding, I was told, though not permitted by convention directly, may take place at a distance. (1936, 274)

What Firth and his teacher Malinowski seem to be after is a kind of summa, a highly textured, totalizing picture anchored in an ethnographic self, where self is understood not as a monolithic scientist-observer but as a multifaceted entity who participates, observes, and writes from multiple, constantly shifting positions. Such are the reflective capacities of this versatile, larger-than-life subject that it can absorb and transmit the richness of a whole culture.[3] In this subject is also anchored the heady optimism both Firth and Malinowski convey about the ethnographic enterprise. There is a significant irony in the fact that the speaking subject in the work of these founders of scientific ethnography, as Malinowski called it, is anything but the self-effaced, passive subject of scientific discourse.

The richly perceptive, but terribly unsystematic, textual being that is the ethnographer in Malinowski and Firth contrasts sharply with the frustrated and depressed figure that appears in some subsequent classic ethnographies, such as those of Edward Evans-Pritchard and David Maybury-Lewis. If Firth shows up as a benevolent eighteenth-century scientist-king, Evans-Pritchard comes onstage in the later guise of the gruff Victorian explorer-adventurer who exposes himself to all sorts of dangers and discomforts in the name of a higher (national) mission. In his famed opening description of field conditions in *The Nuer* (1940), Evans-Pritchard joins a century-long line of grumpy British explorers who lose their supplies and cannot control their bearers. His initial self-representation reads thus:

> I arrived in Nuerland early in 1930. Stormy weather prevented my luggage from joining me at Marseilles, and owing to errors, for which I was not responsible, my food stores were not forwarded from Malakal, and my Zande servants were not instructed to meet me. I proceeded to Nuerland (Leek country) with my tent, some equipment, and a few stores bought at Malakal, and two servants, an Atwot and a Bellanda, picked up hastily at the same place.
>
> When I landed at Yoahuang on the Bahr el Ghazal the Catholic missionaries there showed me much kindness. I waited for nine days on the river bank for the carriers I had been promised. By the tenth day only four of them had arrived. . . . On the following morning I set out for the neighbouring village of Pakur, where my carriers dropped tent and stores in the centre of a treeless plain, near some homesteads, and refused to bear them to the shade about half a mile further. Next day was devoted to erecting my tent and trying to persuade the Nuer . . . to remove my abode to the vicinity of shade and water, which they refused to do. (5)

Such episodes are a commonplace of the African travel and exploration writers of the nineteenth century. Here, for instance, is the eternally cranky Sir Richard Burton, whose expedition recounted in *The Lake Regions of Central Africa* ([1868] 1961) is given much the same inauspicious beginning:

> We were delayed ten days off Wale Point by various preliminaries to departure. Said bin Salim, a half-caste Arab of Zanzibar, who, sorely against his will, was ordered by the prince to act as Ras Kafilah, or caravan-guide, had, after ceaseless and fruitless prayers for delay, preceded us about a fortnight,

for the purpose of collecting porters. . . . He had crossed over, on the 1st of June, to the mainland, and had hired a gang of porters, who, however, hearing that their employer was a Muzungu, "white man", at once dispersed, forgetting to return their hire. About one hundred and seventy men were required; only thirty-six were procurable. . . . It was necessary to leave behind, till a full gang of porters could be engaged, the greater part of the ammunition, the iron boat which had proved so useful on the coasting voyage to Mombasah, and the reserve supply of cloth, wire and beads, valued at 359 dollars. The Hindus promised faithfully to forward these articles. . . . Nearly eleven months, however, elapsed before they appeared. (12)

And so it goes, over and over, till Burton's narrative, like Evans-Pritchard's introduction, reads like one long, frustrating master-servant feud. Evans-Pritchard's choice of this persona is not haphazard. An old military memoir by Evans-Pritchard, brilliantly analyzed by Geertz (1983a), connects Evans-Pritchard directly with the tradition of African colonial exploration and writing.

With respect to discursive conventions, Evans-Pritchard's arrival scene must also be thought of as a hugely degraded version of the utopian arrival found in Bougainville and Firth. He lands in a fallen world where European colonialism is a given, and native and white man approach each other with joyless suspicion. Maybury-Lewis gives a similarly degraded version of the scene in *Akwẽ-Shavante Society* (1967). Here the newcomer does find help with his luggage, but the chief who awaits him is not regal, the opening gift-giving not reciprocal: "A number of Shavante from the village had come to the airstrip when our plane landed and helped to carry our baggage to the post. They set it down at the feet of an elderly man, who we discovered was the chief of the village. He clearly expected us to open the trunks then and there and distribute their contents" (xxiii).

The problem, it turns out, is contamination from outside. The Shavante have been spoiled by Brazilian army officers who fly in to see them as a curiosity and bring "elaborate gifts." Like Evans-Pritchard (his teacher), Maybury-Lewis complains at length about his informants' hostility and uncooperativeness, their refusal to talk to him in private, their refusal to leave him alone, his problems with the language, and so on.

In both these anti-utopian instances, the opening scene, written after the fact, is given by way of explaining the limitations on the ethnographer's ability to carry out his scientific mission. Paradoxically enough, the conditions of fieldwork are expressed as an impediment to the task of doing fieldwork, rather than as part of what is to be understood. The contrast with the upbeat tone of Firth and Malinowski is obvious. Evans-Pritchard and Maybury-Lewis are the heirs of the scientific, professional ethnography Malinowski invented. The scientific ideal seems to press on them acutely, calling for a codified field methodology, professional detachment, and a systematic write-up. Whatever about the other culture impedes these tasks is an obstacle to ethnography, as well as an ethnographic fact. Both writers complain, for instance, about the impossibility of having private conversations with informants, as if private conversation ought to be culturally possible everywhere. As methodology gets increasingly codified, the clash between "objective and subjective practices" becomes increasingly acute.

In Evans-Pritchard's case, the difficulties translate into a rigid separation between personal narrative (his long and vivid introduction) and impersonal description (the rest of the account). Gone is the continually shifting voice of Firth or Malinowski, and gone is the sense of authority. Evans-Pritchard strives for a totalizing picture of the Nuer, centered on cattle, but feels he must emphasize the limitations on his capacities and his achievement. Maybury-Lewis's response, in turn, fills his ethnographic book with personal narrative and suggests that "it is time we abandoned the mystique which surrounds fieldwork and made it conventional to describe in some detail the circumstances of data-collecting" (1967, xx).

Each of these opening narrative self-portraits (Malinowski, Firth, Evans-Pritchard, Maybury-Lewis) comes straight out of the tropology of travel and exploration writing. Even more precisely, they often come out of the specific tradition of writing on the region in which the ethnographer is working (central Africa, the South Pacific). Each offers an emblematic self-portrait that functions as a prelude to, and commentary on, what follows. One of their tasks is to position the reader with respect to the formal description. In this respect, they are not trivial. Often such passages undertake to problematize the reader's position, as they do in Evans-Pritchard and Maybury-Lewis. The ethnographer's trials in working to know another people now become the reader's trials in making sense of the text.

In all the examples I have discussed, the sheer inexplicability and unjustifiability of the ethnographer's presence from the standpoint of the other remain unnamed. Equally unmentioned is the overall context of empire in which the ethnographer, regardless of his or her own attitudes to it, is caught up. This relationship is one of the great silences in the midst of ethnographic description itself. It is the silence that shapes the traditional ethnographic project of trying to describe the culture as it was before Western intervention.

Reinventing Ethnography

I have been making a loose generational argument here and propose to end up with one final example from a more recent generation of ethnographers. Marjorie Shostak's *Nisa: The Life and Words of a !Kung Woman* (1981) was widely admired as one of the more successful experiments in revolutionizing ethnographic writing. Shostak was a late participant in the long-standing Harvard Kalahari Project, founded in 1963 by Richard Lee and Irven DeVore to study the hunter-gatherer societies of the Kalahari Desert in southern Africa. Her ethnography undertakes to capture the life of a !Kung woman using her own words and tracking the developing relationship between Nisa and the ethnographer. The arrival trope is only one of many conventions of ethnographic writing that Shostak upends in her text. The introduction to *Nisa* gives two versions of the conventional arrival scene, one impersonal and one personal. Here is the first:

> Walking into a traditional !Kung village, a visitor would be struck by how fragile it seemed beneath the expanse of sky and how unobtrusively it stood amid the tall grass and sparse tree growth of the surrounding bush. . . . A visitor who arrived in the middle of the cold season—June and July—and just at sunrise would see mounds of blankets and animal skins in front of the huts, covering people still asleep beside their fires. Those who had already awakened would be stoking the coals, rebuilding the fire, and warming themselves in the chilly morning air. . . . A visitor on another morning, in the hot, dry months of October and November, would find people moving about, even at dawn, up early to do a few hours of gathering or hunting before the midday heat would force them to rest in the thickest shade. (7–8)

As with Firth, this hypothetical arrival is at dawn—new day, new place. In a slightly different way, it presents an ethnographic utopia: here is a traditional society doing its traditional thing, oblivious to the alien observing presence. Unlike the other examples considered above, this one is hypothetical and normalized. It represents what "a visitor (not an anthropologist) would experience if . . ." The status of this fantasy is made apparent several pages later when Shostak recounts at great length her own arrival experience, the night she meets Nisa:

> By the time we arrived at Gausha, from Goshi, where we had our main camp, it had long since been dark. We drove the Land Rover past one

!Kung village and stopped at a deserted village site farther down the road. The full moon, high in the sky, appeared small and gave off a cold light. . . . Kxoma and Tuma, two !Kung men traveling with us, suggested we make our camp at this site where Richard Lee and Nancy Howell, other anthropologists, had set their camp four years earlier. Living where someone had lived before was right, they said: it connected you to the past. The slender stick shell of Richard and Nancy's hut was still there. It stood out in the moonlight, a bizarre skeleton set apart from the surrounding bush . . . a traditional !Kung frame. The grass had long since been taken and used in Nisa's village. As it stood, the hut offered no protection from the weather, nor any privacy. (23)

To begin with, this is a nocturnal arrival, relatively rare in both travel writing and ethnography. For the arriving anthropologist, this is the land of the dead—the moon is small and cold; inexplicably, they take themselves past the living village to a deserted one and set themselves up in the skeleton of a hut. Shostak's symbolism contrasts sharply with the !Kung's understanding of what they are doing. For the !Kung guides, the link with the past is a haven. Shostak and her companion are haunted by the ghosts of their anthropological predecessors.

There is no spontaneous native welcome in Shostak's account, but unlike both Firth and Evans-Pritchard, these anthropologists do not want or need one: "It was too late for visiting. They knew us by then; we would still be there in the morning." They unpack by themselves, haunted by the past ("I thought of the time Nancy had found a puff adder in her sleeping bag"). Shostak is thwarting even the pretense of a first encounter. Shostak has come at the end of a long chain of anthropologists. This point gets woefully dramatized when the native welcomers belatedly appear after the luggage work is done and the party is ready for bed: "Nisa wore an old blanket loosely draped over the remnants of a faded, flower-print dress, sizes too big. Bo was wearing a pair of shorts, even the patches of which were worn through in places." There they are, in European clothes they have obviously been wearing for a long time. Instead of giving a welcome speech, Nisa sings the praises of their predecessors. "Richard and Nancy! I really liked them! They liked us too—they gave us beautiful presents and took us everywhere with them. Bo and I worked hard for them. . . . Oh how I wish they were here!" (24–25).

It is an awful scene and a literary tour de force. It lands the reader in a carefully deidealized world. The supposedly primitive others are fallen, corrupted not only as non-Europeans but specifically as ethnographic informants. Bo and Nisa arrive praising the guilty relationship of exchange based on Western commodities, the point at which the anthropologist preserver-of-the-culture is the interventionist corrupter-of-the-culture. The naive informant has turned hustler. In short, Shostak's arrival scene contemplates, painfully and in the dark of night, the aftermath of the ethnographic episode: Indigenous people who, specifically through the ethnographic contact, have acquired a vested interest in westernization and a concrete day-to-day link with the larger structures of exploitation. It is like a bad dream, and Shostak's reaction, as she describes it, is to try to pretend it is not happening and wait for a more standard arrival scene in the morning, complete with the ritual exchange of goods: "That was when we would give [tobacco] to the rest of the !Kung with whom we planned to work" (25).

After long resistance, as she tells it, Shostak ultimately capitulates to this degraded anthropological world and consents to be hustled/seduced by Nisa. Then and only then does she find a fieldwork relationship that is, in fact, enormously productive for ethnographic purposes. Nisa is advertising a genuine talent for storytelling and for reflecting on her own culture and experience. She is a really good informant, and she knows it.[4]

Out of that encounter, Shostak produces a text that dramatically reconfigures the balance between personal narrative and impersonal description laid down by classical ethnography. Personal narrative forms the backbone of Shostak's book but not her text. There, Nisa's voice prevails, edited by Shostak into a life story. Ethnographic generalizing and analysis appear as introductory commentary to each section of Nisa's narrative. The book begins and ends with Shostak's personal story. *Nisa* not only alters the proportions of narration and description but breaks with the latter's monopoly on ethnographic knowledge and authority and proposes a different processing of fieldwork into ethnography. In *Nisa*, the ethnographic interview is processed into an individualized life story of a particularly effective informant, rather than into generalizing description. *Nisa* deploys both of these as valid forms of ethnographic knowledge. In expanding the account of her field experience beyond the customary arrival scene, Shostak proposes a different, though probably no less laborious, way of "traversing the distance," as Malinowski put it ([1922] 1961, 1), from fieldwork to "results," one that instead of transcending the embodied experience of fieldwork declares it a source of knowledge. The terrain of mediation here is the amorphous, polyphonous interaction between ethnographer and informant as it evolves in the deepening relation between them.

Gender has everything to do with Shostak's intervention. The refusal of repression, the foregrounding of women as subjects and agents, the legitimation of personal and embodied experience, the recognition of gender neutrality as androcentrism—all are fundamentals of feminism's epistemic revolution. That revolution profoundly altered the landscape of ethnographic writing in the 1980s and 1990s. Ethnography became less unified and more polyphonous. Totality and synthesis were no longer its ideals.[5]

A utopian element persists, however, for the polyphony Shostak creates is strikingly harmonious. One finds little evidence of struggle among the various voices, despite Shostak's awareness of the intolerable contradictoriness of her position. Conceptions of female solidarity and intimacy seem to be at work, celebrating the bonds between them that transcend culture. To Shostak's credit, the last lines of the book challenge that harmony. Nisa's final words to Shostak are, "My niece . . . my niece . . . you are someone who truly thinks about me." Shostak's are, "I will always think of her and I hope she will think of me, as a distant sister" (Shostak 1981, 371). Each assigns the other a different honorary kinship.

In the darkness that shrouds Shostak's arrival scene, readers may recognize the symbolism of guilt. In part, there is guilt linked to the particularities of Shostak's situation as one of a series of anthropologists working among the !Kung. And, in part, it is guilt that comes down to her from much farther in the past. As with the other examples I have discussed, Shostak's text, and those of her colleagues in the Harvard Kalahari Project, has direct continuities with three long centuries of writing about the !Kung. Again, this is an amateur tradition from which the Harvard anthropologists energetically dissociated themselves (most explicitly by replacing the colonial name for the group, the Bushmen). That tradition documents a long and violent history of persecution, enslavement, and extermination visited on the !Kung as southern Africa was colonized. The contemporary !Kung are survivors of that history; the anthropologists are heirs to its guilt. A few details will illuminate this point.

At the end of the eighteenth century, the Bushmen start turning up in European accounts as objects of (a) ethnographic interest and (b) pathos and guilt. Not surprisingly, this was also the point at which this people definitively lost their struggle against European encroachment on their land and lifeways. Since the seventeenth century, they had existed in European writings as hordes of wild, bloodthirsty marauders fiercely resisting the advancing colonists, raiding their farms at night, turning loose or stealing cattle, and sometimes murdering colonists or their laborers. Given a free hand by colonial authorities, white settlers embarked on a war of extermination against them. Commandos descended on Bushman kraals, often at night, killing men and either killing or enslaving women and children. Gradually the settlers won this war. By the 1790s, "the Bushmen were still numerous along the interior mountain range, but in other parts of the colony there were hardly any left" (Theal 1964, 1:201).[6]

At this point, the discourse on the Bushmen changes, and they become objects of condescension. Late eighteenth-century travelers, like the Swede Anders Sparrman (*Voyage to the Cape of Good* Hope, [1785] 1975) and Englishman John Barrow (*Travels in the Interior of Southern Africa*, [1801] 1968), deplore the brutality of the colonists and the injustice of the extermination campaign (Pratt 1985). These writers construct a new ethnographic portrait of the Bushmen. No longer seen as militant warriors or bloodthirsty marauders, they acquire the characteristics that the powerful commonly find in those they have subjugated: meekness, innocence, passivity, indolence coupled with physical strength and stamina, cheerfulness, absence of greed or indeed desires of any kind, internal egalitarianism, a penchant for living in the present, inability to take initiative on their own behalf. Sparrman describes the Bushmen as "free from many wants and desires, that torment the rest of mankind," "detesting all manner of labour," yet easily induced into slavery by a little meat and tobacco ([1785] 1975, 198–201). Barrow finds they are "mild and manageable in the highest degree, and by gentle usage may be molded into any shape." "In his disposition," says Barrow, "[the Bushman] is lively and cheerful; in his person active. His talents are far above mediocrity. Their constitutions are much stronger, and their lives of longer duration, than those of the Hottentots"; "universal equality prevails in his horde.... [T]hey take no thought for the morrow. They have no sort of management or economy with regard to provisions" ([1801] 1968, 287). This is a portrait of a conquered people, simultaneously acknowledging the innocence and pathos of their condition. It evaluates their potential as a labor pool and legitimates their domination on the grounds that they do not know how to manage themselves.

Caught between celebrating and deploring the Bushmen's condition, Barrow expresses his guilt and anguish in a nocturnal arrival scene that has fascinating points in common with Shostak's, despite being written 180 years earlier. Barrow finds that the only way he can make contact with the terrified Bushmen is by hiring a group of Boer farmers to help him ambush a settlement at night. As with Shostak, the result is a nightmare of contradiction, a descent into hell, and one of the few episodes of personal narrative in Barrow's long book. Barrow describes the raiding party descending from the hillsides onto the sleeping camp: "Our ears were stunned with a horrid scream like the war-whoop of savages; the shrieking of women and the cries of children proceeded from every side" ([1801] 1968, 272). Despite Barrow's instructions, his Boer guides begin shooting down the fleeing people; Barrow's protests are ignored. "'Good God!' [the Boer farmer] exclaimed, 'Have you not seen a shower of arrows falling among us?' I certainly had seen neither arrows or people, but had heard enough to pierce the hardest heart" (272). Later Barrow remarks in shame that "nothing could be more unwarrantable . . . than the attack made by our party upon the kraal" (291).

This scene dramatically disrupts Barrow's highly impersonal account. It explicitly upends the utopian arrival scene and reverses the original image of the Bushman horde descending on European ranches. Its impact in Barrow's text parallels Shostak's, and the two share the same discursive history.[7] Contemporary anthropologists share more than arrival tropes with earlier writers on the Bushmen. Twentieth-century ethnographic descriptions likewise reproduce the discursive legacy, even as they openly repudiate it. Ethnographic writers continued to celebrate and naturalize in the Bushmen/!Kung many of the same characteristics singled out by Barrow, Sparrman, and the rest. Cheerfulness, humor, egalitarianism, nonviolence, disinterest in material goods, longevity, and stamina are all underscored with admiration and affection in both journalistic writings like those of Laurens van der Post (*The Lost World of the Kalahari*, 1958) and ethnographic work, from Elizabeth Marshall Thomas's *The Harmless People* (1959) to that of the writers of the Harvard Kalahari Project. Throughout this literature, the same blazing contradiction turns up between a tendency on the one hand to historicize the !Kung as survivors—victims of European imperialism—and a tendency on the other to naturalize them as primal beings virtually untouched by history. In both cases, they stand doomed to extinction.

For the Harvard Kalahari group, the !Kung were of scientific interest as a putative window on the human evolutionary past, as evidence concerning our human ancestors. Though Shostak makes a serious effort to repudiate the image of the pure primitive—she introduces Nisa clad in a dress and selling her talents on the anthropological free market—she seems to have no other way to legitimate her work. "A study revealing what !Kung women's lives were like today," she tells us, "might reflect what their lives had been like for generations, possibly even for thousands of years." "Although the !Kung were experiencing cultural change, it was still quite recent and subtle and had thus far left their traditional value system mostly intact" (6).

Recent and *subtle* are not the adjectives that come to mind when one ponders the grim history of the Bushmen/!Kung during and after colonialism. This is a history of which Shostak and her colleagues seem at times aware, at

CHAPTER TEN |

times oblivious. Repeatedly, Richard Lee and others warn that the !Kung are not to be created as "living fossils" or "missing links" (Lee 1979, xvii), that their colonial past and changing present must be given full recognition to avoid dehumanization and distortion. Yet the inquiry the group proposes, initiated by primatologists, is explicitly evolutionary, in which the !Kung are important as "evidence which will help in understanding human history" (S. Washburn in Lee and DeVore 1976, xv), as examples of an ecological adaptation "that was until ten thousand years ago, a human universal" (Lee 1979, 1). One is led to think the !Kung have lived in the Kalahari for millennia. In fact, they were driven there by settler colonialism. The Harvard studies focus heavily on physical and biological matters like diet, physiology, use of time, settlement patterns, spacing of births, use of food resources, disease, aging, and so on, naturalizing current !Kung lifeways with a vengeance. The researchers' sincere desire to be sensitive to the !Kung's historical circumstances is simply incompatible with their project of viewing the !Kung as a complex adaptation to the ecology of the Kalahari Desert and an example of how "our" ancestors lived. The use of primarily quantitative methods (producing tables like "average number of childcaring acts by a subject per child per hour of observation"; P. Draper in Lee and DeVore 1976, 214) intensifies the reification.

An outsider reading the history of European contact with the !Kung/Bushmen inevitably questions this image of them as representatives of hunting-gathering life as it was lived ten thousand years ago. Is it not worth even asking whether three hundred years of warfare and persecution at the hands of white settlers had an impact on their lifeways, consciousness, social organization, and even physiology? Did the long-term practice of massacring their men and enslaving their women have no impact on "what women's lives were like" today or on how women saw themselves? What picture of the !Kung would one draw if instead of defining them as remnants of the Stone Age and a complex adaptation to the desert, one looked at them as survivors of capitalist expansion and a delicate and complex adaptation to three centuries of violence and intimidation? The work of decolonization is urgently called on here.

Shostak's *Nisa* was part of a wave of experimentation in ethnographic writing that gradually gathered momentum in the 1980s and became unstoppable in the 1990s. It has continued to open the discipline to creativity, innovation, and decolonization. The drastic, often hostile bifurcation of anthropology in the 1990s triggered by the rise of sociobiology caused enormous harm, not least because sociobiology sought to expel interpretive methods rather than coexist with them. The conflict, in some ways, abetted the experimental, self-reflective stream in ethnography. It built the clash between objective and subjective knowledge into the structure of the discipline itself and the institutional spaces that house it.[8] In what is overall a tragic war, imaginative, challenging experimentation in ethnographic writing has held onto space where it can develop and nourish itself from neighboring fields without killing or being killed by science.

RIGOBERTA MENCHÚ AND
THE GEOPOLITICS OF TRUTH

In the years following its publication in 1983, *Me llamo Rigoberta Menchú y asi me nació la conciencia* (in English *I, Rigoberta Menchú: An Indian Woman in Guatemala*, 1984) attracted a worldwide reception that undoubtedly saved many Guatemalan lives, including Rigoberta Menchú's own. Its appearance marked the beginning of a trajectory through which Menchú became the most famous Indigenous leader in the world. She received the Nobel Peace Prize in 1992 for a decade of international work to end the campaign of military terror in her homeland that had cost some two hundred thousand Indigenous lives.[1] She used the prize money to found the Rigoberta Menchú Foundation, dedicated to promoting an "ethic of world peace through the struggle for justice and democracy, especially for Indigenous peoples."[2] She eventually ran for president of her country. Her activities won her many admirers and also some serious enemies.

Her enemies were undoubtedly pleased when, in December 1998, the global press was gripped by a sensational front-page report in the *New York Times*: an American anthropologist, professor at a prestigious college,

11.1 — Guatemalan activist Rigoberta Menchú. SOURCE: RIGOBERTA MENCHÚ TUM/WHEN THE MOUNTAINS TREMBLE.

claimed on the basis of years of research that *I, Rigoberta Menchú* was a tissue of lies, inventions, and distortions (Rohter 1998). So dramatic were the allegations that the *Times* had sent a reporter to Guatemala to verify sources cited by the researcher, David Stoll. The scoop was advance publicity for Stoll's three-hundred-page book, *Rigoberta Menchú and the Story of All Poor Guatemalans* (1999), which was on its way to bookstores.[3] The *Times* story unleashed a media frenzy, or perhaps a feeding frenzy. The controversy quickly acquired international dimensions, with serious stakes for Menchú and also for the Guatemalan peace process then underway, for Indigenous movements worldwide, and for scholars and teachers in American universities. In general, the immediate public reaction ran heavily against Menchú.

This chapter examines the controversy in ways that I hope will help readers make sense of its multiple contours and grasp its implications. I first situate the controversy in its US academic context, sketching out the role *I, Rigoberta Menchú* acquired in the 1980s and 1990s in the conflicts that raged in higher education between a cultural conservatism taking hold in the Ronald

Reagan years and a progressive multiculturalism with roots in civil rights and anticolonial liberation struggles. These conflicts are an important factor in explaining why the attacks on the book and on Menchú acquired such a high profile, why they elicited such intense reactions, and why they marked a triumph for the political right. In the second part of the essay, I address the main claims in Stoll's book and examine Menchú's *testimonio* in light of his critique. I end with an assessment of Stoll's research and a reflection on the (much better) book he might have written. My aim is to be honest and fair but also partisan. I see Stoll's intervention as a sorry and unjustified act of aggression whose claims are not well borne out. Along with other scholars, I take up the call to work through the issues the controversy raised, including a series of important epistemological, methodological, and ethical questions that go far beyond any particular case. I come to terms with the attack by making it the occasion for a deepened reflection on subjectivity and on what Julie Skurski and Fernando Coronil (1993) have called the "geopolitics of truth."

Reaganism and the Culture Wars

What came to be known as the culture wars in the United States was the result of a fateful collision between two historical processes. On the one hand, the youth of the 1960s arrived on university faculties, a generation shaped by hippie counterculture, feminism, the civil rights movement, and third-world liberation struggles. On the other hand, Ronald Reagan arrived at the White House, along with a political right wing hungry for power. Beginning in about 1975, veterans of the student movements and the counterculture, doctorates freshly in hand, began joining university faculties as junior colleagues of professors whose classes they might once have boycotted. Antiracist and feminist activism had begun forcing open the doors of American higher education to the most diverse student bodies in the history of the country. Affirmative action was making a difference. Many disciplines—most dramatically law, humanities, and social sciences—developed critical wings that questioned the ideological and historical underpinnings of these disciplines. The Cold War had stimulated the study of third-world regions in the universities, through area studies programs that attracted scholars of all ideological stripes. Over the next twenty years, these innovations in higher education would revitalize and reenergize academic disciplines in ways traditional scholars eventually came to value. But at the beginning, tensions abounded. At the same time, a conservative movement humiliated by Watergate and Vietnam had gathered strength and began promoting conservative agendas that were political, religious, and cultural.[4] In the 1980s and 1990s, most universities in the United States were at one time or another thrown into upheaval by these ideological and generational conflicts. In the 2020s, they have arisen again, driven by a newly consolidated conservatism centered more firmly than ever on a white nationalist agenda.[5]

The culture wars acquired considerable visibility at Stanford University, where David Stoll was a doctoral student in anthropology in the 1980s and where he began the investigation that produced *Rigoberta Menchú and the Story of All Poor Guatemalans*. I, too, was at Stanford at that time, a young faculty member in Latin American studies and comparative literature. The conflict at Stanford centered on a yearlong course in Western culture adopted in 1980 and required of all first-year students. The curriculum consisted of a list of thirty-two authors, from Plato to Friedrich Nietzsche via Niccolò Machiavelli and Voltaire. All were European men and standard figures in the Western canon. The stated aims were to familiarize Stanford students with "the roots of their culture" and provide them with a "common intellectual experience." By the mid-1980s, however, owing to a strong commitment to affirmative action, more than half of Stanford's entering classes were students of color—Asian Americans, Chicanos, African Americans, Native Americans. Nearly half of each class were women. It was not possible to persuade such a diversified group that the course represented their cultural roots or to argue that they would have a common intellectual experience in the course. Moreover, this was a moment when students were learning energetically from exploring their differences and were eager to learn about the globalizing world around them. Many minority students saw Western culture as an imperial, assimilationist enterprise. A large and diverse opposition to the course formed, involving faculty, students, and staff. A vigorous debate ensued, leading to a full-fledged institutional crisis that lasted for nearly two years (1987–88).[6] Thanks to Reagan's secretary of education, William Bennett, the Stanford debate became a national cause célèbre.[7] Bennett latched onto it as a platform for his conservative views. On national television and in newspaper articles, he forcefully took sides in favor of the Western culture curriculum and the occidental civilizing mission in general. His crusade touched a nerve in a society confused and anxious about its identity and values (especially among white people) and put the Stanford debate on editorial pages and in magazine stories across the country. As a counterpoint to Bennett, Reverend Jesse Jackson entered the fray in support of the student movement, leading a march through campus in January 1988, with shouts of "Hey hey, ho ho, Western Culture's got to go!" (Bernstein

CHAPTER ELEVEN

1988). When the conflict was finally settled in late 1988, the story was front-page news. Stoll entered Stanford's doctoral program in anthropology at the height of the debate in fall 1987 and received his doctorate in 1992.[8]

A Battle of Books instead of Ideas

The culture wars had the positive effect of opening spaces for new framings of culture and history and making people think about their educational practices. At the same time, one of the strategic successes of the right lay in framing the debate as a battle over book titles rather than over ideas or civic visions. This was a key reason Menchú's book became a target. The country was engaged in an important and legitimate discussion about how to construct an inclusive, grounded, democratic culture. But the media portrayed it as "the battle of the books," and in colleges, universities, secondary schools, and school boards across the country, that is the form it took. New curricular proposals were seen as acts of substitution (or homicide) in which great books written by important European men were displaced by inferior books written by unknown and marginal figures (like Rigoberta Menchú) that had not withstood the test of time. Lists of authors and titles came metonymically to represent Western culture itself, besieged by barbarism in the form of books like *The Interesting Narrative of the Life of Olaudah Equiano*, Frantz Fanon's *The Wretched of the Earth*, Jean Rhys's *Wide Sargasso Sea*, or Juan Rulfo's *Pedro Páramo*. While the classics were studied for their implicit merit and importance, the new books, conservatives said, were prescribed for purely ideological reasons.

Having taken this form, the debate inspired many regrettable moments. Opponents of change were often arguing from ignorance. Why, after all, would they bother to read books the other side was talking about if they already knew them to be unworthy? Even respected conservatives, like C. Vann Woodward and George Will, could be found dismissing writers and books solely on the basis of their non-European origins. Saul Bellow was widely quoted making the disparaging remark that "when the Zulus have a Tolstoy, we will read him."[9] The battle of the books thwarted the possibility of serious dialogue over what was really at stake for American society: How should the United States recognize and develop itself as a multiethnic, heterogeneous, democratic, and postcolonial society? What at the end of the twentieth century was it going to assert as its cultural archive? How was it to educate its citizens to be citizens? How was it going to decolonize its culture? Targeting individual books deflected from what was really at stake. The seriousness of the stakes registered most in the emotional and moral intensity of the discussion.

I, Rigoberta Menchú in its English translation became a reading of choice in humanities and social science courses that explored critical and nonhegemonic perspectives in the context of multiculturalist innovation. In the late 1980s, it began to appear frequently in the first-year composition courses that taught entering students the tools of critical thought and argumentation.[10] *I, Rigoberta Menchú* proved very powerful in classrooms. It still does. It generates difficult, passionate, and revealing dialogues. After teaching the book for many years in Stanford's Europe and the Americas course, anthropologist Renato Rosaldo commented:

> In the classroom Menchú's work has made vivid both Mayan traditions and the more recent trials of Mayan peoples in the face of genocidal military incursions. The work can be read next to the classic Mayan telling of the creation, the Popol Vuh, a narrative whose echoes appear in her life story. Her narrative, not unlike the classic confessions of St. Augustine and Jean-Jacques Rousseau, provides readers with a compelling world view and an impassioned articulation of a historical crisis. . . .
>
> Menchú's work engages students in rich discussions that range from the character of cultural traditions, the impact of military incursions against indigenous peoples, the factors that transform rural, agricultural ways of life, and the struggles of social groups to live their lives with dignity and self-respect. The book brings cultural and social issues to life in a way that is realistic and humanly engaging; it is a gift to the classroom.[11]

Along with teachers all over the country, I witnessed the impact Menchú's text had, and still has, on young readers at colleges and universities. I taught it in several courses over many years. Every time, it was the text students most often named when asked what reading most changed them. The book tended to have a dramatic, sometimes transformative impact. Most undergraduates had never read anything like it. As a personal narrative of life experience, it has the power to break down the distancing strategies that normally muffle young Americans' encounters with their racial and economic others. The extraordinary specificity and vividness of the narrative and its emotive force overcome the recoiling, dehumanizing reflexes that tend to insulate young Americans from the suffering of others. Many students encountered for the first time the notion that the rich are rich *because* the poor are poor, and vice versa. For many, the book shook up their relation with their nation and their government for the first time. They were shocked to learn that a few short years before, genocidal violence had occurred in a nearby country with the tacit collaboration of their own government. "I had no idea!" was a general response to the book, followed often by "What can I do?"

In students from privileged backgrounds, *I, Rigoberta Menchú* often creates a dramatic first engagement with the realities of exploitation, economic vulnerability, and the absence of good choices. The reactions, invariably intense, varied from aggressive rejection to illumination, from guilt to mobilization. Students who came from poor backgrounds or who had lived with everyday violence found that the book vindicated their historical consciousness and social experience, which their studies otherwise rarely engaged. The book's US reception was further shaped by the historic role that autobiographical writing has played in North American literary culture as a vehicle for both individualism and egalitarianism. From Benjamin Franklin and Frederick Douglass to Helen Keller and Hank Aaron, new and emergent subjects in American culture enter the social imagination through the doorway of autobiography or what has come to be called *self-writing*.[12]

Educational conservatives were not mistaken, then, in singling out *I, Rigoberta Menchú* for attack. It is indeed a powerful book. Its capacity to move metropolitan subjects does not derive from the fact that it is the *testimonio* of a young Guatemalan Indigenous woman who suffered many painful experiences.[13] Its impact derives from its expressive power and range; its complex articulation of aesthetic, narrative, ethical, and emotive dimensions; its ability to evoke not only a history and a country but also a cosmos. Some of that power derives, as we shall see, from aspects for which the text was later attacked.

Menchú in the Crosshairs

The book that established *I, Rigoberta Menchú* as a public target in the United States appeared in 1991 when the campaign to nominate Menchú for the Nobel Prize was underway. That book was *Illiberal Education: The Politics of Race and Sex on Campus*, a heated ideological attack on the educational reforms of the 1980s written by Dinesh D'Souza, then a young disciple of the Republican right.[14] In a chapter titled "Travels with Rigoberta," D'Souza denounced Menchú from two contradictory directions: as an ignorant and uneducated Indian woman from whom we have nothing to learn and as a woman whose experiences and life choices were so atypical they disqualified her from representing her people. For academics, responding publicly proved difficult. D'Souza had written his book with full-time support from conservative foundations, and it had the benefit of a national advertising campaign run by professionals. Working academics lacked the time, resources, and media expertise to commandeer the attention of the national media or to respond effectively to its distortions and errors (remember, Facebook, Twitter, and Instagram were undreamed of in 1991). Some of us got calls from fact-checkers for magazines like *U.S. News and World Report* and *Forbes*, with questions like "Is it true that you teach *I, Rigoberta Menchú* in your course? Is she a communist? Do you really believe it is a great book?" We tried to learn about sound bites, but we weren't good at it. We didn't yet know what media training was. Meanwhile, the hostile attention from the right may actually have increased Menchú's presence on bookshelves and course syllabi.

In sum, throughout the 1990s, *I, Rigoberta Menchú* was demonized in some quarters as an example of a destructive and promiscuous multiculturalism, while in others it was treasured as a courageous critique of oppression and a vivid affirmation of justice. Between these poles, it galvanized debates around questions such as how subalterns should be included in academic inquiry, what forms the decolonization of knowledge should take, and whether and how feminist values are pertinent to Indigenous and non-Western societies. During these years Menchú made personal appearances on American campuses, where she displayed eloquence, wit, wisdom, and courage. In the early 1990s, David Stoll also began appearing in academic settings, raising his doubts about the veracity of her text.

The culture wars in general, and D'Souza's attack in particular, built the stage onto which Stoll's book *Rigoberta Menchú and the Story of All Poor Guatemalans* burst in the spring of 1999.[15] Stoll lays out his position in the prologue. One of his three objectives in writing the book, he says, was to oppose a "'new orthodoxy' in the academy whose premise is that Western forms of knowledge, such as the empirical approach adopted here, are fatally compromised by racism and other forms of domination. Responsible scholars must therefore identify with the oppressed, relegating much of what we think we know about them to the dustbin of colonialism. The new basis of authority consists in letting subalterns speak for themselves and agonizing over any hint of complicity with the system that oppresses them, and situating oneself in relation to fashionable theorists" (Stoll 1999, xv). The disparaging tone is obvious. Stoll becomes the metropolitan researcher who stops agonizing about complicity, refuses to privilege subaltern voices, and reaffirms his own authority and access to truth.[16] In his book Stoll is the hero of a quest for truth, battling against forces of deception. He refers to months spent researching in archives; visiting sites all over the Guatemalan highlands where the events in Menchú's *testimonio* took place; interviewing survivors, witnesses, and family members; and trying to piece it all together—getting the facts, ma'am, just the facts. As I argue below, if you actually read Stoll's book from cover to cover, as few do, you encounter a far more complicated and interesting scenario than his polemical prologue suggests. His book could, in other words, have made an entirely different intervention. As I'll discuss below, contrary to its stated aim, Stoll's meticulous research could have produced a compelling study of how slippery facts become in contexts crisscrossed by deep, long-standing, multifaceted conflicts and traumatizing violence.

But Stoll and his publicists chose a different path, promoting a series of sensational claims that poked holes in Menchú's credibility and demolished the image many readers held of her. For example, her family's lack of land, Stoll said, was due not to the greed and cruelty of ladino (white) landowners but to disputes between Menchú's father and her mother's family.[17] The death of her infant brother, described early in the book, said Stoll, never occurred—he had found the brother alive and well in Guatemala. The accusations, big and small, accumulate: Menchú's region was not in economic decline, so there was no justification for militant struggle or for a guerrilla presence there. The army invaded her village not to punish the peasants for defending their land but because the guerrillas had assassinated two ladino landowners. Though Menchú gives an eyewitness description of the death by torture of her brother Petrocinio, she in fact was not present, said Stoll, and heard the account from others. Contrary to her claims, her father, an activist, had been affiliated with the guerrilla movement. He had personally welcomed the guerrillas when they entered his town. When he and his fellow protesters burned to death in the Spanish embassy, it was by their own hand, Stoll claimed, not that of the police. Most damning of all, perhaps, was Stoll's claim that Menchú did not grow up as an illiterate *campesina*. She had received at least four years of schooling, he said, at boarding schools run by Belgian nuns in Uspantán and Guatemala City, a privilege she concealed to gain her readers' sympathies. And since she was at school, he argued, she could not have accompanied her family to harvest coffee at the fincas, as she so vividly describes, nor helped them defend their village from the army, nor worked as a maid in the city, all key experiences in her narrative. (I comment on the validity of these claims below.)

Stoll argued that Menchú's lies and fabrications were motivated by her commitment to the left-wing guerrilla cause, an involvement she always denied. "Rigoberta's secret," as one chapter title calls it, was that she was a pawn of the Guerrilla Army of the Poor (Ejército Guerrillero de los Pobres; EGP), the main Guatemalan guerrilla force, who manipulated her as they had manipulated "all the poor people of Guatemala."[18] Worse still, she and they had manipulated readers all over the world, winning their sympathy by cynically exploiting political stereotypes of victimization.

Behind the attack on Menchú was a concern Stoll had laid out in an earlier book on the Guatemalan conflict, titled *Between Two Armies in the Ixil Towns of Guatemala* (1993). There he disputed analyses that saw the guerrilla movement as a legitimate popular struggle and blamed the Guatemalan army for the campaigns that killed a quarter of a million people, mainly Indigenous peasants. Stoll argued that the guerrillas were often responsible for attracting military violence to Indigenous communities and were criminally indifferent to the consequences. They often left sympathetic villagers facing the army unarmed, he said. Many communities were forced to take sides not out of political allegiance but simply in an effort to survive. Stoll denied that the guerrilla movement had widespread popular support in Guatemala. Though the military had carried out 90 percent of the killings, the guerrilla movement, in Stoll's view, was equally responsible, for they left the army no choice.

Such views, not surprisingly, received a warm welcome among the Guatemalan military, but Stoll's real target was the international solidarity movement, whose support for the guerrilla movement he found naive and reprehensible. In part owing to her compelling presence and willingness to travel, Menchú had become an icon of the solidarity movement and of the broader international human rights movement as a whole. Discrediting her was an effective way for Stoll to bring his case into the international and nonacademic arenas, as well as inserting it into the debates on culture within the United States. In the latter context, it was obvious that the conservative movement would receive the critique as a splendid vindication of its campaign not only against Menchú and her book but against multiculturalism, new social movements, and educational reform in general.

That is indeed what happened. Beginning in December 1998, the media blitz orchestrated by Stoll's publisher was a spectacular success. Dinesh D'Souza weighed in immediately with a sarcastic article ("Well, at least she didn't get the Nobel Prize for literature . . ."). In the spring of 1999, after the book appeared, every major news publication in the world carried the story, generating floods of letters and columns. From his post at the Center for Popular Culture in Los Angeles, conservative activist David Horowitz took out newspaper ads condemning Menchú's book as a fraud and criticizing academics who defended it. On the left, responses varied from impassioned defenses to anger to agonized self-doubt (for examples, see Arias 2001). Readers who lacked knowledge of Guatemala were most disturbed by Stoll's accusations. On the basis of Menchú's text, such readers had constructed a vivid portrait of her and her world in their imaginations and engaged with it on a deep ethical level. Now they were being told it was a deceitful fantasy. Given the timing, at the height of the Monica Lewinsky scandal, analogies with the investigations of President Bill Clinton were unavoidable: liars, however trivial, should be impeached. (How quaint that sounds now, in 2020.)

It is clear from the commentaries that many commentators relied not on the book but on media reports or a skim of early chapters. Few indeed actually read it—the international media blitz fed mainly on itself. This was predictable, and Stoll's publicists surely knew that. For one thing, even for a motivated reader, the book is heavy going. The first two hundred pages review in detail the aspects of Menchú's *testimonio* that Stoll found reason to doubt and argue for alternative versions of the story; the last hundred pages comment on Menchú's trajectory since 1983. The text is a dizzying tangle of names, places, voices, judgments, details, and speculation. For ideologues primarily seeking to police college syllabi and discredit certain forms of knowledge, however, the particulars of Stoll's account did not matter. For them, the history and inhabitants of Guatemala were already of little or no importance. Ironically, then, the most fervent fans of Stoll's critique may be those least likely to care about what he actually found and least likely to read beyond the first chapter.

Let me sum up a little. To a significant degree, in the United States, what was at stake in the controversy around *I, Rigoberta Menchú* was not Menchú and Guatemala but academic authority. New knowledge makers entering the stream of academic discourse have always encountered resistance and reaction, as Menchú did. Scholars of all stripes often create authority for themselves by attacking others, as Stoll did. In this respect, though not in others, the controversy was academic business as usual. It echoed, for example, sociobiologist Derek Freeman's (1983) attack on cultural anthropologist Margaret Mead. Like Menchú, Mead was an international public figure and a respected iconoclast whose strengths and weaknesses were well known within her field. Freeman's attack was directed less at Mead's work than at her status as an icon (on whom, paradoxically, Freeman built his own reputation). The aggressive discrediting of Mead was part of a campaign to establish sociobiology's dominance in the field of anthropology. The humanistic (and female) Mead had to be dethroned as the image of the anthropologist. In similar fashion, it appeared, Menchú had to be destroyed as the image of the subaltern challenger to metropolitan academic authority. The drama confirms Jean Franco's astute observation that the *testimonio* represents "a struggle for interpretive power" (1992, 111).[19]

Addressing Stoll's Claims

But what of Stoll's claims? Facts do matter. All over the world, from South Africa to Peru, countries emerging from periods of extreme state violence have formed truth commissions, precisely in order to establish what happened under cloaks of secrecy and deception. Bringing out the facts is perceived as essential for societies to recover from such collective traumas and relegitimate government. Facts are the key to accountability; secrecy and deception are instruments of the abuse of power. Guatemala, too, had such a commission; its head, Archbishop Juan Gerardi, was murdered in April 1998, two days after turning in his report. (Three army officers were later convicted of the murder.)

Some of Stoll's factual claims have been confirmed, while others have been refuted or remain in dispute. To mention some of the main examples, most Guatemala specialists reject his claim that there was no justification for a guerrilla presence in the area where Menchú lived. Others say he was wrong in associating Menchú's father with the guerrilla army. Menchú admitted that she did not witness her brother's death and told it as she had heard it from the accounts of others. There were indeed disputes about landownership within Menchú's extended family, but it is also true that the unjust distribution of land between Indigenous and ladinos is the root source of inequality everywhere in Guatemala, including where she lived.[20] Menchú said she made no mention of family disputes because they were irrelevant to the story and she had no business airing her family's internal affairs. Menchú insists that the account of her baby brother's death is true and that her parents later gave the same name to another brother, an accepted practice in Latin America. Stoll has since confirmed this (Arias 2001, 407). As for the incineration of the protesters at the Spanish embassy, which Stoll argues was self-inflicted, in January 2015 a Guatemalan court convicted a former police chief of orchestrating the massacre and sentenced him to ninety years in prison. Menchú continues to deny that she supported the guerrilla movement, while others point out that if she had, it would have been suicidally dangerous to say so. In addition to the particulars of Stoll's charges, some scholars of the region doubt that the manner and circumstances in which he carried out his interviews would have permitted a reliable reconstruction of what happened.[21] For some, his failure to systematically identify informants violates the norms governing this kind of research.

On the explosive question of Menchú's schooling, Stoll is both reliable and not. Menchú did study intermittently at boarding schools run by Belgian nuns but apparently not as a regular pupil. She was one of a number of Indigenous girls taken in as servants and given access to basic instruction in exchange for performing domestic labor for the paying pupils. Menchú does not describe this experience in her *testimonio*, but she does refer to it. Contrary to Stoll's claims, the dates Stoll reconstructs for her attendance at school make it quite possible that she went to the fincas to pick coffee when she says she did and worked as a maid in Guatemala City when she says she did. Menchú says she could not discuss the school when she gave her *testimonio* in 1982 for fear of endangering the nuns. State terror in Guatemala was still at its height, and the nuns, who had protested human rights violations, were already under suspicion. These facts were surely evident to Stoll, who nevertheless accused Menchú of deliberately deceiving her readers about who she was.

In sum, some of Stoll's accusations hold up, and others do not. Most of the time, as Stoll often acknowledges, his findings confirm Menchú's account. Many of his most dramatic claims are not borne out by his own findings, while others are exaggerated and distorted by partisanship—the very quality he denounces in Menchú. At the same time, there is no doubt that his revelations require readers to create a more complex relationship to Menchú's text than the naive, totalized embrace. There are many aspects of Guatemala's sociohistorical reality that Menchú does not take up or explore in her *testimonio*. There is no doubt that in some respects, such as reporting things as if she had witnessed them when she had not, Menchú's account violates metropolitan norms and expectations. But then there is the question of genre.

Testimonio/Exposé

To try to line up the facts this way is to overlook a key factor: genre. Neither Menchú's book nor Stoll's aims at producing a definitive, objective, all-encompassing account of the kind we might look for in legal testimony or a truth commission. Each text belongs to a genre governed by its own norms and expectations. Stoll's book, as Kay Warren astutely observes, is written as an exposé, a genre in which a writer seeks "to generate facts that will discredit accepted accounts and interpretations. Facts outside the frame of the immediate quest are ignored" (2001, 206). *Testimonio*, Menchú's genre, is a form of personal narrative produced by a collaboration between a subaltern participant and a lettered intellectual in order to tell the world about a collective trauma of violence and injustice. After taping Menchú's testimony in a series of interviews, her collaborator, the Venezuelan anthropologist Elisabeth Burgos-Debray, transcribed and edited it into the book, a process that did not involve Menchú.

The question of genre is important because Stoll's project could have taken other forms. Indeed, reading *Rigoberta Menchú and the Story of All Poor Guatemalans*, I often found myself imagining other, finer books it could have been, other goals its painstaking findings could have served. As an exposé, the book often seems an act of hubris, that is, an act whose heroic ambitions fatally exceed its powers. While questioning point for point the veracity of Menchú's account, Stoll's text often raises doubts as to its own reliability. He proposes to revindicate empirical research (Stoll 1999, 247) but deploys an intensely partisan rhetoric and hermeneutics. He suggests alternate interpretations but then sets them aside without explaining why. The search for competing facts often leads Stoll into labyrinths of uncertainty that require him to rely on speculation and imagined reconstructions. It is hard not to notice, for example, the way some facts invent themselves in the course of his account. At times, what is introduced initially as one possibility among others later reappears as an empirical truth. In chapter 8, for instance, two eyewitnesses affirm that Menchú's father, Vicente, was not present when the guerrillas first entered his town of Chimel. Two other informants say he was, one of whom appears to be speaking secondhand (110–11). By chapters 12 and 17, however, it has become a fact that Vicente Menchú personally received the guerrillas in Chimel (172, 240). In reverse fashion, other facts mutate into fictions. Early on, the author affirms that Menchú's account of the capture, rape, torture, and death of her mother is "basically true" and gives reasons for this conclusion (125). Nevertheless, in chapter 16 we read that Menchú "imagined" the death of her mother (194)—as if it had not occurred at all! Chapter 17 alludes perversely to "the calvaries through which Menchú puts her mother and brother" (308)—as if her description of their torture was the torture itself.

Frequent incongruities arise between the author's judgments and the historical picture that emerges from his account. For instance, one of Stoll's main claims is that the guerrilla movement in Guatemala never had massive support among Indigenous peasants. From this, he deduces that anyone who did support the guerrilla movement does not represent the experience of the peasants during the war. At another point, however, he speaks of an "inundation of recruits from religious, peasant and labor organizations" in 1981 (174), an expansion of numbers in Santa Cruz del Quiché so massive that it overwhelmed the guerrilla movement's capacity to grow. He tells us the Guatemalan guerrilla movement was the first to attract significant numbers of Indigenous adherents (208). The racial factor is constantly downplayed, especially in the discussion of land disputes, but at the same time we are told that ladino (non-Indigenous) landholders collaborated unanimously with the army and that the lands of Chimel wound up in the hands of a ladino who was able to gain title. Menchú's school is depicted as a cloister "isolated from the outside world," leading to the claim that her political education began only after she left Guatemala. Yet the school is described as "under siege" by the military during the 1980s and surrounded by soldiers threatening the nuns, who were reporting human rights violations (164) and trying to "protect their pupils from reprisals" (191).

The most difficult thing to accept about Stoll's exposé, however, is what might be called the ethical scale of its accusations. By this, I mean that it remains incongruous to measure the discrepancies between Menchú's narrated testimony and the reconstructible facts of her life on the same scale as the mass atrocities of the Guatemalan army, the vast suffering and loss they inflicted, the immense inequalities and injustices of Guatemalan society, the courage and stamina of those who survived, the legitimacy of the demands for peace and justice, and the corrupt complicity of the American government. These are all things Menchú gets right. It is not easy to imagine an ethical compass that orients not toward these truths but toward the truth that Menchú was not physically present when they killed her brother, that she said little about her schooling, and so on. To the extent that Stoll's book asked its readers to make that ethical choice, it did itself an injustice. It impeded reflection on the serious issues the author himself raised, including the important question of the accountability of the guerrillas. Written in the form of an exposé, the book in the end betrayed its own goals, even as it created a sensation in the book market.

So perhaps we should read it otherwise. Far from bearing us upward into the realm of certainty, the whirlwind of voices, details, innuendos, questions, possibilities, and judgments that make up *Rigoberta Menchú and the Story of All Poor Guatemalans* creates a fascinating truth seeker's purgatory from which it does not offer an exit. Stoll's quest for truth reveals a different truth about Guatemala: the truth of the extraordinary difficulty of finding truth in the aftermath of genocidal violence. The dead cannot speak, survivors are traumatized and afraid, language fails, and webs of collective memory have been shredded.[22] Written as a reflection on that reality, Stoll's meticulous investigation could have produced a masterpiece.

Testimonio, Transculturation, and the Personal

Scholarly debate on the *testimonio* still suffers from confusion with respect to the question of genre. Cultural studies scholars have criticized the so-called literary treatment of *testimonios*, arguing that focusing on textual particulars diverts attention from the histories they recount. But perhaps the treatment has not been literary enough. Excellent studies exist, but we still lack well-developed theoretical frameworks for discussing what the *testimonio* is and how it should be read, taught, disseminated, and produced. Irrelevant norms are often applied. For example, in a number of instances, accusations of falsehood, distortion, and partisanship against Menchú are based on the norms that govern legal testimony. But, of course, the *testimonio* is not legal testimony but personal narrative. It does have much in common with autobiography. Both autobiography and *testimonio*, for example, expect truthfulness but also partiality rather than impartiality. Frederick Douglass cannot be faulted for his partisan attitude toward slavery in his autobiography, nor Winston Churchill for his attitudes toward Nazism. Nor is selectiveness against the rules of autobiography. As autobiographers, Jean-Jacques Rousseau and Benjamin Franklin were not required to report on their catastrophic conduct as husbands or fathers, which surely compromised their image as the civic moralists they wanted to be. Such omissions get noted by critics, of course, but they do not make the autobiography fraudulent, to use the language of Menchú's accusers. The autobiographical contract (between writer and reader) assumes the producer is committed to truthfulness qualified by self-interest, partisanship, and the fragility of memory, and the reader is assumed to know this. It is perfectly apparent to Menchú's readers that other participants in the story—say, the military or the landowners—would tell it very differently. It's evident that selection and idealization are involved. Menchú says little or nothing about conflicts and dysfunction within Indigenous communities.[23] The testimonial subject decides what to tell and how to tell it (as with autobiography), and the collaborator decides how to present the material as a text. Specialists on Guatemala, including Stoll, affirm the overall historical fidelity of Menchú's account. At the same time, the intense disappointment and dismay Menchú's readers expressed at the criticisms was real and tells us something really did go wrong. Whether she knew it or not, Menchú made choices that violated the contract most of her readers made with her and her text. Let us consider a little more closely how that came about.

The Transcultural Paradox

Testimonios are produced orally by two people, a person telling their story and a metropolitan intellectual who records it and brings it into publishable form. In Menchú's case, this collaborator was Elisabeth Burgos-Debray, a Venezuelan activist and anthropologist living in Paris. Other genres use this two-person approach, including the life story used by anthropologists, oral history, and as-told-to autobiography. In this dialogic field, the *testimonio* stands out as a genre produced transculturally and geopolitically, across the divides between center and periphery, rich and poor, vernacular and elite, educated and uneducated, white and nonwhite. For this reason, the *testimonio* exists in a state of permanent, and often productive, contradiction. For instance, though testimonial subjects are asked to narrate their individual experience, the testimonial contract understands them to be speaking as members of a group that has lived a shared trauma. Experience is thus governed simultaneously by paradigms of individuality (uniqueness) and of collectivity (exemplarity). According to the testimonial contract, the testimonial subject voluntarily communicates their personal experience to the metropolitan listener/editor. Each is other to the other. But, of course, this concept of "personal experience" is a modern Western existential category that presupposes a subjectivity that the testimonial speaker is expected *not to possess*, for they are its other. This is not at all to say that the idea of personal experience exists only in the West. That is palpably false. The claim is that the coproducers of *testimonios* locate themselves in a process that you might call *transculturation*, or *cultural translation*, or *cultural reconversion*, as discussed in chapter 13 of this book. As a team, they try to align Western concepts of life, experience, subjectivity, and personhood with the experiential and verbal repertory of a non-Western or subaltern subject. What binds the two together is a shared ethical commitment to the project of communicating the subaltern's historical experience to metropolitan publics who are ignorant of it, in a discourse those publics can decipher and with which they will empathize. What Jürgen Habermas (1970, 205) would call "systematically distorted communication" is irremediably built into its geopolitics of truth.

This context of production obliges testimonial subjects to make decisions as to what to relate and how to relate it, always on the basis of an incomplete understanding of the contexts in which they will be read. Menchú apparently decided to present processes and things that happened to other members of the collective as personal or eyewitness experiences of her own, and to present herself as Indigenous in a way she thought non-Indigenous people would recognize.[24] Her intentions, insofar as we know them, were to strengthen the impact and reach of the story. She succeeded. The force of her account derives from the vividness and immediacy of her descriptions and from our sense that these things were happening to her. She transgressed the metropolitan distinction between the personal and the collective and in doing so violated its norms.

It is easy to imagine arguments for and against these moves and easy to imagine ways of producing testimony that avoid or allow them. The important challenge, in my view, is finding ways to comprehend transcultural communicative situations and their epistemic, ethical, and geopolitical aspects. How do the participants in producing a *testimonio* evaluate their communicative situation and make their decisions? How should the results be assessed?[25]

Historically, universities have always privileged lettered knowledge over narrated experience. From academic standpoints, experiential knowledge is often dismissed as anecdote or unreflected spontaneity. The communications revolution from which the *testimonio* arises has undermined this hierarchy. On a global scale, marginalized groups, especially Indigenous and Afro-descended peoples, are insisting on dialogue with lettered knowledge from within their own epistemological grounds. This calls for new ways of thinking about authority, meaning making, knowledge, and truth. The *testimonio* is a rich, problematic form of communication and source of knowledge. This fact is one reason Stoll's sensational exposé, in the end, probably did less damage than expected.

CHAPTER TWELVE

THE POLITICS OF REENACTMENT

From its opening to its closing scene, Icíar Bollaín's film *También la lluvia* (*Even the Rain*; 2010) is punctuated by scenes of white northerners looking at radically unfamiliar southern realities through the windows of moving white SUVs.[1] The film puts filmmaking itself to the test as a form of travel. Specifically, it explores the quest for geohistorical authenticity that is sought by filming on location. Set in 2000, *También la lluvia* centers on a Spanish film crew that travels to Latin America to make a movie about the early years of Spanish colonialism in the Americas. The project is driven by an ethical mission: to recall the brutality and violence of Spanish colonial rule and recognize the handful of dissident priests who bravely condemned the abuses.[2] The film will stage a reenactment of events in Spain's first American colony, founded in 1493 on the island of Hispaniola. Spanish soldiers and colonists are the villains of the piece; the heroes are two Dominican friars who condemned the abuses, Antonio de Montesinos and his famed disciple Bartolomé de las Casas (played by Raúl Arévalo and Carlos Santos, respectively) and the Taíno rebel leader, Hatuey (played by Juan Carlos Aduviri).[3] The director, Sebastián (played by Gael García Bernal), and the producer, Costa (played by Luis Tosar), are the main characters of the frame story. Sebastián sees himself as a contemporary heir of Las Casas and Montesinos, inspired by their actions and pursuing the same moral high ground (which apparently still or again needs to be claimed). For authenticity's sake, they say, they will shoot the film in Spanish, even though English would have brought "twice the funding and twice the audience."[4] Key scenes in the history of the early conquest will form the backbone of the film: Christopher Columbus's initial encounters with natives, his claims to their lands and demands for riches; Indians delivering quotas of gold dust as tribute, the brutal maiming of those who fail to comply; Antonio de Montesinos's famous sermon of December 4, 1511, in which he declares to the landowning elite that their practices of enslavement and cruelty place them in mortal sin; the jungle ambush of a Spanish slave convoy by rebel Taíno and their leader Hatuey; the Spaniards' ruthless pursuit of the escaping Taíno with attack dogs; Taíno mothers drowning their babies to save them from the nightmare; the burning at the stake of Hatuey and a dozen others in 1514, condemned by a distraught but seemingly helpless Las Casas.[5] We witness all these scenes in one phase or another of preparation, from rehearsal to final shoot. In between, we follow the cast's internal dramas and growing logistical nightmares as the contemporary legacy of Spanish colonial politics threatens to engulf their project.

También la lluvia has an unusual history. It began as a proposal by US radical historian Howard Zinn to make a biopic about Bartolomé de las Casas. In the hands of radical Scots/Irish screenwriter Paul Laverty and his longtime collaborator Ken Loach, it acquired its layered structure in which the Las Casas story was embedded in the frame story of the Spanish filmmakers. It thus became a film-on-location within a film-on-location.

On-location filming has an irony (perhaps a cruel joke) at its heart: the realism and authenticity it seeks require logistical contrivance and manipulation on a huge scale in order to turn settings into sets. Nightmare tales of hysterical stars and jungle catering feats are a commonplace of the cinematic lore around on-location films (Francis Ford Coppola's *Apocalypse Now* and Werner Herzog's *Fitzcarraldo* are memorable examples). On-location films require assembling in one time and place disparate sets of people who are often living unconnected realities and histories. Alongside geographic challenges, any cinematic location is living an unfolding history of its own, quite apart from its role as a set for filmmakers. This fractured circumstance provides *También la lluvia* with its central trope: the parallels between colonial violence in the sixteenth century and the twenty-first.

12.1 — Outtake from Icíar Bollaín's film *También la lluvia* (*Even the Rain*). SOURCE: MORENA FILMS.

From the start, the Spanish filmmakers find themselves trammeled by the history they aim to recover: the real Taíno were largely wiped out by the Spanish onslaught (but see Haslip-Viera 2001).[6] There are none left to play themselves in the reenactment. Where in the genocidal empire did Indigenous populations survive in numbers large enough to provide, five centuries later, a pool of extras for a reenactment? Producer Costa comes up with the answer: contemporary Bolivia. Production will be based in the city of Cochabamba, where usable geography, weather, and infrastructure can be found, as well as cheap labor and multitudes of Indians or Indian-looking people.[7] A set of substitutions will be made. Bolivian Quechua will stand in for the now-lost Taíno language. Costumes and makeup will recode the Bolivian actors as tropical Caribs. Cochabamba's lowland forests will stand in for the Caribbean island of Hispaniola. One ex-colonial site can legitimately (and authentically) substitute for another because equivalent elements are present—including exploitable labor pools. Audiences will fail to notice or will suspend disbelief.

Nevertheless, irony prevails: the required elements can be found in Bolivia in 2000 because the colonial story had a different outcome there than it did in Hispaniola. The Quechua people were not wiped out; things unfolded in a different way than in the Caribbean and continue to do so. That continuity provides the frame story in *También la lluvia*, which was indeed filmed in Cochabamba and nearby Villa Tunari. So we have a triple layering: Bollaín makes a film in 2010 on location in Cochabamba about a Spanish crew making a film in 2000 on location in Cochabamba about events that took place in the 1500s in the Caribbean. The film is bookended by travel: it opens with the cast and crew arriving on location and ends with their terrified, precipitous retreat as the history they came to recuperate overwhelms them with its own anticolonial plotline.

Reenactment as Aftermath and Afterlife

Latin Americanists in recent years have made wide use of Peruvian sociologist Aníbal Quijano's concept of the "coloniality of power" (Quijano 2000a, 2000b). Quijano proposed the term to capture the degree to which power in the Americas continues to articulate along colonial lines or in colonial fashion. Such dynamics are foregrounded in *También la lluvia*. By the very conditions of the location and their presence, the fictional film crew finds itself reenacting the colonial hierarchies it came to condemn. This point is made in the opening scene in a way so emphatic as to suggest caricature. Passing through a market in the white vans that will remain the sign of power throughout the film, the crew sees a long line of local people, men, women, young, old. They have replied to the call for extras to play the Taíno in the reenactment; they are a multitude of two hundred, many more than are needed. "I told you not to do an open casting," says producer Costa. "Tell them to leave." Director Sebastián objects, you can't treat them like that. Walking down the line of hopefuls, he selects several people, then tells the rest to disperse. Protest erupts; a man with his young daughter angrily voices the objections—we have been waiting for hours, this paper says everyone will be seen, my daughter needs this opportunity, and we are not leaving until you have seen us all. The crowd agrees. The encounter turns colonial: cruel and indifferent Spaniards, exploited natives demanding redress. Sebastián relents; Costa scoffs. The filming has not begun, and already the colonial divide is in play: the Spaniards are being Spaniards, and the *indios* are being *indios*.

Another layer of complexity must be added. These potential extras for the reenactment are also real extras in Bollaín's film, local people hired by her team to play a crowd of local people and would-be extras. Did Bollaín also do an open casting call? Did many more than these show up? How were they treated? How well or badly were they paid? Both Sebastián's film (set in 2000) and Bollaín's film (shot in 2010) inhabit the late-capitalist neoliberal moment. Cities north and south abound with displaced rural people desperate for paid work and opportunities for their children. Companies are tethered to profit above all else. When fictional producer Costa crows that "here you can negotiate everything," he describes Bollaín's situation as well.

Staging the reenactment both requires and engenders contemporary reprises of colonial relations that continually clash with the filmmakers' ethical, decolonizing goals. In part, such contradictions are in the nature of reenactment. Reenactments are, by definition, part of the aftermath and the afterlife of the events they recall. They happen because the events are still alive in the place where they occurred. Reenactment requires reproducing to a degree the conditions and relations of the original. It is overdetermined, for example, that the European cast are all men in Costa's film and also, with one exception, in Bollaín's, because the Spanish colonists were all men. Like the conquistadores, the filmmakers are in an unfamiliar environment and dependent on local labor. They, too, seek wealth and profit. At the same time, nothing obliges producer Costa to behave with the harshness of an overseer, as he does. It is the coloniality of power, operating through him. On the phone in English with an investor, he gloats about the extras' naive willingness to work for "two fucking dollars a day. Throw in some old trucks when you are done and they're happy. . . . It's fucking great." The echo of Columbus's first letter is unmistakable.[8] In heated arguments in the hotel's colonial-style dining room, served by Quechua-speaking staff, the actors replay debates between Dominican priests and Spanish landowners, defending their characters, peppering their own arguments with lines from the script, moving in and out of character. In rehearsal, Antón, the actor playing Columbus (played by Karra Elejalde), incorporates a young Bolivian catering worker into his scene, converting her at his whim into a gold-bearing fifteenth-century native he has come to exploit. Grabbing her gold earring, he (in character) shouts fiercely into her face, "¿Donde esta el oro?" ("Where is the gold?"). She looks at him in silence. This twenty-first-century encounter between Antón and the nameless worker becomes not just a reenactment but a straightforward repetition of the original encounter, an enactment of colonial power, not a reenactment. Bolivian theorist Silvia Rivera Cusicanqui, discussed in chapter 14, would identify this as an instance of recolonization (Rivera Cusicanqui 2012). Enactment and reenactment become indistinguishable. In another reprise, Daniel, the rebellious man who mobilized the extras line, is cast as the rebel Taíno leader Hatuey, who in 1513–14 led a guerrilla war against the Spaniards in Cuba. For director Sebastián, Daniel's passion and bravura, as well as his Indigenous appearance, make him perfect for the part ("Look at his eyes!"). Costa retorts that he'll regret it: "No vas a poder controlar ese tipo" ("You're not going to be able to control that guy"). Both turn out to be right.

So frequently does the coloniality trope repeat that a *New York Post* reviewer was provoked to call the film a "conquista-bore, . . . the cinematic equivalent of a term paper for Imperialism 101" (K. Smith 2011). Other reviewers find that

Bollaín's artful direction keeps these intersections of past and present from seeming mechanical. But they are schematic and heavy-handed enough that the viewer suspects they must not be the main point. After all, that recolonization point was already made by an obvious antecedent: Werner Herzog's *Fitzcarraldo* (1982), which reenacted on location an epic episode from the Amazon in the 1890s, and Les Blank's simultaneously filmed *Burden of Dreams* (1982), which documented the chaotic making of *Fitzcarraldo*. Blank's documentary depicts the driven Herzog as a modern-day version of the Peruvian rubber baron whose mad feats his film is reenacting.[9] In *También la lluvia*, Laverty and Loach's script, in effect, compresses this layering into a single film and adds more layers. Many of Bollaín's cast members are thus playing double roles, as actors in the frame story and actors in the embedded reenactment. So, for example, Elejalde plays Columbus in the reenactment and the actor playing Columbus in the frame film. On top of that, Costa's film crew includes a videographer, the only woman crew member (played by Cassandra Ciangherotti), who, Les Blank–like, is making a documentary about the making of the film. We frequently see scenes through the lens of her black-and-white video camera.

Loach's complex script wraps another layer of history around the embedded filmmaking drama. Independent of the crew, hotels, vans, extras, and movie sets, a separate historical crisis is unfolding in Cochabamba. It is the Cochabamba Water War (history, not fiction), the uprising that in the spring of 2000 set in motion the revolutionary process that would topple oligarchic rule in Bolivia and bring Aymara-descended president Evo Morales to power. In the frame story, Bollaín stages a vivid on-location reenactment of this event. Inevitably, it echoes and entangles with the reenactment of sixteenth-century events inside the frame.

In early 2000 Cochabamba became a crisis point for neoliberal globalization. Bolivia had been in deep thrall to international lenders since the mid-1980s. A 1998 International Monetary Fund loan required the government of longtime president Hugo Banzer to agree to privatize all public enterprises—railway, telephone, airline, and water systems. The World Bank made one of its loans contingent specifically on the privatization of water systems in the cities of La Paz and Cochabamba, where the public water service notoriously failed to serve poor neighborhoods. Cochabamba's public utility was put up for auction, and the lone bid came from an international consortium whose main players were Bechtel (United States), Edison (Italy), and International Water Limited (England). Under the name Aguas de Tunari, they paid $2.5 billion for a forty-year concession—on which they were guaranteed a 15 percent annual return!—for controlling and administering all water supplies in Cochabamba, including irrigation and communal resources that had never been part of the municipal system. The film's title phrase, "even the rain," references a particularly vivid detail: the law was so broad that people feared they would be charged even for the rainwater they collected from their roofs. Water bills doubled and tripled to amounts completely beyond the reach of the poor majority.[10] Mass protests began. In January 2000 strikes and blockades shut down Cochabamba for four days. For the next three months, unarmed mass protests continued, coordinated by an effective and experienced grassroots organization led by longtime labor activist Oscar Olivera. (The film character Daniel is modeled on Olivera.) Confrontations became increasingly violent as the government called in the police and armed forces. Deaths multiplied; rebellion spread to other cities while the government, pressured from abroad, steadfastly refused to revoke its contract with the consortium.

At last, in April 2000, Banzer capitulated. Control of Cochabamba's water was turned over to the grassroots organization led by Olivera.[11] This popular victory detonated the dramatic political process that in 2006 brought Aymara-descended labor leader Evo Morales to the presidency of Bolivia, wresting political power for the first time from the hands of the white oligarchy. The result has been a wholesale reconstitution of the Bolivian state.[12]

También la lluvia was made in 2010 in the aftermath of this extraordinary transformation. Its on-location reenactment of the Water War, using archival footage and large numbers of local extras, is vivid, gripping, and morally uplifting. These, of course, are the same effects sought by the fictional Spanish crew reenacting the conquest. Did it involve similar exploitive relations, profit motives, and ethical compromises? Presumably we are intended to ask this question. What are the politics and ethics of reenactment? What is its ontological relation to the original event? Its mode of idealization? Its futurity?

Unfolding in the background of the Spanish film crew's activities, the Water War in Bollaín's film occasions a second string of intersections or mirrorings between the sixteenth century and the twenty-first, and between reenactment and enactment. In the 1514 time frame, Spanish soldiers hunt down the rebel Taíno with attack dogs; in the 2000 time frame, a Water War demonstration is disrupted by riot police with attack dogs. The Taíno's forced tribute in gold dust parallels the newly imposed water fees, which also cannot be met.[13] In the Water War, the women of one barrio defend their community water project from police in the name of their children. On the film set, the Bolivian extras playing Taíno women are assigned to perform a scene in which the Taíno mothers drown their babies in a river to save them from enslavement. Crying babies (also extras) in their arms, the Bolivian women refuse to perform the scene. Finally, Daniel, the actor playing the rebel leader Hatuey in the embedded film, turns out to be the leader of the water revolt in the frame story. The film cuts from Montesinos's historic sermon of 1511 to Daniel exhorting resistance through a handheld loudspeaker at a demonstration.

Parallels aside, the Water War quickly entangles and eventually overwhelms the filmmakers, mainly by overtaking the logistics of mobility and location. The popular movement's main weapon is road blockades, which shut the city down and cut it off from commerce, supplies, and reinforcements. So much for the white vans.[14] Daniel is detained. As the violence escalates, the Spanish cast and crew become terrified for their safety and demand to leave the country. Costa and Sebastián struggle to keep things together just long enough to assemble everyone in the jungle set to film the remaining indispensable scene, in which Hatuey and twelve of his men are burned at the stake amid the protests of the distraught Father Las Casas. The logistical nightmare becomes an ethical turning point. Costa and a horrified Sebastián bribe a police chief to free Daniel long enough for him to finish the film. They agree (this is the ethical crisis) to return him to custody when the filming is done. Sebastián sells his soul to finish his film. (Did Bollaín, we are asked to ask, do the same?) In the most damning parallel of all, the Spanish filmmakers will fictionally burn Daniel at the stake as the captured rebel leader Hatuey, then turn him over to the Bolivian police as the real-life captured rebel leader Daniel. For the viewer, the parallels between sixteenth- and twenty-first-century coloniality culminate here.

Not, apparently, for the Bolivians. In a fascinating directorial achievement, Bollaín repeatedly makes clear that for the Bolivians, parallels between the embedded film (sixteenth-century Spanish colonialism) and their lived present (twenty-first-century neoliberalism) do not exist, as real as these may be for the metropolitan filmmakers and their presumed audience. For the most part, Bollaín expresses this disconnect wordlessly through a conspicuous use of the gaze. When Antón, rehearsing Columbus, turns the catering worker into a Taíno woman, the camera focuses in on her face, which remains blank and unresponsive, even when the acting ends and Antón apologizes ("We actors are all egotists"). As the actor playing Montesinos rehearses his sermon, the camera picks up two Bolivian workers looking on, their faces again blank and unmoved. It's the stereotype of the inscrutable other but deployed so blatantly the viewer knows something else is going on.

When the crew's videographer, filming, asks Daniel his reasons for working in the film, a companion replies, "For the money." The Bolivians give no indication that the cinematic reenactment resonates in any way with their own circumstances. They do not appear to find the reenactment revealing or even meaningful, let alone noble, redeeming, or empowering. These are jobs; they are hired help; whatever story these Europeans are constructing for themselves has nothing to do with them. The attack dogs loosed on the Taíno in the movie are trained movie props; the attack dogs loosed on their street demonstrations are trained attack dogs. Bollaín dramatizes the disconnect at one point through an aggressive manipulation of her viewer. On the screen, we see the scene of the Taíno lined up to pay tribute quotas to the Spanish, little bells filled with gold dust. A man who fails to comply is violently hauled aside, and while his young daughter screams in despair, a Spaniard cuts his arm off with an ax. The camera pans outward: we are in a screening room; the filmmakers are screening the rushes. The camera goes straight to the face of the girl Belén (played by Milena Soliz), the Bolivian extra who plays the role of the distraught child in this scene. She is Daniel's daughter. Seated between Costa and Sebastián, her gaze is riveted to the screen. We think (as we are invited to think), "She is connecting this scene to her father. Something horrifying like this could happen to him, now, in the present." We are completely wrong. Belén jumps out of her seat and runs excitedly to her father, delighted by what she has seen. "Muy interesante," she says, "triste, pero interesante. Me gusta mucho" ("Very interesting. Sad, but interesting. I like it a lot"). She has been watching a projection, and we have been projecting onto her. The viewer cannot help but assign directorial intent here: to intercept the workings of the postcolonial meaning machine and signal its grounding in a self-interested metropolitan subjectivity. Belén is responding like an actress, not a colonized subject.

This intercept is imposed on the viewer again near the end. We watch as, despite all the obstacles, the climactic scene of Hatuey's execution is finally filmed. Tied to the stakes at which they will be burned, the condemned rebels are offered baptism so they may go to heaven. "Do the Christians go to heaven?" Hatuey asks the priest. "Some, yes," says the priest. "Then I prefer hell!" Hatuey retorts. He begins shouting in Quechua (alias Taíno), "I despise your god and your greed," and the Taíno multitude (the Bolivian extras) join him while the pyres are lit. The viewer cannot help but construct a whole web of connections with the Water War. But the Bolivians do not. When Sebastián at last yells "cut," everyone on the set, actors, extras, and crew, break into applause. The work is done. Dressed in his "Taíno" loincloth and face paint, Daniel jumps down from the pyre, only to face the police arriving in their own white suv to take him back to jail. The extras, still in costume and makeup, come to his defense, overturning the vehicle and rescuing Daniel. The police draw guns. "This is like a dream," says Sebastián, now a lost soul. The viewer cannot turn off the echo machine: the Taino revolt and the Water War are variants of the same thing; Daniel and the extras are the heirs of Hatuey, as Sebastián is the heir of Las Casas. But Bollaín somehow manages to make clear that for the Bolivians, there are no echoes, layers, or equations. They are defending Daniel from being taken away by the Bolivian police. That they are still dressed in costumes and makeup from the movie shoot is just happenstance. The contrast has already been sharply drawn. "There are things more important than your movie," says Daniel on two occasions. For Sebastián, however, this is not true. At his darkest moment, he insists, "This protest is going to end, but our movie is going to last forever." At that climactic point, it is no longer he who holds the moral high ground.

For the Bolivians, the operative term is not *reenactment* or *reprise* but simply *repetition*, the familiar, mutating continuation of an endless, ongoing conflict between rich and poor. "I already know this story," Daniel tells Costa (in English), after overhearing him crow crassly on the phone in English about how "fucking" cheap the extras are. He has been a migrant laborer in the United States. The Bolivians inhabit a non-Derridean always already: survival is always hard, the story already known. Recovered history reveals nothing they didn't already know. I have often quoted with conviction Gayatri Chakravorty Spivak's (1999, 110) observation that Eurocentrism, ethnocentrism, and colonialist thinking cannot simply be set aside; they must be worked through—the basis for her revindication of deconstructive critique. *También la lluvia* seems to argue differently: there is no working through, no advance, only an ongoing story. "Siempre nos cuesta tanto" (It is always so costly for us), says Daniel at the end. "It's never easy. I wish there were another way, [*ojalá hubiera otra forma*], but there is not." Asked what he will do next, he replies, "Survive. That's what we do best." The survival narrative does not have a beginning, middle, or end; it does not progress; it only goes on.

Against Flow

White suvs versus blockaded roads. The frame story in *También la lluvia* puts to the test global capitalism's celebratory self-image as flow, the free-trade planetary circulation of goods, money, ideas, talent, and human capital from sites of supply to sites of demand, for which the adjective *free* was cynically co-opted. (See chapter 2 for a fuller elaboration of this argument.) The Cochabamba Water War literalized the flow metaphor—it was about real water—and simultaneously discredited it. In Cochabamba water did not flow freely from supply to demand, and the free market made things worse, not better. Early in the film, the young female videographer encounters Daniel and his neighbors hand-digging a ditch seven kilometers long to bring water to their barrio from a distant well they have collectively managed to purchase. Twice, police arrive to shut down the unlicensed operation because it violates the multinational privatization agreement. So much for flow. Water is life, and in this cruel system, many are told their lives are worthless.

It's no accident that the unarmed popular movement's single most powerful weapon in the Water War proved to be its ability to immobilize road transport. Traffic flow was the powerful's point of greatest vulnerability. Unlike rivers, global flows depend not on gravity but on fueled pumps and machines designed for motion and speed. The mere threat of immobilization terrifies, as the film crew discovers through their own wretched panic. A mere pile of rubble on a street or highway can stop them dead. Bollaín captures beautifully the unfolding of the political confrontation through a dialectics of vehicular motion and bodily stasis, of bodies seeking to move and bodies refusing to move. Out the windows of their SUV en route to a reception with the mayor, the crew sees Daniel before a crowd, calling for a blockade of the city. While they flee, he is taking a stand. Costa drives by crews of *cholas* (working-class Bolivian women) building street blockades. The film crew is finally turned back by a police roadblock. "This matter has nothing to do with me," says Costa, climbing into his vehicle after watching a demonstration. "Yes," his videographer replies, "Pero estás aquí" ("But you are here")—on location.

As I discuss in chapter 1, in Western modernity, mobility is the figure for the freedom and autonomy of the rights-bearing individual, and the figure for modern knowing. Modern subjects know the world by exploring, touring, wandering. Postmodernity's ungrounded hybrid subject intensifies this figure. As Sandy Grande (2014) argues, from the Indigenous side of the equation, that figure of modern selfhood is part of the lexicon of Western imperialism. It offers no emancipatory possibilities to Indigenous people. "The notion of fluidity," Grande says, "has never worked to the advantage of indigenous people" (112).

A model of unchanging permanence does not work to their advantage either. It is merely the mobile subject's facile inverse. The reenactment of the Cochabamba Water War in *También la lluvia* impresses by its depiction/

reenactment of the workings of Indigenous and mestizo popular power, the means by which unarmed masses can confront armed state violence and win. In the wake of their triumph, Bolivian Aymara sociologist Pablo Mamani Ramirez (2004) analyzed the practices of Bolivian popular movements, developed over generations of struggle. Bollaín dramatizes several of them. In one scene, a group of mothers confront the police who have come to lock up their water supply. They drive them off not by using weapons but by relentlessly pushing them with the mass of their bodies. In one of the most ethnographically resonant scenes in the film, a popular assembly decides whether to escalate the protest or not. Men and women of all ages give opinions, in a continuous mix of Quechua and Spanish, till a vote is taken. At the height of the violence, Daniel's wife, Teresa (played by Leonidas Chiri), singlehandedly holds up the escaping convoy of white SUVs. By sheer force of emotion, she manages to commandeer both Costa and his vehicle to rescue her daughter from a building where she lies gravely wounded. She achieves this entirely through embodied speech, a relentless torrent of supplication that flows and that we know will not stop until Costa relents and does what she requires. She must compel him to agree that there is something more important than his film, and to risk his life for that thing, to move to the high ground, even as the rest of the crew flee. Moving in the affective sense (e-motion) is an irresistible force. In obeying her demand, Costa also obeys Montesinos's instruction from 1511 to "love them as you love yourselves." But the mother could care less about love or history; she needs his white face and his white SUV to save her daughter.

As Montesinos's paternalist words attest, the moral high ground is no less colonial than the low, even in the twenty-first century. That Costa's race, gender, and vehicle become instruments for good cannot legitimate them or him. Yet the film's denouement appears to do just that, throwing up an unexpected challenge to the anticolonial viewer it has so diligently called forth. Costa, the harsh, exploitive producer, becomes the white savior, heroic rescuer of Daniel's wounded daughter. He does for her what her father cannot do. In the film's final scene, after all is over and victory won, Daniel seeks out Costa to thank him. Looking upward, short, brown man to tall, white one, camera close, he tearfully thanks the Spaniard for saving his daughter's life. A long, full-body embrace follows, both men in tears—moved. "Will you return?" "I don't think so." "I brought you a gift." In the taxi, en route to the airport, the vehicularized, exculpated Costa opens the gift, a wooden box in the style of religious relics. It contains a vial of water. "Yaku," says Costa (the Quechua word for water). Why the fairy-tale ending? Is the intensely sentimental coloniality of this ending ironic on Bollaín's part, or is it possible she fell into a familiar racialized fantasy to resolve her film? Reviewers have tended to conclude the latter. Many find the Indians sentimentalized, and the whites one-dimensional. But a third option exists: simple repetition, the view supplied by the Bolivian characters. This story ends this way because this is the story. Won or lost, the Water War does not change the story; it becomes an event in it. Villain or hero, Costa is the more powerful; Daniel, the survivor. One key detail supports such a reading. In the taxi, when "Yaku" leaves Costa's lips, the camera shifts to the rearview mirror, where the steady, expressionless gaze of the Bolivian taxi driver looks directly at the camera, and so at us. He is driving the car now, but he's going where Costa tells him to go, or so we assume. If the film is indeed the cinematic equivalent of Imperialism 101, the ending unexpectedly affirms the continuing power of imperial hierarchies to organize action and affect, meaning and possibility, life and death. At the same time, it suggests that knowing this quite possibly makes no difference.

TRANSLATION, CONTAGION, INFILTRATION

> Es la traducción un esfuerzo de alteridad. Alteridad
> del cuerpo respirando la música de otra lengua en
> la estricta particularidad de una voz que habla.
>
> Translation is an effort of otherness, otherness of
> the body, breathing the music of another language
> in the strict particularity of a voice that is speaking.
>
> —DIANA BELLESSI, *Lo propio y lo ajeno*

Some of the important advances in humanistic knowledge in the past three decades have been the result of what Argentine poet Diana Bellessi so felicitously calls "esfuerzos de alteridad" (efforts of otherness; quoted in Masiello 2001, 14). As specialists in what I like to call the traffic in meaning, literary scholars have appropriately taken on the task of defining and analyzing such efforts, as well as carrying them out. The past three decades have seen an unprecedented flourishing of translation studies. Like so many of the phenomena under study in this book, it took off in the 1990s (Venuti 1995). Globalization and the emergence of world literature catalyzed this explosion of thought around translation (Apter 2006, 2013; Venuti 1998, 2013). Inevitably, this explosion gave rise to proposals for expanding the reach of the concept beyond its narrowly linguistic meaning. In particular, scholars proposed a concept of cultural translation to refer to the activity of making one culture's values or practices comprehensible to members of other cultures. Was it useful to use the term *translation* to characterize intercultural as well as interlingual transactions? What implications did such a move have for what Venuti (1998) calls the "ethics of difference"?

This chapter reflects on translation and the idea of cultural translation. It begins with an example, a fascinating text from eighteenth-century colonial Peru, a place rich in high-contrast, high-stakes dramas of alterity. I consider the operations in this text through the work of two eminent contemporary thinkers about translation: poet and translator Eliot Weinberger and anthropological theorist Clifford Geertz, considering how it confirms and also troubles their insights. The argument carries forward to a second textual example. The chapter ends with eight critical questions about what analytical work a concept of cultural translation can and cannot do.

Cuzco, May 1781

In November 1780, in the interior of the Viceroyalty of Peru, a large-scale Indigenous rebellion almost overthrew the Spanish colonial regime in the Andes. After years of secret planning, coordinated revolts broke out in towns and villages across the Andean regions of what are now the republics of Peru and Bolivia. In Peru the uprising was led by José Gabriel Condorcanqui, who rebaptized himself Túpac Amaru, after the last Inca ruler. That first Túpac Amaru had fallen to the Spaniards in 1571.

Condorcanqui's spouse, Micaela Bastidas (the subject of chapter 14), was his militant and fearless coconspirator.[1] The rebels' demands included, among others, an end to the Spanish regime's ruthless practices of exploitation, the restoration of the Inca dynastic rule, and an end to slavery. The rebellion lasted until 1782, but Túpac Amaru and Micaela Bastidas were captured a year earlier. In a dramatic public event, they were tried and executed in the main plaza of the city of Cuzco, along with numerous family members and supporters. Túpac Amaru was drawn and quartered, and Bastidas was garroted, technologies of execution that eyewitnesses said they "had never before seen here" (Lewin 1982, 107).[2]

The 1780–81 rebellion shocked the Spanish authorities. Secure in their dominion, they had cultivated relations with a neo-Inca Indigenous elite as

13.1 — Túpac Amaru II, apocryphal portrait.

partners in their exploitation of the masses. The rebellion rose out of symbolic and political terrain they thought they controlled. One of the documents that fascinates people who study this episode is the lengthy sentencing report issued by Spanish judge José Antonio de Areche on May 15, 1781, from the royal court of Lima. In this document Areche lays out the official Spanish response to the revolt. The report specifies in gruesome detail how the captured rebel leaders are to be executed and what is to be done, limb by limb, with their dismembered bodies. It then goes on to prescribe a new policy of wholesale repression of Indigenous symbolic and artistic practices. The targets are dress, emblems, rituals, and art forms such as music, drama, and portraiture—what we now might sum up as expressive culture. The intent, apparently, was to destroy the Indigenous power structure by suppressing its ability to produce meaning, feeling, identity, and empowerment.

Areche's report is addressed to the Spanish Crown. To justify his campaign of cultural repression, he has to name the Andean practices, objects, and meanings that are to be eliminated and explain their function and force. His sentencing document doesn't just name the things to be condemned; it explains their power and significance, offering a vivid example of what schol-

CHAPTER THIRTEEN |

13.2 — Plaza de Armas, city of Cuzco. SOURCE: FLICKR PHOTO BY KARL NORLING.

ars have proposed calling *cultural translation*. Such translation is required to justify their suppression. Here is an excerpt first in the original Spanish and then in English (Spanish spelling as in original; translation mine):

> Se prohíbe que usen los indios los trages de la gentilidad, especialmente los de la noble raza de ella, que solo sirve de representarles los que usaban sus antiguos Incas, recordándoles memorias que nada otra cosa influyen, que en conciliarles más y más odio a la nación dominante: fuera de ser su aspecto ridículo, y poco conforma a la pureza de nuestras reliquias, pues colocan en varias partes el sol, que fue su primera deidad: estendiéndose esta resolución a todas las provincias de esta América meridional, dejando del todo extinguidos tales trages, tanto los que directamente representan las bestiduras de sus gentiles reyes, con sus insignias, cuales son el *unco*, que es una especia de camiseta; *yacollas*, que son unas mantas muy ricas de terciopelo negro o tafetán, *mascapacjcha*, que es un círculo a manera de corona, de que hacen descender cierta insignia de noblesa antigua, significa

en una mota ó borla de lana de alpaca colorada, y cualesquiera otros de esta especie o significación. (reproduced in Lewin 1982, 166)

It is prohibited for the Indians to wear heathen clothes, especially those of their nobility, since these only serve to symbolize those worn by their Inca ancestors, reminding them of memories that serve no other end than to increase their hatred toward the dominant nation. Not to mention that their appearance is ridiculous and very little in accordance with the purity of our relics, since they place in different parts images of the sun, which was their primary deity. This prohibition is extended to all the provinces of this southern America in order to completely eliminate such clothing, especially those items that represent the accoutrements of their heathen kings, through emblems such as the *unco*, which is a kind of vest; *yacollas*, which are very rich blankets or shawls of black velvet or taffeta; the *mascapacjcha*, which is a circle in the shape of a crown from which they hang a certain emblem of ancient nobility signified by a tuft or tassel of red-colored alpaca wool; as well as many other things of this kind and signification.

Notice how Areche's text explicates the logic of Indigenous identity and its symbolism. If cultural translation exists, this is an example of it. Like a good translator (and ethnographer), Areche seeks to capture faithfully the meaning of things to those who use them and then to communicate these meanings to his readers in a language they will understand. Andean clothing, he explains, reminds people of their ancestors and lost rulers; the sun was their primary deity. The Spaniards are the conquering nation; the Indians hate them and intend never to forget why. Key items are named in Quechua—*unco*, *yacollas*, and *mascapacjcha*—and then defined in vivid, even glowing terms, like those the wearers themselves might use. The imperial rhetoric of cultural and religious superiority coexists with a language of explanation. Where the colonial playbook called for condemnation or mockery, there is also recognition and even respect. Indigenous values and language seem to be speaking through the voice of colonial power—even though the whole point of invoking the force of Indigenous symbols is to justify a campaign of destruction against them, precisely because of their force. So the sentencing report tacks back and forth across the colonial divide. It is fractured by that divide and, at the same time, entangled in it, trafficking in its meanings.

After dealing with dress, the document turns its attention to music and performance. Again the mediator attempts to render the original meaning, side by side with a translation that assigns judgment from the colonizer's perspective. Ministers and magistrates, Areche writes, should ensure that

> en ningún pueblo de sus respectivas provincias comedias u otras funciones públicas, de las que suelen usar los indios para memoria de sus dichos antíguos Incas. . . . Del propio modo se prohíben y quiten las trompetas o clarines que usan los indios en sus funciones, á las que llaman *pututos* y son unos caracoles marinos de un sonido extraño y lúgubre con que anuncian el duelo, y lamentable memoria que hacen de su antigüedad; y también el que usen y traigan vestidos negros en señal de luto, que arrastran en algunas provincias como recuerdo de sus difuntos monarcas, y del día o tiempo de la conquista, que ellos tienen por fatal y nosotros por feliz, pues se unieron al gremio de la Iglesia Católica: y a la amabilísima y dulcísima dominación de nuestros reyes. (Lewin 1982, 167)

> in no town of their respective provinces be performed plays or other public functions that commemorate the former Incas. . . . In like manner the trumpets or bugles that the Indians use for their ceremonies shall be prohibited and confiscated, those they call *pututos*, being seashells with a strange and lugubrious sound that celebrate the mourning and pitiful memorial they make for their antiquity. Also prohibited is the custom of wearing black robes as a sign of mourning, which they drag around in some provinces in memory of their deceased monarchs, and of the day or time of the conquest, which they consider disastrous and we consider fortunate, since it brought them into the company of the Catholic Church and the most kind and gentle domination of our kings.

The customs being condemned are simultaneously honored with explanations that acknowledge (translate?) their meaningfulness, their historical logic, specificity, and force. The power of the *pututos* ("strange and lugubrious sound") is evoked with a desire at odds with the will to suppress them. When Areche speaks of the wearing of black for mourning, he evokes a point of intersection of Spanish and Andean customs. In the very next sentence, he codifies their difference—"which they [the Indians] consider disastrous and we consider fortunate." The crisis of the rebellion brings to the surface a fractured, entangled world of imperial power and desire whose textual symptoms include the starkest of face-offs and at the same time the infiltration and contagion of each side by the other. How much of this can a concept of translation grasp? Or, better, how much can it help us grasp it?

Through the Looking Gloss

Areche's report is a manifesto of colonial violence and repression. How disconcerting, then, to note that it also demonstrates what are seen to be translation's most precious creative powers. Let me refer to two magnificent reflections on the subject: a lecture by Eliot Weinberger, the brilliant translator of Latin American poetry, titled "Anonymous Sources: A Talk on Translators and Translation" (2000), and Clifford Geertz's classic essay "Found in Translation: On the Social History of the Moral Imagination" (1983a). For Weinberger, translation is a necessity "for the obvious reason that one's own language has only created, and is creating, a small fraction of the world's most vital books" (2000, 4). His privileged site of translation is, we know, poetry. "The purpose of, say, poetry translation," Weinberger says, "is not, as it is usually said, to give the foreign poet a voice in the translation-language. It is to allow the poem to be heard in the translation-language, ideally in many of the same ways it is heard in the original language. . . . [I]t means that the primary task of a translator is not merely to get the dictionary meanings right—which is the easiest part—but rather to *invent a new music for the text in the translation-language, one that is mandated by the original though not a technical replication of the original*" (8; emphasis mine). How intriguing that Areche's sentencing report should correspond as fully as it does to Weinberger's ideal for poetry—making the original heard in the translation language ("a strange and lugubrious sound"). It's probably not a correspondence Weinberger would have predicted or even wished: to make a music heard in order to justify snuffing it out. Yet, we can see, to legitimate itself, cultural repression requires a moment of translation, a scene in which the original's power (its mandate, in Weinberger's terms) is displayed. "Translation," Weinberger says, "flourishes when writers feel that their language or society needs liberating. One of the great spurs to translation is a cultural inferiority complex or a national self-loathing" (4–5). In a kind of perverse way, that statement illuminates the legitimation crisis Spain was facing in Peru in 1781, in which Areche's text is enmeshed. Certainly, Areche does not feel entitled to claim a monopoly on meaning in the Andes.

While the translator Weinberger speaks about translation in the linguistic sense, the anthropologist Geertz works with a broader idea of it, as a name for the processes by which a human subject seeks to comprehend a distant culture, the "effort of otherness," as Bellessi called it. Intriguingly, Geertz locates this exercise in the realm of the moral imagination, a stance inherited from his literary mentor, Lionel Trilling. Like Weinberger, he sees "imaginative productions" as privileged sites for the translator's work. For Geertz, the most valuable thing that can be "found in translation" is subjective growth: "the growth in range a powerful sensibility gains from an encounter with another one as powerful or more" (1983a, 45). Here both the strength and the limitations of his liberalism, and Trilling's, shine. For Geertz, the mystery of intercultural understanding is that it is possible at all—but, he insists, it is possible. In Geertz's view, the thing to be studied is how cultures can at one and the same time be so deeply and particularly distinctive and yet be comprehensible to those outside them. In his words, the mystery is "how the massive fact of cross-cultural and cross-historical particularity comports with the equally massive fact of cross-cultural and cross-historical accessibility" (48). This is indeed a big, consequential question. Geertz continues, "The truth of the doctrine of cultural (or historical—it is the same thing) relativism is that we can never apprehend another people's or another period's imagination neatly, as though it were our own. The falsity of it is that we can therefore never genuinely apprehend it at all. We can apprehend it well enough, at least as well as we apprehend anything else not properly ours; but *we do so not by looking behind the interfering glosses that connect us to it, but through them*" (44; emphasis mine). If for Weinberger the exemplary site of translation is poetry, for Geertz there are two such sites. One is literary criticism, which he sees as a scene of translation of the past into the present. His iconic figure is Lionel Trilling, from whom Geertz takes the category of the moral imagination (Trilling 1950). The other exemplary site is the ethnographic encounter in its deepest, most potent instance—though not necessarily its professional form. Indeed, as a model text, Geertz analyzes a long excerpt from a Danish traveler's "superbly observed" account of an occasion of *sati*, or widow burning, in Bali in the 1880s (for a discussion of ethnography and travel writing, see chapter 10).

Areche's sentencing document is obviously neither of these, and yet at intriguing points it seems to bear out Geertz's vision. Arguably, it registers the encounter of "a powerful sensibility . . . with another one as powerful or more." It confirms Geertz's claim that cross-cultural particularity can coexist with cross-cultural accessibility—in Areche's text, the Indigenous Andeans remain irremediably alien yet comprehensible and present. Areche would likely have agreed with Geertz's all-important warning: "Whatever use the imaginative productions of other peoples—predecessors, ancestors, or distant cousins—can have for our moral lives, then, it cannot be to simplify them" (1983a, 44). Rather, one sensibility's encounter with another "comes only at the expense of its inward ease" (45). The fractures and entanglements in Areche's text suggest exactly this unease.

Perhaps Geertz's account, too, provides a way to distinguish between Areche's translation project and his own. The path to apprehending the cultural imagination of another people, Geertz says, runs not "behind the interfering glosses that connect us to it, but through them." "The interfering glosses that connect us to it"—what an essential point! What Geertz means is that when translators appear, they are always already connected in some way to the imaginative production to be translated. Some relation across (historical or cultural) distance has brought the original and the translator together. The scene of translation already possesses a meaning or meanings (glosses) in the translator's world. In Areche's text, it is the whole matrix of colonial difference. According to Geertz, such meanings—like "heathen" in Areche's text—can be expected to interfere with apprehension, and yet they are the very things that the connection is made of (heathen vs. Christian, for example). For this reason, they cannot simply be set aside. They must be looked through—that is, the learning and understanding, the successful translation, will occur when translators destabilize their own cultural imagination ("What does heathen mean, anyway?"). Perhaps this is what Areche's text does not do. Perhaps that is a decolonizing move. Perhaps it is what Areche could not do if he was to enforce the interests of the Spanish Crown.

Seeing through one's glosses seems to happen, or nearly happen, in another fascinating document from the same Andean uprising. It is an eyewitness account of the execution of Túpac Amaru and his supporters in the plaza at Cuzco on May 15, 1781, written by a local official. The writer is a criollo (a person of European descent born in the Americas); he holds a status below the European-born Spaniards and above the mixed-race and Indigenous castes. From this in-between standpoint, he apprehends the symbolic force of the execution mainly in Indigenous terms. Moreover, as Geertz predicts, this happens at the cost of his "inward ease." In a gruesome passage, the witness describes the drawing and quartering of Túpac Amaru:

> Cerró la función José Gabriel, a quien se le sacó a media plaza; allí le cortó la lengua el verdugo y despojado de los grillos y esposas lo pusieron en el suelo; atáronle las manos y pies cuatro lazos, y asidos estos a la cincha de cuatro caballos, tiraban cuatro mestizos a cuatro distintas partes; espectáculo que jamás se había visto en esta ciudad. No sé si porque los caballos no fuesen muy fuertes o el Indio en realidad fuese de fierro, no pudieron absolutamente dividirlo, después que un largo rato lo tuvieron

tironeando, de modo que lo tenían en el aire en un estado que parecía una araña. Tanto que el Visitador, movido de compasión, porque no padeciere más aquel infeliz, despachó de la Compañía una orden mandando le cortase el verdugo la cabeza, como se ejecutó. (reproduced in Lewin 1982, 107–8)

The rebel Jose Gabriel ended the event. He was taken out into the middle of the square, where the executioner cut out his tongue, and then, freed of his shackles and handcuffs, he was laid on the ground; to his hands and feet were tied four ropes, the ends of which were fastened to the saddle straps of four horses, which four mestizos were pulling in four different directions, a spectacle that had never before been seen in this city. I don't know if it was because the horses were not very strong, or if the Indian really was made of iron, but they were absolutely unable to completely split him apart, even after they had been tugging at him for some time, so he was held up in the air looking like a spider. So much was the inspector moved to compassion, that he sent an order for the executioner to cut off his head so the poor man might not suffer anymore, and so it was done.

The operation of multiple interpretive systems produces uncertainty for this criollo observer. Making sense of the scene is indeed costing him his inward ease. It requires him to be a translator for his Spanish readers, for the scene has been shaped by Indigenous glosses—the belief that Túpac Amaru is the reincarnated Inca, that he cannot be killed by execution. Everyone is entangled in these glosses. They are what give the spectacle its significance and its very form. The drawing and quartering were aimed at demonstrating once and for all that the rebel was not superhuman and could not rise again.[3] (As it turned out, he could.)

Remarkably, by the end of the eyewitness account, we find the observer translating in the reverse direction—interpreting Indigenous glosses back into the Christian imagination. Here is his closing paragraph:

Suceden algunas cosas que parece que el diablo los trama y dispone, para confirmar a estos indios en sus abusos agüeros y supersticiones. Dígolo porque habiendo hecho un tiempo muy seco y días muy serenos, aquél amaneció tan toldado que no se le vio la cara al sol, amenazando por todas partes a llover; y a hora de las doce, en que estaban los caballos estirando al indio, se levantó un fuerte refregón de viento y tras este un aguacero, que hizo que toda la gente, y aun los guardias se retirasen a toda prisa. Esto ha sido causa de que los indios se hayan puesto a decir

que los cielos y los elementos sintieron la muerte del inca, que los es-
panoles inhumanos e impíos estaban matando con tanta crueldad. (108)

It seems that the devil schemes and arranges certain things to confirm
these Indians in their abuses, omens, and superstitions. I mention this
because after a period of dryness and very quiet days, this particular day
dawned so overcast that the sun's face was hidden and it was threatening to rain everywhere, and around twelve o'clock, when the horses were
pulling on the Indian, there arose a strong gust of wind, and after it a
downpour that forced all the people, even the guards, to withdraw in
haste. This has resulted in the Indians saying that *the sky and the elements
all felt the death of the Inca, whom the inhumane and ungodly Spaniards
were killing with such cruelty.* (emphasis mine)

Read through the Indigenous glosses, the account translates the scene
back into Christian terms, into the scene of the Crucifixion, coding Túpac
Amaru as a Christ figure and the Spanish as cruel pagan Romans. Though
the account indicts the Spanish, the speaker offers no alternative moral vision. In a social formation that has evolved out of more than two hundred
years of colonial relations, a fractured, entangled world exists. Neither side
can make sense of or act in this world without drawing on the cosmic vision
of the other. This colonial scenario differs from the ones translation theorists
usually imagine, yet there is much to be learned from it.

Questioning "Translation"

What are the strengths and limits of translation as a referent and metaphor
for characterizing cultural transactions, the appropriations, negotiations,
migrations, mediations, recodings, and transposings that are now so much
in the purview of us scholars who traffic in meaning? Can the concept of
translation usefully contain all those things? What is lost and gained if it is
asked to do so? Where does the metaphor succeed and fail as it mutates into
theory? What questions does such an approach have to ask? What distinctions have to be made?

As the Andean texts suggest, to think about cross-cultural meaning making, it's essential to attend to fractures and entanglements, the asymmetries,
ethics, histories, interdependencies, distributions of power, and accountability that are in play. This necessity does not mean giving up or giving up
on the pleasures and beauties of translation—the intense, distilled moments
of poetic or ethnographic encounter, the epiphanies of illumination and un-

ease that Geertz, Weinberger, and Bellessi celebrate. The call to translation for these writers is the call to surpass fractures and entanglements, not by rising above them or going around them or trying to erase them but by entering them and working through toward a place "mandated by the original" (Weinberger 2000, 8).

Translation in its primary, linguistic sense seeks some form of equivalence. How helpful is it, then, to treat as translation processes that are aimed at creating nonequivalence? That deliberately translate into music not mandated by the original? For example, what about translation processes that muffle, absorb, appropriate, transpose, or conceal? What about music that captures aspects of the original through modes like parody, mockery, and caricature whose accuracy derives from exaggeration?

What are the uses of a translation model for exploring the migration of art forms, their insertion (grafting?) into new contexts of reception—Indian cinema viewed in Nigeria; Latin American soap operas finding audiences in Egypt; American funk displacing samba in Brazilian neighborhoods; or, for that matter, transatlantic surrealism or the spread of the sonnet in Europe? Do new audiences *translate* these productions into their own imaginations? Is that the right word? For contexts like these, ideas of resonance and intersection seem as useful as the idea of translation. Does a concept of cultural translation (Geertz's vision of seeing through the interfering glosses) help clarify how migrating art forms enter through what is already there and how they get infiltrated by it in the process?

Is translation the right concept for exploring what Néstor García Canclini (1992) calls *cultural reconversion*? This term refers to transpositions where the knowledges, practices, or symbols of one social arena or institution get processed into the contents of another—as when vernacular cultural forms are reconverted into lettered high-culture art forms (like graffiti in galleries), or when vernacular aesthetic categories are appropriated into academic theory, or when communal lifeways are reconverted into folklore, that is, into cultural capital for nation-states? With reconversion, translation again produces something nonequivalent to the original, yet, in some sense, it reproduces the original. Here, too, entanglements matter. When reconversion happens as part of interventions like evangelization or modernization, destroying the original is often part of the process. Argentine cultural historian Beatriz Sarlo (1998) singles out a moment in her country's history when the national government assigned rural schoolteachers the task of collecting local stories and legends and forwarding them to the ministry in written form—folklore. This reconversion signified the preservation of local, oral knowledges and, at the same time, their substitution by a new canon, the knowledges of modern (national) schooling.

Is it helpful or unhelpful to think of commodification as a process of translation? For example, the World Trade Organization created something called *trade-related intellectual property rights*. The term names a process whereby local Indigenous knowledge, especially biomedical knowledge, was converted into ownable, commodified forms (e.g., pharmaceuticals), which could then be sold back as commodities to those who created them in the first place. The ethical vacuum in which such processes occur today takes the anachronism out of Geertz's call on the moral imagination.

Decolonization produces other forms of reconversion that postcolonial critics have brought to our attention.[4] For example, *testimonio* and oral history often involve a kind of self-translation, in which subaltern subjects seek to translate or transpose their knowledge into terms that make it apprehensible to distant metropolitan subjects. Here reconversion has many facets: subalterns perhaps speaking in a second language more powerful than their own, or metropolitan intellectuals reconverting a recorded text into writing. The intersections and resonances between metropolitan genres and the speech repertoire of the testimonial speaker are critical. What counts as a story? Again, in all such instances, the entanglements matter. Anthropologist Ruth Behar explores this question in a study aptly titled *Translated Woman: Crossing the Border with Esperanza's Story* (1993).

The concept of cultural translation bears the unresolvable contradiction that in naming itself, it preserves the distances it works to overcome. Nikos Papastergiadis, for instance, formulates cultural translation as "the process by which communication occurs across boundaries" or "the means by which people with different cultural histories and practices can form patterns of communication and establish lines of contact across these differences" (2000, 127). (Notice how such formulations obliterate the entanglements.) Because it sustains difference, a translation paradigm by definition likely won't lead us to the new subjectivities and interfaces that eventually come out of entanglements sustained over time—as they were in Cuzco. Here we need to refer to other linguistic operations and metaphors—pidginization, creolization, and above all multilingualism, translation's mother but thus also, in crucial ways, its definitive other. The multilingual person is not someone who translates constantly from one language or cultural system into another, though translation is something multilingual subjects are able to do if needed. To be multilingual is above all to live in more than one language, to be one for whom translation is unnecessary. The image for multi-

CHAPTER THIRTEEN |

lingualism is not translation, then, but perhaps *desdoblamiento* (doubling), a multiplying of the self.

Translation is a deep but incomplete metaphor for the traffic in meaning. It is probably not, in the long run, an adequate basis for a theory of cross-cultural meaning making and certainly not a substitute for such a theory. But exploring that metaphor may be a productive way of clarifying what such a theory might look like. Translation can be our constant reminder that the study of cultural mediation will be both a science and a poetics.

THINKING ACROSS THE COLONIAL DIVIDE

Two hours southwest of Cuzco, Peru, there is a small Quechua-speaking town called Tinta, an ancient place located at an altitude of 11,500 feet on what for centuries was a trade route between the Inca capital Cuzco and the mining center Potosí in what is now Bolivia.

Tinta was a prosperous place and an important regional center during both the Inca and Spanish Empires. Today it has around 2,500 inhabitants and maintains many classic features of Andean urbanism, like gently sloping downhill streets where a channel of fresh mountain water runs down the middle as a communal amenity; and an annual cycle of fiestas, processions, and ceremonies. Its population has been affected by out-migration to urban areas and other countries where there are jobs.

Tinta is best known as the home of José Gabriel Condorcanqui, the Indigenous leader who in 1780, under the name Túpac Amaru II, led a rebellion across the Andean region that threatened to overthrow Spanish rule (see figure 13.1). His trial and execution are discussed in chapter 13. His namesake, Túpac Amaru I, the last Inca emperor, in 1571 was defeated by the Spanish

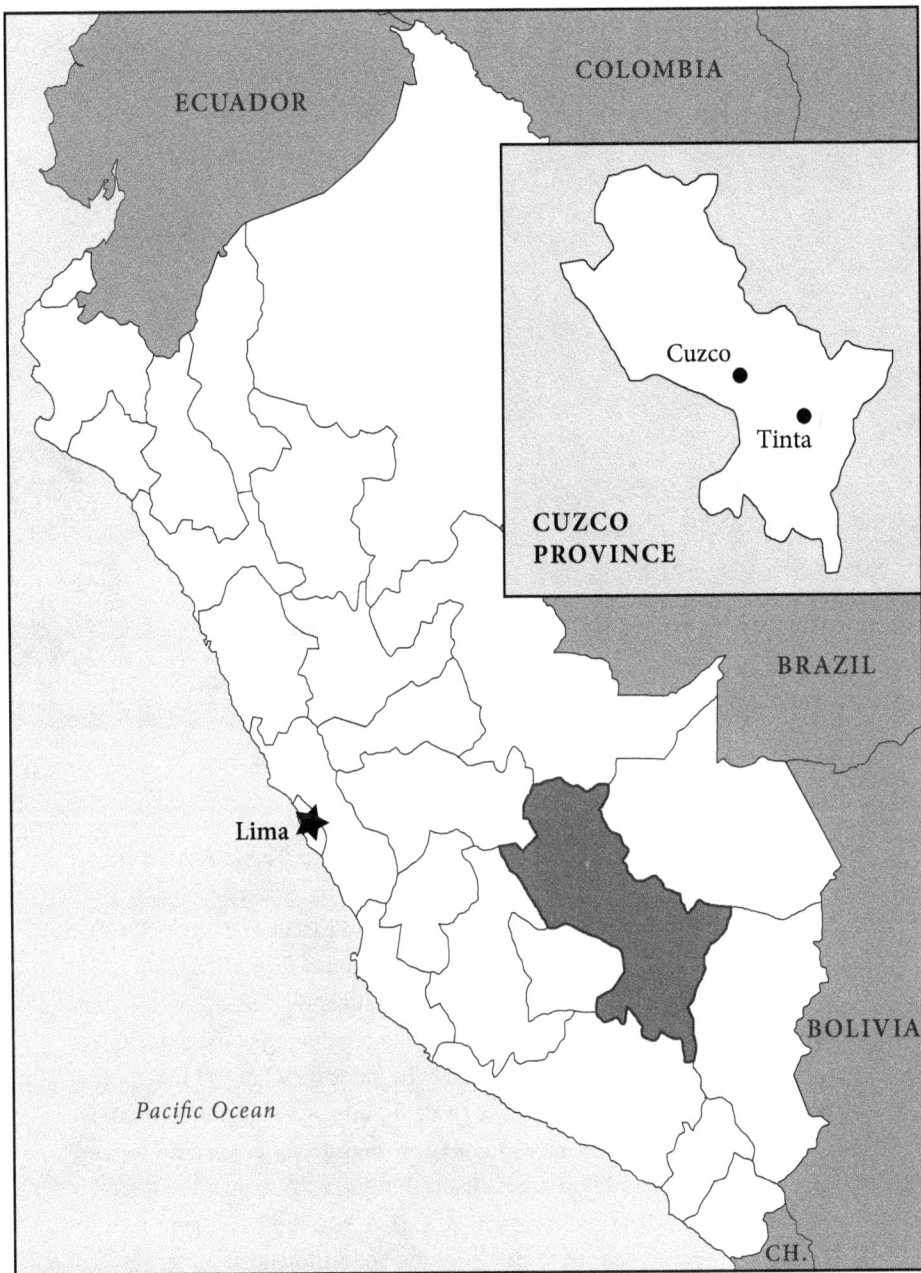

MAP 14.1 — Map of Peru with Lima, Cuzco, and Tinta marked. SOURCE: CHRISTINE RIGGIO.

14.1 — Three women in Andean Indigenous dress. SOURCE: PIKIST.

and executed soon after in the main plaza in Cuzco.[1] Túpac Amaru II was a successful Indigenous farmer and muleteer whose commercial networks extended from Tinta west all the way to Lima and east all the way to La Paz. In the late 1700s, as anger intensified against the many forms of exploitation, taxation, and dispossession imposed by the Spanish regime, these commercial networks became the basis for clandestine organizing of the mass uprising, which took the Spaniards completely by surprise when it broke out in November 1780.[2] As those who have studied Latin American history know (see Walker 2014), Túpac Amaru's forces were defeated after six months, and he was executed, like his predecessor, in the Plaza de Armas in Cuzco in front of a large crowd. If you have visited Cuzco, you will have spent time in this plaza. He was sentenced to death by the Spanish magistrate José Antonio de Areche, whose sentencing document is discussed in chapter 13. As regards his corpse, Areche ordered an elaborate geographic distribution: "His head will be sent to the town of Tinta where, after having been three days on the gallows it shall be placed on a stake at the most public entrance to the

CHAPTER FOURTEEN |

town. One of his arms will go to the town of Tungasuca, where he was chief, where it will be treated in a like manner. And the other in the capital of the Province of Caraballa" (reproduced in Lewin 1982, 164). Areche also prescribed the program of cultural repression discussed in the previous chapter. It prohibited Indians from wearing "heathen clothes" or performing their traditional forms of dance, theater, ceremony, and music.

Though his prohibitions are elaborated in detail, Areche does not tell people what kind of clothing they ought to wear or what musical instruments they are allowed to play. What is known today as traditional Andean dress descends from Andean women's appropriation and adaptation of European peasant dress in response to the repression (see figure 14.1).[3] Out of the attempt to suppress Indigenous music and musical instruments came the distinctive harp, violin, and panpipe music associated with Andean Indigenous culture today. It takes a lot more than an edict to squelch expressive culture.

The Ghosts in the Plaza

When you go to Tinta, you enter the town by crossing the bridge where Túpac Amaru's head was displayed, you look out over the fields he once owned, and you make your way to the plaza, where, no surprise, there stands a bronze statue of the hero, his rebel arm aloft, his young son by his knees.

Even if you explore the plaza, however, you might miss the parts of Tinta's history I'm going to dwell on in these pages. Along with the *héroe de la patria* (hero of the fatherland), two other ghosts inhabit that plaza, both of them women—gifted, powerful women who also made their mark on Peruvian history. One is Micaela Bastidas, Túpac Amaru's wife, coconspirator, and military strategist. She is present, sort of, in the statue (figure 14.2), on her knees behind her husband, at the same height as the child. This subservient image completely distorts her life and her key role in the rebellion, where she recruited and commanded troops, managed spies and clandestine communications, organized troop movements, punished traitors, and devised battle plans (Chauco Arrián 1980; Silva Hurtado 1982). In fact, many historians think that if her husband had followed her instructions and invaded Cuzco quickly, before the Spanish could gather their forces, the rebels might have won. Bastidas was likewise executed in the plaza in Cuzco, not as a wife or mother but as a rebel leader. The criollo eyewitness to the execution (also discussed in the previous chapter) offered the following description of her death. Like her husband, she appears almost impossible to kill: "Then the Indian woman Micaela climbed up to the platform where likewise in the

14.2 — Statue of Túpac Amaru, town of Tinta, Peru. SOURCE: *TOURS VIRTUAL DE TINTA* (BLOG).

presence of her husband her tongue was cut out and she was garroted which lasted a seemingly infinite amount of time since she had a very small neck and the clamp could not strangle her, and the executioners were forced to put ropes around her neck and pull them in opposite directions in order to finish killing her" (Lewin 1982, 107).[4]

No true portraits of Micaela Bastidas exist. They were all imagined long after her death. In addition to Bastidas, nearly two hundred women were punished for their participation in the rebellion of 1780–81 (Silva Hurtado et al. 1982). The women of Tinta today still remember them.

The second female ghost lives in a white, tile-roofed house that is falling into ruin on one side of the plaza, behind the statue of Túpac Amaru. You can see it was once a lovely home, with a front patio shaded by what is now a very old tree. It used to be the post office, my guide told me, but before that it was the house of Clorinda Matto de Turner, probably Peru's most famous

14.3 — Micaela Bastidas, apocryphal portrait. Artist unknown. SOURCE: HISTORIA PERUANA, HTTPS://HISTORIAPERUANA.PE/BIOGRAFIA/MICAELA-BASTIDAS -PUYACAHUA/.

14.4 — Clorinda Matto de Turner, circa 1890. Artist unknown. SOURCE: HTTP://
MUJERICOLAS.BLOGSPOT.COM.ES/2016/10/CLORINDA-MATTO-DE-TURNER
-ESCRITORA.HTML.

woman writer, who lived in Tinta in the 1870s with her husband, Joseph
Turner. Turner was an English expatriate who studied medicine but became
a landowner and businessperson in Peru. Clorinda Matto was born near Cuzco
in 1852 and educated there in a prestigious college for women (Cuadros 1949;
Peluffo 2005). In 1889 she published a landmark novel condemning the mistreatment and oppression of Indigenous people in the Andes by their white
overlords. It was titled *Aves sin nido* (*Birds without a Nest*). Matto went on
to write two more novels, a play, three books of tales and legends, and many
shelves of essays and magazine articles. She was a feminist, and women occupy a central place in her writings. After moving to Lima, she became the
editor of Peru's equivalent of *Time* magazine, *El Perú Ilustrado*, and founded

an all-female printing press called La Equitativa (Gelles 2002; C. Ortiz 2014). She was persecuted by religious authorities for her novels depicting interracial love and sexual misconduct by priests. She was eventually driven into exile and spent her final years in Buenos Aires, where she died in 1909. Only three or four photographs of Matto exist. Her house in Tinta is unrestored and marked only by a tiny plaque.

So in the shadow of the statue of the male hero in the plaza lie these two female presences, one recalled by a ruin and the other by a distortion. I am going to situate them in relation to each other and to coloniality.

Many powerful lines of difference separate these two women, one remembered as a late eighteenth-century Indigenous revolutionary and the other as a late nineteenth-century feminist writer. Bastidas belongs to the colonial period, Matto to the republic (Peru became independent from Spain in 1821). Bastidas lived as a colonized subject; Matto did not. Matto was white; Bastidas was of mixed race, of Indigenous and possibly African descent, a decisive fact in the colonial hierarchy. Bastidas was a warrior and Matto a writer. Matto was a paternalistic reformer, Bastidas an insurgent; Bastidas was Catholic and devout, Matto an anticlerical skeptic. Matto was learned and well educated, including by an English feminist tutor. Bastidas had minimal schooling, though she could read and write. Bastidas died in her thirties in a canonically premodern way: garroted, decapitated, and dismembered in a public plaza. Matto died in her fifties in a strictly modern fashion: after undergoing surgery following a tour of Europe that weakened her health (Peluffo 2015). About Matto, a modern, white republican woman, we know quite a lot. About Bastidas, a colonial woman of color, we know very little.

However, as the Andean historian Nils Jacobsen (1993) observes, for the most part the divides that separate the two women are colonial in origin. They are lines of hierarchy and difference that construct what my title calls "the colonial divide," the binary distinctions that form the epistemic infrastructure of colonial power, upholding unequal access to economic opportunity, resources, social power, wealth, and political control.

So we may pose the question: Is it possible to come up with a different set of descriptors, an epistemic infrastructure that is, if not decolonized, then at least decolonizing? Here is a start. Micaela Bastidas and Clorinda Matto were both *serranas*—highland women in Peru's fractured geography, divided by the long distance between *sierra* and *costa* (mountains and coast). They were *andinas*, Andean women, formed by the dramatic geography and ecology in which they grew up. They were both rural. They were both literate and empowered by their literacy. Bastidas wrote copious letters, edicts, and orders, without which the rebellion could not have taken place. A handful survive. Matto made her living as a modern professional writer and left a copious archive (Gelles 2002).

Both women were bilingual in Spanish and Quechua, and like many Andean people, they lived in both languages. Matto spoke Spanish at home and learned Quechua growing up on her father's hacienda in a place called Paulo Chico, today an hour or so outside Cuzco. There is disagreement about where Bastidas grew up, but her first language was Quechua, and she learned Spanish through schooling and then her work. Both were businesswomen, ambitious and successful. Matto took over her husband's export businesses after he unexpectedly died when she was twenty-eight. She went on to found magazines and her printing press. Bastidas was a full partner in her husband's agricultural and commercial enterprises before co-organizing the revolt (Silva Hurtado et al. 1982; Walker 2014). Both women were abolitionists and anticolonialists. Both were rebellious, courageous, and defiant. "There is no reason," wrote Bastidas in an edict, "for them [the Spanish] to treat us like dogs, but for taking away our goods and possessions through so much tyranny" (que nos traten como perros, fuera de quitarnos con tanta tiranía nuestras posesiones y bienes; Chauco Arriarán 1980, 60; my translation). Both women experienced the violence of war, Bastidas in the insurgency and Matto in the 1873 War of the Pacific between Peru and Chile.[5] As a young bride in her twenties, she turned the house in Tinta into a field hospital.

Both women were violently punished for their political dissent and defiance of gender norms. In both cases, moreover, the punishment focused on their power of speech. Bastidas's execution began with the amputation of her tongue. Matto's house and her all-woman printing house in Lima were invaded by the army and destroyed, her books burned. Both married young, at sixteen, and formed marital relationships marked by high degrees of collaboration, reciprocity, mutual respect, and empowerment. One of them, Bastidas, had children, but neither built her identity around maternity or the domestic sphere. They were both women of power. Bastidas and Túpac Amaru wanted to restore the Inca Empire and rule it. Matto never mentions either of them in her writings, though she wrote a play about an Inca princess named Yma Sumac who is tortured and executed by the Spanish (Cuadros 1949).[6]

Strange as it may seem, the 1780–81 rebellion does not appear explicitly in Matto's writings. Was it forgotten? Not at all. As Francesca Denegri (1996), Cecilia Méndez (1995), and others have shown, the Andean rebellion is present in Matto's novelistic writings as a subtext; that is, it lies underneath them, detectable by secondary effects. The defeat that cost Bastidas her life had a great impact on the highland society into which Matto was born seventy years later. Matto lived, in other words, in the afterlife of the failed rebellion, in a world shaped by it. In similar fashion, the Haitian Revolution of 1791, which overthrew French colonial rule, became an unspoken but omnipresent subtext in nineteenth-century French thought, like a trauma nobody wants to talk about (Buck-Morss 2009; Fischer 2004).

One of my aims in bringing together these two figures is to disturb the disciplinary and imaginative divide that Latin American historiography draws between colonial times and republican times. In the historiography of the Americas, the colonial period before independence and the nineteenth century after independence exist as separate academic fields, distinct historical orders separated by the defeat of the colonial order. (For a discussion of independence as a concept, see chapter 15.) But that pre/postindependence distinction is yet another binary defined by the colonial divide, by coloniality. How, then, to inquire about the continuities that flow across that line—the pathways of daily life, belief, identity, economy, custom, institutions, and knowledge that carry across the scholarly and political break between colony and republic? How to track the enduring forces of geography, ecology, and language? How to interrupt the force of coloniality, decolonize its schema?

The academic cutoff between two historical periods and two academic specialties, we should notice, reproduces the original political break in which the overthrow of colonial rule marks the beginning of a new phase. This means that the academic mapping is constructed from *within* the story the republic wants to tell about itself, a story of emancipation and progress. In that story, a colonial dark age, marked by unenlightenment and cruelty, is overthrown by enlightened republicanism that transforms rigid colonial hierarchies into dynamic modern citizenries. But that story itself needs decolonizing, because much of what supposedly came to an end did not and was never meant to.

Bolivian sociologist and cultural theorist Silvia Rivera Cusicanqui (2010) has pursued this question. Rejecting the republican narrative, Rivera Cusicanqui offers a very different analysis of the eighteenth-century Andes. Despite the harsh restrictions and demands that colonial hyperexploitation imposed on Indigenous Andeans, she argues, by the late eighteenth century a dynamic, innovative society had developed in the Peruvian highlands, with an expansive and diversified economy based on "the long distance circulation of goods, networks of productive communities . . . multicultural highly mixed urban centers" (Rivera Cusicanqui 2010, 53; my translation).[7] She argues that "an emergent indigenous modernity" was being built, steadily expanding its influence and geographic reach, a modernity anchored in Indigenous technology and knowledge and the enduring infrastructure of the Inca Empire. For the sake of its own interests, the Spanish Crown chose to repress this nascent project through taxation and the many other kinds of coercion that motivated the rebellion of 1780–81. The twentieth-century anticolonial thinkers discussed in chapter 16 would recognize these tactics that sought, as they put it, to interrupt the unfolding of the productive forces that were in play at the time.

From Rivera Cusicanqui's perspective, Túpac Amaru and Micaela Bastidas exemplify the expansive, innovative, modern energies she refers to. They were businesspeople, commercial agents who owned extensive lands around Tinta and several hundred mules with which they ran an enterprise producing and distributing a variety of commercial goods. As mentioned earlier, their commercial territory extended from Cuzco west all the way down to the Pacific Coast and east all the way south to Potosí, La Paz, and eventually the Atlantic Coast (Walker 2014). The rebellion they led was directed not against the Spanish Crown itself but against the excesses of financial and labor coercion that impeded the unfolding of the emergent Andean project. As the writings of Bastidas make clear, theirs was not a strictly Indigenous rebellion at all. They sought to mobilize not only Indigenous people but anyone whose aspirations were thwarted by colonial impositions—mestizos, dissident Spaniards, clerics, chieftains, local bosses. And such people did join in, along with hundreds if not thousands of women (Silva Hurtado et al. 1982). The rebellion itself was *abigarrada* (piebald; see note 7), a modern, alternative hegemonic project. It was defeated, but it changed the political trajectory of Peru. "To say indigenous Andeans lost the rebellion," says Jacobsen, "is only half true" (1993, 332).

Decolonization. Who Needs It?

From the Bolivian sociologist Silvia Rivera Cusicanqui, to the North American historian Nils Jacobsen, to the Peruvian sociologist José Guillermo Nugent (discussed in chapter 1), scholars tend to agree on what came next in the Andes, and it can't meaningfully be called decolonization. After gaining independence from Spain in 1824, Peru did not, in fact, proceed to develop a modern citizenry or a modern social contract. Jacobsen puts it like this: "Instead of decolonizing, in the highlands (*altiplano*) colonial structures and relations were revitalized." The "colonial cleavages" persisted, reinscribing, again and again, the "polarized vision of society" that structures colonial power (Jacobsen 1993, 5–6). In Rivera Cusicanqui's words, instead of decolonization, there was recolonization. Examples abound. In 1854, thirty years after independence, the reviled Indian tribute system was finally abolished. But it was replaced almost immediately with a taxation system that overwhelmingly fell on Indigenous communities. As might be expected, that imposition triggered a rebellion, this time in the city of Puno, near Lake Titicaca (the Huancano Rebellion, 1867). Although public corporal punishment, like that inflicted on Bastidas, had been abolished in the 1820s, the Puno rebels were nevertheless publicly strangled and burned at the stake (Monsalve Zanatti 2012, 252). The colonial playbook, in other words, was still very much in force—or at least there in the cultural cache, ready to be taken out when needed.

Rivera Cusicanqui pursues the idea of *recolonization*, as the way coloniality unfolds through time: "The modernizing efforts of the European (white) elites in the region resulted in successive processes of recolonization" that "recycled old practices of exclusion and discrimination" (2010, 53, 56). For Rivera Cusicanqui, the whole historical sequence—from the eighteenth-century Bourbon reforms, to nineteenth-century republicanism, to twentieth-century modernization and progress, to late twentieth-century postmodernism, multiculturalism, and hybridity—represents "waves of recolonization," a continuous retooling of colonial relations of domination, exploitation, and exclusion.[8] In the Andes, she argues, these processes produced elites that were not modern or progressive but *arcaicos* (archaic), anchored in "feudal and rentier modes of domination" (53). In the Andean countries, including her native Bolivia, Rivera Cusicanqui says, it is white elites, not Indigenous people, who need to be decolonized and integrated into modernity. As we saw in chapter 1, the Peruvian sociologist José Guillermo Nugent arrives at a similar conclusion, though he speaks not of recolonization but of countermodernity (Nugent 1992). Thinking across the colonial divide, Bastidas struggled against colonization, and Matto against recolonization. As it turns out, their lives can tell us a lot about how this came about on the ground.

It came about through the very processes that drew Peru into the capitalist export economy that boomed globally in the second half of the nineteenth century (Beckman 2012). The export commodity in question was wool; the mode of production was the hacienda; the commercial infrastructure was British.[9] The history of wool in the Andes is ancient. Micaela Bastidas and Clorinda Matto are beads on a string of yarn that goes back three thousand years and forward to the present.

In the late eighteenth century, with hundreds of mules, Túpac Amaru and Micaela Bastidas trafficked in wool, among other products, in a vast internal market that, as described earlier, stretched from Lima to La Paz. No international wool market existed in the eighteenth century. Spain and

England both had their own wool industries that supplied the domestic demand. After 1820, with the mechanization of the textile industry and the expansion of wage work in England, the demand for raw wool exploded to feed the new mills and the growing Eurasian market (Jacobsen 1993, 197). The search for raw wool brought British wool merchants to highland Peru. Exports of Peruvian wool took off after 1830 and expanded so fast that in only twenty years, by 1850, wool rather than minerals had become the main source of foreign earnings in Peru (Miller 1982).

The rapid expansion of the wool market triggered a vast land grab in the Andes. White elites dispossessed Indigenous communities of their grazing and crop-growing lands in order to consolidate extensive holdings that could sustain large herds of sheep and alpacas. Haciendas proliferated in zones like Tinta, where they had not existed before. As Jacobsen notes, this transfer of land did not occur through modern capitalist buyer-seller transactions but in colonial fashion, through violent and irregular usurpations. Once again, dispossession was justified by the supposed lack of productivity of Indigenous inhabitants, their supposed failure to make good use of the land. In a familiar script, the dispossessed *indios* were then recruited and coerced to become the workforce for this profit-making enterprise. But, again, they were not recruited as modern salaried workers free to sell their labor on a competitive labor market. They entered into the semifeudal arrangements of peonage. In the face of what Rivera Cusicanqui would call a recolonization, Indigenous communities, Jacobsen says, reinvested in their own traditional structures of communal solidarity. They circled their wagons, strengthening communitarian forms to defend their autonomy and their remaining lands. In the world of commerce, business relations based on clientelism, *compadrazgo* (friendship), kinship, and the handshake prevailed, not the fierce competitive energies of capitalism (Jacobsen 1993; Miller 1982). Tinta had been a center for textiles under Inca rule; wool continued to be a source of prosperity for Túpac Amaru and Micaela Bastidas in the eighteenth century, and for Clorinda Matto and Joseph Turner a hundred years later. Jacobsen suggests a further connection: "After 1850, the wool economy helped define a common Southern Peruvian identity, *an identity that first appeared in the political struggle around the Túpac Amaru rebellion*" (1993, 334; emphasis mine). That Andean identity is one of the threads that crosses the colonial divide from Bastidas to Matto.

Through the hacienda system, wool became the commodity that "incorporated highland Peru into the international market" (Jacobsen 1993, 197). The infrastructure for distribution and transportation remained much as it was in Bastidas's time. This changed in 1874, when Clorinda Matto was twenty-two and living in Tinta. A railway opened between Puno in the high-lands and the port city of Arequipa three hundred miles away, permitting a scalar expansion of the wool trade. That railway replaced the mule-driven transportation system that had made Bastidas and her husband prosper-ous. It was also the system that created Joseph Turner's profession as a wool merchant. Serving the export industry, Turner became one of a corps of pur-chasing agents who circulated from town to town in the Andes, buying wool for five English commercial houses that ran the Peruvian wool trade from their base in Arequipa. Turner worked for Stafford House, the commercial family that gave its name to Staffordshire in England. With the arrival of the railway, these British enterprises set up wool markets at train stations in the altiplano. Wool cultivators brought their wares to sell to the agents. Each commercial house owned its agents, often binding them through debt (Jacobsen 1993, 190). It was a ruthless trade. Agents routinely used fraud and deception against local vendors, who in turn exploited Indigenous herders. In this harsh commercial world, some prospered, and many did not. Joseph Turner's enterprise did not, neither in his hands nor in those of Clorinda, who took over the business when her husband unexpectedly died in 1881. After two years, she lost the business when she was defrauded by her own lawyers. She left Tinta and the Andes in 1883 and never returned.

So it was that at the end of the nineteenth and the beginning of the twen-tieth century, "across the altiplano, neocolonial hierarchical power relations were resurrected . . . just as commercial networks were becoming more dense, and competition for land was intensifying" (Jacobsen 1993, 5).[10] This world, born out of the defeat of the project that Túpac Amaru and Micaela Bastidas died for, is the world into which Clorinda Matto was born and in which she grew up and lived half her life. It is the world that formed her as a dissident woman, an anticolonialist, an antiracist, a feminist, and an Andean. It is a neocolonial world where decolonization and recolonization seem to become indistinguishable. While elites recolonized labor and prop-erty, anticolonial dissidents like Matto or the Sociedad Amigos del Indio (Society of Friends of the Indian; Monsalve Zanatti 2012) saw only one path to justice, equality, and citizenship for Indigenous people: assimilation to white and mestizo culture, especially through education. Here, too, decolo-nizing energies recolonized. Viewed across the colonial divide, paternalistic assimilationist programs look like variants of Areche's suppression of In-digenous culture in 1781. Across the colonial divide, the Andean rebellion appears to share a similar decolonizing/recolonizing contradiction. After overthrowing Spanish rule, the rebels' project was none other than to restore the Inca dynasty from which Túpac Amaru was descended. The antidote to Spanish imperial domination was to be Inca imperial domination. Empire, too, crossed the colonial divide.

In commonsense semantics, the difference between colonization and decolonization is that the latter undoes or dismantles the former. But the more consequential difference, perhaps, is that we know what the former looks like but not the latter. As with the concept of independence explored in chapter 15, decolonization is an exercise in futurology. There is no script, no recipe, for what is supposed to happen once colonial rule ends. There is no theory of decolonization, no picture of what a decolonized society should look like, no telos that recognizes when the new state has been achieved. Decolonization is a future that lies over the horizon.

Perhaps we are looking at a paradox. If colonialism can be overthrown only through the imposition of a new hegemonic project, then that imposition will invariably be experienced by some as a recolonization, a new wave of domination and coercion. In Peru, for example, the wool export boom lasted well into the 1930s.[11] The hacienda system lasted until 1969, when it was dismantled by the left-wing dictatorship of Juan Velasco. Velasco's government bought eleven million hectares of land from hacienda owners and distributed them among cooperatives and communities. The great hacienda houses that dotted the spare landscape of the altiplano were abandoned as elites headed to Lima to seek their fortunes in banking and other businesses. Surely Velasco must have thought this was decolonization at last. But for Andean peasantries ordered to reorganize themselves into the alien form of Soviet-style agricultural cooperatives, it was the opposite. Migrants flooded to the coastal cities; the Andes became a backwater and a crucible for the unfathomably cruel Maoist guerrilla movement, the Shining Path.[12]

If, in contrast, decolonization occurs as a bottom-up process in which ex-colonial groups collectively decide their possibilities and their paths, then there can be no formula, script, or paradigm for it.[13] There can, however, be practices and principles of decolonization. Rivera Cusicanqui suggests a few:

1 It is the privileged who need to be decolonized, not subalterns. The privileged need to be saved from themselves, and the world from their mindless depredations.

2 "There can be no discourse of decolonization, no theory of decolonization, without a decolonizing practice" (Rivera Cusicanqui 2010, 71). New intellectual paradigms that leave privileged white intelligentsias in their place and their intellectual authority unquestioned will

CHAPTER FOURTEEN |

never be enough. There has to be transformative energy and political urgency. Decolonizing practices, Rivera Cusicanqui argues, do exist and can be invented, even though there is no knowing where they will lead. Over many years, Rivera Cusicanqui herself developed a pedagogy based on deep analyses of Aymara concepts and cosmovision, which are then placed in dialogue with Western concepts, with the aim of retooling the imaginations of her students.

3 Decolonization cannot be carried out only in the languages of the colonizers. It requires working in and between the languages of colonizers and colonized. For Rivera Cusicanqui, serious translingual intellectual work is a source for the new social visions decolonization requires. Those visions, she argues, can only come out of the conflicting but intersecting histories that produced the colonial experience—across the colonial divide. Obviously, this requires deep encounter not just between languages and concepts but between minds and bodies. Rivera Cusicanqui is not a native speaker of Aymara, though she grew up hearing it. Her knowledge of it is the result of long, hard work, driven by a sense of responsibility and a refusal to appropriate.

Language brings us back to Clorinda Matto and Micaela Bastidas. Neither of these remarkable women seems to have placed any particular value on her bilingualism, even though it was essential to both their achievements. Bastidas could not have marshaled so many social sectors in support of the revolt without both languages, nor grasped so well the workings of colonial power. Matto, without them, likewise could not have achieved her critical grasp of colonial abuses and her passion for denouncing them.

Rivera Cusicanqui speaks of recolonization coming in "waves," from the defeat of the 1780–81 rebellion all the way down to late twentieth-century multiculturalism and twenty-first-century decolonial thought. In some respects, the Andean concept of time, which she also discusses, offers a more generative grasp on this recycling and reengineering. As in so many cultures, Andean temporality is cyclical and spiral. The present is both a repetition and an overcoming of the past; the present is the past of a future that is unknown but will be recognizable when it arrives because pasts will be repeating themselves there. The colonial divide spirals through pasts, presents, and futures, mutating but always recognizable. It is easy to imagine the connectedness of Micaela Bastidas and Clorinda Matto in this temporality. What, then, of decolonization? Is it, too, the mutating redeployment of possibilities that existed, realized or unrealized, in the past? No wonder the academy so readily replaced demand for decolonization with the simplifying, linear adjective *postcolonial*.

Coda

Those southern Andean haciendas, fallen into ruin, are still there in the Peruvian altiplano. Driving aimlessly outside Cizco one day in 1992, my companions and I noticed one that appeared to be still occupied. Smoke rose from a chimney. We asked our driver to turn in, and the result was a memorable lesson in thinking across the colonial divide. A tall, thin man, middle-aged, white, and quite nervous, came out of the big house. His clothes were threadbare, his hair long and unkempt, his teeth in need of care. He never had visitors, he told us nervously; his Spanish was getting rusty. He was a son of the wealthy family that had owned the hacienda. After the agrarian reform in 1969, they had all gone to Lima. Except him. I couldn't leave this place, he told us; this is my home, I'm a product of this land, this place; I belong here, I could never live anywhere else. He shared the house with a group of Quechua campesinas and campesinos who lived on the ground floor, maintained the household, and farmed what were now their fields. He lived in a section of the upper floor, looking over the courtyard where the cooking and washing went on. The household lived in Quechua. There was no electricity or plumbing. A clear, cold stream of water ran down a cement trench in the middle of the central patio. A spacious, once-elegant salon was now a storeroom for the barley crop that was his sole source of cash. Behind the house, under tangled trees and underbrush, the former hacienda owner showed me what had once been a splendid tiled swimming pool. Denouncing the land reform, he waved his hand to a field across the road where an ancient John Deere threshing machine stood, some of its green paint intact. "Do you know the only difference now between me and them?" he asked (referring to the campesinos). "Esa máquina" (that machine). The mutating, endlessly adaptive colonial divide was here, on life support, sustained, barely, by a creaky machine that he and not they owned, and gave him the ability to produce a greater surplus than they could. This remarkable person fully knew he was a remnant. Stereotypes suppose that only Indigenous people, not colonizers, become inextricably embedded in landscape, ecology, and place. But of course that is entirely false. In that ruined house, the chronotopic power of geography and history, for better or worse, held them all.

THE FUTUROLOGY OF INDEPENDENCE

For English speakers, the greatest mystery of Spanish grammar seems to be the subjunctive voice. More than any other, it is the reef on which students shipwreck. When I was teaching Spanish, one of my favorite ways of introducing this grammatical formation was through the vast archive of Spanish love songs, where subjunctives naturally abound: romantic love is the homeland of hypothetical, potential, unrealized, hoped-for, lost, and impossible but longed-for states of being and therefore the subjunctive voice: "Ay, cuanto diera por verte una vez más" (Ay, what I would give to see you once again); "Por lo que tú más quieras, dime cuando" (In name of what you most love, tell me when); "Que te den lo que no pude darte / aunque te haya dado de todo" (Let them give you whatever I could not, though I gave you everything); "Cuando lejos te encuentres de mí, cuando quieras que esté yo contigo" (When you find yourself far from me, when you want me to be with you).[1]

To teach Spanish future verb tenses, in turn, there is no richer corpus than the vast archive generated by Spanish American struggles for independence from Spain in the late eighteenth and early nineteenth centuries. Here, as in all decolonizing literatures, prophetic voices call futures forth as historical necessities, demands, and political prescriptions—"Seremos libres, seremos hombres, seremos nación" (We will be free, we will be men, we will be a nation; Miranda 1801; see also Beccone, Mondolfi, and Ruiz 1991). And yet, in the literatures of independence, these resounding nonsubjunctives are projected into a political field of radical uncertainty, instability, and unpredictability. Those verbs postulate futures at a moment when what is genuinely possible is unknown, unknowable, even unimaginable. Independence is a traveling idea. It shows up as futurity, as possibility, wherever colonialism has moved in and taken over, but it does not come with a script in its suitcase or a playbook in its hand. These pages reflect on independence as an exercise in futurology. I examine the contrasting cases of South America, the Philippines, and Santo Domingo (Haiti/Dominican Republic). But these cases will be of interest for anyone thinking about the improvisational arts of decolonization.

Independence as Concept

In the modern imperial geopolitical order, independence came to be thought of as a step—an essential step—in a script of decolonization. Independence enacts the change of state from colony to ex-colony; it is a telos. This formula for decolonization persists down to the present, most recently in the case of Namibia's independence from South Africa in 1990, for instance, or the independence many Puerto Ricans still seek for their island.[2] In the Americas, independence provided the starting point for the national narratives that Doris Sommer (1991) so brilliantly named *foundational fictions*. This futurological narrative inhabits our common sense: the nations of the Americas were founded through the historic act of throwing off the colonial yoke and claiming the territory for those who lived there—or for at least some of those who lived there. One version of the story is oedipal: the son defeats the father and claims the motherland and the means of production. Another variant is paternalistic: the loving imperial father/mother at last recognizes that the child is ready to take responsibility for its own future and grants it self-determination. Another variant is gestational: colonialism comes to fruition in the "birth" of nations in blood and pain, with colonial dependence left behind like a placenta. The multiplicity of the metaphors and their allegorical, abstract nature are, of course, what makes them serviceable. They are all called forth by the inevitable man-on-horseback statues that, as Benedict Anderson (1983) taught us to notice, dot the plazas of Spanish America's towns and cities, depicting *el héroe de la patria* (the hero of the fatherland).

Imagining independence as a telos of colonialism, an end point toward which it steadily unfolds, is possible, however, only in retrospect. As the case of Namibia makes clear, even in 1990 there was still no script or formula for exiting colonial status, any more than there was in 1790, when the Venezuelan Francisco de Miranda decided to devote his life to ending Spanish rule in the Americas. In a spirit of experimentation, I imagine independence differently here, as a projection into an unknown, unknowable future—in Elizabeth Grosz's words (see the introduction), into "possibilities of being otherwise" that "lie beyond the horizon of the given real" (2011, 79). *Independence* names struggles to exit colonial status. Such struggles are launched into radical uncertainty, with almost no idea how things will unfold, where they will end up, how long it will take, or how it ought to be done. From this perspective, *independence* names not a process but a concept that gets concretized, above all through improvisation and risk. "We need concepts," says Grosz, "to think our way in a world of forces that we do not control" (78). Rather than thinking of independence as a telos, one can think of it as a concept that arises when a colonial regime is no longer able to contain the generative, self-realizing energies of the subjects and collectivities it has brought into being through its own orderings of life and matter. This becomes the "pressing problem" (81) that brings the concept into play. Independence turns up when colonial orders go into crisis, a crisis that their own asymmetrical orderings have generated.

Grosz's analysis of concepts, outlined in the introduction, is especially pertinent here not only because concepts for her are key instruments of radical social change but also because their work is primarily the work of futurology, of enabling the living to imagine things otherwise, to move toward futures that lie beyond existing horizons. Grosz's language illuminates remarkably well the way independence operates in the generally tumultuous processes through which colonies seek an exit from colonial status and a path to a different future. Concepts for Grosz make bridges between "forces which relentlessly impinge on us from the outside to form a problem, and those forces we can muster . . . by which to address problems" (80). They "carve out for us a space and time in which we may become what can respond to the indeterminate particularity of events" (80).

Independence continues to operate in this way in places where it has not been achieved. It operated this way for the people living the crisis and chaos of the decaying colonial order in Spanish America in the late eighteenth and early nineteenth centuries. Without offering a script, independence enabled people to "surround themselves with possibilities of being otherwise"

15.1 — Francisco de Miranda. SOURCE: SHAREALIKE 4.0 INTERNATIONAL.

and transform the forces around them "into new and different forces that act in the future" (82).

We can test this approach in the writings of one of the founding figures of Spanish American independence, Francisco de Miranda. Born in Caracas in 1750, Miranda received a commission in the Spanish army in 1772 and served in North Africa, southern Spain, and Cuba. In Cuba he entered into contact with Spain's British rivals and with the newly independent United States. He traveled extensively in the United States, met George Washington, and, from then until his death in 1816, dedicated his life to pursuing independence for Spain's American colonies. For years, he traveled around Europe, avoiding Spanish arrest, seeking allies, and lobbying the British government to support an invasion of South America from bases in the Caribbean. Miranda's eventful, unpredictable, and driven but unscripted life exhibits the essentially futurological force of independence and the intensely improvisational activity it set in motion. Nobody ever lived more relent-lessly oriented to the future than Miranda, and no one faced more often than he the fact that (a) you never know what's going to happen, (b) things rarely turn out as planned, and (c), nevertheless, you need a plan.

In 1790 Miranda wrote William Pitt, prime minister of England, an im-passioned proposal for support to address the problem to which indepen-dence is connected. Symptomatically, Miranda describes the problem in highly specific terms, but the solution is pure abstraction:

> La América española desea que la Inglaterra le ayude a sacudir la opre-sión infame en que la España la tiene constituida; negando a sus natura-les de todas las clases el que puedan obtener empleos militares, civiles o eclesiásticos de alguna consideración y confiriéndoles sólo a españoles europeos de baja esfera por lo general, que vienen allí únicamente para enriquecerse, ultrajar, y oprimir los infelices habitantes, con una rapaci-dad increíble, prohibiendo aun a la nobleza americana, el que pase a Es-paña ni a ningún otro país extranjero, sin licencia particular del Rey. . . . La América se cree con todo derecho a repelar una dominación igual-mente opresiva que tiránica y formarse para sí un gobierno libre, sabio y equitable. (Miranda 1801)

> Spanish America wishes for England to assist them in shaking off the infernal oppression into which Spain has confined her, denying her in-habitants of all classes access to military, civilian, and ecclesiastical offices of significant rank, conferring these only on European Spaniards of gen-erally low standing, who come there only to enrich themselves, abuse and oppress the hapless natives with an incredible rapacity, prohibiting even American nobility from traveling to Spain or any other foreign country without express permission from the King. . . . America believes she has full rights to fend off a domination as oppressive as it is tyrannical, and to form for herself a government that is free, wise, and equitable. (my translation)

Miranda, at this point, has a great deal of clarity about the conditions that have become intolerable. Yet he does not and could not have a road map for the continent-wide process of change he wants to set in motion, or any certainty about what that "gobierno libre, sabio y equitable" would look like. He can, however, articulate concretely the factors that impede the pro-cess. These amount to the colonial condition itself: "No hay caminos para comunicarse por tierra . . . ni una sola gaceta por donde comunicar de una a otra provincia . . . imposible actuar de acuerdo" (105; There are no roads for communicating by land . . . and not a single newspaper communicating between one province and another . . . impossible to act collaboratively). How, then, to get from here to there, from colonialism to independence? Not only is there no road map, there are literally no roads.

A decade later, in 1801, the possibilities for being otherwise have acquired more precise contours in Miranda's discourse, though not in reality. Miranda again writes Pitt, saying the colonies are at the point of insurrection. This time, he offers a model for a provisional, continent-wide, ex-colonial government. The model is surprisingly detailed, an ambitious exercise in futurology and a hypothetical recipe for "transforming the forces of the present into new and different forces," to again use Grosz's language (2011, 81). It is also an utter fantasy. In robust future tenses, Miranda calls for establishing a central government in a new capital city to be built on the Isthmus of Panama, called Colombo.[3] Executive power will be invested in two individuals elected by landowners over forty years of age, and these two leaders will be called Incas. The Incas will name two *cuestores* (treasurers), two *ediles* (councilors) for road construction and repair, and six *censores* who will take charge of the census, public instruction, and "la conservación de las buenas costumbres" (the preservation of good customs). In instances of grave national crisis, the two Incas may, for a one-year term, name a *dictador* who may rule by fiat. The model specifies multiple levels of elective offices with rules for voting eligibility at each level, according to sex, age, parentage, annual income, and land tenure. There are rules to govern the clergy, militias, and taxation.

Read today, Miranda's model has a delirious quality; it is a hallucinatory mix of extreme specificity and complete unreality. That delirious quality is perhaps the most unequivocal expression of the moment of radical change when people must imagine new forms of order but can do so only using elements of the known in new ways. In such scenarios, imaginations must shift into overdrive. Goals must be declared to organize collective action at a moment when the future is unknown, even unimaginable. It is overdetermined that, in retrospect, revolutionary futurologies convey a quality of delirium and excess.

Independence and Decolonization

The historiography of the Americas normalized independence as the mechanism for exiting colonial status. But there were other competing strategies. Here we can learn by comparing Spanish America with another Spanish colony, the Philippines, also colonized by Spain in the sixteenth century. Until

1821 the Philippines were governed from Mexico (then New Spain) and controlled through a monopolized sea route from Acapulco to Manila—the famed Manila Galleon. The aspiration to independence did not take root in the Philippines in the early 1800s.[4] After Mexican independence in 1821, the Philippines remained a Spanish colony and transferred to direct rule from Spain, a change that placed the Philippines politically nearer but geographically farther from the imperial administrative center in Madrid. As the nineteenth century unfolded, Spanish America and the Philippines, while sharing many challenges and aspirations, including the desire to decolonize, followed very different political trajectories.

Like the Americas, the Philippines had a colonial system that privileged the Spanish-born, restricted the possibilities of a growing native-born creole elite, and brutally subordinated Indigenous populations, which in the Philippines were also called *indios*. As in the Americas, the Catholic Church was extremely powerful in all spheres. It controlled education and was the biggest landholder. Unlike the Americas, the Philippines had visible populations of Chinese traders and Muslims (called *moros*)—we know little as yet about the presence of these groups in Spanish America. Despite, or maybe because of, the example of the Americas, anticolonial pressures in the Philippines developed along strikingly different lines. The main points of contrast are these:

1 The call for equality and freedom took the form not of a demand for separation from Spain but the opposite: a demand for full incorporation into the Spanish state, as a province on equal footing with, say, Catalonia or Asturias. In the Philippines, dissident Creoles were nationalists, not *independentistas*. They were futurologists like Miranda, driven by many of the same pressures, but they organized themselves toward a different imagined possibility.

2 As in the Americas, a network of dissident creole men of arms and letters developed the revolutionary program. But the Philippine radicals did their plotting in the imperial capital, Madrid, where the subversives—led by José Rizal—fled the persecution of the colonial church.[5]

3 For the Philippine creoles, Spain represented not a decadent power associated with the Inquisition, slavery, and archaic tribute systems but modern liberalism. It was to liberal Spain that the Philippines sought to affiliate. This Spanish liberalism, developed from the late eighteenth century, was not absent from the American equation. It was encoded in the Cortes de Cádiz (1810), which reworked Spanish colonialism.

For some American creoles, Spanish liberalism, not colonial domination, was the true threat to their privilege. For many Indigenous peoples, Spanish liberalism made continuing Spanish rule more desirable than independence.

As the Spanish colonial system melted into crisis, the Philippine nationalists made a different bet than the Spanish American revolutionaries. They bet that Spanish liberalism would overthrow the archaic infrastructure of colonialism *from within Spain*, especially the outrageously broad powers of the Catholic religious orders. They demanded recognition of the Philippines as a Spanish province, equal treatment of Filipinos, freedom of the press, curtailment of Guardia Civil (Civil Guard) abuses, representation at the Spanish court, and secularization of local governance.[6] For the Philippine radicals, the imagined path toward decolonization passed through *acercamiento* (rapprochement) to the colonial state, not separation from it.

In some key respects, the Philippine radicals were right. During the nineteenth century, the Philippines modernized along many of the same lines as the new Spanish American nation-states: Spain freed them for international trade in 1834, established free primary instruction for all children in 1863, encouraged filipinization of the priesthood and teaching, and encouraged the proliferation of journals and newspapers (Francia 2010, 103). Roads and bridges were built, and a national literature developed, all under progressive Spanish rule. Americanist historiography associates such modernizing projects with postindependence nation building and state building, but in the Philippines these developments took place in the absence of independence. Contrary to common assumptions, then, independence and statehood are not necessary conditions for liberalism and modernity or for decolonization. Indeed, by remaining a colony, the Philippines avoided the decimating territorial wars and racialized genocides that accompanied state building in the Americas.[7]

And yet a picture of liberalism emanating from the mother country to its colonies is a picture that needs to be decolonized.[8] The Philippines were a stage on which the struggle over liberalism took place. Philippine creoles inspired by Spanish liberalism were empowered players in that struggle within Spain against conservative elites and the Roman Catholic hierarchy. Though the Philippines remained a colony, the contours of this struggle were not simply dictated from Madrid. As Philippine historian Luis Francia (2010) demonstrates, across the nineteenth century, laws and policies changed continuously as one side or the other came to power. As late as 1871, for example, conservatives attempted to restore forced labor and tribute in the Philippines.

Nevertheless, as Anna Lowenhaupt Tsing (2005) reminds us, the new can establish itself in a place only by gaining traction with something that is already there. In the Philippines, liberalism's handholds kept getting knocked off. By the 1890s, equality and freedom still seemed beyond reach. "The feudal system with all its exploitative features . . . and the religious, remained intact," says Francia, "essentially unchanged since the conquest that began in the late 16ᵗʰ century" (2010, 123–24). By the late nineteenth century, liberalism was not winning in the Philippines, nor in Spain either.

Nineteenth-century Spanish American historiography hinges on the same epic struggle between liberals and conservatives, famously registered in Gabriel García Márquez's classic *One Hundred Years of Solitude*. In Spanish America this struggle appears as a result of independence. The Philippine case obliges us to rethink this analysis because there the struggle was not connected to independence. In other words, liberalism could be, and was, fought for from either side of the independence debate. There could be pro- and anti-independence liberalisms. For a Latin Americanist, this is a fascinating observation.

As it happens, pro- and anti-independence liberalisms very nearly met on the battlefield in Cuba, in an extraordinary encounter that might have happened but, in the end, did not. In 1895 the Philippine nationalist hero José Rizal was arrested by Spanish government forces in Barcelona on false charges of being a supporter of independence and revolution in the Philippines. A medical doctor, Rizal was on his way to Madrid to join the Spanish army against the independence rebellion in Cuba. That rebellion was led by Cuban nationalist hero José Martí. Rizal was returned to Manila and executed for treason. Imagine the scene that did not occur but might have. If Rizal had been able to fulfill his mission, the two decolonizing, liberal nation builders, Rizal, aged thirty-four, and Martí, aged forty-two, could have met on a battlefield in Cuba, on opposite sides of the fight for independence but on the same side of everything else. Both men offered and lost their lives fighting for freedom, equality, autonomy, the secular state, and a thousand other shared ideals. Rizal was executed in Manila in 1895, and Martí died in battle in Cuba a year later.

Almost immediately, Cuba and the Philippines were both swept into the imperial designs of the United States. After the United States declared war on Spain in 1898, it backed the Philippine independence movement, pursuing its own imperial designs. In the early 1800s, Britain and France had supported South American movements in the same way.

These conjugations of independence with empire created brutal ironies. When in 1898 the Philippine revolutionaries declared independence from Spain, they spoke as allies of the United States. Their declaration began,

"Under the protection of the mighty and humane North American nation..." (quoted in Francia 2010, 139). The next step, as we know, was a betrayal—the United States cut a deal with Spain that placed the Philippines under US control in exchange for $20 million. The independence movement was completely excluded from the negotiations. Full political independence in the Philippines finally came in 1946.

The Language Factor

This story has another twist. Philippine cultural historian Vicente Rafael argues that the unfolding of the colonial exit in the Philippines was driven to a significant degree by language. Rafael has developed this argument in two fascinating books, *Contracting Colonialism* (1988) and *The Promise of the Foreign* (2005).[9] In the Americas, when we think of linguistic imperialism, we think about European languages imposed on Indigenous populations and policies to undermine and eradicate Indigenous languages. In the Philippines, linguistic imperialism took a different route. Instead of imposing Spanish on Indigenous populations, Philippine colonial institutions withheld it. The Spanish language remained in sole possession of the Spaniards. The religious orders proselytized and educated in Indigenous languages, ensuring that Indigenous populations had no independent access to administrative power or colonial authorities, no bilingual mediators, and no imperial lingua franca with which to communicate with one another. This distribution of linguistic resources placed the Catholic religious orders in command of local governance as well as education (Rafael 2005). Since local populations lacked Spanish, colonial authorities were compelled to communicate with them through the friars. Despite Spanish government policies calling for the spread of Spanish, after three hundred years of Spanish colonialism, Rafael says, only 1 percent of the population in the Philippines spoke it. This is a stunning fact. While, in the Americas, decolonization called for empowering Indigenous languages to interrupt the colonial script, in the Philippines, taking possession of Spanish became the decolonizing move—which the colonizing forces fiercely resisted. As Grosz (2011) argues, the same concept can give rise to any number of alternative futures.

Though Rafael does not phrase it this way, the religious orders in the Philippines made themselves indispensable to all sides by securing a monopoly not on Castilian per se but on Spanish/Indigenous bilingualism. In this scenario, for the native population, the path to independence lay through claiming Castilian. Indigenous languages marked the continuation of colonial rule. But let me again underscore here that the power struggle is not between Castilian and Indigenous but over access to Spanish/Indigenous bilingualism. Who will command this power? In the postcolony, what will be the lingua franca that enables the nation? Over and over, the nationalists, led by Rizal, argued for access to the Spanish language for all. Resolutely, the religious orders resisted and refused, while local authorities complied.

To promote his case, Rizal famously wrote two foundational national novels in Castilian Spanish. But as Rafael shows, in the end, the Philippines' linguistic and literary future lay elsewhere. Preventing the spread of Castilian, he argues, empowered local Philippine languages. Instead of remaining isolated or marginal, as they did elsewhere, they became dynamic and extroverted, open to absorbing elements from the metropole. They became infused with "the promise of the foreign." For example, as Rafael shows in a fascinating chapter, a unique tradition of Spanish *comedias* written and performed in Tagalog and other Indigenous languages developed and continued into the twentieth century. The Tagalog language hosted a Spanish literary form. Used in this way, Rafael argues, the vernacular creates in colonized subjects "the possibility of becoming other than what the colonial order says they are supposed to be" (2005, 97).

The outcome of this story can seem strange to those of us who think about independence and decolonization from the Americas. When the United States took over the Philippines in 1898, English by law became the language of public instruction. The requirement was written into the Philippine constitution, and it is still there. Castilian, out of reach of all but educated elites, remained the language of the courts and legislature until 1941, when it was replaced by English. Manuel Quezon, president in the 1930s, spearheaded a retooling of Tagalog so that it could become a national lingua franca in a country of some 170 languages. This program adopted an ingenious lexical strategy. It chose to expand the Tagalog lexicon with terms borrowed from other Philippine languages so that all citizens would hear in it both the foreign and the familiar (Rafael 2005, 132). Through this brilliant move, the new national Tagalog belonged to no one and to everyone, whatever their mother tongue. Tagalog would make the nation, and English would connect it to the world outside, as indeed it has.

Santo Domingo/Saint Domingue

Nowhere is the unscripted, improvisational churn of independence futurologies more apparent than on the island of Hispaniola, known in colonial times as Santo Domingo in Spanish and Saint Domingue in French. Hispaniola's western side was colonized by France, today the Republic of Haiti, while the eastern side was colonized by Spain, today the Dominican Republic. Haiti was the first colony in Latin America to achieve independence. It did so by a path that had neither precedents nor sequels and that struck terror into the Euro-imperial world. Haiti's decolonization began with an organized mass revolt of slaves and people of color that overthrew French colonial rule in 1791 and opened an entirely new range of possibilities and unknowables. An extraordinary path of experimentation followed. Haiti, led by former slaves, undertook to refound society on antislavery, egalitarian principles. In search of social models, it adopted seven constitutions between 1801 and 1816 (Fischer 2004), all of them exercises in futurology. After abolishing slavery, it declared itself an empire, then a monarchy, then a republic. It neutralized race: the constitution of 1805 declared all Haitian citizens Black. It forbade white inhabitants from owning property and parents from disinheriting their children; it required all citizens to learn a mechanical art.[10] In a groundbreaking study, Sibylle Fischer (2004) shows that mainstream historiography has systematically occluded the Haitian story, denying the significance of Haiti's project of "revolutionary anti-slavery." Yet, Fischer argues, the shadow of the disavowed Haitian Revolution explains the shape creole *independentismo* eventually took.

Haiti's bold revolutionary trajectory impacted the futurologies of independence that developed on the other side of Hispaniola. Independence in Santo Domingo came to mean the possibility of being absorbed into Haiti's radical project. While this path appealed to many Dominicanos, the elites frantically sought alternative futurologies. They wanted to find a way to exit colonial status while retaining the empire's protection against Haiti. Again, there was no script. The result is a story even more tumultuous than most.

Famed as Christopher Columbus's first stop in the Americas, Santo Domingo remained a Spanish colony till Spain ceded it to France in 1795 after being defeated by Napoleon. In 1808 the population rebelled against French rule and demanded not independence but a return to Spanish rule, named a *reconquista* in official history. This path proved disappointing. Spain took little interest in its recovered colony, and other possibilities came into play. In 1821, under José Núñez de Cáceres, Santo Domingo claimed what official history calls its *primera independencia* (first independence), also known more colorfully as its *independencia efímera* (ephemeral independence). Núñez de Cáceres's goal was to incorporate

Santo Domingo into Simón Bolívar's project of unifying South America into a Gran Colombia. But this imagined path evaporated when it became clear that a majority of the population preferred to merge with the Republic of Haiti. The reason? Above all, slavery. Daylet Domínguez, in a brilliantly researched study, demonstrates that the Dominicans aspired to follow the Haitian revolutionary program of equality, fraternity, and, above all, the immediate abolition of slavery. Abolition was not part of Núñez de Cáceres's political program. So it was that Santo Domingo first exited colonial status in 1822 not through independence but by "voluntary incorporation" (Domínguez 2021, 306) into its neighboring ex-colony. Slavery was indeed abolished. For the next twenty-two years, the two sides of the island together formed the independent Republic of Haiti (a name of Indigenous origin). This story is so at odds with the standard futurologies of independence that official history still records it as a conquest of Santo Domingo by Haiti. Domínguez's new study provides convincing evidence that it was not.

But the story does not end there. In 1844 Santo Domingo embarked on yet another uncertain path. It separated from Haiti, an act recorded today as its *segunda independencia* (second independence). But the ex-colony failed to prosper on its own, and elites continually feared Haiti. Under dictator Pedro Santana, Santo Domingo offered itself—and its deepwater ports—as a protectorate, first to England, then to France, then to Spain, and then to the United States. In effect, it sought to resume colonial status. Spain finally agreed, and in 1861 Santo Domingo reannexed itself to Spain, on the same conditions sought by the Philippine radicals. The arrangement lasted but four years. Alarmed by the costs of defending its new acquisition, Spain cut Santo Domingo loose in 1865, and thus, in an act of rejection, not liberation, was the independent Dominican Republic finally born, after exhausting all alternatives.[11]

These examples lead to a conception of independence as a field of futurological speculation and speculative action in which an indeterminate range of possibilities surge and swirl, gaining traction at one spot, disappearing from view at another. Decolonization involves embarking down paths that, as Grosz (2011) observes, one knows lead beyond the limits of existing imaginations. Abolition, for example, was imaginable as a legal action, but postslave society was unknown and unknowable. What could it look like? What could it become? One is reminded of the Polynesian navigators famous for carrying out long sea journeys without instruments. They do so, they explain, by sailing toward an imagined point below the visible horizon. It is not a point you intend to reach, just one you aim for in order to take and hold a direction. Today, more than ever, we know we do not know the route out of the legacies of slavery and coloniality; we navigate toward imaginary points in what we hope is that direction.

CHAPTER SIXTEEN |

REMEMBERING ANTICOLONIALISM

The postcolonial paradigm that consolidated itself in metropolitan universities in the 1990s displaced a corpus of anticolonial, anti-imperial, global
liberationist thought that thrived in the 1960s, 1970s, and 1980s, developed
in Africa, Asia, and Latin America in connection with third-world emancipation struggles. The political decolonization struggles of the 1940s, 1950s,
and 1960s set in motion a decolonization of knowledge that amounted, in
Edward Said's words, to a "huge and remarkable adjustment in perspective
and understanding" (1993, 243).

For these anticolonial and anti-imperial thinkers, many of whom led
struggles to overthrow colonial orders, the work of decolonization required,
among its foundational steps, diagnosing the colonial system itself. It was
necessary to discredit the self-congratulatory European myth of modernity
as the natural diffusion of an inherently superior civilizational model. It was
necessary to reveal the imperial project, to diagnose colonialism in a way
that pointed to futures beyond subordination and dependency. This body
of thought was energized by key terms that postcolonialism would set aside:

imperialism, *liberation*, *self-determination*, and the *third world*. The latter term asserted the planetary, worldmaking aspirations of these thinkers. Fara Dabhoiwala puts it well, speaking of Black Anglophone anticolonialists in Africa and the Americas: "It was not enough simply to free people from alien rule. Their full liberation from external domination, both economic and political, would also require a radical transformation of the international order. Decolonization had to be a project of worldmaking as well as nation-making" (2020, 62).

By now, well into the twenty-first century, the postcolonial paradigm has given what it had to give, and the long-banished concept of decolonization is energized anew. The imperative for a radical transformation and world making on a planetary scale is again before us, not least because of the persistent imperial design of the international order. It is a worthy moment to revisit this body of critical and emancipatory thought, to hear again these pre-postcolonial voices. The pages that follow make a modest step in that direction. They examine how a range of anticolonial and anti-imperial thinkers in the 1960s, 1970s, and 1980s diagnosed colonialism, neocolonialism, and the path toward decolonized futures. Rather than examine the corpus author by author, I distill five recurring arguments that drove the anticolonialist analysis of how colonialism and imperialism worked and how they could be undone.[1]

Interruption

Angolan liberationist Amílcar Cabral, assassinated by the Portuguese in 1973, summed up in Marxist terms a narrative of interruption that anticolonial thinkers consistently emphasize: "The principal characteristic, common to every kind of imperialist domination, is the negation of the historical process of the dominated people, by means of violently usurping the free operation of the process of development of the productive forces" (Cabral 1973, 41–42).[2] European expansionism is seen as having interrupted the ongoing development of societies, derailing them from the historical trajectories on which their internal forces and existing histories were embarked. European expansionism cuts off this unfolding, and they become frozen in time. Those interrupted histories often included interaction with Europe but not of an imperialist kind (empire in Cabral's definition refers to a takeover of the productive forces of one society by another).

Interruption is an important element in another key anticolonial text, Kwame Nkrumah's 1964 decolonization manifesto *Consciencism*. Nkrumah was a revolutionary who led Ghana to independence from Britain in 1957 and served as its first president. In his rereading of African history, Nkrumah argues that Africa's precolonial social structures and values coincided to a great degree with the prescriptions of contemporary socialism. Africa, he says, was on a socialist path before colonization interrupted its line of development, making revolution the only route back to it. (A similar suggestion has been made, controversially, about the Incas. Certainly, there is no reason to think that the principles of socialism were invented only once, and in Europe.) Nkrumah argued that autochthonous socialist values continued to operate in African societies in his own time, though they were no longer hegemonic. Socialist revolution, he argued, would therefore find a "disposition of forces which will enable African society to digest the Western and the Islamic and the Euro-Christian elements in Africa and develop them in such a way that they fit into the African personality" (1964, 79). The futurology of anticolonialism lies in recovering the unrealized, perhaps unimagined, possibilities of the past.

In another anticolonial classic, *The West and the Rest of Us* (1975), Nigerian historian Chinweizu views colonial interruption as a process that continues over time. Colonial regimes, he argues, actively prevent industry and trade relations from developing in colonized regions. The metropole itself coercively manufactures the underdevelopment that modernization is supposed to correct. Left alone, Chinweizu argues, Africa would have industrialized and modernized more fully than colonialism would ever allow it to do. This argument, that the condition of underdevelopment was something Euro-imperial modernity produced for its own benefit, not a problem it offered to solve, became a fundamental insight of anticolonial thought.

South Asian anticolonialists have an equally emphatic version of the narrative of interruption. They retrieve the history of India's sophisticated scientific, philosophical, and literary traditions and its cosmopolitanism. As soon as these civilizational achievements are recognized, they argue, the idea of India as a backward society that needed European intervention in order to advance becomes insulting and absurd. Jawaharlal Nehru, who led India's independence struggle and became its first prime minister, gave this version of colonial interruption: "When the British came to India, though technologically somewhat backward, she was still among the advanced commercial nations of the world. Technical changes would undoubtedly have come and changed India as they had changed some Western countries. But her normal development was arrested by the British power. Industrial growth was checked. . . . [T]he normal power relationships of society could not adjust themselves and find an equilibrium as all power was concentrated in the alien authority which based itself on force" (quoted in Chatterjee 1986, 137).

Ideas of "normal development" and "normal power relationships" are obviously critical to this analysis of interruption. The interruption trope marks colonialism and imperial intervention as inherently illegitimate and aberrant. They produce abnormal relations marked by lack of reciprocity, imbalances of power, use of force, and disruption of productive forces.

Appropriation

Anticolonial thinkers also reanalyzed Europe's rise to global dominance. The rise of Europe was the result not of its own superior civilizational endowments, as Europeans liked to think, but of its success in appropriating knowledge from other places. This claim no longer startles, but for post–World War II anticolonial thinkers, it was an important challenge to standard historical accounts that treated "the rise of Europe" as a sui generis phenomenon that gestated internally and then diffused outward to the rest of the world. (This issue is discussed at length in chapter 1.) Anticolonial thinkers tell the story in reverse: Europe was backward until knowledge arriving from other places changed its course. Chinweizu opens his book with this argument, expressed with his characteristic militancy: "For nearly six centuries now western Europe and its diaspora have been disturbing the peace of the world. Enlightened, through their Renaissance, and the learning of the ancient Mediterranean; armed with the gun, the making of whose powder they had learned from Chinese firecrackers, equipping their ships with lateen sails, astrolabes and nautical compasses, all invented by the Chinese and transmitted to them by Arabs; fortified in aggressive spirit and an arrogant, messianic Christianity . . . and motivated by the lure of enriching plunder, white hordes have sallied forth from their European homelands" (1975, 3). Who are the barbarians now? Europe's imperial expansion, then, included great ingestions of knowledge from elsewhere, used to develop its own productive forces and expand its power. As with other resources, this is knowledge taken by pillage, not necessarily given or exchanged. In Cabral's words, in the rich countries "imperialist capital increased the productive creativity of man and brought about a total transformation of the means of production. This in turn translated into loss of creativity in the colonized world" (1973, 58). Thus, in empire's wake, the original sources of the new knowledge would look, and become, backward. That Europe's empowerment was a joint creation is either lost from view or deemed unimportant.[3]

In a later book, *Aborted Discovery* (1984), the Sri Lankan historian of science Susantha Goonatilake denounced the notion that Europe had a monopoly on science and indeed invented it. Scientific inquiry, Goonatilake observed, flourished in parts of Asia well before it made its way to Europe: "Until 1500, the flow of scientific knowledge was from east to west" (49). He documents the European borrowings from Asia that made European expansion possible: navigation, astronomy, warfare, arithmetic, algebra, trigonometry, and much more.[4]

In anticolonial thought, this process of knowledge transfer is both a precondition that made the rise of Europe possible and an ongoing dynamic that reinforces imbalances of power over time. It is how the colonial world system works. Chinweizu (1975, 188) argues, for instance, that slavery sapped human vitality and creativity away from African societies and shipped these energies across the Atlantic to infuse them into the nascent colonial societies of the Americas. While metropolitan common sense imagined imperialism as a centrifugal force diffusing outward from its European center, anticolonial and anti-imperial thinkers argue that it is equally, perhaps chiefly, a centripetal force, sucking in and devouring everything it can, processing it into additional productivity, wealth, and power.

Obliteration

Anticolonial thinkers also developed insights into the way the transfer of knowledge from colonized to colonizer gets systematically disguised in Western historiography. The agency of colonized people is willfully obliterated from the history colonizers tell about themselves. Jack Weatherford (1988), an anticolonial historian based in the United States, shows that knowledge transfer was often disguised as simply the transfer of raw materials. Historians depicted Spain's American colonies as sources of substances, whether precious metals or new materials like guano, cochineal dye, hemp, coffee, tobacco, chocolate, potatoes, and corn. Weatherford points out that the really consequential transfer involved not the raw materials themselves but the specialized knowledge and infrastructure for extracting or growing and processing them into consumable commodities. This was knowledge developed in the Americas over centuries. Europe's so-called discovery of guano as a fertilizer involved not an encounter with mountains of composted bird excrement but an appropriation of knowledge from Indigenous agriculturalists who, through long-term interaction with their environment, had come to know its fertilizing properties and how to make use of them. Naturalists' objectivized descriptions of flora and fauna often recode Indigenous knowledge as scientific observation. In this way, the agency and even the presence of Indigenous peoples are obliterated from history. Those thus erased experience this obliteration, in the words of Eritrean philosopher Tsenay Serequeberhan, "as death and destruction, the effective creation of vacuity. . . . The subjugated experienced Europe as the putting into question of their very existence" (1997, 143).

Feminist historian of science Sandra Harding is one of the few metropolitan scholars who address such processes of appropriation and annihilation from within science. Harding speaks of the "predatory conceptual frameworks of European science" (1997, 64). She identifies their "persistent substitution of abstract for concrete, locally situated" knowledges, and their concept of nature that "sucks up local features of local knowledge systems into apparently universal features of 'real sciences'" (64). European natural science, says Harding, turns specific environments into instances of an abstract nature and uses them as laboratories. The process appropriates not only environments but also knowledges and ways of knowing developed by their inhabitants over time. Europe's self-ascribed monopoly on the scientific method itself is, for Harding, an instance of manufacturing the universal: "Such everyday practices as inducting, deduction, trial and error reasoning" are devices "everyone in the world uses all the time" (64). Reified into scientific methodological principles seen as the property of a very few, these practices produce "the illusion that only modern science can generate knowledge claims that are useful" (63). The construction of the imperial universal, this argument claims, depends on the denial of equivalence between formal and vernacular and between occidental and nonoccidental knowledges. Those denials underwrite the diffusionist narrative and expel from the picture the history of Europe's interactions with the rest of the world.

This epistemic critique has a long history among anticolonialist thinkers from Asia. The Indian political scientist Partha Chatterjee cites the nineteenth-century Indian intellectual Asok Sen, who in the 1880s passionately condemned "that monstrous claim to omniscience which certain Europeans put forward for themselves. No knowledge is to them true knowledge unless it has passed through the sieve of European criticism. All coin is false coin unless it bears the stamp of a Western mint. Existence is possible to nothing which is hid from their searching vision. Truth is not truth, but noisome error and rank falsehood, if it presumes to exist outside the pale of European cognizance" (quoted in Chatterjee 1986, 61). In the same vein, Goonatilake argues that Europe, India, and China for many centuries followed roughly parallel and highly similar stages in scientific and philosophical development until Europe began to differentiate in the seventeenth century. "In common with the cultures in Europe," he argues, "there was [in Asia] a constant and enduring search for valid knowledge. This search was accompanied by a constant test of map against reality" (1984, 3). How could it have been necessary to say this in the 1980s? But it was. The pain and anger in these thinkers' words is obvious.

In 1986 third-world scientists held a remarkable conference in Penang, Malaysia, titled the Crisis in Modern Science to address this enduring issue. Attended by scholars from throughout the third world, the conference produced an eighty-page declaration that proposed a road map for decolonizing knowledge production. The papers from this remarkable conference appeared as a book aptly titled *The Revenge of Athena* (Sardar 1988b). In one pain-filled declaration, rural development specialist S. N. Nagarajan summarized the problem of the West's obliteration of the knowledge of others. "What does western science tell us, the traditional people of the world?" he asks (quoted in Sardar 1988b, 9).

It tells us that:

Your crafts are useless.
Your crops and plants are useless.
Your food is useless.
Your houses are useless.
Your cropping patterns and agricultural patterns are useless.
Your education is useless.
Your knowledge is useless.
Your religion and ethics are absolutely useless.
Your culture is useless.
Your soil is useless.
Your medical system is useless.
Your forests are useless.
Your irrigation system is useless.
Your administration is useless.
You are finally a useless fellow.

Substitution

Alongside obliteration, anticolonial thought repeatedly identifies knowledge substitution, that is, the substitution of Western knowledge and education for local or traditional ones, as a key instrument of the colonial system. Critic Peter Amato puts it this way: "The West has spent several hundred years attempting to wipe out what has remained of indigenous intellectual culture in order to substitute its own. It has regarded their traditional authors as its enemy and as the enemy of intellectual culture as such, since they have been an obstacle to its own authority, which has been understood as carrying forward the inevitable march of universal, traditionless human history" (1997, 73). Serequeberhan asserts the anticolonial position starkly: "In its global invasion and subjugation of the world, European modernity found the reality of myriad non-capitalist social formations which it promptly shattered and replaced with its own replication of itself" (1997, 143). Amato notes the way this process of substitution/subjugation was interpreted in the metropole: first, as inevitable and automatic, "as if the economic and political realities of the modernization of Europe had to create this modern Africa only insofar as it is their byproduct," and, second, as requiring "broad scale cultural replacement" (1997, 73). Colonialism in Africa, says Chinweizu, aimed to "refashion Africa in some debased image of Europe" (1975, 78). While imperial ideology normalized this process as replacing an inferior paradigm with a superior one, anticolonial accounts code it as purposeful, invasive intervention combining physical and epistemic violence. At the same time, anticolonial thinkers are quick to point out that terms like *substitution, replacement,* and *replication* in no way describe what actually occurred. Imperial substitution does not produce a replica or an equivalent, first, because it is not really intended to and, second, because this is impossible. As a matter of principle, diffusion does not produce replicas because it cannot make what was already there simply go away. As I discussed in chapter 1, even at its most aggressive, imperial diffusion is negotiated, interactive, dependent on what precedes it.[5]

Reversal

As they disassemble the diffusionist paradigm, anticolonial thinkers argue that metropolitan ideas, institutions, and principles often produce effects that differ entirely from those found in the metropole, often, in fact, their exact opposite. For example, Goonatilake underscores that the industrialization of European countries had as a consequence the deindustrialization of colonial areas to eliminate competition (1984, 93). Chinweizu (1976, 188) argues that European expansion produced not advancement in Africa but decline, isolation, and devastation. European contact with Africa was so destructive, he says, that ex-colonial Africa had to "go back to the sixteenth century situation as an element from which to build" (188). The universities that had made Africa an intellectual center in the late sixteenth century, he tells us, were destroyed, causing knowledge to "degenerate into esoteric mysteries" (188) and ritual. The decline of the trans-Sahara trade cut Africa off from the European Enlightenment, even as maritime contact developed around commodities and the slave trade.

In the 1990s, anticolonial thinkers identified liberalism as another instance of this kind of reversal. Over and over, they argue that liberalism, when deployed abroad along imperial and colonial lines, produces its opposites—bondage and inequality, not freedom and equality. In the European imperial center, the argument goes, liberalism established the individual as the basis for claims of equality among persons; in the colonial world, that same mechanism became a device for producing social disaggregation, vulnerability to exploitation, and inequality. For instance, studying the nineteenth-century intelligentsia in India, Chatterjee argues that the rigid hierarchies colonialism required were incompatible with modern democratizations of power: "The nineteenth century intelligentsia may have genuinely welcomed the new ideas of reason and rationality, and some may even have shown considerable courage and enterprise in seeking to 'modernize' social customs and attitudes. But the fundamental forces of transformation were absent in colonial society. As a result there was no possibility for the emergence of a consistently rational set of beliefs or practices. Liberalism stood on highly fragile foundations, 'reason' dwindled to merely individual means for self-gratification" (1986, 25). This argument is made repeatedly in the Americas as well. For example, Quebecois anthropologist Pierre Beaucage says with reference to Mexico: "In Western Europe and North America liberalism as a social and political philosophy had been the product of the slow maturation of a capitalist economy and a bourgeois worldview. In order to be put into practice in nineteenth-century Mexico, liberalism's basic principles—a maximum of economic and political freedom for the individual and a minimum of state presence—had to be turned into their opposites" (1998, 10–11). Far from diffusing spontaneously, Beaucage argues, liberal values had to be installed in Mexico through permanent state intervention (anathema to liberalism) and violence against the citizenry they supposedly were to liberate. These were mainly peasants, whose "aspirations (having land to till and maintaining village life) clashed with the liberal view of a nation of autonomous, individual citizens" (11). At times, the illiberal effects of liberalism in the colonies were a matter of deliberate policy. Chinweizu cites a South African document declaring a deliberately cruel policy intended to "break up the tribal system which gives solidarity and some political and economic strength to native life, set the Kaffir on an individual footing as an economic bargainer to which he is wholly unaccustomed, take him by taxation or other 'stimulus' from his locality, put him down under circumstances where he has no option but to labour at the mines" (1975, 58). In other words, in the colony, a free labor market becomes a mechanism for disempowering individuals, not empowering them. Liberalism supports not freedom but opportunities for bondage and exploitation. The "individual" being created in the colonial legislation was specifically a male worker obliged to sell his labor, not the self-realizing citizen-subject that inhabited metropolitan liberal theory.[6]

Conclusion

In 1905 Max Weber grounded his epic synthesis, *The Protestant Ethic and the Spirit of Capitalism,* in a myth of Western civilization whose acceptance he could take for granted. The book opens thus: "A product of modern European civilization, studying any problem of universal history, is bound to ask himself to what combination of circumstance the fact should be attributed that in Western civilization and Western civilization only, cultural phenomena have appeared which (as we like to think) lie in a line of development having universal significance and value" (13). At the time Weber was writing, the rise of the West was a fact, its most glorious and unique creation being a set of universal values and principles capable of unifying all humanity. Human progress, or in Kantian terms the upward unfolding of the human spirit, was the story of the diffusion of this unique, European-driven project and these European-derived principles across the planet. Yet the last clause of Weber's statement contains a pregnant parenthesis. The story is something "we like to think," and possibly no more than that. Who is that "we" whose interests might not be those of all of humanity but uniquely its own? This subject is "bound" to ask for explanations of his historical privilege, yet he apparently suspects there may be answers to the question he will not like—which of course is what binds him to ask.

In this scene of knowing in 1905, the modern European asks himself, because there is no one else to ask. In fact, in this mythic universe, no one else even knows the question exists. Who is the "they" implied by the "we" in Weber's pregnant parenthesis? Who could tell the story otherwise? Who could question the European's self-invention as the monopolist of the universal? Who could introduce the alternative futurologies, the possibilities for being otherwise? For Weber in 1905, this subject could be posited but not specified.

The anticolonial thinkers I have been considering here offer answers to the questions Weber's subject was asking himself. They lay out concrete replies to the question of what "combination of circumstance" produced the West's claim to a monopoly on the universal. They are not answers the Europeans are able to supply. They demonstrate that from sites outside Europe the narrative of diffusion could not be naturalized. What appeared natural and universal to them was what was happening in their homelands before Europeans took over. There never was nor ever will be a straightforward "line of development," to use Weber's term. The anticolonial subject of imperial European modernity was unknown to Weber in 1905, but this subject existed, as it had in sixteenth-century New Spain, bearing the knowledge that the metropolitan subject was required to obliterate or deny, before also denying the denial.

CODA |

AIRWAYS, THE POLITICS OF BREATH

June 2020.

The twenty-minute qigong routine I follow every morning on YouTube is all about breathing. "If you want more energy, the best place to start is your breathing," says my adorable guide, arms floating above his head, then sweeping down to a crouch. Qigong came back into my world with the COVID-19 lockdown, a ritual to inaugurate yet another day in the bunker. We were all seeking small ways to affirm life.

Is it uncanny or overdetermined that the two epic events that upset the United States and the world in the summer of 2020—the COVID-19 pandemic and the filmed public murder of George Floyd—were both about suffocation? Of the hundreds of thousands killed by the coronavirus in the United States, nearly all died of suffocation as their lungs failed, or of the devastating effects of being placed on breathing machines. Like Eric Garner and so many others, George Floyd also suffocated because a police officer threw him to the ground, knee on his neck, blocking his airway long enough to kill him. Classic lynchings used to strangle by hanging; the contemporary version involves choke holds. They are one and the same, public spectacles using blocked airways as an instrument of racial terror.

Like most mammals, human bodies have two lungs, two eyes, two kidneys, and two ears but only a single airway that lies close to the surface of the body. If it is blocked—by a grape, a choke hold, or a noose—you agonize horribly and you die. Strangulation is one of the few ways humans can kill other humans without using a weapon. In the case of COVID, it is the lungs that fail, unable to absorb oxygen. Here, too, people agonize horribly while they die.

We've been living the politics of breath—who gets held down and strangled by police and who does not; who has to fear that and who does not; who gets access to oxygen, respirators, and ventilators and who does not; who are told to stay home and who are required to expose themselves; who are trapped in crowded institutions and who can self-isolate; who are provided protection and who are not; who can get tested and who cannot. People's oxygen meters sit next to their toothbrushes. At this extraordinary moment, the question of which lives are expendable is worked out in the administration of airways. Carried on the breath. Language twists; to be *essential* is to be at risk. At risk, because you are essential to the virus, too, for it requires a living host.

The virus kills through airways but also propagates through airways. The force of living breath transports it from host to host. With the pandemic, the social contract mutates into a pure matter of how people administer their own breathing. Civic responsibility boils down to not breathing on others. Deliberately breathing on others becomes a weapon and a crime. Sociality twists; physical separation becomes the primal expression of civic solidarity, as well as of friendship and love. Governments pass laws requiring it—there is legal and illegal breathing. Opponents of government of course decline these terms. They insist on the previral social contract—the right to gather, the right to infect and be infected, to breathe on and be breathed on, with no state regulation. Churches demand special status and lose in the Supreme Court by a single vote. Only divine intervention could make a church service safe. As a group of Washingtonians learned, choir practice can kill you.

When the virus hit northern California in March 2020, many people already had N95 masks. They had used them during the wildfires of 2018 that filled their neighborhoods with smoke and incinerated everything in their path at temperatures never before seen in forest fires. Though viruses are alive and fire is not, both are primed to spread, and both require oxygen to do that. When forest fires kill people, they, too, do so by suffocation. The only way to stop a forest fire is to suffocate it, deprive it of oxygen. Otherwise, like the virus, you have to let it burn till it runs out of fuel. Like COVID, like tear gas, like polluted air, smoke attacks the lungs. It harms by riding the breath into the body. Masks help but won't save you. Eighty-five people died in the Camp Fire of 2018, plus countless wild creatures. Here the politics of life and breath generated two questions analogous to those generated by the virus: Should governments try to suffocate wildfires or let them burn? Should people be prohibited from living in places prone to fires, or is it their civic right to do so, whatever the risk?

Air pollution of course is the elephant in the room when it comes to the politics of breath. It is one of the reasons Black, brown, and poor people are more likely to die of COVID-19, for they are more likely to suffer already from pollution-related lung ailments. There is a political geography of breath, and it, too, can twist. In many cities the COVID shutdown reduced air pollution enough to bring beloved landmarks back into view—one could see the stars in Mumbai, the Andes from Santiago, Mount Everest from Kathmandu. Breath came more easily, even with a mask. Soundscapes changed too. One could hear birds in Brooklyn, and silence. For many people, the lockdown brought pleasures, some new, some long-lost.

All over the world, in locked-down cities, people retained shreds of collectivity in two-minute cheering sessions held at a specific hour each evening. Nonessential and therefore protected citizens en masse honored the essential and therefore endangered citizens providing their care and upkeep. People filled their empty cityscapes not with bodies but with breath—shrieks, shouts, and whistles, along with banged pots, sirens, and applause. Those still breathing on their own stood in for those who were not.

And yet other love-driven sounds did not echo on those communal airwaves—the shrieks and wails of mourning. In another cruel twist, the virus made it dangerous for the living to mourn the dead, to whisper or sing to them as they died. Of all the damage and devastation the pandemic has left behind, this stymied grief may be the deepest and most long-lasting. The dying using their last breaths to say goodbye into a cell phone held by a staff member waiting to move on to the next gasping fatality. Family members deprived of the chance to say the unsaid and watch someone slip away. Staff members overwhelmed with the weight of these unfulfilled farewells. Survivors unable to gather in rituals for which there is no alternative. Like the virus itself, mourning rolls out on the breath, in words and song, in sighs, moans, screams, sobs, and bellowing rage. No 7 p.m. ritual has emerged for this, at least not yet.

Grief and rage, I think, gave George Floyd's brutal death, also unaccompanied, also by suffocation, the power to bring so many millions into the streets around the world. We were already mourning, for months haunted and

C.1. George Floyd protest, June 2020. SOURCE: FLICKR PHOTO BY EDEN, JANINE AND JIM.

surrounded by death. Out of the murder, and the film of the murder, an imperative came forth that overwhelmed the imperatives of the virus. There was no staying home. Politics of breath: the need to live in a world free of the virus was overwhelmed by the desire to live in a society free of racial terror. The sacrifices required to quell the virus would not be compensated by a mere return to a social world in which deaths like Floyd's continue to be routine. The extremity of the response to the virus made possible extreme demands in the street, for weeks. Defund the Police, Abolish the Police, End Systemic Racism, We Have Had Enough, The Real Pandemic Is Racism, We Can't Breathe. Tear gas was another player in the weaponized struggle over breath. Masks, too—the police refused to wear them, even when they got in your face.

The George Floyd uprising was the result of years of filmed episodes of police brutality, years of activism against it, years of failed attempts at police reform, years of organizing, especially by the Black Lives Matter movement.

It was a response to white supremacist movements actively supported by a racist president and his party. It reflected the raised consciousness of many white people, mostly under fifty, who have learned to reflect on their whiteness as an instrument of injustice. They showed up in droves. There was an important shift: the marches were not about white people coming out in support of the Black community. It was not about coalition. It was about a huge proportion of the citizenry demanding not to live in a society founded on racial terror. All these people made a choice: either continue to stay home to avoid spreading the virus or take to the streets to march and shout, knowing it may spread the virus. Save your breath, or put it to work. Viruses have no intentions, but people do. For the most part, the choice does not seem to have been difficult to make, and the country and the world overwhelmingly supported it. It was a consequential choice: a price, we were sure, would be paid. We did not know how great, but we knew what it was for, and we were okay with it. Freedom requires risk. Of course, this is precisely what white conservatives were saying about going to beaches and car rallies and end-the-lockdown rallies. Is this the elusive common ground? Whose knee is on their necks?

Surprisingly, the George Floyd marches produced no spike in COVID-19 cases in New York. The US death toll continued to rise, reaching 200,000 in September 2020, one-fifth of the known deaths worldwide. Readers of this book will know how it all turned out.

NOTES |

INTRODUCTION

1 The Alfa y Omega translations are mine. For an ethnography of Alfa y Omega, see Gogin (2005).

2 For a moving and vivid documentary account of this economic shock in Lima, see Heddy Honigmann's 1994 documentary *Metaal en Melancholie* (*Metal and Melancholy*).

3 Some readers may be reminded here of the concept of teleiopoiesis (*teleio* = end-directed, *poiesis* = making) introduced by Jacques Derrida in *The Politics of Friendship*, a third text that appeared in 1994. Derrida evokes a similar figure of an indecipherable future. Speaking of a "time out of joint," he imagines a state of "messianicity without messianism" and "an anticipatory poiesis that may lead us to experience the impossible" (3).

4 The feat took place at a campaign stop in Chicago on November 1, 2020. See "'That's What I Do': Barack Obama Hits Silky Three-Pointer on Campaign Trail," Northwestern High School, November 1, 2020, https://www.youtube .com/watch?v=Akqoxeu-RHE.

5 Scientists estimate that the separation of the continents took place around 200 million years ago.

6 Performance studies theorist Diana Taylor (2003) makes a related distinction between *archive* and *repertoire*.

7 Alfa y Omega, accessed March 16, 2005, www.alfayomega.com.pe/noguerra .htm (link no longer working).

8 *GeoHumanities* is the title of a journal founded by the American Association of Geographers in 2015.

9 Masao Miyoshi (2001) documents a similar experience. In his account as in mine (below), Edward Said's Orientalism marks a watershed.

10 Chinua Achebe had already given, in 1975, his earthshattering lecture, "An Image of Africa: Racism in Conrad's *Heart of Darkness*," at the University of Massachusetts. It, too, appeared in print in 1978, another watershed moment in literary history (Achebe 1978).

11 For example, see Ashcroft, Griffiths, and Tiffin (1989); Pratt ([1992] 2007); Said (1993); and Spurr (1993). For early critiques of the postcolonial paradigm, see McClintock (1992) and Shohat (1992).

12 The field of transatlantic studies emerged to fill this gap.

13 Bell, panel discussion, Center for Advanced Studies in the Behavioral Sciences, Stanford University, April 28, 2021.

14 In 2020 Muskogee poet Joy Harjo was named poet laureate of the United States, the first Native American to hold this position. That year she edited a comprehensive anthology of Native nations' poetry titled *When the Light of the World Was Subdued, Our Songs Came Through*.

15 Pérez is one in a line of Chicana feminist theorists whose books in the 1980s and 1990s animated the radical reimagining of the Americas from the literal or figurative site of the US-Mexico border. They include Gloria Anzaldúa, Norma Alarcón, Cherríe Moraga, Chela Sandoval, and Alicia Gaspar de Alba, among others.

16 Recent book listings, for example, include volumes on decolonial feminisms, decolonial linguistics, decolonial futures, and decolonial love, as well as a decolonial travel guide and Mignolo's own *The Politics of Decolonial Investigations* (2021).

CHAPTER ONE. MODERNITY'S FALSE PROMISES

This chapter is based on "Modernity and Periphery: Toward a Global and Relational Analysis," in *Beyond Dichotomies: Histories, Identities, Cultures, and the Challenge of Globalization*, edited by Elisabeth Mudimbe-Boyi (Albany: State University of New York Press, 2002), 21–47.

1 These compendiums of elements were gathered from the canonical academic literature on modernity, including such classics as Appadurai (1996), Berman (1982), Buell (1994), Calinescu ([1977] 1987), Habermas (1985), Held (1983), Heller (1990), Latour (1991), Toulmin (1990), and Touraine (1988, 1992). I also draw on surveys of metropolitan theories of modernity by Brunner (1987), Calderón (1988a), Lechner (1991), Lander (1991), and Larraín Ibañez (1996).

2 This erasure from history contrasts dramatically with the Andean eighteenth century, when elaborate power-sharing arrangements prevailed between criollo elites and Indigenous nobility, and the Indigenous masses participated in a relentless series of revolts, culminating in the pan-Andean Túpac Amaru–Túpac Katari rebellion discussed in chapters 13 and 14. Indigenous elites were disempowered in the wake of this revolt.

3 A parallel claim is made for political movements. Anarchism, an urban phenomenon in Europe, had powerful rural variants in Latin America, notably that of the Flores Magón brothers in Mexico.

4 Julie Skurski and Fernando Coronil (1993), in an important study of Gallegos's novel *Doña Barbara* (1928), argue that the text exemplifies a "return to the rural," which was an attempt to resolve ambivalent relations to the high modernism of the center. The Venezuelan countryside—the periphery of the periphery—became the site of an elite's effort to resolve the double consciousness of its dependent condition.

5 *Malandro* means roughly "scoundrel" in Brazil. *Cholo* and *chola* in the Andean countries refer to Indigenous-descended people, usually urban migrants from rural backgrounds. In the United States, *cholo* and *chola* are used differently, usually referring to street gang members and their female counterparts.

CHAPTER TWO. WHY THE VIRGIN OF ZAPOPAN WENT TO LOS ANGELES

This chapter originated in *Images of Power: Iconography, Culture and the State in Latin America*, edited by Jens Andermann and William Rowe (New York: Berghahn, 2005), 273–89.

1 The Lost Boys label was borrowed from *Peter Pan*. The rescue operations in the Sudan, carried out by international Christian charities, were sharply criticized for exacerbating the problems they were trying to solve (see, for example, the *New York Times* [2001] editorial, "Redemption of Sudanese Slaves"). The money paid to purchase the enslaved Dinka boys increased incentives for increased enslavements by the government-sponsored militias who were primarily responsible for the practice. .

2 The 2018 Australia-based Global Slavery Index estimated that 40 million people in the world were enslaved, of whom two-thirds were female and a fourth were children. The transatlantic slave trade is estimated to have transported 15 million individuals over 150 years. In the United States, estimates that some 100,000 girls and women were being trafficked into the country yearly in the sex trade led Congress to pass the Victims of Trafficking and Violence Protection Act in 2000. See Global Slavery Index, accessed September 24, 2021, https://www.globalslaveryindex.org.

3 In 2019 a photo of the entwined corpses of two Salvadoran migrants, Oscar Alberto Ramírez Martinez and his twenty-three-month-old daughter, drowned crossing the Rio Grande, similarly fed outrage about the Trump administration's border cruelty.

4 The 1988 Penang Declaration on Science and Technology made similar calculations: "In 1985 alone . . . US $74 billion left the Third World on its debt account alone: it obtained only $41 billion in new loans but had to pay $114 billion in debt servicing." If the profits of multinationals are added in, the figure goes up to $230–$240 billion, without counting a $65 billion loss due to falling commodity prices. See Penang Declaration in Sadar 1988, 329. My original sources for this data are no longer available. Thorough discussion of the Ecuadorian crisis can be found in a series of articles published in 2000 by the *Economist*, January 15, 2000 ("Desperation in Ecuador"), and January 27, 2000 ("A Warning from Ecuador).

5 My original source for this data is no longer available. For a detailed discussion of the effects of NAFTA on households in Mexico, see González de la Rocha (2000).

6 At the same time, metropolitan literatures became diasporic. Contemporary French and English fiction has been dominated in recent years by ex-colonial writers writing for metropolitan audiences about nonmetropolitan places and times. To a great degree, it is a literature of storytelling bringing tales from afar that admit both decolonizing and exoticist readings.

7 In July 2001 Mexico was rocked by news of the capture of "La Rana" (the frog), a notorious hit man employed by one of the country's most powerful narco cartels. Unbeknownst to police, he had been in custody for some time in a Tijuana jail. Plastic surgery and the removal of forty pounds of fat by liposuction had made him unrecognizable. See *La Jornada* (2001).

8 Bruno Latour mentions the idea of trunk lines and the effects of their severing in *We Have Never Been Modern* (1993). Ferguson discusses nodality in *Expectations of Modernity* (1999).

9 Half the potato farmers in the United States were forced out of business between 1995 and 2000, and the picture has been about the same for US producers of other things, from soybeans to pigs and cranberries. In my home country, Canada, after free-market governments suspended rules on foreign ownership of farmland, a wave of German and Swiss buyers swept in, bought up family farms, and consolidated them into large landholdings. At the same time, outside its borders, Canadian mining companies, like the one discussed in chapter 5, were becoming first-class international predators in other countries.

10 Noncapitalist modes of production found within capitalism range, they argue, from household labor to volunteer work, prison labor, self-employment, theft, slavery, hobbies, scavenging, donating care work, and others.

11 In 2000, the seventy thousand residents of the Tambo Grande Valley in Peru found that their $110 million a year crop of mangoes and limes had become dispensable in the eyes of the Manhattan Minerals Corporation, which wanted to turn their land into an open-pit mine that would employ at most five hundred people. Ironically, the mango and lime enterprise had been introduced fifty years earlier through a World Bank irrigation project. Manhattan Mineral's proposal, which then president Fujimori approved, included no plans for the tens of thousands who would lose their homes and livelihoods to the mining project. See *Noticias Aliadas* (Lima, Peru) 38, April 13, 2001.

An earlier version of this chapter appeared in Spanish as "Los que se que-
dan," in *Los viajeros y el Rio de la Plata: Un siglo de escritura* edited by Jean-
Philippe Barnabé, Lindsey Cordery and Beatriz Vegh (Montevideo: Linardi y
Risso, 2010), 356–78.

1 This case was communicated to me by the Mexican anthropologist Lourdes
   Portillo in Zocoalco, Mexico, 2009.
2 In addition to slavery, the world today faces international trafficking of young
   women into marriage, prostitution, and domestic labor; of athletes, including children, by international sports federations; of infants and children in
   adoptions; of body parts, from corneas to kidneys. These are all commercial
   transactions.
3 On contemporary Mixtecos and migration, see Stephen (2007). I am indebted
   to her presentation at New York University in April 2009.
4 I am grateful to Lourdes Trujillo of the Program in Rural Studies at the Autonomous Metropolitan University Xochimilco for sharing these impressions
   (August 2004).
5 Ironically, the girl is vulnerable to the assault because a priest has forbidden
   her to work alongside her *novio*, or fiancé, attempting to suppress the Andean
   tolerance for premarital sex. When the pregnancy becomes apparent, the
   girl's father expels her from home. The rape dispossesses him of his authority
   over his daughter in the community.
6 The mother's relentless remaining parallels the contemporary use (especially by
   women) of blockades and occupations as weapons of social protest in Indigenous areas of Latin America. They have proved to be among the most effective
   weapons for unarmed groups responding to ruthless economic regimes. A few
   logs or immobilized vehicles can disrupt the all-important flow of goods.
7 For a broad and detailed study of the contemporary "politics of presence" in
   Mexico and Central America, see Taylor (2020).
8 Jacques Derrida (1998) briefly mentions the sexual violence implicit in traditional patriarchal models of hospitality in *De l'hospitalité*.
9 This statement by Subcomandante Marcos is widely quoted. Here it is taken
   from Ejercito Zapatista de Liberación Nacional (2005).

CHAPTER FOUR. FIRE, WATER, AND WANDERING WOMEN

An earlier version of chapter 4 appeared in Spanish as "Tres incendios y
dos mujeres extraviadas: El imaginario novelístico frente al nuevo contrato
social," in *Espacio urbano, comunicación y violencia en América Latina*,
edited by Mabel Moraña (Pittsburgh: Instituto Internacional de Literatura
Iberoamericana, 2002), 91–106.

1 These were mass movements that coalesced around issues that had had no
   place in conventional politics, such as women's rights, gay and lesbian liberation, ethnic or religious identities, and regional formations such as those

of landless peoples in Brazil, coca producers in Bolivia, or waste recyclers in Buenos Aires (see Obarrio et al. [2011] for an excellent overview of these movements). These new social movements created new ways of doing politics, as orthodox left politics was defeated and states withdrew from commitments to citizen well-being. Among many landmarks in the unfolding of this process, the AIDS crisis stands out.

2 The exception is the bond between Alexis and his mother, toward whom he feels responsibility, particularly economic responsibility, in the role of provider.

3 The concept of the West appeared frequently in Augusto Pinochet's speeches, as a cultural referent for Chile and as the name of a civilizing project that the dictatorship was in charge of defending.

CHAPTER FIVE. PLANETARIZED INDIGENEITY

1 The Zapatista revolutionary movement, which erupted in Chiapas in 1992, is named after Emiliano Zapata, a major peasant leader in the Mexican Revolution of 1910. From the state of Morelos, he was a mestizo who spoke Nahuatl and recruited many Indigenous peasants to his army. His dedication to agrarian revolution made him the icon of the contemporary Zapatista movement.

2 The Maoist Shining Path guerrilla movement that terrorized the Andes in the 1980s and 1990s supported the eradication of traditional Andean culture, which it regarded as backward and colonial, setting the young Andeans who made up its ranks in opposition to their parents.

3 The most comprehensive account of the residential school system and how it was experienced is found in the 2015 report of Canada's Truth and Reconciliation Commission. Appointed in 2007, the commission spent six years traveling to different parts of the country holding hearings, gathering testimony, and reviewing historical documents. See Government of Canada (2021).

4 The report of Canada's Truth and Reconciliation Commission (2015) begins thus: "For over a century, the central goals of Canada's Aboriginal policy were to eliminate Aboriginal governments; ignore Aboriginal rights; terminate the Treaties; and, through a process of assimilation, cause Aboriginal peoples to cease to exist as distinct legal, social, cultural, religious, and racial entities in Canada. The establishment and operation of residential schools were a central element of this policy, which can best be described as 'cultural genocide'" (8).

5 For an overview, see the World Directory of Minorities and Indigenous Peoples, Minority Rights Group International, accessed December 10, 2020, https://minorityrights.org/directory/. Some states, such as Indonesia, have vigorously resisted the category of Indigenous eager to avoid the friction it generates (Tsing 2004). Some peoples resist the label, such as the Tibetans, whose colonized relation to the Chinese could enable them to claim Indigenous power.

6 In spring of 2019 the Waorani, a major Amazonian group, announced a historic victory in Ecuadorian courts, banning the government from selling their lands to oil companies. The decision protects 500,000 acres of Ama-

zonian rain forest from oil exploitation. The case was fought for seven years (Scozza and Nenquimo 2021). In June 2020 the US Supreme Court recognized the legal jurisdiction of the Muskogee people over half of the state of Oklahoma (Healey and Liptak 2020).

7 Warrior (1995), Weaver (1996), Alfred (1999), Mamani (2005), Vizenor (2008), Paredes (2008), Goeman (2013), Simpson and Smith (2014), Kopinawa (2015), and de la Cadena (2015) give an idea of the range of this work. Broader, more generalized approaches to contemporary indigeneity include de la Cadena and Starn (2007), Bengoa (2000), Sandoval (2008), and Johnson (1999).

CHAPTER SIX. ANTHROPOCENE AS CONCEPT AND CHRONOTOPE

This chapter draws in part on "Coda: Concept and Chronotope," in *Arts of Living on a Damaged Planet: Ghosts and Monsters of the Anthropocene*, edited by Anna Lowenhaupt Tsing, Heather Swanson, Elaine Gan, and Nils Bubandt (Minneapolis: University of Minnesota Press, 2017), 169–74.

1 The Anthropocene would mark the end of the Holocene, the geological era posited to have begun after the last ice age ended close to twelve thousand years ago.

2 One cannot help juxtaposing this 2001 document with another Amsterdam Declaration that appeared in 2002, an Official Statement of World Humanism, a reaffirmation of principles first put forth by Humanists International in 1952. Fifty years later, those canonical humanist principles codify the anthropocentrism that the climate scientists argue has become suicidal. See Humanists International 2002.

3 In *The End of the Myth* (2019), cultural historian Greg Grandin argues that the new national obsession with a border wall signals the exhaustion of the frontier myth and the beginning of what Bakhtin would call a new national chronotope.

4 Recent successful experiments include Peter Wohlleben's *Hidden Life of Trees* (2016), Alissa York's novel *Fauna* (2010), and Richard Powers's *The Overstory* (2018), awarded the 2019 Pulitzer Prize for Fiction.

CHAPTER SEVEN. MUTATIONS OF THE CONTACT ZONE

1 "Arts of the Contact Zone" first appeared in 1992 in *Profession*, a journal of the Modern Language Association. It has been reprinted dozens of times in essay collections, handbooks, textbooks, and course readers.

2 Institute for Saxon History and Cultural Anthropology, Dresden, Germany.

3 These recent travels are no doubt due in part to the translation of *Imperial Eyes* (Pratt [1992] 2007) into Spanish, Portuguese, Polish, Chinese, and Korean.

4 Annual Meeting, Association of American Geographers, Boston, April 5–9, 2017.

Chapter 8 appeared in an earlier form in *American Quarterly* 68, no. 3 (2016): 557–62.

CHAPTER NINE. AUTHORITARIANISM 2020

This chapter is revised and rewritten from "Overwriting Pinochet: Undoing the Culture of Fear in Chile," *Modern Language Quarterly* 57, no. 2 (1996): 151–62.

1 The plebiscite mandates establishing by popular vote a 155-person body that will form a constitutional convention charged with drafting a new constitution. This body must be half women and half men and include no sitting politicians.

2 P g R (@Pikaya61), "The Pinochetization of America cometh," replying to @thenation, Twitter, July 17, 2020, 1:18 p.m., https://twitter.com/Pikaya61 /status/1284190775564283906.

3 The coup overthrew the socialist coalition Unidad Popular (Popular Unity), headed by President Salvador Allende Gossens, replacing it with a military junta made up of four generals. Allende died during the coup. He had pursued a socialist model of national development, including nationalizing the Chilean copper industry and appropriating 50 percent of arable land for redistribution to small farmers. The US government through the Central Intelligence Agency was heavily involved in bringing down his government and installing the dictatorship.

4 This and all translations are mine. The regime also published its official views on gender in a booklet, *Valores patrios y valores familiares* (Secretaría Nacional de la Mujer 1982).

5 In the campaign against the Unidad Popular government, right-wing parties and the military sought to mobilize middle- and upper-class women, whose opposition would appear apolitical. When a truckers' strike supported by the Central Intelligence Agency created shortages of food and household needs, women mobilized in protest marches, banging empty pots. More specifically, a network of highly placed military wives was organized to call for the military to restore order. The coup could then be presented as a response to the demands of a politically disinterested sector.

6 Chilean scholars have produced a vast and rich literature on the question of culture, authoritarianism, and redemocratization in Chile, on which this essay relies and by which it is framed. In addition to the works cited in the main text, see Brunner (1981, 1985); Richard (1992); Riquelme (1990); Subercaseaux (1991); Vidal (1985, 1989); and Garretón, Sosnowsi, and Subercaseaux (1993).

7 Archibald, class lecture on Pía Barros in the context of the Pinochet regime, Stanford University, May 1994. See also Munizaga (1983).

8 According to Grinor Rojo (2016), *testimonios* circulated clandestinely in Chile as early as 1975 and openly after 1981.

9 These events are vividly captured in the lengthy documentary *La batalla de Chile (The Battle of Chile)*, produced by Patricio Guzmán and directed by

Federico Elton in 1973. The film was banned in Chile until the mid-1990s. In a moving sequel, *Chile: La memoria obstinada* (*Chile, Obstinate Memory*, 1997), Guzmán documented the first showings of the film in Chile, more than twenty years after the events took place.

10 The filmed footage was edited into a four-hour TV series as well as the two-hour film and circulated widely on international circuits. Shortly after the book appeared, on Pinochet's orders, fifteen thousand copies were burned by the Ministry of the Interior in Valparaiso.

11 Vidal (1985) speaks at length of the medieval quality of the Pinochet dictatorship.

12 The title puns on the adjective *homérica* (Homeric) and the phrase *lumpen América*.

13 The Southern Cone regimes often described their work as that of healing a diseased national body. Communism, for example, was a cancer that had to be removed by self-inflicted surgery.

14 For a comprehensive study of literary and visual artistic production in the transitional period in Argentina and Chile, see Masiello (2001).

15 Gessen follows the Hungarian sociologist Bálint Magyar, who finds that autocracies follow a trajectory from an autocratic attempt to an autocratic breakthrough to autocratic consolidation. Many writers use the terms *autocratic* and *authoritarian* interchangeably. I do not see them as synonymous, but both adjectives apply to the figures I am discussing here.

16 The Trump administration engaged in all of these. The installation of an unbalanced right-wing majority on the US Supreme Court was completed on October 26, 2020, the day after the Chilean plebiscite and days before the US election. It was a process as illegitimate as the one by which the dictatorship established the 1980 constitution in Chile. That antidemocratic imbalance will likely last as long as Pinochet's constitution did and may restructure US society to much the same degree.

CHAPTER TEN. THE ETHNOGRAPHER'S ARRIVAL

This chapter is a revised and expanded version of "Fieldwork in Common Places," in *Writing Culture: The Poetics and Politics of Ethnography*, edited by James Clifford and George Marcus (Berkeley: University of California Press, 1986), 27–50.

1 This book, incidentally, should have generated a scandal of its own. Its editor-transcriber, Ettore Biocca, claimed it as his own and inexcusably failed to credit Valero adequately for her own story. Her name appears nowhere on the cover, and there is no indication she was receiving any royalties. At the story's end, Valero is on her own in a Brazilian city, struggling to get her children through school. In August 1996 contact with Valero was renewed by a Brazilian health worker, Marinho de Souza, traveling with anthropologist Patrick Tierney, who was investigating abuses of the Yanomamo by anthropologists.

Valero was living near a missionary outpost in Yanomamo country, destitute, hungry, and nearly blind. She had returned to Amazonia, preferring the hardships of her jungle home over the prospects she had encountered elsewhere. In his vehement critique of thirty years of Yanomamo anthropology, Tierney likewise expresses indignation at the field for thirty years of collaboration in "the theft of Valero's singular achievements" and the suppression of her expertise because "it would have detracted from their own mystique" (2000, 248–49).

2 Hernán Cortés's conquest of Mexico was made possible by the mediation of a Spanish castaway, Gerónimo de Aguilar, whom he retrieved from captivity in the Yucatán. Aguilar had learned a Maya language, which made him able to communicate with Cortés's concubine, Doña Marina, who was bilingual in Maya and Nahuatl. The three-way translation circuit, and Marina's strategic genius, made it possible for Cortés to recruit Indigenous allies to help him overthrow the Aztec Empire. See Díaz de Castillo ([1568] 1963, 64–65).

3 James Clifford has made similar observations about Malinowski, and I am indebted to his work here (see Clifford 1985).

4 The contrast could hardly be starker between this fallen nocturnal world and the visión of the !Kung offered in a feature film being made at the same time, South African Jamie Uys's international hit *The Gods Must be Crazy* (1980), a celebratory reincarnation of the sun-drenched primitivist Bushman stereotype, and a quaint and paternalistic reinstription of apartheid values.

5 Shostak's (1981) text coincided with other experimental texts, including Vincent Crapanzano's *Tuhami: Portrait of a Moroccan* (1980) and Kevin Dwyer's *Moroccan Dialogues* (1982), and was followed by such landmarks as Ruth Behar's *Translated Woman: Crossing the Border with Esperanza's Story* (1993) and Anna Lowenhaupt Tsing's *In the Realm of the Diamond Queen* (1993).

6 My remarks here on the history of Bushman-European contact are based mainly on George McCall Theal's *History of South Africa, 1892–1919*.

7 Interestingly, Shostak's predecessor and colleague Richard Lee also uses a nocturnal arrival scene to introduce his third visit to the !Kung (Lee 1979, xvii).

8 It is fair to say that the emergent field of sociobiology aggressively undertook to displace cultural anthropology as the center of the discipline, resulting in conflicts so harsh that in some universities the two separated into different departments.

CHAPTER ELEVEN. RIGOBERTA MENCHÚ AND THE GEOPOLITICS OF TRUTH

This chapter is based on "*I, Rigoberta Menchú* and the Culture Wars," in *The Rigoberta Menchú Controversy*, edited by Arturo Arias (Minneapolis: University of Minnesota Press, 2001), 29–48.

1 This was the conclusion of the United Nations Commission for Historical Clarification (1999), whose report, titled "Guatemala: Memory of Silence," was presented by its director, the German Christian Tomuschat, in February 1999. The commission was established as part of the peace negotiations

between the Guatemalan army and the guerrilla Unidad Revolucionaria National Guatemalteca(Revolutionary Nationala Unit of Guatemala)in 1996. The commission concluded that 93 percent of the killings were the work of the army, which responded to a guerrilla uprising with a campaign of genocide. The death toll reflects only a fraction of the violence, which included the widespread use of torture, forced conscription into the army and civilian patrols, and the forced displacement of tens of thousands of people.

2 Fundación Rigoberta Menchú Tum, Facebook, accessed September 17, 2021, https://www.facebook.com/fundacionrmt/. The foundation does not maintain a website at this time.

3 For press coverage, see, for example, Rohter (1998), reprinted in Arias (2001, 58). Other press documents are included in Arias's collection.

4 We now know that this movement had its roots in the Barry Goldwater campaign of 1968 and developed through generously sponsored College Republican organizations that became increasingly vocal after Reagan's election in 1980. Many prominent conservative activists, including Karl Rove, Roger Stone, and Peter Thiel, got their start in the College Republicans.

5 In the fall of 2020, President Donald Trump by executive order prohibited required diversity training and announced in addition his intention to prohibit the teaching of materials that reflected negatively on the United States. See Federal Register, "Combating Race and Sex Stereotyping," Executive Order 13950, September 28, 2020, https://www.federalregister.gov/documents/2020/09/28/2020-21534/combating-race-and-sex-stereotyping.

6 For a fuller discussion of this debate, see Pratt (1990).

7 Bennett published a series of influential books on virtue, but his influence waned in the late 1990s when the press revealed he had used his book proceeds to pay $2 million in losses in casinos. See Seelye (2003).

8 Stoll's doctoral thesis (1993) advanced the arguments that reappear in the Menchú book: (a) most campesinos during the Guatemalan civil war saw themselves as caught between the army and the guerrilla movement, neither of which they genuinely supported; and (b) the guerrillas were heavily responsible for the suffering and loss of life because they initiated the confrontation and failed to defend the campesinos.

9 The key term here is undoubtedly "we." Many thought this quotation was apocryphal. However, its authenticity was recently confirmed in Bellow's obituaries. See, for example, Gussow and McGrath (2005). According to his obituaries, Bellow made the remark on a radio interview.

10 For an entire volume dedicated to classroom approaches to *I, Rigoberta Menchú*, see Carey-Webb and Benz (1996).

11 Public statement, January 1999, in response to Stoll's accusations, issued at Center for Advanced Research in Anthropology (CIESAS), Guadalajara, Mexico.

12 The particular role of autobiography in US lettered culture undoubtedly shaped the reception of the book in ways neither Menchú nor her editor, Elisabeth Burgos-Debray, could possibly have anticipated. Certainly it had

much to do with the intensity of the response to Stoll's accusations among US readers. As is customary with testimonio, Burgos-Debray taped Menchu's oral account, then transcribed and edited the manuscript for publication. *Testimonio* is an autobiography collaboratively produced. The process is explored in more detail in Pratt (1996).

13 Following Anna Lowenhaupt Tsing (2005), I use the term *move* in a dual sense: triggering an emotional response and repositioning subjects, taking them from a known place to a new one.

14 Later a fellow of the American Enterprise Institute and president of a Christian college, D'Souza found his voice at Dartmouth College in a chain of conservative student newspapers founded by the Republican right in the 1980s as a seed ground for young activists. Candidates received internships, salaries, and training in how to create controversy around left-wing, minority, and gay faculty members. D'Souza has written sixteen books and made several films. Wikipedia currently describes him as a "far-right political commentator, provocateur, author, filmmaker, and conspiracy theorist." Dinesh D'Souza, Wikipedia, accessed August 9, 2021, https://en.wikipedia.org/wiki/Dinesh_D%27Souza.

15 The book had consequences in many other contexts as well, notably the European solidarity movement and the peace process within Guatemala. Kay Warren (2001) expresses her concerns about the book's effects on political processes in Guatemala.

16 Rereading it in 2019, one cannot help but hear the echo of the Trumpian style, then in the making on television.

17 For discussion of these and other claims, see Arias (2001). In that important collection, the essay by W. George Lovell and Christopher Lutz, "The Primacy of Larger Truths," is particularly fascinating, documenting sixteenth-century Maya deliberations on such matters as land tenure, torture, schooling, identity of children, and other colonial issues that appear as contemporary concerns in both Menchú's and Stoll's books. Other writers in the collection (Duncan Earle, Carol Smith, Danilo Rodríguez, Kay Warren, and Rosa Morales) also address these factual disputes.

18 Such an accusation was very serious for a recipient of the Nobel Peace Prize. In awarding her the prize, the Nobel Committee had satisfied itself that Menchú had not been a supporter of armed struggle or guerrilla warfare, though she had advocated civilian self-defense.

19 Warren (2001), however, contrasts anthropological polemics between peers like Mead and Freeman with the situation in which an American anthropologist uses academic authority to discredit an Indigenous leader and public figure.

20 Guatemala has one of the most inequitable land distributions in the world. Its large rural Indigenous population has long suffered from a critical land shortage. This inequality, combined with climate change, is the main motive for massive out-migrations of Guatemalan campesinos since 2000. For analysis of land tenure and its consequences in Guatemala, see Jonas (1991), and for discussion of Guatemalan migration to the United States, see Jonas and Rodríguez (2015).

21 Scholars have asked, for example, whether Stoll's relations with informants were affected by the fact that he did not know Indigenous languages and was obviously a white foreigner. He also required military permission to travel where he went and was working in areas under martial law. See Warren (2001), C. Smith (2001), Rodríguez (2001), and others in Arias (2001).

22 Perhaps for this reason, in Guatemala exhumation by forensic anthropologists has been the officially recognized mechanism for documenting loss of life. After 2010, with international support, the Guatemalan legal system laid down an extraordinary record of accountability for the atrocities of the war.

23 Duncan Earle (2001) claims that the deepest internal division in Maya society is religious, between Christians and practitioners of traditional religion.

24 It is probably worth recalling that at the time she gave her testimony, Menchú was twenty-two years old, living in exile in Chiapas after suffering the family losses narrated in her text. She had no experience of other parts of the world. The context of her testimony, recorded in Burgos-Debray's apartment in Paris, was very unfamiliar to her.

25 Alongside the metropolitan cult of the fact, we all rely on the common practice that, in the absence of dispute, verisimilitude counts as veracity—that is, if something is plausible, it is likely taken to be true. This is how we "believe" the news, for instance. Under what conditions, we can ask, does that equation break down, as in the case of Menchú after Stoll? When does it not?

CHAPTER TWELVE. THE POLITICS OF REENACTMENT

This chapter appeared in an earlier form in *Motion Pictures: Travel Ideals in Film*, edited by Andrew McGregor and Gemma Blackwood (Bern: Peter Lang, 2016), 15–30.

1 Widely reviewed, the film was nominated for thirteen Spanish Academy Awards. Scholarly treatment has been scarce, but see Paszkiewicz (2013).

2 In anticipation of the Columbus Quincentenary in 1992, Spain embarked on an energetic transatlantic campaign to revindicate Spanish imperialism as a benign "encuentro de dos culturas" (encounter of two cultures). In Latin America the campaign backfired, provoking among other things the first continent-wide assembly of Indigenous people, catalyzing the transnational Indigenous movement discussed throughout this book.

3 Antonio de Montesinos (or Antonio Montesino) was a Spanish Dominican friar on the island of Hispaniola (now the Dominican Republic and Haiti) who, with the backing of his Dominican community, preached against the enslavement and mistreatment of the native people of the island. Montesinos's preaching led Bartolomé de las Casas to join the Dominican Order. See "Antonio de Montesinos," Wikipedia, accessed August 9, 2021, http://en .wikipedia.org/wiki/Antonio_de_Montesinos.

4 All translations here are mine.

5 "Tell me, by what right or by what interpretation of justice do you keep these Indians in such a cruel and horrible servitude? By what authority have you

waged such detestable wars against people who were once living so quietly and peacefully in their own land?" See "Antonio de Montesinos," Wikipedia.

6   In fact, the renowned actor and director Gael García Bernal is Mexican, not a Spaniard. This fact does not appear to be in play in this film, though García Bernal's spoken Spanish is clearly from the Americas.

7   The Bolivian extras, though Indigenous in appearance, would not necessarily identify as Indians or as Indigenous, even those who speak Indigenous languages. People of Indigenous descent, once they leave subsistence agricultural communities, often reidentify as mestizo or *cholo* in Bolivia and other Andean countries. The term *indio* remains stigmatized.

8   From Columbus's famed letter on his first voyage to the Americas: "They are so unsuspicious and so generous with what they possess, that no one who had not seen it would believe it. They never refuse anything that is asked for . . . with any trifle of whatever kind, they are satisfied" (Columbus 1493). Antón, the actor playing Columbus, quotes this text early in the film.

9   *Fitzcarraldo* reenacts a feat attempted by Peruvian rubber baron Carlos Fermín Fitzcarrald, to bring an entire steamship overland to a rubber-rich Amazon River tributary in the 1890s. As Blank's documentary revealed, because of Herzog's own reckless ambitions, the reenactment reproduced some of the colonial abuses Fitzcarrald was accused of, notably dangerous and exploitive working conditions and relentless demands. At least one worker was killed in the filming.

10 Fees for water access rose to $20 a month, completely out of range for the many households. Monthly incomes hovered around $100.

11 The bibliography on this subject in Spanish is vast. For an account in English, see Olivera and Lewis (2004). For broader context, see Bennett, Dávila-Poblete, and Rico (2005).

12 A new Bolivian constitution, the result of a two-year constitutional convention in which all sectors of the society participated, was approved in 2009. Among many changes, it defines Bolivia as a plurinational, secular state, gives recognition to Indigenous languages, and requires Indigenous representation in all branches of government.

13 The connection is reinforced by the fact that the gold comes from rivers, the same rivers that the contemporary communities count on for water.

14 Alongside blockades, the other traditional tool of Bolivian popular movements has been *la marcha*, long treks on foot from the hinterlands to the capital, endurance feats often hundreds of miles long. Here again, the operative marker of subaltern power is political agency predicated on the absence of vehicles.

CHAPTER THIRTEEN. TRANSLATION, CONTAGION, INFILTRATION

This chapter originated as "The Traffic in Meaning: Translation, Contagion, Infiltration," *Profession* (2002): 25–36.

1   In what is now Bolivia, the rebellion was led by another couple, Túpac Katari and Bartolina Sisa. Both of them have given their names to prominent political groups in Bolivia. Túpac Amaru's name, in turn, was adopted by a

Peruvian guerrilla movement, the Movimiento Revolucionario Túpac Amaru, and was also shared by the American rapper Tupac Amaru Shakur.

2 The central plaza of Cuzco was the place where two centuries before (1572), the first Túpac Amaru was executed after losing his last stand against the Spanish invasion. Today this plaza looks much as it did in 1781.

3 This strategy did not succeed. Andean mythology adjusted, and the story spread that the Inca's body was reassembling itself under the ground in order to rise again. Similarly, the prohibition of Indigenous clothing resulted, according to some scholars, in the adoption of a set of European elements—the gathered skirt and bowler hat, for example—that today constitutes "authentic, traditional" Andean dress (see figure 14.1).

4 One instance is the rewriting of metropolitan literary works by colonial, ex-colonial, or anticolonial subjects. The corpus of such rewrites is large and, from a metropolitan perspective, both overdetermined and strange: there is J. M. Coetzee rewriting *Robinson Crusoe* (*Foe*), V. S. Naipaul rewriting *Heart of Darkness* (*A Bend in the River*), Derek Walcott rewriting *The Iliad* (*Omeros*), and Jean Rhys rewriting *Jane Eyre* (*Wide Sargasso Sea*). This practice would seem to fall outside the purview of translation, even in a metaphoric sense.

CHAPTER FOURTEEN. THINKING ACROSS THE COLONIAL DIVIDE

1 The US rapper Tupac Amaru Shakur was named by his parents after Túpac Amaru II.

2 Ten years after the Andean rebellion, the Haitian Revolution broke out and ultimately succeeded in overthrowing French colonial rule in 1804. Mainstream historiography religiously remembers the (white) French and US revolutions and relentlessly ignores the Andean and Haitian ones.

3 The discussion in chapter 13 explores whether it is useful to think of this kind of appropriation as a form of translation.

4 Twelve years after Bastidas's execution, the French radical Olimpe de Gouges was publicly guillotined in Paris for her antislavery, antimonarchist, and feminist writings. Here, too, an anonymous witness reported, "She approached the scaffold with a calm and serene expression on her face, and forced the guillotine's furies, which had driven her to this place of torture, to admit that such courage and beauty had never been seen before." "Olympe de Gouges," Wikipedia, accessed August 2, 2021, https://en.wikipedia.org/wiki/Olympe_de_Gouges accessed July 22, 2019

5 The War of the Pacific (1879–84) was fought between Chile, on the one hand, and Bolivia and Peru, on the other, over trade, boundaries, and resources. Chile gained possession of the Atacama desert, and Bolivia lost its access to the ocean.

6 Some readers will remember the extraordinary Peruvian singer and film star of the 1950s and 1960s who adopted the name Yma Sumac.

7 *Abigarradas* is Rivera Cusicanqui's preferred adjective to speak of the mix alluded to by terms like *hybrid* and *mestizo*. The closest English equivalent is the evocative word *piebald*.

8   In Rivera Cusicanqui's view, the flourishing of Latin American cultural theory after 1980 was also driven to a significant degree by recolonizing energies that produced new cultural visions but left privileged white intelligentsias in their place. Indigenous people and minority groups become "adornments for neoliberalism" (2010, 75).

9   Both the British and French governments supported Spanish American independence struggles, with the aim of gaining commercial access to the region. By the 1880s, British banks were in control of the Peruvian economy. See chapter 15.

10 Nineteenth-century Peru is by no means the only place where the over-throw of colonial rule released recolonizing energies that entangled with or prevailed over the work of decolonization. The world's second great wave of independences, in Africa and Asia after World War II, led similarly to models of development that kept the new nation-states in colonial orbits and reinscribed exploitive economic relations across the colonial divide. Indeed, in both nineteenth-century Latin America and twentieth-century Africa and Asia, ex-colonial status left new nations open to even more external actors, whose access was no longer blocked by mother-country monopolies.

11 The web of wool that links Bastidas and Matto of course extends far back in time, long before the Incas. Textile art in Peru goes back ten thousand years; Andean weavers were world masters of the arts of wool by 1000 BCE. Their creative mastery extends into the present as well, in the unique luxury knitting found in the shops of Cuzco and the breathtaking weavings from Bolivia.

12 The 1969 agricultural reform resulted in a precipitous decline in Peru's agricultural production. Recipients of land had no capital with which to work it, no machines, no way to buy seed, and little technological expertise. As rural people flooded to cities, they established self-organized squatter cities and became both an exploitable workforce and a force to be reckoned with. In the highlands, the power vacuum set the stage for the Maoist Shining Path guerrillas, whose project included eradicating Indigenous culture in the name of a Maoist modernity.

13 J. K. Gibson-Graham explore this kind of practice in their original and fascinating book *A Postcapitalist Politics* (2006).

CHAPTER FIFTEEN. THE FUTUROLOGY OF INDEPENDENCE

1   These are lines from the classic ballads "Quizás," "Que te vaya bonito," "Julieta," and "No volveré."

2   Namibia became an independent state after twenty-two years of international maneuvering and guerrilla warfare waged by the South West African People's Organization. This outcome was a direct unfolding of the Scramble for Africa in the 1880s, when Namibia became a German colony and was then passed to South Africa. Javier Pérez de Cuéllar, then secretary-general of the United Nations, administered the oath of office to the first Namibian president, Sam Nujoma.

3　For the text of the plan, see Miranda (1801).

4　My discussion of Philippine history is based on the recent history by Luis Francia (2010).

5　The café where the conspirators met is located just off the Plaza Santa Ana; it is still open for business and mostly unchanged except for the plaque outside.

6　These demands were laid out in the magazine *La Solidaridad* (Solidarity), published in Spain and financed from Manila from 1889 to 1895, discussed in Francia (2010, 116 and passim).

7　It is noteworthy that the term *state* does not appear anywhere in the discourse of the *independentistas*. They did not name state building as an aspiration; *la nación* was the ideal to be realized.

8　For a lengthy discussion of the problematic of modernity and coloniality in Latin America, see chapter 1 in this volume.

9　See also Rafael's *Motherless Tongues* (2016).

10　For the full text of the Constitution of 1805, see Christophe et al. (1805).

11　Citing Fischer (2004, 132), Domínguez (2021, 80) concludes, "La convulsa vida política dominicana hace imposible enmarcar su historia decimonónica a través de una narrativa de progreso y desarrollo, basada primero en la independencia y luego en la construcción del estado nación" (The tumultuous political life of the Dominican Republic makes it impossible to frame its nineteenth century history as a narrative of progress and development based first on independence and then on the construction of the nation state). The Dominican dream of imperial protection did not evaporate in 1865. In 1869 President Buenaventura de Baez negotiated annexation to the United States, but it was again rejected, this time by abolitionists in the US Senate. The Dominican Republic was still a slave state, and powerful elites were as desperate to hold on to that status as many citizens were to end it. In 1915 the minister of defense organized a coup whose purpose was to trigger a US occupation of the island. It worked. The United States occupied the Dominican Republic until 1924.

CHAPTER SIXTEEN. REMEMBERING ANTICOLONIALISM

Chapter 16 draws in part on "The Anti-colonial Past," *Modern Language Quarterly* 65, no. 3 (2004): 443–56.

1　I have been helped in this work by two excellent collections assembling work by scholars from Asia and Africa, *The Revenge of Athena* (Sardar 1988) and *Postcolonial African Philosophy* (Eze 1994). In a recent book, *Imperial Delusions* (2020), Amos Getachew undertakes a return to anticolonial thought of the kind I call for here.

2　Cabral was head of the Party for the Independence of Cabo Verde and Guinea Bissau. He was forty-nine years old at the time of his murder.

3　Eurocentrism continues to shape metropolitan discussions of modernity and universals to a surprising degree, across the ideological spectrum. Discussions commonly contain no reference to the non-European world or to fundamental relationships of imperialism, colonialism, or slavery. Diffusion is rarely problematized. This is one of the few features shared by books as diverse as Louis Dupré's *Passage to Modernity* (1993), Bruno Latour's *We Have Never Been Modern* (1993), Alain Touraine's *Critique de la modernité* (*Critique of Modernity*; 1992), and Judith Butler, Ernesto Laclau, and Slavoj Žižek's *Contingency, Hegemony, Universality* (2000). The norms of the metropole still do not require or expect scholars to attend to the writings of scholars based in Latin America, Africa, or Asia. The circuits of knowledge today retain an imperial configuration established in the sixteenth century.

4 As evidence, Goonatilake refers to the three major Ayurvedic texts dating from the period beginning in the fifteenth century BC. The volume on medicine, the *Charaka Sanhitha* alone, he observes, is "three times the size of the entire surviving medical literature of ancient Greece" (1984, 8).

5 American anthropologist James Scott (1998) observes that modernization can execute itself only in projects that depend entirely on the continuity and effectiveness of local knowledges and practices.

6 In a similar example, colonial laws in West Africa substituted tribal marriage systems, which automatically gave couples land when they married, with a policy distributing land by individual ownership. The aim was not to install individualism but to compel young men into wage labor in order to assemble the basics to marry.

CODA

The coda was published in electronic form by the Hemispheric Institute of Performance and Politics and also appeared as "Airways," *Anthropology Now* 12, no. 2 (2020): 1–4.

REFERENCES

Achebe, Chinua. 1978. "An Image of Africa: Racism in Conrad's *Heart of Darkness*." *Research in African Literatures* 9 (1): 1–15.

Aira, César. 2001. *La Villa*. Buenos Aires: Emecé Editores.

Aira, César. (2001) 2013. *Shantytown*. Translated by Chris Andrews. New York: New Directions.

Alfa y Omega. 2001. *Divina Revelación, Alfa y Omega, Divinas Leyes: El matrimonio, la familia, la educación y la moral*. Lima: Alfa y Omega.

Alfred, Taiaiake. 1999. *Peace, Power, Righteousness: An Indigenous Manifesto*. Toronto: Oxford University Press.

Amato, Peter. 1997. "African Philosophy and Modernity." In *Postcolonial African Philosophy: A Critical Reader*, edited by Emmanuel Chukwudi Eze, 71–100. Cambridge, MA: Blackwell.

Anderson, Benedict. 1983. *Imagined Communities: Reflections on the Origin and Spread of Nationalism*. London: Verso.

Appadurai, Arjun. 1996. *Modernity at Large: Cultural Dimensions of Globalization*. Minneapolis: University of Minnesota Press.

Apter, Emily. 2006. *The Translation Zone: A New Comparative Literature*. Princeton, NJ: Princeton University Press.

Apter, Emily. 2013. *Against World Literature: On the Politics of Untranslatability*. New York: Verso.

Arguedas, José María. 1958. *Los ríos profundos*. Buenos Aires: Editorial Losada.

Arguedas, José María. 2002. *Deep Rivers*. Translated by Frances Horning Barraclough. Long Grove, IL: Waveland.

Arias, Arturo, ed. 2001. *The Rigoberta Menchú Controversy*. Minneapolis: University of Minnesota Press.

Arriagada, Genaro, ed. 1989. *La campaña del no: Vista por sus creadores*. Santiago, Chile: Melquíades.

Asante, Molefi Kete. 2006. "The Rhetoric of Globalisation: The Europeanisation of Human Ideas." *Journal of Multicultural Discourses* 1 (2): 152–58. https://doi .org/10.2167/md054.0.

Ashcroft, Bill, Gareth Griffiths, and Helen Tiffin. 1989. *The Empire Writes Back: Theory and Practice in Post-colonial Literatures*. London: Routledge.

Asturias, Miguel Ángel. (1946) 2020. *El señor presidente*. New York: Penguin Vintage Español.

Asturias, Miguel Ángel. 1949. *Hombres de maíz*. Madrid: Alianza Editorial, El Libro del Bolsillo.

Asturias, Miguel Ángel. 1995. *Men of Maize*. Translated by Gerald Martin. Pittsburgh: University of Pittsburgh Press.

Bakhtin, Mikhail. 1981. *The Dialogic Imagination: Four Essays*. Edited by Michael Holquist. Translated by Caryl Emerson and Michael Holquist. Austin: University of Texas Press.

Barboza, David. 2001. "Misery Is Abundant for Potato Farmers; Bumper Crops Turned into Fertilizer." *New York Times*, March 17, 2001.

Barker, Joan, ed. 2017. *Critical Sovereignty: Indigenous Gender, Sexuality, and Feminist Studies*. Durham, NC: Duke University Press.

Barrow, John. (1801) 1968. *Travels in the Interior of Southern Africa in the Years 1797 and 1798*. New York: Johnson Reprint.

Baudelaire, Charles. (1957) 2018. *Les Fleurs du mal*. Niort, France: Atlantic Editions.

Bearden, David. 2005. *Vieques and Culebra Island: An Analysis of Environmental Cleanup Issues*. RL32533. Congressional Research Service, US Library of Congress, July 7, 2005. https://fas.org/sgp/crs/natsec/RL32533.pdf.

Beaucage, Pierre. 1998. "The Third Wave of Modernization: Liberalism, Salinismo, and Indigenous Peasants in Mexico." In *The Third Wave of Modernization in Latin America: Cultural Perspectives on Neoliberalism*, edited by Lynne Phillips, 3–27. Wilmington, DE: Scholarly Resources.

Beccone, Horacio, Edgardo Mondolfi, and David Ruiz, eds. 1991. *Miranda: La aventura de la libertad; Antología*. Caracas: Monte Ávila.

Becker, Elizabeth. 2013. *Overlooked: The Exploding Business of Travel and Tourism*. New York: Simon and Schuster.

Becker, Marc. n.d. "History of United States Interventions in Latin America." Marc's House of Knowledge, accessed July 20, 2015. http://www.yachana.org /teaching/resources/interventions.html.

Beckman, Ericka. 2012. *Capital Fictions: Latin American Literature in the Export Age*. Minneapolis: University of Minnesota Press.

Behar, Ruth. 1993. *Translated Woman: Crossing the Border with Esperanza's Story*. Boston: Beacon.

Bellatin, Mario. 1994. *Salón de belleza*. Mexico City: Tusquets.

Bellatin, Mario. 2009. *Beauty Salon*. Translated by Kurt Hollander. San Francisco: City Lights Books.

Bellessi, Diana. 1996. *Lo propio y lo ajeno*. Buenos Aires: Feminaria.

Ben-Ghiat, Ruth. 2020. *Strongmen: Mussolini to the Present*. New York: Norton.

Bengoa, José. 2000. *La emergencia indígena en América Latina*. Santiago, Chile: Fondo Cultura Economia.

Benjamin, Walter. 1999. *The Arcades Project*. Translated by Howard Eiland. Cambridge, MA: Harvard University Press.

Bennett, Vivienne, Sonia Dávila-Poblete, and María Nieves Rico, eds. 2005. *Opposing Currents: The Politics of Water and Gender in Latin America*. Pittsburgh: University of Pittsburgh Press.

Berman, Marshall. 1982. *All That Is Solid Melts into Air*. New York: Simon and Schuster.

Bernstein, Richard. 1988. "In Dispute on Bias, Stanford Is Likely to Alter Western Culture Program." *New York Times*, January 19, 1988. https://www.nytimes .com/1988/01/19/us/in-dispute-on-bias-stanford-is-likely-to-alter-western -culture-program.html.

Bhabha, Homi K. 1988. "Race, Time and the Revision of Modernity." *Oxford Literary Review* 13 (1): 193–219.

Bhabha, Homi K. 1994. *The Location of Culture*. Oxford: Routledge.

Biocca, Ettore, and Helena Valero. 1969. *Yanoáma: The Narrative of a White Girl Kidnapped by Amazonian Indians*. New York: E. P. Dutton.

Blank, Les, dir. 1982. *Burden of Dreams*. Los Angeles: Flower Films.

Bollaín, Icíar, dir. *También la lluvia*. 2010. Los Angeles: Paramount Home Entertainment.

Bonneuil, Christophe, and Jean-Baptiste Fresse. 2016. *The Shock of the Anthropocene: The Earth, History, Us*. Translated by David Fernbach. London: Verso.

Bougainville, Louis Antoine de. (1771) 1967. *A Voyage round the World*. Ridgewood, NJ: Gregg.

Bronte, Charlotte. (1847) 2010. *Jane Eyre*. New York: Harper Collins.

Brunner, José Joaquín. 1981. *La cultura autoritaria en Chile*. Santiago, Chile: Facultad Latinoamericana de Ciencias Sociales.

Brunner, José Joaquín. 1985. *Políticas culturales para la democracia*. Santiago, Chile: Centro de Indagación y Expresión Cultural y Artística.

Brunner, José Joaquín. 1987. "Notas sobre modernidad y lo posmoderno en la cultura latinoamericana." *David y Goliat* 17 (52): 30–39.

Brunner, José Joaquín. 1988. "¿Existe o no la modernidad en América Latina?" In *Imágenes desconocidas: La modernidad en la encrucijada postmoderna*, edited by Fernando Calderón, 95–100. Buenos Aires: Centro Latinoamericano de Ciencias Sociales (CLACSO).

Brunner, José Joaquín. 1994. *Bienvenidos a la modernidad*. Santiago, Chile: Editorial Planeta Chilena.

Bubandt, Nils. 2017. "Haunted Geologies: Spirits, Stones, and the Necropolitics of the Anthropocene." In *Arts of Living on a Damaged Planet: Ghosts and Monsters of the Anthropocene*, edited by Anna Tsing, Heather Swanson, Elaine Gan, and Nils Bubandt, G121–G141. Minneapolis: University of Minnesota Press.

Buck-Morss, Susan. 2009. *Hegel, Haiti, and Universal History*. Pittsburgh: University of Pittsburgh Press.

Budiman, Abby, and Phillip Connor. 2018. "Migrants Send a Record Amount of Money to Their Home Countries in 2016." Pew Research Center, January 23, 2018. https://www.pewresearch.org/fact-tank/2018/01/23/migrants-from -latin-america-and-the-caribbean-sent-a-record-amount-of-money-to-their -home-countries-in-2016/.

Buell, Frederick. 1994. *National Culture and the New Global System*. Berkeley: University of California Press.

Burton, Richard F. (1868) 1961. *The Lake Regions of Central Africa: A Picture of Exploration*. New York: Horizon.

Burton, Tim, dir. 2001. *Planet of the Apes*. Los Angeles: Twentieth Century Fox.

Burtynsky, Edward. n.d. "Edward Burtynsky: Photographs." Edward Burtynsky. Accessed September 2, 2021. https://www.edwardburtynsky.com/projects /photographs.

Butler, Judith, Ernesto Laclau, and Slavoj Žižek. 2000. *Contingency, Hegemony, Universality: Contemporary Dialogues on the Left*. London: Verso.

Buzard, James. 1993. *The Beaten Track: European Tourism, Literature, and the Ways to "Culture," 1800–1918*. New York: Oxford University Press.

Cabral, Amílcar. 1973. *Return to the Source: Selected Speeches of Amilcar Cabral*. Edited by African Information Services. New York: Monthly Review Press.

Caldeira, Teresa. 2001. *City of Walls: Crime, Segregation and Citizenship in São Paulo*. Berkeley: University of California Press.

Calderón, Fernando. 1988a. "Identidad y tiempos mixtos o cómo pensar la modernidad sin dejar de ser boliviano." In *Imágenes desconocidas: La modernidad en la encrucijada postmoderna*, edited by Fernando Calderón, 25–29. Buenos Aires: Consejo Latinoamericano de Cienciaa Sociales.

Calderón, Fernando, ed. 1988b. *Imágenes desconocidas: La modernidad en la encrucijada postmoderna*. Buenos Aires: Consejo Latinoamericano de Ciencias Sociales.

Calinescu, Matei. (1977) 1987. *Five Faces of Modernity*. Durham, NC: Duke University Press.

Camus, Albert. 1957. *Exile and the Kingdom*. Translated by Justin O'Brien. New York: Knopf.

Carey-Webb, Allen, and Stephen Benz, eds. 1996. *Teaching and Testimony: Rigoberta Menchú and the North American Classroom*. New York: State University of New York Press.

Carpentier, Alejo. 1953. *Los pasos perdidos*. Mexico City: EDIAPSA.

Carpentier, Alejo. (1953) 1956. *The Lost Steps*. Translated by Harriet de Onís. New York: Knopf.

Catalán, Carlos, and Giselle Munizaga. 1986. *Políticas culturales estatales bajo el autoritarismo en Chile*. Santiago, Chile: Centro de Indagación y Expresión Cultural y Artística.

Chagnon, Napoleon. 1968. *Yanomamo: The Fierce People*. New York: Holt, Rinehart and Winston.

Chakrabarty, Dipesh. 2009. "The Climate of History: Four Theses." *Critical Inquiry* 35 (2): 197–222.

Chagnon, Napoleon. 1974. *Studying the Yanomamo*. New York: Holt, Rinehart and Winston.

Chatterjee, Partha. 1986. *Nationalist Thought and the Colonial World: A Derivative Discourse*. London: Zed Books.

Chauco Arriarán, Rubén. 1980. *Micaela Bastidas*. Lima: Editorial Universo.

Chinweizu. 1975. *The West and the Rest of Us: White Predators, Black Slavers and the African Exile*. New York: Vintage.

Christophe, Henri, et al. 1805. "Constitution of Hayti, 1805." Wikisource. https://en.wikisource.org/wiki/Constitution_of_Hayti_(1805).

Clifford, James. 1982. Review of *Nisa: The Life and Words of a !Kung Woman*, by Marjorie Shostak. *Times Literary Supplement*, September 17, 1982.

Clifford, James. 1985. "On Ethnographic Self-Fashioning: Conrad and Malinowski." In *Reconstructing Individualism: Autonomy, Individuality, and the Self in Western Thought*, edited by Thomas C. Heller, Morton Sosna, and David E. Wellbery, 140–63. Stanford, CA: Stanford University Press.

Clifford, James 1986. "On Ethnographic Allegory." In *Writing Culture: The Poetics and Politics of Ethnography*, edited by James Clifford and George Marcus, 98–121. Berkeley: University of California Press.

Clifford, James. 2013. "The Story of Ishi." In *Returns: Becoming Indigenous in the Twenty-First Century*, 91–192. Cambridge, MA: Harvard University Press.

Clifford, James, and George Marcus, eds. 1986. *Writing Culture: The Poetics and Politics of Ethnography*. Berkeley: University of California Press.

Coetzee, J. M. 1987. *Foe*. New York: Penguin.

Columbus, Christopher. 1493. "The Letter of Columbus to Luis De Sant Angel Announcing His Discovery." February 15, 1493. Ushistory.org, http://www.ushistory.org/documents/columbus.htm.

Conrad, Joseph. (1904) 1960. *Nostromo*. New York: New American Library.

Conrad, Joseph. (1899) 2007. *Heart of Darkness*. Edited by Robert Hampson and Owen Knowles. London: Penguin.

Cook-Lynn, Elizabeth. 2007. *New Indians, Old Wars*. Urbana: University of Illinois Press.

Coppola, Francis Ford, dir. 1979. *Apocalypse Now*. Los Angeles: United Artists.

Corradi, Juan, Patricia Weiss Fagen, and Manuel Antonio Garretón, eds. 1992. *Fear at the Edge: State Terror and Resistance in Latin America*. Berkeley: University of California Press.

Crapanzano, Vincent. 1980. *Tuhami: Portrait of a Moroccan*. Chicago: University of Chicago Press.

Cuadros, Manuel E. 1949. *Paisaje y obra, mujer e historia, Clorinda Matto de Turner*. Lima: Rozas.

Dabhoiwala, Fara. 2020. Review of *Imperial Delusions* by Amos Getachew. *New York Review of Books*, June 10, 2020, 59–62.

De Andrade, Mário. (1922) 2017. *Paulicéia Desvairada*. São Paulo: Penguin Companhia das Letras.

De Andrade, Mário. (1926) 2016. *Macunaíma: O Herói sem Nenhum Caráter*. São Paulo: Penguin Companhia das Letras.

De Andrade, Oswald (1928) 2017. *Manifesto Antropófago e Outros Textos*. São Paulo: Penguin Companhia das Letras.

"Declaración de Quito." 2000. Center for International Environmental Law, May 6, 2000. https://www.ciel.org/Publications/QuitoDeclaracionSpanish.pdf.

de Certeau, Michel. 1975. *L'écriture de l'histoire*. Paris: Gallimard.

de Certeau, Michel. 1984. *The Practice of Everyday Life*. Translated by Steven F. Rendall. Berkeley: University California Press.

Defoe, Daniel. (1719) 1995. *Robinson Crusoe*. London: Penguin Classics.

De Holmes, Rebecca B. 1983. "*Shabono*: Scandal or Superb Social Science?" *American Anthropologist* 85 (3): 664–67. https://doi.org/10.1525/aa.1983.85.3.02a00130.

de la Cadena, Marisol. 2015. *Earth Beings: Ecologies of Practice across Andean Worlds*. Durham, NC: Duke University Press.

de la Cadena, Marisol, and Orin Starn, eds. 2007. *Indigenous Experience Today*. Oxford: Berg.

De la Torre, Renée. 2008. "La religiosidad peregrina de los jaliscienses: vírgenes viajeras, apariciones en los no lugares y santos polleros." *Emisférica* 5 (1). https://hemisphericinstitute.org/en/emisferica-5-1-traveling/5-1-essays/la-religiosidad-peregrina-de-los-jaliscienses-virgenes-viajeras-apariciones-en-los-no-lugares-y-santos-polleros.html.

Deleuze, Gilles, and Félix Guattari. 1994. *What Is Philosophy?* Translated by Hugh Tomlinson and Graham Burchell III. New York: Columbia University Press.

Denegri, Francesca. 1996. *El abanico y la cigarrera: La primera generación de mujeres ilustradas en el Perú*. Lima: IEP/Flora Tristán.

Denzin, Norman K., Yvonna S. Lincoln, and Linda Tuhiwai Smith, eds. 2008. *Handbook of Critical and Indigenous Methodologies*. Thousand Oaks, CA: Sage.

Derrida, Jacques. 1994. *The Politics of Friendship*. Translated by George Collins. London: Verso.

Derrida, Jacques. 2000. *Of Hospitality: Anne Dufourmantelle Invites Jacques Derrida to Respond*. Translated by Rachel Bowlby. Stanford, CA: Stanford University Press.

Descartes, René. (1637) 2009. *Discourse on Method*. Translated by Ian MacLean. Oxford: Oxford University Press.

Díaz de Castillo, Bernal. (1568) 1963. *The Conquest of New Spain*. Translated by John M. Cohen. London: Penguin.

Diocese of San Juan de los Lagos. 1997. *Devocionario del migrante*. San Juan de los Lagos, Mexico.

Dirlik, Arif. 1999. "The Past as Legacy and Project: Postcolonial Criticism in the Perspective of Indigenous Historicism." In *Contemporary Native American Political Issues*, edited by Troy R. Johnson, 73–97. Lanham, MD: AltaMira.

Domínguez, Daylet. 2021. *Ficciones etnográficas: Literatura, ciencias sociales y proyectos nacionales en el Caribe hispano del siglo xix*. Madrid: Vervuert.

Donner, Florinda. 1982. *Shabono: A True Adventure in the Remote and Magical Heart of the South American Jungle*. New York: Laurel Books.

Dostoevsky, Fyodor. (1864) 1993. *Notes from Underground*. Translated by Richard Pevear and Larissa Volokhonsky. New York: Vintage Classics.

D'Souza, Dinesh. 1991. *Illiberal Education: The Politics of Race and Sex on Campus*. New York: Free Press.

D'Souza, Dinesh. 1998. "I, Rigoberta Menchu . . . Not!" *Washington Examiner*, December 28, 1998. https://www.washingtonexaminer.com/weekly-standard /i-rigoberta-menchu-not.

Dumont, Jean-Paul. 1976. *Under the Rainbow*. Austin: University of Texas Press.

Dumont, Jean-Paul. 1978. *The Headman and I*. Austin: University of Texas Press.

Dupré, Louis. 1993. *Passage to Modernity: An Essay in the Hermeneutics of Nature and Culture*. New Haven, CT: Yale University Press.

Dussel, Enrique. 1993. "Eurocentrism and Modernity: Introduction to the Frankfurt Lectures." *boundary 2* 20 (3): 65–76. https://doi.org/10.2307/303341.

Dwyer, Kevin. 1982. *Moroccan Dialogues: Anthropology in Question*. Baltimore, MD: Johns Hopkins University Press.

Earle, Duncan. 2001. "Menchú Tales and Maya Social Landscapes: The Silencing of Words and Worlds." In *The Rigoberta Menchú Controversy*, edited by Arturo Arias, 288–307. Minneapolis: University of Minnesota Press.

Echeverría, Bolívar. 1991. "Modernidad y capitaismo (quince tesis)." In *Debates sobre modernidad y postmodernidad*, edited by Norbert Lechner, 73–122. Bogotá: Nariz del Diablo.

Egan, Timothy. 2001. "As Others Abandon Plains, Indians and Buffalo Come Back." *New York Times*, May 27, 2001.

Ejercito Zapatista de Liberación Nacional. 1997. *Documentos y comunicaciones*. Mexico City: Ediciones Era.

Elias, Amy J., and Christian Moraru. 2015. "Introduction." In *The Planetary Turn*, edited by Amy J. Elias and Christian Moraru, i–xxxviii. Evanston, IL: Northwestern University Press.

Elias, Amy J., and Christian Moraru, eds. 2015. *The Planetary Turn: Relationality and Geoaesthetics in the Twenty-First Century*. Evanston, IL: Northwestern University Press.

Ellis, Warren, and Jon Cassaday. 2014. *Planetary Omnibus*. New York: DC Comics.

Eltit, Diamela. 1983. *Lumpérica*. Santiago, Chile: Ediciones de Ornitorrinco.

Eltit, Diamela. 1989. *El Padre Mío*. Santiago, Chile: Francisco Zegers.

Eltit, Diamela. 1994. *Los vigilantes*. Santiago, Chile: Sudameriana.

Eltit, Diamela. 2002. *Mano de obra*. Santiago, Chile: Seix Barral.

Eltit, Diamela. 2005. *Custody of the Eyes*. Translated by Helen Lane and Ronald Christ. Santa Fe, NM: Lumen.

Eltit, Diamela. 2008. *E. Luminata*. Translated by Ron Christ. Santa Fe, NM: Lumen Books.

Enloe, Cynthia. 1990. *Bananas, Beaches, and Bases: Making Feminist Sense of International Politics*. 2nd ed. Berkeley: University of California Press.

Epstein, Edward, and David Pion-Berlin, eds. 2006. *Broken Promises? The Argentine Crisis and Argentine Democracy*. Lanham, MD: Lexington Books.

Equiano, Olaudah. (1789) 2004. *The Interesting Narrative of the Life of Olaudah Equiano: Or Gustavus Vassa, the African*. New York: Modern Library.

Evans-Pritchard, E. E. 1940. *The Nuer*. Oxford: Oxford University Press.

Eze, Emmanuel Chukwudi, ed. 1997. *Postcolonial African Philosophy: A Critical Reader*. London: Wiley-Blackwell.

Fabian, Johannes. 1983. *Time and the Other: How Anthropology Makes Its Object*. New York: Columbia University Press.

Fanon, Frantz. (1963) 2004. *The Wretched of the Earth*. Translated by Richard Philcox. New York: Grove Press.

Featherstone, Mike, ed. 1990. *Global Culture: Nationalism, Globalization and Modernity*. London: Sage.

Ferguson, James. 1999. *Expectations of Modernity: Myths and Meanings of Urban Life on the Zambian Copperbelt*. Berkeley: University of California Press.

Ferguson, James. 2002. "Of Mimicry and Membership: Africans and the 'New World Society.'" *Cultural Anthropology* 17 (4): 551–69.

Firth, Raymond. 1936. *We, the Tikopia*. London: Allen and Unwin.

Fischer, Sibylle. 2004. *Modernity Disavowed: Haiti and the Cultures of Slavery in an Age of Revolution*. Durham, NC: Duke University Press.

Fox, Ben. 2012. "Vieques Cleanup: Island at Odds with U.S. Government Declaration That 400-Acre Bomb Site Cleanup Is Complete." *Huffington Post*, October 5, 2012. http://www.huffingtonpost.com/2012/10/05/vieques-cleanup -bomb-site_n_1942107.html.

Francia, Luis. 2010. *A History of the Philippines: From Indios Bravos to Filipinos*. New York: Overlook.

Franco, Jean. 1967. *The Modern Culture of Latin America: Society and the Artist*. Westport, CT: Praeger.

Franco, Jean. (1978) 1999. "From Modernization to Resistance: Latin American Literature, 1959–1976." In *Critical Passions: Collected Essays of Jean Franco*, edited by Mary Louise Pratt and Kathleen M. Newman, 285–310. Durham, NC: Duke University Press.

Franco, Jean. 1992a. "Gender, Death, and Resistance: Facing the Ethical Vacuum." In *Fear at the Edge: State Terror, and Resistance in Latin America*, edited by Juan Corradi, Patricia Weiss Fagen, and Manuel Antonio Garretón, 104–20. Berkeley: University of California Press.

Franco, Jean. 1992b. "Si me permiten hablar: La lucha por el poder interpretativo." *Revista de Crítica Literaria Latinoamericana* 18 (36): 111–18.

Franco, Jean. 2013. *Cruel Modernity*. Durham, NC: Duke University Press.

Frank, André Gunder. 1976. *Economic Genocide in Chile: Monetary Theory versus Humanity; Two Open Letters to Arnold Harberger and Milton Friedman.* Nottingham, UK: Spokesman.

Frank, André Gunder. 1981. *Reflections on the World Economic Crisis.* New York: Monthly Review Press.

Fredriksen, Aurora. 2019. "Encounters in the Ebb and Flow: Knowing Marine Ecologies in the Intertidal Contact Zone." *Environment and Planning E: Nature and Space* 2 (4): 761–80.

Freeman, Derek. 1983. *Margaret Mead and Samoa: The Making and Unmaking of an Anthropological Myth.* Cambridge, MA: Harvard University Press.

Fuentes, Carlos. (1962) 2008. *La Muerte de Artemio Cruz.* Mexico City: Punto de Lectura.

Fuentes, Carlos. (1962) 2009. *The Death of Artemio Cruz.* Translated by Alfred MacAdam. New York: Farrar, Straus and Giroux.

Gallegos, Rómulo. (1929) 2012. *Doña Bárbara.* Madrid: Vintage España.

Gallegos, Rómulo. (1929) 2020. *Doña Bárbara: A Novel.* Translated by Robert Malloy. Chicago: University of Chicago Press.

Gan, Elaine, Anna Tsing, Heather Swanson, and Nils Bubandt. 2017. "Introduction: Haunted Landscapes of the Anthropocene." In *Arts of Living on a Damaged Planet: Ghosts and Monsters of the Anthropocene*, edited by Anna Lowenhaupt Tsing, Heather Swanson, Elaine Gan, and Nils Bubandt, G2–G29. Minneapolis: University of Minnesota Press.

García Canclini, Néstor. 1990. *Culturas híbridas: Estrategias para entrar y salir de la modernidad.* Mexico City: Grijalba.

García Canclini, Néstor. 1992. "Cultural Reconversion." In *On Edge: The Crisis of Contemporary Latin American Culture*, edited by George Yúdice, 29–44. Minneapolis: University of Minnesota Press.

García Márquez, Gabriel. (1967) 2009. *Cien años de soledad.* New York: Vintage Español.

García Márquez, Gabriel. (1967) 2006. *One Hundred Years of Solitude.* Translated by Gregory Rabassa. New York: Harper Perennial Modern Classics.

García Márquez, Gabriel. 1986. *La aventura de Miguel Littín, clandestino en Chile: Un reportaje.* Buenos Aires: Editorial Sudamericana.

Garretón, Manuel Antonio, Saúl Sosnowski, and Bernardo Subercaseaux, eds. 1993. *Cultura, autoritarismo y redemocratización en Chile.* Mexico City: Fondo de Cultura Económica.

Gaviria, Víctor, dir. 1990. *Rodrigo D: No futuro.* Berlin: Kino International.

Gaviria, Víctor, dir. 1998. *La vendedora de rosas.* Bangalore: Nirvana Films.

Geertz, Clifford. 1983a. "Found in Translation: On the Social History of the Moral Imagination." In *Local Knowledge: Further Essays in Interpretive Anthropology*, 36–54. New York: Basic Books.

Geertz, Clifford. 1983b. "Slide Show: Evans-Pritchard's African Transparencies." *Raritan: A Quarterly Review* 2 (1): 62–80.

Gelles, Soledad. 2002. "Escritura, género y modernidad: El trabajo cultural de Clorinda Matto de Turner y Dora Mayer de Zulen." PhD diss., Stanford University.

Germani, Gino. 1969. *Sociologia de la modernización*. Buenos Aires: Paidós.

Gessen, Masha. 2020a. "By Declaring Victory, Donald Trump Is Attempting an Autocratic Breakthrough." *New Yorker*, November 5, 2020. https://www.newyorker.com/news/our-columnists/by-declaring-victory-donald-trump-is-attempting-an-autocratic-breakthrough.

Gessen, Masha. 2020b. *Surviving Autocracy*. New York: Riverhead.

Getachew, Amos. 2020. *Imperial Delusions: The Rise and Fall of Self-Determination*. Princeton, NJ: Princeton University Press.

Ghosh, Amitav. 2016. *The Great Derangement: Climate Change and the Unthinkable*. Chicago: University of Chicago Press.

Gibian, Peter, ed. 1997. *Mass Culture and Everyday Life*. New York: Routledge.

Gibson-Graham, J. K. 1996. *The End of Capitalism (As We Knew It): A Feminist Critique of Political Economy*. Oxford: Wiley-Blackwell.

Gibson-Graham, J. K. 2006. *A Postcapitalist Politics*. Minneapolis: University of Minnesota Press.

Gide, André. (1902) 1970. *The Immoralist*. Translated by Richard Howard. New York: Vintage.

Gilman, Sander L. 1982. *On Blackness without Blacks: Essays on the Image of the Black in Germany*. Boston: G. K. Hall.

Gilroy, Paul. 1993. *The Black Atlantic: Modernity and Double Consciousness*. Cambridge, MA: Harvard University Press.

Goeman, Mishuana. 2013. *Mark My Words: Native Women Mapping Our Nations*. Minneapolis: University of Minnesota Press.

Gogin, Georgina. 2005. "De las nuevas religiosidades urbanas: La Divina Revelación Alfa y Omega." Master's thesis, Pontificia Universidad Católica del Perú, Lima, Peru. http://tesis.pucp.edu.pe/repositorio/bitstream/handle/20.500.12404/66/GOGIN_SIAS_GEORGINA_RELIGIOSIDADES_URBANAS_ALFA_OMEGA.pdf?sequence=2&isAllowed=y.

Gómez-Barris, Macarena. 2017. *The Extractive Zone: Social Ecologies and Decolonial Perspectives*. Durham, NC: Duke University Press.

González de la Rocha, Mercedes. 2000. *Private Adjustments: Household Responses to the Erosion of Work*. Conference Paper Series. New York, UN Bureau for Development Policy.

Goonatilake, Susantha. 1984. *Aborted Discovery: Science and Creativity in the Third World*. London: Zed.

Gorriti, Juana Manuela. 1907. "Si haces mal no esperes bien." In *Sueños y realidades*, 2:146–74. Buenos Aires: Imp. y Estereotipia de la Nación. https://evergreen.loyola.edu/tward/www/mujeres/gorriti/sihaces/si1.htm.

Government of Canada. 2011. "Truth and Reconciliation Commission of Canada." Last modified June 11, 2021. https://www.rcaanc-cirnac.gc.ca/eng/1450124405592/1529106060525.

Graeber, David. 2011. "Occupy Wall Street Rediscovers the Radical Imagination." *Guardian*, September 25, 2011.

Grande, Sandy. (2004) 2014. *Red Pedagogy: Native American Social and Political Thought*. 10th anniv. ed. Lanham, MD: Rowan and Littlefield.

Grandin, Greg. 2019. *The End of the Myth: From the Frontier to the Border Wall in the Mind of America*. New York: Metropolitan Books.

Grosz, Elizabeth. 2004. *The Nick of Time: Politics, Evolution and the Untimely*. Durham, NC: Duke University Press.

Grosz, Elizabeth. 2011. *Becoming Undone: Darwinian Reflections on Life, Politics, and Art*. Durham, NC: Duke University Press.

Guimarães Rosa, João. 1956. *Grande Sertão: Veredas*. Rio de Janeiro: José Olympio.

Guimarães Rosa, João. (1956) 1963. *The Devil to Pay in the Backlands*. Translated by James L. Taylor and Harriet de Onis. New York: Knopf.

Güiraldes, Ricardo. 1966. *Don Segundo Sombra: Shadows on the Pampa*. Translated by Harriet de Onís. New York: New American Library.

Güiraldes, Ricardo. (1926) 2004. *Don Segundo Sombra*. Buenos Aires: Stockcero.

Gussow, Mel, and Charles McGrath. 2005. "Saul Bellow, Who Breathed Life into the American Novel, Dies at 89." *New York Times*, April 6, 2005.

Guzmán, Patricio, dir. 1975. *La Batalla de Chile*. Buffalo, NY: Miramax.

Guzmán, Patricio, dir. 1997. *Chile: Memoria Obstinada*. Brooklyn, NY: Icarus Films.

Habermas, Jürgen. 1970. "On Systematically Distorted Communication." *Inquiry: An Interdisciplinary Journal of Philosophy* 13 (3): 205–18.

Habermas, Jürgen. 1985. *The Philosophical Discourse of Modernity: Twelve Lectures*. Translated by Frederick G. Lawrence. Cambridge: Polity.

Hannerz, Ulf. 1990. "Cosmopolitans and Locals in World Culture." In *Global Culture: Nationalism, Globalization and Modernity*, edited by Mike Featherstone, 237–52. London: Sage.

Harding, Sandra. 1997. "Is Modern Science an Ethnoscience? Rethinking Epistemological Assumptions." In *Postcolonial African Philosophy: A Critical Reader*, edited by Emmanuel Chukwudi Eze, 45–70. Oxford: Blackwell.

Harjo, Joy, ed. 2020. *When the Light of the World Was Subdued, Our Songs Came Through*. New York: Norton.

Harper, Ken. 2000. *Give Me My Father's Body: The Life of Minik, the New York Eskimo*. South Royalton, VT: Steerforth.

Haslip-Viera, Gabriel, ed. 2001 *Taino Revival: Critical Perspectives on Puerto Rican Identity and Cultural Politics*. Princeton, NJ: Markus Wiener.

Healey, Jack, and Adam Liptak. 2020. "Landmark Supreme Court Ruling Affirms Native American Rights in Oklahoma." *New York Times*, July 7, 2020.

Hegel, G. W. F. (1807) 2016. *The Phenomenology of Spirit*. Translated by J. B. Baillie. London: Pantiano Classics.

Held, David, ed. 1983. *States and Societies*. Oxford: Martin Robertson and the Open University.

Heller, Agnes. 1998. "What Is Modernity?" Lecture series at the Universidad de Guadalajara, Mexico, October 1998.

Heller, Agnes. 1999. *A Theory of Modernity*. Hoboken, NJ: Wiley-Blackwell.

Herzog, Werner, dir. 1982. *Fitzcarraldo*. Munich: Werner Herzog Filmproduktion.

Honigmann, Heddy, dir. 1994. *Metaal en Melancholie*. Brooklyn, NY: Icarus Films.

Howe, LeAnne, Lisa Brooks, and Tol Foster. 2008. *Reasoning Together: The Native Critics Collective*. Norman: University of Oklahoma Press.

Humanists International. 2002. "2002 Amsterdam Declaration." Accessed September 10, 2021, https://humanists.international/what-is-humanism/the-amsterdam-declaration.

Hunt, Dee Dicen. 2006. "Didipio Says NO to Mining." *Kasama* 27 (3). https://cpcabrisbane.org/Kasama/2006/V20n3/DidipioSaysNoToMining.htm.

Iñárritu, Alejandro G., dir. 2015. *The Revenant*. Los Angeles: Twentieth Century Fox.

International Geosphere-Biosphere Programme. 2001. "2001 Amsterdam Declaration on Earth System Science." Accessed September 10, 2021, http://www.igbp.net/about/history/2001amsterdamdeclarationonearthsystemscience.4.1b8ae20512db692f2a680001312.html.

International Labour Organization (ILO). 1957. Indigenous and Tribal Populations Convention, 1957. Number 107. Geneva: International Labour Organization. https://www.ilo.org/dyn/normlex/en/f?p=NORMLEXPUB:12100:0::NO::P12100_ILO_CODE:C107.

International Labour Organization (ILO). 1989. Indigenous and Tribal Peoples Convention, 1989. Number 169. Geneva: International Labour Organization. https://www.ilo.org/dyn/normlex/en/f?p=NORMLEXPUB:12100:0::NO::P12100_ILO_CODE:C169.

Isaacs, Jenny R. 2019. "The 'Bander's Grip': Reading Zones of Human-Shorebird Contact." *Environment and Planning E: Nature and Space* 2 (4): 732–60.

Isaacs, Jenny R., and Ariel Otruba, eds. 2019. "More-Than-Human Contact Zones" (themed section). *Environment and Planning E: Nature and Space* 2 (4).

Jacobsen, Nils. 1993. *Mirages of Transition: The Peruvian Altiplano, 1780–1930*. Berkeley: University of California Press.

John Paul II. 2001. "Message of John Paul II for the 22nd World Day of Tourism 2001." June 20, 2001. https://www.vatican.va/content/john-paul-ii/en/messages/tourism/documents/hf_jp-ii_mes_20010619_giornata-mondiale-turismo.html.

Johnson, Troy R., ed. 1999. *Contemporary Native American Political Issues*. Lanham, MD: Rowman and Littlefield.

Jonas, Susanne. 1991. *The Battle for Guatemala: Rebels, Death Squads and U.S. Power*. New York: Routledge.

Jonas, Susanne, and Nestor Rodríguez. 2015. *Guatemala-U.S. Migration: Transforming Regions*. Austin: University of Texas Press.

Kafka, Franz. (1915) 1972. *The Metamorphosis*. Translated by Stanley Corngold. New York: Bantam Dell.

Kaplan, Caren. 1990. *Questions of Travel: Postmodern Discourses of Displacement*. Durham, NC: Duke University Press.

Kenny, Zoe. 2006. "Philippines: New Mine Could Be Environmental Catastrophe." *Green Left Weekly*, July 26, 2006.

Kingsley, Mary. 1897. *Travels in West Africa*. London: Macmillan.

Kingsley, Mary. 1899. *West African Studies*. London: Macmillan.

Kolbert, Elizabeth. 2021. *Under a White Sky: The Nature of the Future*. New York: Crown.

Kondo, Dorinne. 2018. *Worldmaking: Race, Performance, and the Work of Creativity*. Durham, NC: Duke University Press.

Kopenawa, Davi, and Bruce Albert. 2013. *The Falling Sky: Words of a Yanomami Shaman*. Cambridge, MA: Harvard University Press.

La Jornada. 2011. "Identifican a *La Rana*, jefe de sicarios del *cártel* de Tijuana, preso bajo distinta identidad en BC." *La Jornada*, July 11, 2001. https://www.jornada.com.mx/2001/07/11/047n1soc.html.

Lander, Edgardo. 1991. *Modernidad y universalismo*. Caracas: Nueva Sociedad.

Larraín Ibañez, Jorge. 1996. *Modernidad, razón e identidad en América Latina*. Santiago, Chile: Andrés Bello.

Larsen, Neil, ed. 1983. *The Discourse of Power: Culture, Hegemony, and the Authoritarian State*. Minneapolis: Institute for the Study of Ideologies and Literatures.

Latour, Bruno. (1991) 1993. *We Have Never Been Modern*. Translated by Catherine Porter. Cambridge, MA: Harvard University Press.

Lawrence, D. H. (1926) 1954. *The Plumed Serpent*. New York: Vintage.

Lechner, Norbert. 1990. "¿Son compatibles la modernidad y la modernización? El desafío de la democracia latinoamericana." Documento de trabajo, Facultad Latinoamericana de Ciencias Sociales (FLACSO,) no. 440. Santiago, Chile: FLACSO.

Lechner, Norbert, ed. 1991. *Debates sobre modernidad y postmodernidad*. Bogotá: Nariz del Diablo.

Lee, Richard. 1979. *The !Kung San: Men, Women, and Work in a Foraging Society*. New York: Cambridge University Press.

Lee, Richard, and Irven DeVore. 1976. *Kalahari Hunter-Gatherers: Studies of the !Kung San and Their Neighbors*. Cambridge, MA: Harvard University Press.

Lewin, Boleslao. 1982. *Túpac Amaru, su época, su lucha, su hada*. Buenos Aires: Leviatán.

Littín, Miguel, dir. 1986. *Acta General de Chile*. Madrid: Alfil Uno Cinematográfica and Televisión Española.

Lovell, W. George, and Christopher H. Lutz. 2001. "The Primacy of Larger Truths: Rigoberta Menchú and the Tradition of Native Testimony in Guatemala." In *The Rigoberta Menchú Controversy*, edited by Arturo Arias, 171–97. Minneapolis: University of Minnesota Press.

Lynas, Mark. 2000. "Letter from Zambia." *Nation*, February 14, 2000.

Malinowski, Bronislaw. (1922) 1961. *Argonauts of the Western Pacific*. New York: E. P. Dutton.

Mamani, Pablo. 2004. *El rugir de las multitudes: La fuerza de los levantamientos indígenas en Bolivia/Qullasuyu*. La Paz, Bolivia: Aruwiyiri: Ediciones Yachaywasi.

Mamani, Pablo. 2005. *Geopolíticas indígenas*. El Alto: CeS.

Mandeville, John. (1356, approx.) 1983. *The Travels of Sir John Mandeville*. Translated by C. W. R. D. Moseley. London: Penguin.

Marcos, Subcomandante Insurgente. 1999. *Desde las montanas del sureste mexicano*. Mexico City: Plaza y Janes.

Mariátegui, José Carlos. (1928) 1971. *Seven Interpretive Essays on Peruvian Reality*. Translated by Marjory Urquidi. Austin: University of Texas Press.

Mariátegui, José Carlos. (1928) 2009. *Siete ensayos de interpretación de la realidad peruana*. Barcelona: Linkgua.

Martín-Barbero, Jesús. 1991. *De los medios a las mediaciones*. Mexico City: G. Gil.

Masiello, Francine. 2001. *The Art of Transition: Latin American Culture and Neoliberal Crisis*. Durham, NC: Duke University Press.

Matto de Turner, Clorinda. (1889) 2014. *Aves sin nido*. Barcelona: Linkgua.

Maybury-Lewis, David. 1965. *The Savage and the Innocent*. Cleveland: World Publishing.

Maybury-Lewis, David. 1967. *Akwẽ-Shavante Society*. Oxford: Clarendon.

Mayorgal, René. 1988. "Las paradojas e insuficiencias de la modernidad y el proceso de la democracia en América Latina." In *Imágenes desconocidas: La modernidad en la encrucijada postmoderna*, edited by Fernando Calderón, 139–44. Buenos Aires: Consejo Latinoamerican de Ciencias Sociales.

McCaffrey, Katherine T. 2002. *Military Power and Popular Protest: The U.S. Navy in Vieques, Puerto Rico*. New Brunswick, NJ: Rutgers University Press.

McCaffrey, Katherine T. 2006. "The Battle for Vieques' Future." CENTRO *Journal* 18 (1): 125–47.

McClintock, Anne. 1992. "The Angel of History: Pitfalls of the Term 'Postcolonialism.'" *Social Text*, nos. 31–32: 84–98.

McDevitt, Andrew. 2009. "Research Report: The Argentine Financial Crisis (2001–2002)." Birmingham, AL: Government and Social Development Resource Center. https://gsdrc.org/publications/argentine-financial-crisis-2001-2002/.

McGowan, Dan. 2020. "Chance for Chile to Forge New Path in Vote to Scrap Pinochet-Era Constitution." *Guardian*, October 20, 2020. https://www.theguardian.com/world/2020/oct/22/chileans-pinochet-constitution-referendum.

Meléndez, Mariselle. 2011. "Micaela Bastidas' Legible Body: Public Spectacle, Violence, and Fear in the Tupac Amaru Insurrection." In *Deviant and Useful Citizens: The Cultural Production of the Female Body in Eighteenth Century Peru*, 11–40. Nashville: Vanderbilt University Press.

Melville, Herman. (1853) 2004. *Bartleby the Scrivener*. Brooklyn, NY: Melville House Publishing.

Menchú, Rigoberta. (1983) 2007. *Me Llamo Rigoberta Menchú y así me nació la conciencia*. Edited by Elisabeth Burgos-Debrary. Guatemala City: Siglo Veintiuno Editores.

Menchú, Rigoberta. (1983) 2009. *I, Rigoberta Menchú: An Indian Woman in Guatemala*. Edited by Elisabeth Burgos-Debray. Translated by Ann Wright. London: Verso.

Méndez, Cecilia. 2000. "Incas sí, indios no: Apuntes para estudio del nacional-ismo criollo en el Perú." Instituto de Estudios Peruanos, https://repositorio.iep.org.pe/handle/IEP/865.

Mignolo, Walter D. 2011. *The Dark Side of Modernity: Global Forces, Decolonial Options*. Durham, NC: Duke University Press.

Mignolo, Walter D. 2021. *The Politics of Decolonial Investigations*. Durham, NC: Duke University Press.

Miller, Rory. 1982. "The Wool Trade of Southern Peru, 1850–1915." *Ibero-amerikanisches Archiv* 8 (3): 297–311. http://www.jstor.org/stable/43392347.

Mintz, Sidney. 1985. *Sweetness and Power: The Place of Sugar in Modern History*. New York: Viking.

Miranda, Francisco de. 1801. "Planes de Gobierno." Available at *Constitutcion Web*, accessed September 23, 2021, http://constitucionweb.blogspot.com/2010/04/planes-de-gobierno-francisco-de-miranda.html.

Mistral, Gabriela. (1967) 1996. *Poema de Chile*. Santiago, Chile: Editorial Universitaria.

Mitchell, Tim. 2011. *Carbon Democracy: Political Power in the Age of Oil*. London: Verso.

Miyoshi, Masao. 2001. "Turn to the Planet: Literature, Diversity, and Totality." *Comparative Literature* 53 (4): 283–97.

Monsalve Zanatti, Martín. 2012. "Opinión pública, sociedad civil y la 'cuestión indígena': La Sociedad Amiga del Indio (1867–1871)." In *Pensar el siglo XIX desde el siglo XXI: Nuevas miradas y lecturas*, edited by Ana Peluffo, 237–56. Chapel Hill: University of North Carolina Press.

Montaldo, Graciela. 1997. "Strategies at the End of the Century: A Review Essay." *Organization* 4 (4): 628–34.

Montejo, Victor. 1999. "Tied to the Land: Maya Migration, Exile and Transnation-alism." In *Identities on the Move: Transnational Processes in North America and the Caribbean Basin*, edited by Liliana Goldin, 185–202. Albany, NY: Institute for Mesoamerican Studies, University at Albany.

Montejo, Victor. 2005. *Maya Intellectual Renaissance: Identity, Representation and Leadership*. Austin: University of Texas Press.

Montero, Mayra. 1995. *Tú, la oscuridad*. Barcelona: Tusquets.

Montero, Mayra. 1997. *In the Palm of Darkness*. Translated by Edith Grossman. New York: HarperCollins.

Montoya, Rodrigo. 1992. *Al borde del naufragio: Democracia, violencia y problema étnico en el Perú*. Madrid: Talasa.

Moore, Jason. 2018. "Unearthing the Capitalocene: Towards a Reparations Ecol-ogy." *Resilience*, January 4, 2018. https://www.resilience.org/stories/2018-01-04/unearthing-the-capitalocene-towards-a-reparations-ecology/.

Moore, Michael, dir. 2002. *Bowling for Colombine*. New York: Dog Eat Dog Films.

Munizaga, Giselle. 1983. *El discurso público de Pinochet, 1973–1976*. Buenos Aires: Consejo Latinoamericano de Ciencias Sociales.

Munizaga, Giselle. 1993. "El sistema comunicativo chileno y los legados de la dictadura." In *Cultura, autoritarismo y redemocratización en Chile*, edited by Manuel Garretón, Saúl Sosnowski, and Bernardo Subercaseaux, 89–99. Mexico City: Fondo de Culutra Económica.

Murillo, Mario. 2001. *Islands of Resistance: Puerto Rico, Vieques, and U.S. Policy.* New York: Seven Stories.

Naipaul, V. S. 1989. *A Bend in the River.* New York: Vintage International.

Navarro, Mireya. 2009. "New Battle on Vieques over Navy's Cleanup of Munitions." *New York Times,* August 7, 2009. http://www.nytimes.com/2009/08 /07/science/earth/07vieques.html.

New York Times. 2001. "Redemption of Sudanese Slaves." *New York Times,* April 27, 2001.

Nkrumah, Kwame. 1964. *Consciencism: Philosophy and Ideology for Decolonization and Development with Particular Reference to the African Revolution.* New York: Monthly Review Press.

Nkrumah, Kwame. 1965. *Neocolonialism: The Last Stage of Imperialism.* London: Thomas Nelson and Sons.

Nugent, Guillermo. 1992. *El laberinto de la choledad.* Lima, Peru: Fundación E. Ebert.

Nyamnjoh, Francis B. 2007. "'Ever-Diminishing Circles': The Paradoxes of Belonging in Botswana." In *Indigenous Experience Today,* edited by Marisol de la Cadena and Orin Starn, 305–32. Oxford: Berg.

Obarrio, Juan Manuel, Valeria Procupez, Patricia Funes, and Axel Lazzari. 2011. "Los nuevos movimientos sociales en América Latina." Buenos Aires: Ministerio de Educación, Ciencia y Tecnología. Available at *El Blog de la Prof. Miriam Piendibene,* https://miriampiendibene.files.wordpress.com/2011/06 /movimintos-sociales.pdf.

Ochoa V., Fr. Angel S., O.F.M. 1961. *Breve historia de Nuestra Señora de Zapopan.* Zapopan, Mexico: Jal.

Olivera, Oscar, and Tom Lewis. 2004. *¡Cochabamba! Water War in Bolivia.* Boston: South End.

Ortiz, Carolina. 2014. "Felipe Guaman Poma de Ayala, Clorinda Matto de Turner, Trinidad Enríquez y la teoría crítica: Sus legados a la teorización social contemporánea." In *Des/colonialidad y bien vivir: Un nuevo debate in America Latina,* edited by Aníbal Quijano, 101–36. Lima, Peru: Universidad Ricardo Palma.

Palestro, Sandra. 1991. *Mujeres en movimiento, 1973–1989.* Serie Estudios Sociales 14. Santiago, Chile: Facultad Latinoamericana de Ciencias Sociales.

Papastergiadis, Nikos. 2000. *The Turbulence of Migration: Globalization, Deterritorialization, and Hybridity.* Cambridge: Polity.

Paredes, Julieta. 2008. *Hilando fino: Desde el feminismo comunitario.* La Paz: Centro de Defensa de la Cultura (CEDEC).

Park, Mungo. (1799) 1860. *Travels in the Interior Districts of Africa.* London: Blackwood's.

Paszkiewicz, Katarzyna. 2013. "Del cine épico al cine social: El universo metafílmico en *También la lluvia* (2010) de Icíar Bollaín." *Lectora,* no. 18: 227–40.

Pateman, Carole. 1988. *The Sexual Contract.* Stanford, CA: Stanford University Press.

Patzi, Félix. 2004. *Sistema comunal: Una propuesta alternativa al sistema liberal; Una discusión teórica para salir de la colonialidad y del liberalismo*. La Paz: Comunidad de Estudios Alternativos.

Peluffo, Ana. 2005. *Lágrimas andinas: Sentimentalismo, género y virtud republicana en Clorinda Matto de Turner*. Pittsburgh: Instituto Internacional de Literatura Iberoamericana.

Peluffo, Ana. 2015. "'That Damned Mob of Scribbling Women': Gendered Networks in Fin de Siecle Latin America (1898–1920)." In *Cambridge History of Latin American Women's Literature*, edited by Ileana Rodríguez and Mónica Szurmuk, 181–95. Cambridge: Cambridge University Press.

"Penang Declaration on Science and Technology." 1988. Third World Network. Penang, Malaysia. In Sardar 1988, 323–55.

Pérez, Emma. 1999. *The Decolonial Imaginary: Writing Chicanas into History*. Bloomington: Indiana University Press.

Picchi, Debra. 1983. "*Shabono*: A Visit to a Remote and Magical World in the Heart of the South American Jungle." *American Anthropologist* 85 (3): 674–75.

Piglia, Ricardo. 1997. *Plata quemada*. Barcelona: Planeta.

Piglia, Ricardo. 2003. *Money to Burn*. Translated by Amanda Hopkinson. London: Granta.

Pinochet Ugarte, Augusto. 1976. *Mensaje a la mujer chilena: Texto del discurso*. Santiago, Chile: Editorial Nacional Gabriela Mistral.

Polo, Marco. (1300) 1958. *The Travels of Marco Polo*. Translated by Ronald Latham. London: Penguin

Povinelli, Elizabeth A. 2016. *Geontologies: A Requiem to Late Liberalism*. Durham, NC: Duke University Press.

Powers, Richard. 2018. *The Overstory*. New York: Norton.

Pratt, Mary Louise. 1979. "Un mapa ideológico: Gide, Camus y Argelia." *Escritura* 7: 77–92.

Pratt, Mary Louise. 1985. "Scratches on the Face of the Country; Or, What Mr. Barrow Saw in the Land of the Bushmen." *Critical Inquiry* 12 (1): 119–43.

Pratt, Mary Louise. 1990. "Humanities for the Future: Reflections on the Western Culture Debate at Stanford." In *The Politics of Liberal Education*, edited by Darryl Gless and Barbara Herrnstein Smith, 13–32. Durham, NC: Duke University Press.

Pratt, Mary Louise. 1991. "Arts of the Contact Zone." *Profession* 1991:33–40.

Pratt, Mary Louise. (1992) 2007. *Imperial Eyes: Travel Writing and Transculturation*. 2nd ed. London: Routledge.

Pratt, Mary Louise. 1996. "'Me llamo Rigoberta Menchú': Autoethnography and the Recoding of Citizenship." In *Teaching and Testimony*, edited by Alan Carey-Webb and Stephen Benz, 57–72. New York: State University of New York Press.

Pratt, Mary Louise. 2002. "Modernity, Mobility and Excoloniality." In *Seuils et traverses: Enjeux de l'écriture du voyage; Actes du Colloque de Brest*, edited by Centre de Recherche Bretonne et Celtique, 13–30. Brest, France: Unité Mixte de Recherche, Centre national de recherche scientifique.

Pratt, Mary Louise. 2005. "Los imaginarios planetarios." In *Los saltos de Minerva: Intelectuales, género y estado en América Latina*, edited by Mabel Moraña and Maria Rosa Williams, 269–83. Berlin: Vervuert.

Quijano, Aníbal. 1988. "Modernidad, identidad y utopía en América Latina." In *Imágenes desconocidas: La modernidad en la encrucijada postmoderna*, edited by Fernando Calderón, 17–24. Buenos Aires: Consejo Latinoamericano de Ciencias Sociales.

Quijano, Aníbal. 2000a. "Colonialidad del poder, eurocentrismo y América Latina." In *La colonialidad del saber: eurocentrismo y ciencias sociales. Perspectivas latinoamericanas*, edited by Edgardo Lander. Buenos Aires: Consejo Latinoamericano de Ciencias Sociales. En: http://bibliotecavirtual.clacso.org .ar/ar/libros/lander/quijano.rtf.

Quijano, Aníbal. 2000b. "Coloniality of Power, Eurocentrism, and Latin America." *Nepantla: Views from South* 1 (3): 533–80.

Rabinow, Paul. 1975. *Symbolic Domination: Cultural Form and Historical Change in Morocco*. Chicago: University of Chicago Press.

Rabinow, Paul. 1977. *Reflections on Fieldwork in Morocco*. Berkeley: University of California Press.

Rabinow, Paul. 1989. *French Modern: Norms and Forms of the Social Environment*. Chicago: University of Chicago Press.

Rafael, Vicente. 1988. *Contracting Colonialism: Translation and Christian Conversion in Tagalog Society under Early Spanish Rule*. Ithaca, NY: Cornell University Press.

Rafael, Vicente. 2005. *The Promise of the Foreign: Nationalism and the Technics of Translation in the Spanish Philippines*. Durham, NC: Duke University Press.

Rafael, Vicente. 2016. *Motherless Tongues: The Insurgency of Language amid Wars of Translation*. Durham, NC: Duke University Press.

Rama, Ángel. 1984. *La ciudad letrada*. Hanover, NH: Ediciones del Norte.

Rhys, Jean. (1966) 2001. *Wide Sargasso Sea*. Edited by Hilary Jenkins. London: Penguin.

Ribeiro, Darcy. (1976) 1984. *Maíra*. Translated by E. H. Goodland and Thomas Colchie. New York: Vintage.

Ribeiro, Darcy. (1976) 2015. *Maíra*. São Paulo: Global Editora.

Richard, Nelly. 1992. "Cultura, política y democracia." *Revista de Crítica Cultural*, no. 5: 5–7.

Riquelme, Horacio, ed. 1990. *Era de nieblas: Derechos humanos, terrorismo de estado y salud psicosocial en América Latina*. Caracas: Nueva Sociedad.

Rivera Cusicanqui, Silvia. 2008. *Pueblos originarios y estado*. Lima: Azul Editores.

Rivera Cusicanqui, Silvia. 2010. *Ch'ixinakax utxiwa: Una reflexión sobre prácticas y discursos descolonizadores*. Buenos Aires: Tina Limón.

Rivera Cusicanqui, Silvia. 2012. "*Ch'ixinakax utxiwa*: A Reflection on the Practices and Discourses of Decolonization." *South Atlantic Quarterly* 111 (1): 95–109.

Robertson, Roland. 1990. "Mapping the Global Condition: Globalization as the Central Concept." In *Global Culture: Nationalism, Globalization and Modernity*, edited by Mike Featherstone, 15–30. London: Sage.

Rodríguez, Ileana. 2001. "Between Silence and Lies: Rigoberta Va." In *The Rigoberta Menchú Controversy*, edited by Arturo Arias, 332–50. Minneapolis: University of Minnesota Press.

Rohter, Larry. 1998. "Tarnished Laureate: Nobel Winner Finds Her Story Challenged." *New York Times*, December 15, 1998.

Rojo, Grinor. 2016. *La novela de la dictadura y la posdictadura chilena*. Santiago: LOM.

Rouse, Roger. 1991. "Mexican Migration and the Social Space of Postmodernism." *Diaspora* 1 (1): 8–23.

Rowe, William, and Vivian Schelling. 1991. *Memory and Modernity*. London: Verso.

Rulfo, Juan. (1955) 1994. *Pedro Páramo*. Translated by Margaret Sayers Peden. New York: Grove Press.

Rulfo, Juan. (1955) 2019. *Pedro Páramo*. New York: Vintage Español.

Said, Edward. 1978. *Orientalism*. New York: Pantheon.

Said, Edward. 1993. *Culture and Imperialism*. London: Chatto and Windus.

Sandoval, Miguel Angel. 2008. *De Iximche a Ixiche: El recorrido reciente de las luchas indígenas*. Guatemala City: F&G Editores.

Santiago, Silviano. 1996. "The Course of Literary Modernity in Brazil." *Journal of Latin American Cultural Studies* 5 (2): 175–82.

Sardar, Ziauddin, ed. 1988. *The Revenge of Athena: Science, Exploitation and the Third World*. London: Mansell.

Sarlo, Beatriz. 1988. *Una modernidad periférica: Buenos Aires 1920 y 1930*. Buenos Aires: Nueva Visión.

Sarlo, Beatriz. 1998. *La máquina cultural: Maestras, traductores y vanguardistas*. Buenos Aires: Arid.

Scazzi, Margharita, and Oswando Nenquimo. 2021. *From Spears to Maps: The Case of Waorani Resistance in Ecuador for the Defence of Their Right to Prior Consultation*. London: International Institute for Environmental Development.

Schaffner, Franklin, dir. 1968. *Planet of the Apes*. Los Angeles: Twentieth Century Fox.

Schmidt, Wolfgang. 1991. "En los límites de la modernidad." In *Debates sobre modernidad y postmodernidad*, edited by Norbert Lechner, 57–72. Bogotá: Nariz del Diablo.

Schwarz, Roberto. 1992a. "Brazilian Culture: Nationalism by Elimination." In *Misplaced Ideas: Essays on Brazilian Culture*, 1–19. London: Verso.

Schwarz, Roberto. 1992b. *Misplaced Ideas: Essays on Brazilian Culture*. London: Verso.

Scott, James C. 1998. *Seeing Like a State: How Certain Schemes to Improve the Human Condition Have Failed*. New Haven, CT: Yale University Press.

Secretaría Nacional de la Mujer. 1982. *Valores patrios y valores familiares*. Santiago, Chile: Secretaría Nacional de la Mujer.

Seelye, Katharine Q. 2003. "Relentless Moral Crusader Is Relentless Gambler Too." *New York Times*, May 3, 2003. https://www.nytimes.com/2003/05/03/us/relentless-moral-crusader-is-relentless-gambler-too.html.

Serequeberhan, Tsenay. 1997. "The Critique of Eurocentrism and the Practice of African Philosophy." In *Postcolonial African Philosophy*, edited by Emmanuel Chukwudi Eze, 141–61 London: Blackwell.

Shohat, Ella. 1992. "Notes on the 'Post-colonial.'" *Social Text*, nos. 31–32: 99–113.

Shostak, Marjorie. 1981. *Nisa: The Life and Words of a !Kung Woman*. Cambridge, MA: Harvard University Press.

Silva Hurtado, Nélida, Delia Vidal de Villa, Famel Guevara Guillén, and Ana Bertha Vizcarra. 1982. "La mujer en la revolución de 1780." In *Actas del Coloquio Internacional Túpac Amaru y Su Tiempo*, 285–348. Lima: Comisión Nacional del Bicentenario de la Rebelión Emancipadora de Túpac Amaru.

Simpson, Audra, and Andrea Smith, eds. 2014. *Theorizing Native Studies*. Durham, NC: Duke University Press.

Skurski, Julie, and Fernando Coronil. 1993. "Country and City in a Postcolonial Landscape: Double Discourse and Geo-politics of Truth in Latin America." In *Views beyond the Border Country: Raymond Williams and Cultural Politics*, edited by Dennis L. Dworkin and Leslie G. Roman, 231–60. New York: Routledge.

Smith, Carol. "Why Write an Exposé of Rigoberta Menchu?" In *The Rigoerta Menchu Controversy*, edited by Arturo Arias, 141–55. Minneapolis: University of Minnesota Press.

Smith, Kyle. 2011. "Even the Rain." *New York Post*, February 18, 2011. http://nypost .com/2011/02/18/even-the-rain/.

Smith, Linda Tuhiwai. 1999. *Decolonizing Methodologies: Research and Indigenous Peoples*. London: Zed.

Sommer, Doris. 1991. *Foundational Fictions: The National Romances of Latin America*. Berkeley: University of California Press.

Sommer, Doris, ed. 2006. *Cultural Agency in the Americas*. Durham, NC: Duke University Press.

Sparrman, Anders. (1785) 1975. *Voyage to the Cape of Good Hope*. New York: Johnson Reprint.

Spivak, Gayatri Chakravorty. 1999. *A Critique of Postcolonial Reason: Toward a History of the Vanishing Present*. Cambridge, MA: Harvard University Press.

Spivak, Gayatri Chakravorty. 2003. *Death of a Discipline*. New York: Columbia University Press.

Spurr, David. 1993. *The Rhetoric of Empire: Colonial Discourse in Journalism, Travel Writing, and Imperial Administration*. Durham, NC: Duke University Press.

Staden, Hans. (1557) 1874. *The Captivity of Hans Stade of Hesse in A.D. 1547–1555 among the Wild Tribes of Eastern Brazil*. London: Hakluyt Society.

Stephen, Lynn. 2007. *Transborder Lives: Indigenous Oaxacans in Mexico, California, and Oregon*. Durham, NC: Duke University Press.

Stoll, David. 1993. *Between Two Armies in the Ixil Towns of Guatemala*. New York: Columbia University Press.

Stoll, David. 1999. *Rigoberta Menchú and the Story of All Poor Guatemalans*. Boulder, CO: Westview.

Subercaseaux, Bernardo. 1991. *Historia, literatura y sociedad*. Santiago, Chile: Centro de Indagación y Expresión Cultural y Artística.

Sumida Huaman, Elizabeth, and Nathan D. Martin, eds. 2020. *Indigenous Knowledge Systems and Research Methodologies: Local Solutions and Global Opportunities*. Toronto: Canadian Scholars Press.

Sutherland, Colin R. 2019. "Encountering the Burn: Prescribed Burns as Contact Zones." *Environment and Planning E: Nature and Space* 2 (4): 781–98.

Taylor, Diana. 2003. *The Archive and the Repertoire*. Durham, NC: Duke University Press.

Taylor, Diana. 2020. *¡Presente! The Politics of Presence*. Durham, NC: Duke University Press.

Theal, George McCall. 1964. *History of South Africa, 1892–1919*. 11 vols. London: Allen and Unwin.

Thomas, Elizabeth Marshall. 1959. *The Harmless People*. New York: Knopf.

Thoreau, Henry David. (1854) 2016. *Walden*. London: Macmillan Collector's Library.

Tierney, Patrick. 2000. *Darkness in El Dorado: How Scientists and Journalists Devastated the Amazon*. New York: Norton.

Tomaselli, Keyan G., Lauren Dyll, and Michael Francis. 2008. "'Self' and 'Other': Auto-Reflexive and Indigenous Ethnography." In *Handbook of Critical and Indigenous Methodologies*, edited by Norman K. Denzin, Yvonna S. Lincoln, and Linda Tuhiwai Smith, 347–72. Los Angeles: Sage.

Torres Rivera, Alejandro. 2003. *Visión de Vieques: El uso del territorio nacional puertorriqueño por parte de las fuerzas armadas de Estados Unidos*. San Juan: Ateneo Puertorriqueño, Editorial LE.

Toulmin, Stephen. 1990. *Cosmopolis*. New York: Free Press.

Touraine, Alain. 1988. "Actores sociales y modernidad." In *Imágenes desconocidas: La modernidad en la encrucijada postmoderna*, edited by Fernando Calderón, 175–78. Buenos Aires: Consejo Latinoamericano de Ciencias Sociales.

Touraine, Alain. 1992. *Critique de la modernité*. Paris: Fayard.

Touraine, Alain. 1994. "Mutations of Latin America." *Thesis Eleven* 38 (1): 61–71.

Trilling, Lionel. 1950. *The Liberal Imagination: Essays on Literature and Society*. New York: Viking.

Truth and Reconciliation Commission of Canada. 2015. "Honouring the Truth, Reconciling for the Future." Ottawa: Government of Canada. Accessed September 6, 2021, https://nctr.ca/records/reports/.

Tsing, Anna Lowenhaupt. 1993. *In the Realm of the Diamond Queen: Marginality in an Out-of-the-Way Place*. Princeton, NJ: Princeton University Press.

Tsing, Anna Lowenhaupt. 2005. *Friction: An Ethnography of Global Connection*. Princeton, NJ: Princeton University Press.

Tsing, Anna Lowenhaupt, Heather Swanson, Elaine Gan, and Nils Bubandt, eds. 2017. *Arts of Living on a Damaged Planet: Ghosts and Monsters of the Anthropocene*. Minneapolis: University of Minnesota Press.

UN Commission for Historical Clarification. 1999. "Guatemala: Memory of Silence." Accessed September 3, 2021. https://hrdag.org/wp-content/uploads/2013/01/CEHreport-english.pdf.

UN *News*. 2003. "Development Funds Moving from Poor Countries to Rich Ones, Annan Says." UN *News*, October 30, 2003. https://news.un.org/en/story/2003/10/84012-development-funds-moving-poor-countries-rich-ones-annan-says.

UN World Tourism Organization. 2015. "UNTWO Tourism Highlights, 2015 Edition." https://www.e-unwto.org/doi/pdf/10.18111/9789284416899.

US Department of Labor. 2004. "2003 Findings on the Worst Forms of Child Labor—Côte d'Ivoire," April 29, 2004. https://www.refworld.org/docid/48c8caof3c.html.

Uys, Jamie, dir. 1980. *The Gods Must Be Crazy*. CAT Films.

Vallejo, Fernando. 1994. *La virgen de los sicarios*. Bogotá: Alfaguara.

Vallejo, Fernando. 2001. *Our Lady of the Assassins*. Translated by Paul Hammond. London: Serpent's Tail.

Vallires, Pierre. 1968. *Nègres blancs d'Amérique*. Montreal: Éditions Typo.

Van der Post, Laurens. 1958. *The Lost World of the Kalahari*. London: Hogarth.

Vargas Llosa, Mario. 1966. *La casa verde*. Barcelona: Seix Barral.

Vargas Llosa, Mario. (1966) 2005. *The Green House*. Translated by Gregory Rabassa. New York, Rayo.

Venuti, Lawrence. 1995. *The Translator's Invisibility: A History of Translation*. New York: Routledge.

Venuti, Lawrence. 1998. *The Scandals of Translation: Towards an Ethics of Difference*. New York: Routledge.

Venuti, Lawrence. 2013. *Translation Changes Everything*. New York: Routledge.

Vidal, Hernán. 1983. "La declaración de principios de la junta militar chilena como sistema literario: La lucha antifascista y el cuerpo humano." In *The Discourse of Power: Culture, Hegemony, and the Authoritarian State*, edited by Neil Larsen, 43–66. Minneapolis: Institute for the Study of Ideologies and Literatures.

Vidal, Hernán. 1985. *Cultura nacional chilena: Crítica literaria y derechos humanos*. Minneapolis: Institute for the Study of Ideologies and Literatures.

Vidal, Hernán. 1989. *Fascismo y experiencia literaria: Reflexiones para una recanonización*. Minneapolis: Institute for the Study of Ideologies and Literatures.

Vizenor, Gerald. 1999. *Manifest Manners: Narratives on Post-Indian Survivance*. Lincoln: University of Nebraska Press.

Vizenor, Gerald. 2008. *Survivance: Narratives of Native Presence*. Lincoln: University of Nebraska Press.

Wachtel, Nathan. 1994. *Gods and Vampires: Return to Chipaya*. Chicago: University of Chicago Press.

Walcott, Derek. 1990. *Omeros*. New York: Farrar, Straus and Giroux.

Walker, Charles. 2014. *The Túpac Amaru Rebellion*. Cambridge, MA: Harvard University Press.

Wallerstein, Immanuel. (1974) 1979. *The Capitalist World-Economy*. Cambridge: Cambridge University Press.

Warren, Kay B. 2001. "Telling Truths: Taking David Stoll and the Rigoberta Menchú Exposé Seriously." In *The Rigoberta Menchú Controversy*, edited by Arturo Arias, 198–218. Minneapolis: University of Minnesota Press.

Warrior, Robert. 1995. *Tribal Secrets: Rediscovering American Indian Intellectual Traditions*. Minneapolis: University of Minnesota Press.

Weatherford, Jack. 1988. *Indian Givers: How the Indians of the Americas Transformed the World*. New York: Fawcett Columbine.

Weaver, Jace, ed. 1996. *Defending Mother Earth: Native American Perspectives on Environmental Justice*. Maryknoll, NY: Orbis.

Weaver, Jace. 1998. *Native American Religious Identity: Unforgotten Gods*. Maryknoll, NY: Orbis.

Weber, Max. (1905) 1958. *The Protestant Ethic and the Spirit of Capitalism*. New York: Charles Scribner.

Weinberger, Eliot. 2000. "Anonymous Sources: A Talk on Translators and Translation." *Encuentros*, no. 39: 1–14.

Williams, Raymond. 1976. *Keywords: A Vocabulary of Culture and Society*. London: Croom Helm.

Wilson, Helen F. 2019. "Contact Zones: Multispecies Scholarship through *Imperial Eyes*." *Environment and Planning E: Nature and Space* 2 (4): 712–31.

Wohlleben, Peter. 2016. *The Hidden Life of Trees: What They Feel, How They Communicate—Discoveries from a Secret World*. Translated by Jane Billinghurst. Vancouver: Greystone.

Wolff, Janice, ed. 2002. *Professing the Contact Zone*. Urbana: National Council of Teachers of English.

Woolf, Virginia. 1923. *Mrs Dalloway*. New York: Penguin.

Woolf, Virginia. (1927) 2005. *To the Lighthouse*. New York: Harcourt.

York, Alissa. 2010. *Fauna*. Toronto: Random House Canada.

Yujra Mamani, Carlos. 2005. *Laq'a achachilankan jach'a tayka amuyt'awinkapa/ Los grandes pensamientos de nuestros antepasados*. La Paz: C&C Editores.

INDEX

climate fiction, 121

Clinton, Bill, 73, 199

Cochabamba, Bolivia, 209, 212–17, 219

Cochabamba Water War. *See* Cochabamba, Bolivia

Cold War, 23

Colectivo Acciones de Arte (Art Actions
Collective), 152, 161

College Republicans, 290n4

Colombian Drug Trade, 92

colonial condition, 46, 255

colonial divide, 18, 210, 228, 241, 243,
245–50

colonial experience, 249

colonialidad del poder (coloniality of
power). *See* Quijano, Aníbal

colonial imagination, 14–22, 208, 216, 230,
258

colonialism: and the academy, 196; in Africa, 267, 272; and Bushmen/!Kung, 186;
as a concept, 248, 256; concept of, 15, 19,
21, 41; diagnoses of, 265–66; and empire,
20; European, 179; French, 14–15; in
India, 273; and Indigenous activism,
114; and interruption, 268; as an object
of study, 14; playbook of, 252; settler, 16,
120, 126, 132, 187, 245, 248, 267; sexual
scripts of, 88; Spanish, 14, 16, 22, 207,
209, 214, 257–58, 260; telos of, 253; trope
of, 85. *See also* decolonization; imperialism; neocolonialism; postcolonialism;
recolonization

coloniality, 20–22, 25, 29, 34, 53, 211, 241,
243, 245, 264

colonial order, 243, 253, 261, 265

colonial power, 19, 43, 224, 226, 241, 244,
249, 256, 258, 262. *See also* colonialism

colonial script, 209, 224, 245, 260

colonial state, 243–44, 258, 260, 262, 267,
271

colonial violence, 26, 208, 226

colonized people. *See* colonized subject

colonized subject, 241, 269. *See also*
colonizer-colonized relationship

colonizer-colonized relationship, 18–19,
215, 225, 249–50

colonizers, 19, 26, 86, 249–50, 269

colony, 25

Columbus, Christopher, 208, 211–12, 262,
294n8

Columbus Quincentenary, 109, 113

commerce, 41, 78

Committed Outsider, 129

complementarity, 44, 53

concepts (Grosz), 12–14, 19, 119, 124, 252–53

Conrad, Joseph: *Heart of Darkness*, 16;
Nostromo, 16

Consciencism (Nkrumah), 266

conservatism, 198. *See also* conservative
movement

conservative movement, 191–92

consulta ciudadana (citizens' consultation), 88

contact zone: common use of, 130; concept
of, 11, 13, 125–27, 132, 135; conferences
on, 130; dialogues of, 129; human, 134;
interspecies, 131–32, 134; multispecies,
133–34; shared knowledge in, 128

continuity, cultural, 9, 72

Cooper, Sarah, 161

Coronil, Fernando, 191, 283n4

corporate work culture, 143

corridos (Mexican ballads), 67

Cortes de Cádiz, 257

cosmopolitanism, 12–13, 63, 267

countercultures, 45

countermodernity, 48, 50, 245

COVID-19 virus, 67, 276–80

créolité, 45, 54

creolization, 232

criollo, 228–29

Crisis in Modern Science conference
(Malaysia), 271

critical pedagogy, 19, 80

Crutzen, Paul, 117

Cuba, 259

cultural matrices, 121

cultural translation, 22, 205, 221–32

Culture and Imperialism (Said), 15. *See also*
Said, Edward

culture wars, 191, 193, 196

curriculum, 126

Cuzco, Peru, 1, 14, 221, 223, 228, 235–37, 250, 294n2

danzantes (dancers), 56
de Andrade, Mário, 52
de Andrade, Oswald, 51
de Areche, José Antonio, 222, 224–28, 236–37
death and survival tales, 69, 216
de Certeau, Michel, 76–77, 79
"Declaración de Quito," 110
Declaration of Indigenous Rights, 112–13
decolonization, 282n16; in the Americas, 260–61; in the Andean region, 244; art of, 252; in Canada, 27; colonization, as distinct from, 248; as a concept, 250; and epistemic infrastructure, 241; Euro-American out-migration, 70; as a force, 7, 14; of Haiti, 262; of knowledge, 196; Ministry of, in Bolivia, 113; and mobility, 89; in the Philippines, 22, 257–58; practices of, 249; "pressing problem" of, 126; processes of, 62; project of, 266; and reconversion, 232; in Spanish America, 22; speculative, 263–64; strategies of, 17, 88; struggle for, 19, 21; translation, 228; work of, 20. *See also* colonialism
Defoe, Daniel, 75, 78
de Gouges, Olympe, 295n4
De Holmes, Rebecca, 166–68
Deleuze, Gilles, 12
democratic ideals, 49
demodernization, 69–70
Department of the Interior (US), 140
Derrida, Jacques, 281n3, 285n8
Descartes, René, 36
desdoblamiento (doubling), 73, 233. *See also* bilingualism; multilingualism
Deskaheh (Levi General), 109
de Souza, Marinho, 289n1
desplazado (displaced), 80
Devocionario del migrante (Migrant's prayer book), 82
diaspora, 59–60, 66
diasporic communities. *See* diaspora
Dickinson, Emily, 80

dictatorship, 147–49, 151, 157, 159
differentiation, 44–45, 53
diffusion, 45–49, 51, 54, 272
diffusionist narrative. *See* narrative of diffusion
disciplines, 37, 243. *See also* area studies
Domínguez, Daylet, 297n11
Dominican Republic, 262–63, 297n11
Doña Marina, 290n2
Donner, Florinda, 166–69, 176
Dostoyevsky, Fyodor, 80
drug trade. *See* Mexico
D'Souza, Dinesh, 195–96, 198, 292n14
Dussel, Enrique, 40
dystopia, 12

Earle, Duncan, 293n23
eco-logic, 12
ecological balance, 72
ecological catastrophe, 5–6, 10, 13–14, 97
ecological standpoints, 11
education, 126, 195
El Alto, Bolivia, 111
el derecho a no migrar (the right not to migrate), 81–82, 84
El laberinto de la choledad (The labyrinth of cholitude) (Nugent), 47–48
El Padre Mío (Eltit), 149, 151, 153, 161. *See also* Eltit, Diamela
El Perú Ilustrado, 240
El Salvador, 74
Eltit, Diamela, 5, 92, 99, 102–5, 145, 148–49, 151, 153–54, 156–58, 161
emancipation processes, 71
empire: and colonialism, 20; and coloniality, 15; dynamics of, 14; and environmental degradation, 140; and ethnography, 180; and gender, 27; genocidal, 209; and geography, 25; in Haiti, 262; and imperialism, 15; and knowledge, 268; late capitalist, 63; neocolonial forms of, 16; novels of, 78; outposts of, 143; stages of, 66; study of, 126, 131; US, 138; work of, 142. *See also* colonialism; imperialism
empiricism, 24

futurity: alternative sense of, 72; and Chile, 156; crisis of, 7, 10–11, 13, 26, 29, 115, 157; ex-and neocolonial, 53; and force, 7; gap, 26; and independence, 252; and neoliberalism, 74; pessimist standpoint of, 124; as progress, 46; and reenactment, 213

futurologist, 156, 257; *futurólogo*, 6

futurology: alternative, 44, 274; and the Anthropocene, 121–22; of anticolonialism, 267; of catastrophe, 121; and Chile, 158; exercise in, 248, 252, 256, 262; as a force, 254; in Haiti, 263; idealized, 12; and identitarianism, 40; independence, 261; and modernity, 39, 42, 49; postmodern, 34; revolutionary, 256; twenty-first century, 123; work of, 253

Galápagos, 141

Galeano, Eduardo, 54

García Bernal, Gael, 208, 294n6

García Canclini, Néstor, 46, 54, 231

García Márquez, Gabriel, 47, 151, 259

Gaviria, Víctor, 94

gay movement, 98

Geertz, Clifford, 221, 226–28, 231–32

gender: and agency, 183; embodied, 93, 96, 98, 100; equality, 25; fraternal order, 98; marker of, 154; masculinity, 147, 160; and meaning making, 41; and modernity, 6, 41; neutrality, 184; norms, 242. See also *mujer chilena* (Chilean woman)

generation, 23, 26

genocide, 286nn3–4, 289n1

genre, 201–2, 204–5

geoaesthetics, 11

geohistorical authenticity. *See* geohistorical forces

geohistorical forces, 142, 207

geohumanities, 11

geolinguistics, 11

geontology, 11, 117

geontopower, 11

geopolitical conditions, 17, 141, 191

geopolitics of truth, 205

Gerardi, Juan (Archbishop), 200

Germani, Gino, 46

Germany, 130

Gessen, Masha, 145, 159, 289n15

Ghana, 266

Ghosh, Amitav, 29, 121, 124

Gibson-Graham, J. K., 9, 71, 73–74

Gide, André, 14, 80

gift economy, 77

Gilman, Sander, 37

Gilroy, Paul, 39–40, 45, 50

global division of labor, 44

globality, 59

globalization, 8, 11, 59, 61–71, 80, 88, 212, 220

Global South, 66

Gods Must Be Crazy, The (dir. Uys), 289n4

González, Elián, 60–61

Goonatilake, Susantha, 268–70, 272, 298n4

Gorriti, Juana Manuela, 85–86

Graeber, David, 88

Grande, Sandy, 19, 79–80, 82, 84, 217

Grandin, Greg, 287n3

Gran Televisor Solar, 4; Great Solar TV, 4, 10, 29

Great Derangement, The (Ghosh), 29, 121

Greenlanders, 73

grenouille de sang (blood frog). *See* transspecies story

grid: form of, 70–71; of hospitality, 77

Grosz, Elizabeth, 12, 119, 126, 253, 256, 260, 263

Guadalajara, Mexico, 56–57

Guantánamo Bay (Gitmo), 138, 142–43

Guatemala, 52, 111, 190, 197–201, 203–4, 289n1, 292n20, 293n22

Guattari, Félix, 12

Guerrilla Army of the Poor, 197–98, 200, 202–3

Guimarães Rosa, João, 53

Güiraldes, Ricardo, 51

Gutenberg, Johannes, 35

Habermas, Jürgen, 205

Haiti, 96–97, 243, 262–63

Hannerz, Ulf, 63

Harding, Sandra, 270

Harjo, Joy, 282n14

Harvard Kalahari Project, 181, 184, 186–87
Hegel, G. W. F., 36–37
Heller, Agnes, 37, 50
Herzog, Werner, 212, 294n8
Heston, Charlton, 120
heterosexual contract. *See* sexual contract
Highland Scots, 26
hip-hop culture, 72
Hiriart de Pinochet, Lucía, 146
Hispaniola, 207, 209, 261–62
Holocene, 117–18, 287n1
homosexuality. *See* sexuality
Horowitz, David, 198
hospitality, 77, 88. *See also* stayers
humanists, 24
human migrancy, 11
hybridity, 17, 19–20, 45, 54, 80

I, Rigoberta Menchú. See Menchú, Rigoberta
Ifugao, Philippines, 113–14
illiberal democracy, 159
Illiberal Education (D'Souza), 195
Ilongots, 113–14
imagined community, 128–29
immigration, 66, 74. *See also* migration
immobilization, 217
Immoralist, The (Gide), 14–15, 80
Imperial Eyes (Pratt), 287n3
imperial ideology. *See* imperialism
imperialism: anti-, 265; concept of, 15, 211; designs, 259; European, 25, 48, 126, 186, 262, 269, 273; in filmmaking, 219; French, 15; ideology of, 272; and intervention, 268; linguistic, 260; paradigm of, 126; and power, 225; projects of, 265; study of, 266; universal, 270; US, 25; Western, 19, 80, 217. *See also* colonialism; empire
imperial substitutions. *See* imperialism
improvisation, 129
Iñárritu, Alejandro, 120
Inca Empire, 14, 221, 224–25, 230, 234, 242, 244, 246, 248, 267
independence: of Cuba, 259; of the Dominican Republic, 262–63; futurology

and, 28, 248; of Haiti, 262–63; of the Philippines, 256–61; South American, 243–44, 251–54
India, 112, 267
indigeneity, 294n7; in the Americas, 7; Andean, 237; and the colonial encounter, 17, 85; and coloniality, 20, 86; as a concept, 13, 18, 80, 84, 115; as a force, 7, 11, 14, 19, 84, 107–8, 112–14; and identity, 17–18, 224; and language, 224; in literature, 84; and mobility, 80; and placedness, 88, 111; as a planetary discourse, 84; values of, 224
Indigenous activism, 109–11, 114–15, 221
Indigenous agency, 17–19
Indigenous and Tribal Populations Convention, 109
Indigenous being, 20. *See also* indigeneity; Indigenous agency
Indigenous environment, 170
Indigenous people: agriculturalists, 269; Andean, 240, 243, 244; in Argentina, 48; in Bolivia, 245; and citizenship, 247; and colonial optic, 19; and colonial power, 19; and the colonial script, 86; communities of, 245–46; and epistemology, 206; and history, 47, 110, 270; and international labor migration, 111; justice for, 189; languages of, 260–61; marches and demonstrations of, 87; and militarism, 194; and modernity, 108; and the notion of fluidity, 217; populations of, 257, 260; and resistance, 110, 244–45; rights of, 112, 114; and Spanish liberalism, 258; stereotypes of, 250; and westernization, 183; and world making, 17
Indigenous Peoples' Rights Act (Philippines), 113–14
Indigenous principles, 46
Indigenous rebellion. *See* Indigenous activism
Indigenous thinkers and thought, 9, 17, 80, 114–16. *See also* indigeneity; Indigenous agency
indio, 108, 294n7
industrialization, 36

intellectual commons, 116
International Decade of the World's Indigenous Peoples, 112
International Labour Organization (ILO), 109
International Monetary Fund, 64, 76
international rules of trade, 6
international solidarity movement, 198
interpreters. *See* interpretive power
interpretive power, 38–40, 45, 73
interruption trope. *See* narrative of interruption
interspecies studies, 132
irrationality, 38
Ishi, 72
Islam, 50
Ivory Coast, 61

Jackson, Jesse (Reverend), 192
Jacobsen, Nils, 241, 244, 246
Jalisco, Mexico, 58
January 6th insurgency of US Capitol, 159
John Paul II (Pope), 63
Joyce, James, 52–53
junta, 146, 152–53, 156

Kafka, Franz, 80
Kahlo, Frida, 91
Kalimantan, Indonesia, 8
Kant, Immanuel, 274
Kaplan, Caren, 79
Katari, Túpac, 294n1
K'emé Chay, Rigoberto, 113
Kennedy, John F., 27
Keywords. See Williams, Raymond
killer bees, 66, 68
Kirchner, Néstor, 142
knowledge: African, 272; anticolonial, 269; belief, as distinct from, 4; the crisis of, 5; humanistic, 220; Indigenous, 17, 232, 269; making, 7, 14, 23, 199; modern, 217; narrated experience, as distinct from, 206; new, 6, 268; objective and subjective, 188; search for, 271; situated, 270; traditional, 6; transfer, 269; of the world, 79

Kolbert, Elizabeth, 11
Kondo, Dorinne, 9
Korean Ministry of Education, 130
Korean Research Foundation, 130
!Kung peoples, 181–84, 186–87, 289n5, 289n7
Kurdi, Alan, 61

La aventura de Miguel Littín, clandestino en Chile (Garcia Márquez), 151
La batalla de Chile (dir. Guzmán), 288n9
Lacandon jungle, Chiapas, 87–88
ladino (white/nonindigenous), 197, 200, 203
Lake Chapala, 58
Lake Regions of Central Africa, The (Burton), 173–74, 178–79
La Moneda Palace, 150
language, 134, 232, 249, 260. *See also* multilingualism
La Paz, Bolivia, 212, 236, 244
la peregrina (the pilgrim). *See* Virgin of Zapopan
Larraín, Jorge, 55
Latin America, 16, 22–25, 33–36, 42–54, 80, 140–42, 207, 226, 243, 262. *See also* colonialism; *and specific countries*
Latin American literature, 5, 11, 15, 29, 52–53, 66, 90, 98
Latour, Bruno, 284n8
La Villa (*Shantytown*) (Aira), 5
La virgen de los sicarios (*Our Lady of the Assassins*) (Vallejo), 92–94, 97, 98
Lechner, Norbert, 46
Lemebel, Pedro, 91
liberalism, 40, 70, 103, 257–59, 273–74
liberal social contract, 103
lifeways, 6, 9, 72, 166, 169–70, 176, 184, 187, 231
lifeworld, 105
Lima, Peru, 85, 222, 235–36, 240, 242
literature: African, 29; American, 120; Andean, 230; children's British, 25; death and survival, 61; decolonizing, 252; European, 14, 28; of exile, 84; of independence, 252; literary criticism, 227;

literature (*continued*)
modern European, 52; modern Mexican, 52; South American, 22; of the South Sea explorations, 174; of suffering and loss, 62; travel, 60, 76–77, 177; world, 220. *See also specific authors*
Littín, Miguel, 151, 153
Little Grand Rapids, 135
logocentrism, 133–34
longings: planetary, 14, 22; utopian, 12
Los Angeles, California, 56, 59, 73
Lost Boys of Sudan, 60–61, 283n1
Los vigilantes (*Custody of the Eyes*) (Eltit), 5, 92, 99, 102–5
Lumpérica (Eltit), 153, 156–58

Machu Picchu, 141
Macunaíma (M. de Andrade), 52
Madrid, Spain, 257–59
magical realism, 54
male bodies. *See* gender
male-female relations. *See* sexual contract
male fraternal order. *See* gender
Malinowski, Bronislaw, 165, 167, 169, 171, 173, 176–78, 180
Mamani, Pablo, 112, 218
Manhattan Minerals Corporation, 284n11
Manila, Philippines, 259
Manila Galleon, 257
Manitoba, Canada, 135
Mano de obra (*Workforce*) (Eltit), 157
Mapuche, 111–12
Mares of the Apocalypse, 91
Mariátegui, José Carlos, 108
Martí, José, 259
masculinity. *See* gender
mass extinction, 119, 131
mass society, 36
Matto de Turner, Clorinda, 238, 240–43, 245, 247, 249
Maya, 292n17
Maya mythology, 52, 111. *See also* Latin American literature
Maybury-Lewis, David, 169, 178–80
Mayorgal, René Antonio, 43
Mead, Margaret, 199–200

meaning making, 41, 230, 233
Medellín, Colombia, 92, 94, 97
Melville, Herman, 80
Menchú, Rigoberta, 22, 113, 189–205, 293n24
Meratus, 8
mestizo peoples, 45, 47, 80, 218, 229, 244, 247
metropoles, 61, 74, 261, 267, 272
Mexico, 57, 59, 65–67, 81, 88, 108, 113, 142, 257, 273, 289n2
Mexico City, 99
Mignolo, Walter, 20–21, 282n16
migration, 8, 45, 59–66, 80–81, 84, 111, 234, 248
milagrosa. See Virgin of Zapopan
militarism, 137, 140–43, 149
militarized geopolitics. *See* geopolitical conditions
millennial moment, 4, 8, 14
mimicry, 17, 19. *See also* Bhabha, Homi; colonialism
Ministry of Decolonization (Bolivia), 113
Mintz, Sidney, 45
Miranda, Francisco de, 253, 255–57
mirrorings, 213. *See also* mimicry
Mitchell, Tim, 118
Mixteco, 81–82, 84
Miyoshi, Masao, 10, 282n9
mobility: and colonial relations, 19, 88; and freedom, 8, 65, 72, 76–80, 86, 102; and globality, 59; human, 130; image of, 63, 89; and knowledge, 79; and modernity, 214, 217; and placedness, 11, 79, 87; and the politics of belonging, 84–87; and the Virgin of Zapopan, 73. *See also* citizenship; freedom; indigeneity; migration
modernism, 36, 52–53
modernity: in the Americas, 36, 41, 45–47, 51, 53–54, 140–42, 150; capitalist, 5, 29, 53, 80, 118, 132, 150, 286n3; Cold War, 137; colonial, 11, 20, 44–45, 47–48, 54, 62, 86, 126, 131; environmental, 131, 133–34; European, 14–22, 34, 38, 40–50, 80–81, 108, 217, 265, 267, 272, 275, 297n2; expectation of, 70; features of, 35, 38; as a force, 7, 43;

global, 9, 34, 41, 43–44, 46–48, 68, 71–72, 84; human, 134; as identity discourse, 39–40; Indigenous, 17, 114, 243, 245; migration and, 79, 111; modernization and, 46; otherness and, 40, 48–49; peripheral, 41–42, 47, 49; study of, 5–6, 14–21, 33–44, 47, 50, 54, 61–62, 85. *See also* capitalism; colonialism; Eurocentrism; futurity; globalization; neoliberal economics

modernization, 42, 46, 70, 267, 298n5

Modern Language Association, 125, 128

modern literary system, 122

modern world system, 39

monosexual. *See* sexuality

Monroe Doctrine, 16, 140

monsters, 66–69, 74

Montaldo, Graciela, 33–34

Montejo, Victor, 73

Montero, Mayra, 92, 96–98, 102

Montoya, Rodrigo, 46

Moore, Jason, 118

Moore, Michael, 66

Morales, Evo, 212–13

Morelos, Mexico, 78

more-than-human agents, 132, 135

more-than-human beings. *See* nonhuman entities

more-than-human encounters, 131, 134–35

Morocco, 50

movers, 77–79, 86. *See also* hospitality; migration; stayers

Movimiento Revolucionario Túpac Amaru, 294n1

mujer chilena (Chilean woman), 147–48, 150

multicentric totality, 12

multiculturalism, 191, 198

multilingualism, 28, 232

multinational enterprises, 6, 8, 65, 81, 110

multipolar temporality, 122

multispecies interaction, 131, 134–35

Munizaga, Giselle, 146, 149–50

Muslim populations. *See* Islam

myth of Western civilization. *See* Western civilizing project

Namibia, 252–53, 296n2

narrated testimony. *See testimonio*

narrative of diffusion, 44, 270, 275

narrative of emancipation, 44

narrative of interruption, 267–68

narrative of origin, 35–36, 38–39, 42

narratives of isolated survivors, 66

National Secretariat for Women (Secretaría Nacional de la Mujer), 146

Native American Graves Protection and Repatriation Act, 73

Native Americans, 143, 286n3

nature writing, 121

Nègres blancs d'Amérique (White Negroes of America), 27

Nehru, Jawaharlal, 267

neocolonialism, 16, 41, 53, 86, 145, 247, 266. *See also* postcolonialism; tourism

neoliberal economics, 210. *See also* neoliberalism

neoliberalism, 63, 70–72, 74, 99, 103, 107, 152, 157

Neruda, Pablo, 15

new authoritarians, 158–59

New Mexico, 143

new planetary order. *See* planetarity

Nicaragua, 109, 141–42

Nietzsche, Friedrich, 37

Nisa: The Life and Words of a !Kung Woman (Shostak), 181–87

Nkrumah, Kwame, 266–67

Nobel Peace Prize, 189, 195, 292n18

Nobel Prize in Literature, 15, 52, 198

nonanalogue state, 7, 118–19, 124

nonhuman entities, 131. *See also* agency

North American Free Trade Agreement (NAFTA), 65–67, 73, 81, 111

novel, 11, 53, 66, 93–99, 101–6, 155, 157–58

Nuer, The. See Evans-Pritchard, Edward

Nugent, Guillermo, 47–48, 50, 53, 244–45

Núñez de Cáceres, José, 262

Nyamnjoh, Francis, 114

Oaxaca, Mexico, 81, 111

Obama, Barack, 6

Oceania, 16

Official Statement of World Humanism, 118, 287n2
Olivera, Oscar, 213
One Hundred Years of Solitude (García Márquez), 47, 259
on-location films, 208, 212–13, 217
organ theft. *See* "stolen kidney"
Orientalism (Said), 15
otherness, 17, 34, 36–40, 42, 47–51, 53–54, 97, 220, 226

pan-Indigenous public. *See* Indigenous people
Park, Mungo, 173, 177
paternalism, 148
patio de atrás (backyard), 141
patriarchal ideologies, 148
patronage, 49
Paulicéia Desvairada (*Hallucinated City*) (M. de Andrade), 52
Paz, Octavio, 50
pedagogy. *See* education
Penang Declaration in Sadar, 284n4
Pérez, Emma, 21, 282n15
Pérez de Cuéllar, Javier, 296n2
performativity, 129
periphery, 40–46, 48, 50, 53. *See also* center-periphery relations
Permanent Forum on Indigenous Issues (UN), 112
personal experience, 170, 205
personal narratives, 166–71, 173, 180, 183, 185, 194, 202, 204
Peru, 20, 46, 48–49, 68, 108, 226, 241, 244–46, 248, 284n11, 296n10, 296n12
Pew Institute, 74
Philippine independence movement, 259–60, 297n7
Philippines, 16, 64, 113–14, 256–59, 261, 263
Picchi, Debra, 168
pidginization, 232. *See also* language
Piglia, Ricardo, 92, 94–96, 98, 101–2, 104
Pinochet, Augusto, 11, 112, 144–61, 286n3
pishtako. *See* monsters
Pitt, William, 255–56
pivot, 8, 14

placedness, 11, 84, 86–88
planetarity, 4, 6, 9–13, 17, 20, 29, 43, 61, 112, 118
planetary force. *See* planetarity
planetary longings, 14, 22
Planetary Turn, The (Elias and Moraru), 12
planetary turning point. *See* planetarity
Planet of the Apes (dir. Schaffner), 120
Plata quemada (*Money to Burn*), 94–96, 98, 101–2
Platt Amendment, 16
pluridiversity, 12
policing, 143, 145
policing at the border, 283n3. *See also* Border Patrol
Polo, Marco, 173
Portillo, Lourdes, 285n1
Portland, Oregon, 145
Portuguese (language), 22, 28
Postcapitalist Politics, A (Gibson-Graham), 9, 71, 296n13
postcolonialism, 15–22, 40, 80, 215, 232, 261, 265–66. *See also* colonialism
postmillennial divide, 11
postmodern, term, 33–34, 46, 55, 59, 79, 217
Povinelli, Elizabeth, 8, 11, 117
Practice of Everyday Life, The (de Certeau), 76–77
precolonial being, 18
premodern imaginaries, 122
premodern societies, 37–38
pre-postcolonial moment, 15
privatization initiatives, 6. *See also* neoliberal economics
progress, 42, 45–46
Protestant Ethic and the Spirit of Capitalism, The (Weber), 274
Puerto Rico, 138–39

Quebec, Canada, 27
Quechua, 209, 211, 215, 218, 234, 242, 250
Quijano, Aníbal, 20, 46, 210

Rabinow, Paul, 50
racism, 27, 50, 53. *See also* colonialism; otherness

Ramírez Martínez, Oscar Alberto, 283n3
Ratana, T. W., 109
rationality, 38, 46
Reagan, Ronald, 107, 191–92
realist storytelling, 122
reception, 45, 47–49, 51, 53, 231
recolonization, 14, 17, 212, 244–46
reenactment, 211–13, 215–17
refugees. *See* migration
remesas (remittances), 82
residential schools, 286nn3–4
resistance, 45, 148, 151–52, 161
Rigoberta Menchú and the Story of All Poor Guatemalans. See Stoll, David
Rio de Janeiro, Brazil, 22–23
Rio Grande, 63
Rivera Cusicanqui, Silvia, 211, 243–46, 248–49, 295n7, 296n8
Rizal, José, 16, 257, 259, 261
Roosevelt, Teddy, 142
Rosaldo, Renato, 113, 194
Rough Riders, 142, 143
Rouse, Roger, 73
Rousseau, Jean-Jacques, 49
rural literature in Latin America, 52, 66. *See also* backwardness

sacaojos, 68–69
Said, Edward, 14–15, 29, 265
Salón de belleza (*Beauty Salon*) (Bellatin), 92, 98–99, 102–5
San Cristóbal de las Casas, Mexico, 88
Santiago, Chile, 148, 152–54, 161
Santiago, Silviano, 43, 51, 53
Santo Domingo, 261–63
São Paulo, Brazil, 52
Sarlo, Beatriz, 33, 41, 231
Sarmiento, Domingo Faustino, 48
Savage and the Innocent, The (Maybury-Lewis), 169
Schaffner, Franklin, 120–21
Schopenhauer, Arthur, 37
Schwarz, Roberto, 43, 45, 47–50, 53
scientific position of speech, 170
Scott, James, 298n5
segregation, 50

self-duplication, 59, 74
selfhood, 77, 154, 156, 217
self-mutilation, 154–55
Seoul, South Korea, 130
settler colonialism, 16, 120, 132. *See also* colonialism; modernity
sexual contract, 93–94, 97–98
sexuality, 6, 93–97, 285n5
sexual privilege, 96
Shabono (Donner), 166–69
Shakur, Tupac Amaru, 295n1
Shining Path guerrilla movement, 4, 108, 248, 286n2
Shostak, Marjorie, 181–87, 290n5, 290n7
"Si haces mal no esperes bien" (He who does evil should expect no good), 85
Sisa, Bartolina, 294n1
Skurski, Julie, 191, 283n4
slavery, 7, 21, 45, 49, 61, 69, 80, 221, 262–64, 269, 283n2
Smith, Linda Tuhiwai, 18
Smithsonian Institution, 72
social contract, 93, 97, 99, 103–4, 277
socialism, 267
social media, 160
socio-sexual order, 103
Sommer, Doris, 9, 252
Sorbonne, the, 52
Southern Cone, 148, 289n13
Spain, 16, 138, 226, 244–45, 251, 256–59, 262–63, 289n2
Spanish (language), 28, 242, 251, 260–61, 293n2
Spanish Empire, 176, 234, 236, 247–48, 253, 257–58, 262
Sparrman, Anders, 185–86
species extinction, 97
Spivak, Gayatri Chakravorty, 9–10, 20, 216. *See also* futurity
Staden, Hans, 171–73, 176
standard account, the, 34–36, 38–40, 42–45, 47–49, 51, 54, 268
Standing Rock Sioux, 87–88
Stanford University, 192–94
stayers, 77–79, 86
Stoermer, Eugene, 117

161, 191–92, 199, 254, 259–61; and *I,
Rigoberta Menchú*, 195, 199; immigration to, 59–66; Indigenous populations
in, 109, 113, 286n3; and killer bees, 66;
and migratory diaspora, 66, 70, 73–74;
and modernity, 33; postcolonial society
in, 193. *See also* Americas, the; colonialism; Cuba; Latin America; Philippine
independence movement; Puerto Rico;
settler colonialism
urbanization, 36, 50–51
US Fish and Wildlife Service, 140
US Information Agency, 68
US invasion of Iraq, 10
US-Mexico border detention center,
McAllen, Texas, 160
US Navy, 137–38, 143
utopia, 174, 176, 179, 181, 184
utopian longings, 12

Valdivia, Pedro de, 153
Valero, Helena, 167–68, 176, 289n1
Vallejo, Fernando, 92–94, 96–98, 104
Velasco, Juan, 248
vernacular culture, 54, 60, 66
verticalization, 65
Vieques, Puerto Rico, 137–40
Virgin of Zapopan, 56–59, 73–74
visiting, 77–78
Vizenor, Gerald, 18. *See also* survivance
Voyage to the Cape of Good Hope (Spar-
rman), 185–86

Wallerstein, Immanuel, 36, 39
Waorani, 286n6
War of the Pacific, 242, 295n5
Warren, Kay, 292n15, 292n19
We, the Tikopia (Firth), 173–77, 179–82
Weber, Max, 273, 275

Weinberger, Eliot, 221, 226–27, 231
West and the Rest of Us, The (Chinweizu),
267–69, 272–73
Western civilizing project, 46, 183, 274,
286n3. *See also* aesthetics; colonialism
Western culture, 192–93
Western literary canon, 80, 192
"What is Modernity?" (Heller), 37–38
whiteness, 14, 85, 120, 280
white supremacy, 21, 39, 160, 280. *See also*
Eurocentrism
Wilder, Laura Ingalls, 122
Will, George, 193
Williams, Raymond, 24, 54
witchcraft, 154
women's movements, 71. *See also* gender
Woodward, C. Vann, 193
wool, 245–48
Woolf, Virginia, 51
Working Group on Indigenous Popula-
tions, 109, 112
World Bank, 64, 212
world-making, 8–13, 17–18, 21, 93–94, 98,
104–6, 266
World Tourism Day, 63
World Trade Organization, 232
World War I, 25, 27
World War II, 25

X-Files, The (TV series), 67, 69

Yahi, 72
Yanoáma (Biocca and Valero), 167
Yanomamo, 166–69, 289n1

Zambia, 69–71
Zapatismo, 71, 286n1
Zapatistas, 87–89, 108, 113, 285n9
Zinn, Howard, 208

PUBLICATION HISTORY |

Chapter 1 is based on "Modernity and Periphery: Toward a Global and Relational Analysis," in *Beyond Dichotomies: Histories, Identities, Cultures, and the Challenge of Globalization*, edited by Elisabeth Mudimbe-Boyi (Albany: State University of New York Press, 2002), 21–47.

Chapter 2 originated in *Images of Power: Iconography, Culture and the State in Latin America*, edited by Jens Andermann and William Rowe (New York: Berghahn, 2005), 273–89.

Chapter 3 is based on "Los que se quedan," in *Los viajeros y el Rio de la Plata: Un siglo de escritura*, edited by Jean-Philippe Barnabé, Lindsey Cordery, and Beatriz Vegh (Montevideo: Linardi y Risso, 2010), 356–78.

Chapter 4 is based on "Tres incendios y dos mujeres extraviadas: El imaginario novelístico frente al nuevo contrato social," in *Espacio urbano, comunicación y violencia en América Latina*, edited by Mabel Moraña (Pittsburgh: Instituto Internacional de Literatura Iberoamericana, 2002), 91–106.

Chapter 6 draws in part on "Coda: Concept and Chronotope," in *Arts of Living on a Damaged Planet: Ghosts and Monsters of the Anthropocene*, edited by Anna Lowenhaupt Tsing, Heather Swanson, Elaine Gan, and Nils Bubandt (Minneapolis: University of Minnesota Press, 2017), 169–74.

Chapter 8 appeared in an earlier form in *American Quarterly* 68, no. 3 (2016): 557–62.

Chapter 9 is revised and rewritten from "Overwriting Pinochet: Undoing the Culture of Fear in Chile," *Modern Language Quarterly* 57, no. 2 (1996): 151–62.

Chapter 10 is a revised and expanded version of "Fieldwork in Common Places," in *Writing Culture: The Poetics and Politics of Ethnography*, edited by James Clifford and George Marcus (Berkeley: University of California Press, 1986), 27–50.

Chapter 11 is based on "*I, Rigoberta Menchú* and the Culture Wars," in *The Rigoberta Menchú Controversy*, edited by Arturo Arias (Minneapolis: University of Minnesota Press, 2001), 29–48.

Chapter 12 appeared in an earlier form in *Motion Pictures: Travel Ideals in Film*, edited by Andrew McGregor and Gemma Blackwood (Bern: Peter Lang, 2016), 15–30.

Chapter 13 originated as "The Traffic in Meaning: Translation, Contagion, Infiltration," *Profession* (2002): 25–36.

Chapter 16 draws in part on "The Anti-colonial Past," *Modern Language Quarterly* 65, no. 3 (2004): 443–56.

The coda was first published in electronic form by the Hemispheric Institute of Performance and Politics and also appeared as "Airways," *Anthropology Now* 12, no. 2 (2020): 1–4.

www.ingramcontent.com/pod-product-compliance
Lightning Source LLC
Chambersburg PA
CBHW071014280326
41935CB00011B/1343